ENDURING TERRITORIAL DISPUTES

STUDIES IN SECURITY AND INTERNATIONAL AFFAIRS

ENDURING TERRITORIAL DISPUTES

Strategies of Bargaining,

Coercive Diplomacy,

and Settlement

KRISTA E. WIEGAND

The University of Georgia Press
Athens and London

© 2011 by the University of Georgia Press

Athens, Georgia 30602

www.ugapress.org

All rights reserved

Set in 10/14 Minion Pro by Graphic Composition, Inc.

Printed and bound by Thomson-Shore

The paper in this book meets the guidelines for
permanence and durability of the Committee on
Production Guidelines for Book Longevity of the
Council on Library Resources.

Printed in the United States of America

15 14 13 12 11   P   5 4 3 2 1

Library of Congress Cataloging-in-Publication Data

Wiegand, Krista Eileen, 1971–

  Enduring territorial disputes : strategies of bargaining,
coercive diplomacy, and settlement / Krista E. Wiegand.

       p. cm. — (Studies in security and international affairs)

  Includes bibliographical references and index.

  ISBN-13: 978-0-8203-3738-8 (hardcover : alk. paper)

  ISBN-10: 0-8203-3738-2 (hardcover : alk. paper)

  ISBN-13: 978-0-8203-3946-7 (pbk. : alk. paper)

  ISBN-10: 0-8203-3946-6 (pbk. : alk. paper)

  1. Pacific settlement of international disputes.

2. Boundary disputes. 3. Territory, National. I. Title.

  JZ6010.W54 2011

  327.1—dc22

                                        2011010516

British Library Cataloging-in-Publication Data available

to Michael

CONTENTS

PREFACE

Territory—it is the backbone of our lives on this planet. Without territory, a homeland, a place to put down our roots, we would be lost, wandering like the tribes of Israel so long ago. Territory is highly valued on many different levels, ranging from material, economic value to symbolic, intangible value. The fact that so many countries have been involved in disputes over territory for centuries should not therefore be surprising. What is surprising is why so many disputes continue to endure for decades and sometimes more than a century, when the resolution of such disputes seems to be in everyone's best interest. The persistence of territorial disputes makes it difficult for states to cooperate on simple bilateral issues like immigration, trade, fishing rights, and joint security.

This book is about the endurance of territorial disputes, and why they last for years and years, while others are resolved over time. This puzzle is a critical question for policy makers and scholars alike because multiple past studies of international conflict have demonstrated that the presence of territorial disputes is the most important factor in explaining armed conflict compared to all other issues about which states can potentially disagree. Therefore, territory is important not only to the citizens of the countries where territory is disputed, but also to the international community of states. Understanding the strategies used by governments involved in territorial disputes is critical to working toward peace. This book is an attempt to broaden our knowledge of this important topic and to answer some of the important questions of our time.

My study of territory started not as an academic exercise but from an early fascination with maps. From the age of eight I had a map of the world hung in my room, where I would study the countries, with their pink, green, blue, and yellow colorings, and wonder why some countries were so big and others so tiny they could hardly be seen on the map. I decided early on that one of my life goals would be to visit as many of those countries as possible. Over time, some of the countries that I visited, such as Czechoslovakia and Yugoslavia, eventually disappeared, only to reappear as new countries. So far, I have visited sixty-one countries, many of which have at some point been involved in territorial disputes. Traveling to the borders of disputed states such as Guatemala and Belize, Argentina and Chile, or more hostile borders like Israel and Lebanon, and talking to people living in states involved in territorial disputes about their concerns and views have provided me with a real-world, on-the-ground understanding of some of the dynamics and consequences of territorial disputes. Academic studies and a dedication to the field of conflict management, specifically territorial disputes, seemed a natural progression for me.

The research in this book began many years ago in a very different format but evolved over the years into the culmination that is presented here. In my first semester of graduate school at Duke University, I was searching for a topic for a research paper for the course International Conflict when Christopher Gelpi, my professor at the time, recommended a recent book on territorial disputes written by Paul Huth, *Standing Your Ground: Territorial Disputes and International Conflict*. I read the book with fascination and intrigue, knowing this was exactly what I wanted to study. From that point forward, I wrote almost all of my graduate papers on some topic related to territorial disputes, culminating in my dissertation about territorial dispute strategies. Having published a number of articles gleaned from the dissertation, initially I had not thought of writing a book on territorial disputes, but my passion for the subject motivated me to delve deeper and broader than I ever had. Knowing it was time to write this book, I read every study written about some aspect of territory or territorial disputes that I could get my hands on, I spent years presenting different aspects of the theories in this book at political science conferences, I collected articles about dozens of real-world cases in the news, and, finally, I began the writing, a task that I enjoyed immensely and will miss now that the manuscript is completed. I will continue my study of territorial disputes and am eager to delve into different aspects that I have not yet explored.

In writing this book, I had help from many people over the years. First, I thank Christopher Gelpi, who planted the idea of studying territorial disputes in my head many years ago and Hein Goemans, who shares the same interest in territory. Robert Keohane, my dissertation advisor, worked diligently with me to hone my research methods skills and writing in general, and his influence is still present in my research and writing today. John Vasquez generously advised me about the best fit for a publisher, leading me to Nancy Grayson, my editor at the University of Georgia Press. From the time I submitted the original manuscript to the time of publication, Nancy and others at the Press were nothing but efficient and enthusiastic about guiding me through the review and publishing process.

I am grateful to several colleagues who provided me with valuable comments and insights about different aspects of the material covered in this book, including David Carter, David Dreyer, Taylor Fravel, Hein Goemans, Paul Hensel, Sara McLaughlin Mitchell, Daniel Morey, Emilia Justyna Powell, William Reed, Christine Sixta, David Soskice, Jaroslav Tir, John Tures, John Vasquez, and anonymous reviewers. John Harper Publishing in London graciously provided copyright permission for use of three maps from their publication *Border and Territorial Disputes*, fourth edition, edited by Peter Calvert (2004). Jie Tian of the Department of Geology and Geography at Georgia Southern University was kind enough to create the map of Shebaa Farms. Zack Anderson, Katie Brookins, Christine Dalton, Ryan Pickerell, and Kayla Whaley, students in an honors seminar on territorial disputes, frequently listened to my ideas about the book beyond their regular obligations. I am greatly appreciative of editorial work done by my research assistant Kathryn J. Harrison, who spent countless hours carefully reading the manuscript and providing useful editorial suggestions. Finally, I thank my family, particularly my husband Michael, who is also passionate about geography, history, international politics, and armed conflict. As a military reporter who has traveled to many war zones, Michael provided unique insights based on personal experiences that we as academics sometimes overlook. His unending patience regarding the time I have spent on my research is greatly valued.

Dr. Krista E. Wiegand
Savannah, Georgia
September 2010

ABBREVIATIONS

AU	African Union
CBM	confidence building measures
CCP	Chinese Communist Party
EC	European Community
ECAFE	(United Nations) Economic Commission for Asia and the Far East
ECU	European Currency Unit
EEZ	exclusive economic zone
EU	European Union
IBRU	International Boundary Research Unit
ICBM	intercontinental ballistic missile
ICJ	International Court of Justice
ICOW	Issue Correlates of War
IDF	Israel Defense Forces
IR	International Relations
JDA	Japanese Defense Agency
LDP	Liberal Democratic Party
MID	militarized interstate dispute
MSA	Maritime Safety Agency
NATO	North Atlantic Treaty Organization
NEFA	Northeast Frontier Agency
OAU	Organization of African Unity
PFT	(Sino-Japanese) Peace and Friendship Treaty
PLA	People's Liberation Army
PLO	Palestine Liberation Organization
PRC	People's Republic of China
PTBT	Partial Nuclear Test Ban Treaty
ROC	Republic of China, Taiwan
SDF	Self Defense Forces
SEATO	Southeast Asian Treaty Organization
SLA	South Lebanese Army

UAE	United Arab Emirates
UCD	Union of the Democratic Centre
UK	United Kingdom of Great Britain and Northern Ireland
UN	United Nations
UNCLOS	United Nations Convention on the Law of the Sea
UNESCO	United Nations Educational, Scientific, and Cultural Organization
UNIFIL	United Nations Interim Force in Lebanon
US	United States of America
USSR	Union of Soviet Socialist Republics
WTO	World Trade Organization
COW	Correlates of War
ECU	European currency unit

ENDURING TERRITORIAL DISPUTES

CHAPTER ONE

The Endurance of Territorial Disputes

Despite the rise of globalization and an increasingly interdependent economy where borders seem to matter less and less (Ruggie 1993), the persistence of dozens of active territorial disputes worldwide suggests that territory still matters. States can potentially dispute many issues—type of government, resources, trade, and weapons proliferation, among others—but territorial disputes are by far the most detrimental type of interstate dispute, and they are at the root of many other disputes such as those involving arms, nuclear proliferation, and resources. Many states invest heavily in their military capabilities to deal specifically with territorial disputes. Unless their sovereignty is secure, states involved in territorial disputes cannot effectively deal with other international relations issues such as trade, environmental concerns, resources, or economic development. Enduring territorial disputes are particularly problematic because they cause continual bilateral, regional, and international tensions and threaten international security. Even when armed conflict does not occur, the "negative peace" of an enduring dispute is quite distinct from the "positive peace" between states that have no disputes (Gibler and Tir 2010; Klein, Goertz, and Diehl 2008).

Of all interstate disputes, those over territory tend to be the most salient for states and the most likely to lead to armed conflict (Hensel 2001; Vasquez and Henehan 2001). What appears to be a minor dispute can easily flare up: "the danger is that political or social tensions in a claimant country may provide the tinder by which an islet dispute could become a serious international relations issue rather than a tempest in a teacup" (Morrison 1997, 8). Numerous studies have found that disputed territory is the primary factor influencing the likelihood of militarized interstate disputes (MIDs) and war, particularly in enduring rivalries and among developing countries (Colaresi, Rasler, and Thompson

2007; Forsberg 1996; Goertz and Diehl 1992; Hensel 1999; Huth 1996; Kocs 1995; Tir and Diehl 2002; Vasquez 1993). In the last two centuries, almost one-third of all territorial disputes have escalated to war, a much higher percentage than the universe of all international disputes. Territorial disputes are nearly twice as likely as other issues to escalate to interstate war (Hensel 1999).

Fortunately, many states have peacefully settled territorial disputes. Since 1953, states have successfully resolved ninety-seven territorial disputes through bilateral negotiations, third-party mediation, arbitration, or adjudication at the International Court of Justice (ICJ). These settled disputes provide many benefits, mainly long periods of peace between former adversaries (Henehan and Vasquez 2011; Huth 1996; Kocs 1995; Vasquez and Henehan 2010). Overall, long periods of universalist peace (Wallensteen 1984) are associated with the existence of fewer territorial disputes (Vasquez and Henehan 2010). Settled disputes are also beneficial in that they are more likely to allow the emergence of democratic regimes (Gibler 2007) and increased trade (Simmons 2005). Despite the clear benefits of settled territorial disputes, seventy-one territorial disputes are ongoing today, the vast majority of which have endured several decades. They exist in every region of the world and involve 41 percent of all sovereign states. Some disputes, such as Eritrea v. Ethiopia and Serbia v. Croatia, have lasted only a few years, while others, such as the Falklands/Malvinas dispute between Argentina and the United Kingdom (UK), are enduring disputes, having lasted more than 175 years. What these disputes have in common is that the states involved have been unwilling to attempt settlement or to make or agree to territorial concessions that would lead to settlement. The more enduring the dispute, the greater the likelihood that continued tense relations will spiral into armed conflict.

Why have some states or their decision makers successfully settled almost two-thirds of the territorial disputes since 1953, while so many other states have continuing territorial disputes?[1] Why are government officials in some states willing to offer territorial concessions to resolve their territorial disputes, while others are unwilling or unable to? This book is about why territorial disputes become enduring, with a focus on dispute strategies—primarily the reasons why states are willing to attempt settlement in some cases, or why, in other cases when negotiations do occur, states are unwilling to offer territorial concessions. Enduring disputes are considered to be territorial disputes that last more than ten years, with or without militarized conflict.[2] This study also explores why states engage in diplomatic and military threats or uses of force while involved in territorial disputes, contributing to their endurance. In each case, the lack of initial settlement attempts, the lack of territorial concessions, and the continued use of diplomatic or militarized threats or the use of force make it difficult for states to resolve territorial disputes.

Some ongoing territorial disputes have never been subjected to settlement attempts or attempts by the challenger state, the state making the territorial claim, to change the status quo through force. For example, though representatives of China and Japan have met to discuss procedural issues or issues related to the disputed Senkaku/Diaoyu Islands in the East China Sea, the two states have never discussed sovereignty or potential settlement of the dispute. Likewise Canada and Denmark have never attempted to negotiate the sovereignty of Hans Island near Greenland, and Egypt and Sudan have never been willing to discuss sovereignty at the bargaining table regarding the disputed Wadi Halfa/Hala'ib Triangle along their border. Though these states have held bilateral negotiations, the focus has been on related issues such as maritime issues and resource management or unrelated bilateral issues. In these and many other cases, the problem is therefore not that states fail to bargain successfully in order to settle disputes. Rather, the problem is that initial attempts to resolve the disputes never occur. This seems puzzling considering that the assumed purpose of a territorial claim is for the challenger state to acquire the disputed territory. Since acquiring territory through force is typically too costly and risky, peaceful resolution methods are the only feasible means by which the status quo can change. It is not clear why challenger states in these cases in particular bother with their territorial claims without making any active attempt to resolve the disputes.

In other cases, when states have attempted peaceful settlement, the bargaining process has failed, so disputes continue to prevail. The two adversaries are unable to find a bargaining space where there is some overlap of the preferences of each state, meaning that neither or both states are willing to offer or agree to territorial concessions that would shift the status quo, whether by dropping a territorial claim, ceding territory, or dividing disputed territory. Because of the level of salience that territory has for most states, it is difficult for states to agree on territorial concessions, especially when the territory has value or there is domestic accountability, theories that are discussed at length in the next chapter. As a result of the failure of bargaining, these disputes have become enduring disputes. The dispute between Spain and the UK over Gibraltar, the Kurile Islands/Northern Territories dispute between Japan and Russia, and

Guatemala's claim for the territory of Belize have been subjected to many failed settlement attempts, none of which has brought the adversaries close enough to a mutually agreed bargaining space where some concessions could be exchanged to end the disputes. What this implies is that one or both states involved have refused the terms of settlement for some reason. In successfully resolved disputes like the border and territorial dispute between China and the Soviet Union/Russia, these states were eventually willing to offer and accept territorial concessions, leading to the settlement of the dispute. Understanding the factors that make it likely for states to consider territorial concessions is critical to understanding the problem of enduring territorial disputes.

The offer of nonterritorial concessions could potentially help entice an adversary to reconsider territorial claims. Yet, even when a target state is willing to share economic revenue from resources located in or near disputed territories, many challenger states refuse to drop their territorial claims. For example, even after the UK expressed willingness to share revenue from oil deposits discovered near the disputed Falkland/Malvinas Islands in the mid-1990s if Argentina gave up its claim to sovereignty, Argentina's leaders continued to demand full sovereign rights despite the state's continuous economic instability. China has also refused proposals by Japan to jointly exploit oil deposits in the waters around the disputed Senkaku/Diaoyu Islands, despite both states' significant interest in oil resources. The implication is that the territory itself is valued more than potential economic payoffs, or the endurance of the territorial dispute provides some other benefits to the state.

This study builds on previous research on territorial disputes by presenting a theory of territorial disputes as bargaining leverage. This theory attempts to explain variation in territorial dispute strategies, mainly attempted settlement— why states sometimes pursue settlement but under different conditions do not, leading to the endurance of territorial disputes. The theory of territorial disputes as bargaining leverage attempts to outline conditions that make settlement attempts in territorial disputes more or less likely to occur. The central argument is that challenger states in particular can actually benefit from the endurance of disputes when other salient disputed issues exist. Such conditions provide an opportunity for states to pursue a strategy of issue linkage and coercive diplomacy. By pursuing this strategy, challenger states can attempt to use territorial disputes as bargaining leverage to gain concessions in other disputed issues. Under these circumstances, challengers have little incentive to settle the disputes and more incentive to pursue diplomatic and militarized threats and limited uses of force against the target during the ongoing disputes. In other words, it may be efficient in some conditions for states to "play the border card" (Danhui 2005, 91), purposely maintaining territorial disputes as ongoing rather than attempting to resolve them. The implication is that though territorial disputes are an underlying cause of tensions between states, it may not necessarily be the disputed territory that is driving the dispute, but instead other salient disputed issues linked to the territorial disputes.

By persisting in a territorial dispute, a challenger state can make some threat or use limited force as a form of coercive diplomacy. The challenger can simultaneously pursue a strategy of issue linkage, in which it links the territorial dispute with other disputed issues, such as an adversary's military activity (unrelated to the territorial dispute) or third-party security or economic agreements with other adversaries. The challenger can use diplomatic or militarized threats or minor uses of force in the territorial dispute, such as threatening to use force in a territorial law, deploying troops to a border, or launching missiles over disputed territory as a way to compel the target state to halt or change its behavior or policy on another disputed issue. By linking the persistence of territorial disputes to other disputed issues, challenger states can gain bargaining leverage over target states, helping them to achieve nonterritorial concessions in other disputed issues. Such bargaining leverage makes challenger states unwilling to attempt settlement of their territorial disputes since they can take advantage of the disputes. Therefore, when other disputed issues exist at a particular time, challenger states should be more likely to initiate diplomatic or militarized threats or uses of force and less likely to attempt settlement by offering territorial concessions, making territorial disputes enduring. On the other hand, when other disputed issues do not exist or are resolved, we should expect to see a decreased likelihood of diplomatic or militarized threats or uses of force and an increased likelihood of attempted settlements with more offers of concessions, making resolution of territorial disputes more likely. In other words, when states can use territorial disputes as bargaining leverage acquired through the use of coercive diplomacy and issue linkage, challenger states should be less willing to resolve territorial disputes. However, when challenger states are unable to link territorial disputes to other disputed issues, they should be willing to attempt settlement and resolve their territorial disputes once and for all.

The theory of territorial disputes as bargaining leverage attempts to more effectively explain the variation of territorial dispute settlement and threats or uses of force as dispute strategies. I test the theory against two sets of alternative theories used in previous literature to explain the variation of territorial dispute strategies: 1) value of territory and 2) domestic accountability and mobilization. The main premise of the first explanation is that different values of territory will influence dispute strategies including uses of force and settlement (Hensel 2001; Huth 1996). The domestic accountability and mobilization arguments link domestic vulnerability to dispute strategies (Chiozza and Choi 2003; Fravel 2008; Huth and Allee 2002; Tir 2010). These theories explain some of the variation in territorial dispute strategies, but they are insufficient in explaining much of the variation. The theory of bargaining leverage attempts to fill this gap in the literature.

TYPES OF DISPUTED TERRITORY

There are two types of territorial disputes—interstate and intrastate. Interstate territorial disputes occur when there is a disagreement between government officials of two or more sovereign states who make official claims for territory or defend against attempts to change the territorial status quo. Intrastate territorial disputes occur within a state when domestic groups seek autonomy or secession from the state. While domestic-level intrastate disputes are as important to study, the focus of this book is interstate territorial disputes. There are many informative studies of intrastate-level disputes, focusing on the pros and cons of partition and secession, the role of territory in ethnic and civil conflict, and enduring internal rivalries (Fearon 2004; Furhmann and Tir 2009; Horowitz 1985; C. Johnson 2008; C. Kaufmann 1996, 1998; Kumar 1997; Tir 2002, 2005a, 2005b, 2006; Toft 2002, 2003). Explaining dispute strategies in domestic-level disputes is outside the scope of this study, and while the theories discussed in this book could likely apply to such disputes, the differences are significant enough that they merit their own study.

Disputed territory in interstate disputes can include a variety of types of territory. For the purpose of this study, I created three general types of disputed territory: 1) uninhabited island disputes, 2) border disputes, and 3) disputes over inhabited tracts of territory. It is important to distinguish which type of territory is disputed because the claims and consequences of the dispute may be directly affected by type of territory and because leaders are expected to make different strategic choices regarding a territory such as a heavily inhabited area like Hong Kong compared to a desolate border river where no one lives, making the exchange of territory less detrimental to the population. For example, uninhabited island disputes can linger on for decades without much cost to the involved parties and little or no costs to the public since they generally involve little security and people's lives are not directly affected by the dispute.

On the other hand, the costs and consequences of disputes over inhabited tracts of territory are generally much higher since people living in those territories will be directly affected by the dispute and any potential territorial exchange. For example, the British residents of the Falkland Islands would be living under Argentine rule if the UK had ceded the islands to Argentina as was planned in the late 1970s or if Argentina had succeeded in maintaining control of the islands in the early 1980s. Such a territorial exchange would have major effects on the Falklands residents, a key reason why the UK today is unwilling to consider any concept of shared sovereignty with Argentina. Another reason for the distinction of territorial disputes as uninhabited islands, borders, and inhabited tracts of territory is that it provides for a further test of salience separate from only examining strategic, ethnic, or economic value. There are certainly other ways to categorize territorial disputes, such as homeland versus colonial or dependent territories, and mainland territory versus island and territorial waters (Hensel 2001). The case studies do reflect some variance of these categories of disputed territory as well, but the main focus is on the actual types of territory based on inhabitance and whether the exchange of territory would have significant impact on the states involved.

Uninhabited islands are generally barren, small, rocky, and without resources. Small and uninhabited islands tend to be left off maritime maps, and in the past states did not go to great efforts to claim such islands due to their lack of value. Only when states began recognizing maritime resources accessible only by ownership of islands did acquisition become significant in most cases. Therefore, the real dispute over islands is usually not about the islands themselves, but about the maritime borders that result from sovereignty of certain islands, as well as maritime resources such as oil, natural gas, fish, and minerals. Sovereignty of the islands, and hence maritime access around the islands, most often provides economic benefits in the form of maritime resources and shipping access. As a result, many island disputes were initiated because of the realized potential for access to maritime resources otherwise inaccessible.

Without clearly delimited international maritime borders, it becomes difficult, if not impossible, to pursue maritime resources without provoking the opposing state. For example, in 1971, when China began showing interest in the Senkaku/Diaoyu Islands in the East China Sea, Japan halted applications for drilling rights for potential oil resources in the vicinity of the islands. Since then, neither state has attempted to drill for oil in the disputed waters, preventing both states from accessing the resources. Until the sovereignty of disputed islands is settled, the secure, legal access to maritime resources is limited or completely inaccessible for states involved in disputes over uninhabited islands. Sovereignty of these islands can sometimes provide security, such as control of a strategic shipping lane like the Strait of Hormuz. Legal ownership of the Abu Musa Islands disputed between Iran and the United Arab Emirates (UAE) is critical to the security of the shipments of oil from the Persian Gulf to the rest of the world. For Canada, sovereignty of tiny Hans Island is critical to shipping and naval access to the Arctic region.

Disputed borders are disagreements about the delimitation of the location of an international border or boundary between sovereign states. There are several reasons that border disputes arise. Typically, there are ambiguous historic treaties signed by colonizers and not by the postcolonial sovereign states (Murphy 1991). Such border disputes are very common in Africa and the Middle East in particular, where European colonizers drew artificial lines in the sand with little reference to ethnic divisions or geographic landmarks. In many cases, historic treaties did not clarify exactly where a border should be located. In other cases, one state claims lost autonomy because a colonizing state drew the border in a different location than that state's prior autonomous region. In noncolonized states, sometimes the course of a river, a common way to delimit borders, shifts over time so that the border becomes disputed. This was the case in the now-settled border dispute between Mexico and the United States (US) over the Rio Grande. Another factor is when a heavily forested border region is so dense or difficult to reach that demarcation never occurs, leading to future claims. Even if demarcation occurred in the past, such boundary markers are sometimes destroyed, moved, or worn down to the point where the legal border must be redrawn. Whatever the justification for the territorial claim, identifying the legal location of an international border is critical for security, economic, and ethnic reasons.

Inhabited tracts of territory are considered to be areas where people are actively residing, working on the land, or using the territory for commerce. States initiate claims to inhabited tracts of territory generally because there is an ethnic link to the people in the target state or the territory was once part of the challenger state's conception of a homeland. It is important to differentiate between inhabited territory and uninhabited territory because disputes over inhabited territory directly affect people living in the territory. These territories tend to be mainland territories, but can include island territories that are inhabited, such as Hong Kong, Goa, or the Falkland/Malvinas Islands. A dispute over uninhabited islands or an uninhabited border region in the mountains, along a river, or in a rainforest does not have a direct effect on the lives of people, making the dispute less costly. In disputes over inhabited territory, threats issued about the territory have a direct impact on the inhabitants, sometimes forcing them to flee the territory if the threat is militarized. The very idea of a state making a threat to acquire the territory where people in another state live is stressful. For the people living in Taiwan, Kashmir and Jammu, and South Korea, the threat of military force by China, Pakistan, and North Korea, respectively, is always on their minds. In these types of disputes, the territories are not merely pawns in a strategic game; the disputes threaten the very livelihood of thousands or millions of people.

INITIATION OF TERRITORIAL DISPUTES

Regardless of which type of territory is disputed, there are many cases where the status of the territory is ambiguous, and recognized, definitive sovereignty is lacking. In atlases and international maps, disputed territory is usually labeled as occupied by one state, claimed by another. The Falkland/Malvinas Islands in the South Atlantic Sea are usually labeled as British territory claimed by Argentina, the Golan Heights is labeled as Israeli-occupied territory, claimed by Syria, and Kashmir and Jammu is often noted as Indian territory disputed with Pakistan.[3] In other cases, the territory is clearly recognized by the international community as sovereign territory of one state or the other, and the opponent's claim is generally dismissed. Examples of these cases are Lebanon's claim for Shebaa Farms, Guatemala's claim for Belize, and Taiwan's claim for the Senkaku Islands, owned by Japan. In any case, the dispute must be official and active; this means that the governments of both the challenging and defending states have recognized a dispute between them.

A territorial dispute is initiated when a state makes an official claim for a portion or all of the territory of another sovereign state, a state questions the location of an existing border and requests a revision of the border, or a state contests the right of another state to exercise sovereignty over a certain territory (Huth 1996). Territorial disputes exist for several reasons. First, there could be a disagreement about the legal validity of a treaty signed under duress or by third-party states. An example of such a disagreement is Japan's claim that signing away the Northern Territories Islands to the Soviet Union as part of 1951 postwar peace treaty was unfair. As a result, Japan claimed the islands as theirs from a point immediately following the signing of the treaty. Another reason for the initiation of territorial disputes occurs when a colonizer or another third party cedes control of some tract of territory, and two or more newly independent states claim the territory. For example, China and Vietnam both claimed the Paracel and Spratly Islands after Japan imparted the islands as part of the 1951 postwar peace treaty (Fravel 2008).

Different interpretations of a treaty delineating territorial boundaries are another reason why territorial disputes exist. Uruguay and Brazil, for instance, each identify different streams as the waterway that is defined in an 1851 treaty delineating their border at the end of the Uruguayan civil war. An additional explanation for the initiation of territorial disputes is the discovery of new geological data showing the actual territorial markers that were noted in a boundary treaty, but never actually cited. This discovery can cause a state to challenge previously decided borders or ownership. An example is Ecuador's exposure in 1950 to newly released US satellite photos of a previously unknown river in the border area with Peru, activating a latent territorial claim that eventually led to armed conflict in the 1990s. Similarly, in the 1890s, Mexico initiated a claim against the US after discovering that the course of the Rio Grande had shifted. This dispute was peacefully resolved in the 1960s.

When a state gains independence and claims territory that was not included as sovereign as determined by a former colonizer, a state can also initiate a territorial dispute. For instance, in 1949, upon Indonesia's independence, it claimed West Irian, a territory in New Guinea, which it could not previously claim as a colonized state. Other claims for territory could occur as a result of partition, when a neighboring state claims the disputed territory for irredentist reasons. In some cases, a rump state continues to seek disputed territory from a state that has seceded, like Ethiopia's continued claim of disputed territory along the border with Eritrea (Tir 2005b). Pakistan's claim to Kashmir and Jammu, and Rann of Kutch after the 1947 partition, and accession of these territories to India also illustrates this type of dispute. Another well-known case is Ireland's claim to the six provinces of Northern Ireland after the 1922 partition of the island, which was dropped as part of the Good Friday Peace Accords in 1998.

Lastly, states can actually initiate territorial claims specifically to gain bargaining leverage against a target state, a theory discussed in chapter 3. In this case, a state will deliberately challenge the territorial rights of its adversary in order to use the dispute as a means of issue linkage. An example of such an initiation is China's seizure of some of the Paracel Islands in the South China Sea from Vietnam, so that China could use the dispute over the islands as leverage in the Sino-Vietnamese border dispute and preempt Vietnam's claim to the islands (Burton 1979; C.-K. Lo 1989).

TERRITORIAL DISPUTE STRATEGIES

States involved in territorial disputes have several strategy options for how to deal with their territorial claims. Challenger states can choose to use force to acquire disputed territory from the target state, they can maintain the dispute as ongoing but take no action, or they can take some action to peacefully resolve the dispute by dropping the territorial claim or attempting to settle the dispute through bilateral negotiations with the target or some type of third-party involvement such as mediation or adjudication by the ICJ. Maintaining the dispute but not engaging in conflict or settlement attempts falls into the category of negative peace, where the dispute is unsettled, but the adversaries are not engaging in any conflict (Klein, Goertz, and Diehl 2008). Though the objective of a state involved in a territorial dispute is usually to acquire or defend all of the disputed territory, providing the highest payoffs to one state and none to the other, this is difficult to achieve through both war and peaceful settlement. Despite attempts by one state to actively settle a dispute, settlement cannot occur without consent of the opposing state. Such a predicament means that one state agreeing to concede all of the disputed territory to the other is not nearly as likely as a state agreeing to divide the territory or not settle at all.

Threats or Uses of Force

At any point during a territorial dispute, challenger states can threaten to use some type of force or initiate and engage in armed conflict at varying levels. Challenger states can threaten or use force for many reasons, including actual attempts to change the status quo through the acquisition of disputed territory by force. More frequently, challenger states threaten or use force to signal resolve to the target state about the seriousness of their claim to the disputed territory or to compel the target state to take an action of some type. Threats or displays of force can include shows of potential force such as mobilization of troops, movement of troops in proximity to the disputed territory, war games or maneuvers related to the territorial dispute, or missile launches across disputed waters. Uses of force can range from low-intensity force involving clashes of troops along a border with no or few casualties to wars involving strong use of force resulting in high numbers of fatalities and destruction. Qatar's 1986 attack on a Bahraini coast guard station under construction on the disputed shoal of Fasht al-Dibal is an example of low-intensity conflict. Qatar's escalatory actions included shooting live fire from helicopters at the construction site, the rounding up and imprisonment of 29 foreign construction workers, and the occupation of the island by up to 150 Qatari soldiers. Wars over territory include the Arab-Israeli wars in 1948, 1967, and 1973 between Israel and Egypt, Syria, and Jordan, the Korean War from 1950 to 1953, the Iran-Iraq War from 1980 to 1988, and the Football War between El Salvador and Honduras in 1969.

Kashmir and Jammu, the Falkland/Malvinas Islands, the Ethiopia-Eritrea border—these are just some of the other enduring territorial disputes that have caused major wars between adversaries. The dispute over Kashmir and Jammu in the northern border region between India and Pakistan is the most heavily militarized territorial dispute in the world (Central Intelligence Agency 2008). This dispute has led to three major wars fought in 1947, 1965, and 1971, numerous armed clashes at the border, a multitude of terrorist attacks and assassinations, and the acquisition of nuclear weapons by both states. The first two wars were fought directly over the disputed territory of Kashmir and Jammu, occupied by India and claimed by Pakistan, while the third war involved intense fighting in the disputed territory in addition to other disputed border regions between India and Pakistan. The first two wars led to the combined deaths of almost 10,000 Indian and Pakistani troops, while the third war resulted in approximately 300,000 deaths in all locations of the war. Though no war has been fought there since 1971, there have been numerous Pakistani terrorist and guerrilla attacks in Kashmir and Jammu, resulting in continued tension between the two adversaries.[4] The likelihood of resolution is low due mostly to the determination of both states to stand firm in their claims of sovereignty.

The Falkland/Malvinas Islands dispute in the South Atlantic is based on Argentina's unrelenting claim for the islands since 1833. In April 1982, Argentina invaded the islands in an attempt to provoke the UK into sovereignty negotiations, which had stalled in 1968, and to allegedly divert attention of the public from domestic crises with which the government was dealing.[5] As the British navy sailed to the South Atlantic Sea, mediation attempts failed to end the crisis, and war commenced, leading to the deaths of nearly 1,000 Argentine and British servicemen. Despite the improbability of further armed conflict in this dispute, its very endurance continues to adversely affect Argentine-British relations and acts as a thorn in the side of the British. Even though the likelihood of acquiring the islands is low, Argentina continues to regularly press its territorial claim.

The border dispute between Ethiopia and Eritrea, "a conflict once described as so pointless that it was like two bald men fighting over a comb" (Rice 2005), led to a nasty border war from May 1998 to June 2000, resulting in an estimated 70,000 deaths, mass displacement of refugees, and hundreds of millions of dollars spent by both sides. The outcome of the war led to only minor border changes. Ethiopia won the military part of the war, while Eritrea won concessions from the Permanent Court of Arbitration. A United Nations (UN) boundary commission awarded a small disputed border area, the remaining disputed territory after the war, to Eritrea, but the territory continues to be occupied by Ethiopia. In 2005, and again in 2008, tensions rose between the two states when Eritrea expelled UN peacekeeping troops from the border. The UN was fearful of a relapse of armed conflict, yet the institution voted later that year to withdraw its peacekeeping forces from the border region. The dispute continues at a deadlock with no immediate progress or resolution evident. These are just a handful of enduring territorial disputes that have involved major armed conflict, mass casualties, and massive destruction of homes, infrastructure, and cities. In these and many other disputes, there is no question that disputed territory is a major problem for the states involved and, inadvertently, the international community.

A study by Huth and Allee (2002) of all territorial disputes from 1919 to 1995 found that challenger states threatened or used force in 6 percent of the observations of territorial disputes. Though this percentage seems low, it is relatively high compared to nonterritorial disputes. To provide perspective, Vasquez and Henehan (2001) find that compared to policy disputes, territorial disputes are three times more likely to lead to war. Senese and Vasquez (2003) show that states with territorial claims are seven times more likely to engage in armed conflict compared to those without territorial claims. Senese and Vasquez (2008) also demonstrate that territorial disputes are more likely to lead to war compared to disputes over policy, regime, or other disputed issues. Identifying the reasons why challenger states engage in threats or uses of force in territorial disputes is a key aspect of this study.

Settlement Attempts

At any point during a dispute, decision makers also have the opportunity to drop the claim or attempt peaceful settlement through bilateral negotiations or third-party involvement. When a challenger state drops its territorial claim for disputed territory, this means that the challenger officially accepts the status quo in which the challenger recognizes the target state's legal ownership of the formerly disputed territory, sometimes without having to engage in negotiations or a third-party resolution method.[6] Attempting settlement is not merely an attempt by a state to negotiate some aspect about the disputed territory but an actual attempt to negotiate the terms of *sovereignty* by offering some type of territorial concession, whether minor or major.

Most territorial disputes are resolved through some offer of concessions in bilateral negotiations (Huth and Allee 2002; Powell and Wiegand 2010), but disagreements over territory can also be subject to resolution by a third party through mediation, conciliation, good offices, inquiry, or more formal mechanisms, arbitration or adjudication. Bilateral negotiations do not involve any third party and are the least formal and legalized, involving flexibility for the states involved (M. Shaw 2003). Nonbinding third-party dispute resolution methods include good offices, conciliation, inquiry, and mediation, all of which involve a third-party actor examining the merits of the evidence presented by both sides in the dispute and making a recommendation to the disputants regarding settlement (Bercovitch and Rubin 1992; Cassese 2005; M. Shaw 2003). Binding third-party methods, arbitration and adjudication, are more legalized and formalized, involving interpretation of international law (Powell and Wiegand 2010). In each binding method, both the challenger and target state must agree to turn over the dispute to an arbitrator, which issues an award, or a court, which issues a judgment.

Though states do sometimes negotiate or engage in third-party resolution methods at the same time as threatening or using force, there are few cases in which settlement of the territorial dispute occurred immediately after use of force. Rather, when negotiations or third-party methods of settlement attempts occur, they generally deal with terms of de-escalation but rarely lead to settlement. Many actors engage in procedural negotiations in which they agree to meet again at a further date, agree to open a border to allow the flow of trade or people, or agree to deal with other issues related to the territorial dispute. Though these negotiations may achieve some intended goal, they do not represent significant likelihood of change in the status quo. Rather, negotiations and third-party resolution methods specifically involving the sovereign status of the disputed territory and potential territorial concessions are the only means by which states can attempt actual settlement of territorial disputes. The Huth and Allee (2002) study found that challenger states offered territorial concessions in about 37 percent of the cases, with target states offering territorial concessions in 36 percent of the observations. These authors also find that many rounds of disputes generally have to occur before challenger states are willing to consider offering concessions. Understanding why it takes so long, if ever, for challenger states to consider offering concessions through bilateral negotiations or nonbinding or binding third-party resolution methods is the major point of this study.

ORGANIZATION OF THE BOOK

To understand why different dispute strategies are used by challenger states in territorial disputes, it is necessary to first frame the question in the context of previous research on territorial disputes, presented in chapter 2. The previous research examined here focuses particularly on theories about value of territory and domestic accountability and mobilization, tested as alternative theories in this study. The main premise of the explanation about value of territory is that certain values could prevent or promote threats or uses of force and the peaceful attempt of settlement in territorial disputes. The domestic accountability explanation argues that leaders of states avoid territorial concessions, threats, or uses of force when they are most vulnerable so that they can avoid domestic punishment if the settlement is an unpopular choice. This argument is rooted in the international relations (IR) literature about domestic audience costs and rally-round-the-flag theories and follows the same logic as the democratic costs literature, in which leaders are expected to be punished for unpopular foreign policy choices, such as settlement of territorial disputes. A subsequent explanation of domestic mobilization predicts that leaders can use the salience of territorial disputes to mobilize the domestic populace to increase public support.

Chapter 3 presents the theoretical framework for the theory of bargaining leverage. The theory introduced in this study discusses how states benefit from the endurance of territorial disputes, using them as bargaining leverage in other disputed issues. This chapter first discusses strategies of compellence and coercive diplomacy, concepts from international security literature, and explains the concept of issue linkage, a concept from the international institutions and international law literature. Because I am applying concepts from various aspects of IR to the theory, I first provide precise definitions of these terms and then outline the logic of how these combined strategies provide challenger states with bargaining leverage, which can explain the endurance of territorial disputes.

In chapter 4, I outline the research design used to assess the theory of bargaining leverage against the theories of value of territory and domestic accountability/mobilization and describe the characteristics of all territorial disputes since the middle of the twentieth century. The primary method used by this study is a qualitative analysis of the strategies of challenger states in three enduring territorial disputes and one settled dispute. The first part of the chapter focuses on the justification for selecting certain cases, the unit of analysis, the dependent, independent, and control variables, and the overall strengths and limitations of using the chosen methods. In the second section of this chapter, I provide descriptive inferences of ongoing disputes, most of which are enduring, and settled disputes since 1953, including information about region, duration, types of territory, states' involvement in threats or uses of force, and attempted settlements.

Chapters 5, 6, 7, and 8 comprise the four case studies used to test the theory of bargaining leverage versus the value of territory and domestic accountability and mobilization explanations. Though it is impossible to prove that bargaining leverage is the most applicable theory in these cases, the chapters provide a significant amount of evidence to strongly suggest this is the case, while simultaneously demonstrating that the value of territory and domestic accountability/mobilization explanations partially explain dispute strategies or are weak or falsified. Chapter 5 focuses on the Senkaku/Diaoyu Islands dispute between China and Japan and monthly observations of Chinese settlement attempts and threats and uses of force from 1971 to 2008. Chapter 6 looks at the Shebaa Farms border dispute between Lebanon and Israel and all settlement attempts and diplomatic threats made by Lebanon, as well as uses of force made by the nonstate actor Hezbollah from 2000 to 2008. Chapter 7 examines the dispute between Morocco and Spain over the North African enclaves Ceuta/Sebta and Melilla/Melilia and all Moroccan dispute strategies from 1956 to 2008. The last case study, presented in chapter 8, is about the eastern and western borders between China and the Soviet Union/Russia, as well as a large swathe of Russian territory claimed by China. This case reviews all settlement attempts and threats and uses of force pursued by China from 1963 to 2008. Each chapter begins with an overview of the geography and history of the territorial dispute and its initiation, examines the claims of both the challenger and target states, and outlines the dispute strategies of the challenger states. The remaining sections analyze how each theory could explain the disputes and assesses the validity of each theory by examining bilateral strategic interactions.

Chapter 9 examines the feasibility of the strategy of issue linkage and coercive diplomacy, the applicability of the theory of bargaining leverage, and how it affects the endurance of territorial disputes. This chapter also provides an assessment of generalization of the theory and a discussion of how the theory of bargaining leverage adds to previous theories about territorial dispute strategies. The concluding section provides a discussion of the reasons why enduring territorial disputes are an important policy issue and the options for policy makers about territorial disputes for both those directly involved and also potential mediators in such disputes, specifically focusing on confidence-building measures.

CHAPTER TWO

Previous Research on Territorial Dispute Strategies

Though territorial disputes are considered to be the most obvious illustration of zero-sum conflicts (Kratochwil 1985), the majority of states involved in territorial disputes in the twentieth century have attempted to resolve their disputes peacefully, and very few have been resolved through armed conflict. Territory is also generally considered to be the most salient issue and the issue most likely to cause armed conflict compared to other disputed issues (Diehl 1991, 1992; Forsberg 1996; Gochman and Leng 1983; Goertz and Diehl 1992; Hensel 1999, 2001; Herz 1957; Huth 1996; Luard 1970; Senese 1999; Senese and Vasquez 2008; Vasquez 1993; Vasquez and Henehan 2001). Though the outbreak of armed conflict is the significant focus of considerable international relations research, the likelihood of peaceful settlement of international disputes should also be emphasized since peaceful settlement is the ultimate objective. Many states have been able to successfully settle territorial disputes peacefully, without engaging in any armed conflict. Yet, most of the literature on territorial disputes has focused on armed conflict and not as much on the management or the peaceful settlement of the disputes (Frazier 2006; Hensel 2001; Powell and Wiegand 2010). Figuring out the conditions that increase the likelihood of resolution would help to prevent conditions from worsening and states from turning to armed conflict.

The existing research on territorial disputes has examined a wide range of aspects of the disputes. Most of the earlier scholarship, mainly reflecting the dominant realist paradigm, focused on the likelihood of armed conflict (Midlarsky 1975; Richardson 1960; Starr 1978; Starr and Most 1976, 1980, 1983). Later research not only relaxed realist assumptions but also began focusing on other aspects of territorial disputes rather than armed conflict, probing at questions about the role of territory as an issue distinct from other types of issues disputed between states, initiation of territorial disputes, likelihood of resolution, effects of territorial changes and peaceful territorial transfers, the link between territory and enduring rivalries, and degree of third-party intervention (Allee and Huth 2006; Ben-Yehuda 2004; Forsberg 1996; Gibler 2007; Gibler and Tir 2010; Goertz and Diehl 1992; Hensel 1996, 2001; Hensel, Mitchell, Sowers, and Thyne 2008; Huth 1996; Huth and Allee 2002; Kacowicz 1994; Kocs 1995; Mandel 1980; Powell and Wiegand 2010; Rasler and Thompson 2006; Senese 1996, 2005; Senese and Vasquez 2003, 2008; Starr and Most 1983; Tir 2003, 2006; Tir and Diehl 2002; Vasquez 1993, 1996; Vasquez and Henehan 2001; Wiegand and Powell 2011). Factors believed or found to be influential on the likelihood of MIDs and territorial dispute settlement include value of territory, history of militarized conflict, record of peaceful territorial transfers, regime type, past win/loss record, number of democracies in the international system, domestic factors, and domestic legal system.

Much has been written about the effects of peaceful transfers of territory on the likelihood of armed conflict in territorial disputes. The initial argument in this area was that peaceful transfers of territory would likely lead to future peace (Goertz and Diehl 1992), specifically if the transfers were mutually acceptable to the adversaries and did not occur during militarized confrontations (Vasquez 1993). A related argument is that (legally) settled borders were more likely to lead to future peace between adversaries (Huth 1996; Kocs 1995). A key finding of Kocs (1995) is that unresolved territorial claims increased the likelihood of armed conflict by forty times compared to other disputed issues. Yet, despite hopes that there was a link between past transfers and future conflict, Goertz and Diehl (1992) show that there was actually no difference between the effect of peaceful changes to borders relative to violent changes regarding future peace. Tir (2003, 2006) reworked the model based on this earlier finding by taking a different approach and fleshing out peaceful transfers, violent transfers, and transfers that involve overwhelming victories. The key finding by Tir is that violent transfers of territory are, in fact, much more likely to lead to future armed conflict compared to transfers that resulted from overwhelming victories, and that peaceful transfers are associated with future peace because such transfers constrain leaders from using force in the future (Gibler and Tir 2010; Tir 2003, 2006).

In looking at the causes of settlement, specifically peaceful territorial change, Kacowicz (1994) demonstrates that consensus on international norms influences the likelihood of peaceful territorial change, but diplomatic intervention and past experience in armed conflict do not have such influence. Likewise, regime type, power distribution, and third-party threats do not seem to play a conclusive role in the likelihood of peaceful territorial change. Also examining the feasibility of peaceful settlement, Hensel, Allison, and Khanani (2009) examine the effect of past territorial integrity obligations as measured by settlement treaties on the effects of territorial changes. Their finding is that both violent and peaceful territorial treaties have no systematic effect on the likelihood of future peaceful or violent territorial change.

Focusing more specifically on type of settlement attempt, a history of failed settlement attempts in a particular dispute is found to increase the probability of subsequent third-party assistance, and a history of successful settlement attempts increases the probability of bilateral negotiations (Hensel 1999). Recent peaceful settlement in a particular dispute plays an important role, as previous failed attempts at peace subsequently increase pressure to undertake further action to settle a particular dispute (Hensel et al. 2008). Past conflict may also lead to peaceful efforts, since states might have learned that peaceful settlement is less costly and could perhaps offer greater prospects for success than militarized conflict (Hensel 2001). Similarly, Hensel et al. (2008, 127) find that states are more likely to pursue peaceful settlements in general "when they have a history of recent militarized conflict over the same issue and/or a history of recent failed attempts to settle the same issue peacefully." Other research has shown that a challenger state's past win/loss record greatly influences the choice of resolution method (bilateral negotiations, arbitration, adjudication) in attempts to settle territorial disputes (Wiegand and Powell 2011).

Regime type, domestic factors, and domestic legal systems are also thought to influence dispute strategies in territorial disputes. Kacowicz (1994) argues that peaceful territorial changes resulting from dispute settlement are more likely to occur when the disputing states have the same or similar type of political regime. Yet as noted, the cases examined do not provide support for this correlation. Mitchell (2002) makes a systemic level argument, which shows that third-party settlement is more likely for nondemocratic dyads when the proportion of democracies in the system increases. In a more recent study of territorial disputes, Allee and Huth (2006) find that the likelihood of legal dispute resolution triples when the disputing states possess democratic political institutions. Allee and Huth (2006, 286) also show that state leaders facing a territorial dispute often seek legal dispute resolution as a form of "'political cover' that

helps them to counter domestic political opposition to a controversial settlement agreement." Another type of domestic factor is the domestic legal system
of a state—civil, common, Islamic, or mixed legal systems, which have some influence on the choice of resolution method (Powell and Wiegand 2010).

In terms of the effect of democracy on the likelihood of territorial MIDs,
there are mixed results despite the solid finding about the link between democracy and decreased likelihood of armed conflict in the democratic peace
literature. For example, one finding is that mixed regimes or low-level democracies with Polity scores of 0–5 are more likely to initiate or prolong MIDs compared to stronger authoritarian regimes or democracies (Huth and Allee 2002).
More specifically, a change in net democracy scores for a challenger state from
highly nondemocratic (-10) to highly democratic (10) decreases the likelihood
of initiation of force by 70 percent (Huth and Allee 2002). Using a "weak link"
measure, which is considered to be the lowest Polity score in a dyad, Gibler
(2007) shows that democracy reduces the likelihood of MID onset for post–
World War II dyads. However, when controlling for border factors—ethnic
group divided by a border, terrain differences, and same colonial master before
independence—democracy is found to be positive but insignificant, indicating that democracy has little or no effect on the onset of MIDs when certain
factors related to the territorial dispute are taken into account (Gibler 2007).
Similar results are shown by James, Park, and Choi (2006) in that the existence of a democratic dyad does not influence the likelihood of MID initiation
when such factors as issue salience, past attempts at settlement, and recent MIDs
are considered. Based on these mixed findings, it is difficult to make any thor-
ough assessments of the influence of democracy on MID initiation in territorial disputes.

The most extensive findings in the literature about factors that affect territorial dispute strategies are studies about value or salience of territory and domestic accountability. This study builds on these two dominant themes, set out
in particular by Huth (1996), Huth and Alee (2002), Hensel (2001), and Hensel et al. (2008). In addition to reexamining these theories, this book provides
a novel explanation that builds on previous research to more thoroughly explain variation in territorial dispute strategies by providing a theory of territorial disputes as bargaining leverage for other disputed issues, discussed in the
next chapter. All three explanations assume that salience plays an influential
role, but in different ways.

VALUE OF TERRITORY

Perhaps the most logical explanation for states' decisions about whether to attempt settlement of a territorial dispute or to threaten or use force is the value of the disputed territory to the state. Kacowicz (1994, 55) argues that "the importance of the territory in question might make a substantial difference upon the prospects to resolve peacefully or not the territorial issue." How willing a state is to compromise or to provide concessions may depend on the value of the disputed land. The more valuable the disputed land, the higher the price a state will pay when considering compromise or offers of concessions (Fravel 2008).

Territory by itself has little value unless people or states infer value. For millennia, hunter-gatherer societies trekked through territories taking what they needed from the land and moving on. Not until humans settled on specific tracts of territory and began associating it as homelands did territory become important to own. In terms of economic value, it was not until people realized a demand for oil and other major resources that territory gained significant economic value. Territory has also had value in terms of power; for many centuries, acquiring territory was a major step in achieving relative power in the international system. European states scrambled to obtain masses of territory in the Americas, Africa, Asia, the Middle East, and Oceania to demonstrate supremacy through territorial control.

Though the association of territory and power is thought to have dwindled in the latter part of the twentieth century, owning territory has continued to provide multiple benefits. Besides providing the state with a right to interact in the international community, sovereign territory also provides for the foundation of a homeland from which to form a national identity, secure borders to protect the state's citizens, means to survive through access to water and agricultural land, and economic gain resulting in exploitation of the earth's natural resources such as oil, diamonds, and minerals. Territory can be considered valuable or salient both *across issues,* comparing territory to other disputed issues, and *within issues,* examining specific value that disputed territories have. Hensel (2001) argues that because of different salience that different disputed issues in international relations have, they should be treated distinctly in research. *Across issues,* Hensel et al. (2008) show that issue salience is a major factor in determining the likelihood of both militarized conflict and peaceful settlement attempts. Comparing different disputed issues—maritime claims, river claims, and territorial claims, Hensel et al. (2008) show that territorial claims and river claims that have the highest levels of salience are significantly more likely to be subject to peaceful settlement attempts and militarized conflict compared to maritime claims. At the same time, they also point out that though frequency of attempts at settlement is more likely with issues of higher salience, such attempts are also less likely to be successful.

Within issues, when only examining territory, that territory can have tangible or intangible value or some combination of each. Tangible value can include valuable economic resources, strategic value, mainland territory status compared to offshore islands, and a permanent population. Intangible value can include ethnic links to the land, homeland territory status compared to dependency status, or symbolic, nationalist value based on lost autonomy or feelings of attachment to the territory (J. Anderson 1988; Diehl 1992; Hensel 2001; Hensel and Mitchell 2005; Murphy 1991). One way to measure tangible and intangible value is to use a composite scale index of different values inferred upon the territory ranging from 0 to 12 (Hensel 2001). The more values that are present in disputed territory, the higher the salience score. Understanding the value or salience of territory can help to predict dispute strategies.

Tangible Value

The most commonsense tangible value, economic value, refers to territory that has significant natural resources that can be extracted to provide significant economic gains for one or both disputing states, such as fishing grounds, oil, iron, copper, or diamonds. Territory with significant economic value is defined as territory with natural resources that could generate export earnings, trade routes, key ports, and industry (Huth 1996; Tir 2006). Natural resources include oil, manganese, iron ore, lead, titanium, cobalt, tin, uranium, sulfur, copper, water, zinc, phosphate, diamonds, lead, chromium, bauxite, gold, silver, nickel, and tungsten. If the disputed territory is an island, rich fishing grounds and seabed minerals are included in measuring economic value. Economic gain from farming, markets, and other types of businesses located on the territory do not qualify the territory as having significant economic value.[1] The key factor is that the resources are considerable enough that extraction would contribute a significant amount to the gross domestic product of a state. For example, fishing grounds must be so rich that they contribute enough to the economy of a state that it makes a difference in the state's economic health. The major benefit of successfully defending or acquiring territory with economic value is obvious—significant economic gain for the state. Even if the disputed territory is divided, both states have the capability to achieve potential gains.

Strategic value of territory is often based on its location or characteristics, such as mountains, swamps, or deserts, which can provide territorial buffers for a state (Tir 2006). Territory can also have strategic value if it is located at or near military bases, major shipping lanes, or choke points for ships. Control of territory with strategic value strengthens the military position of a state by enhancing power projection, establishing military presence in shipping lanes or choke points, providing a defensive perimeter around military bases, and denying the adversary access to territory where it could project its own military force (Huth 1996). Sometimes disputed territory can have both economic and strategic value, such as Abu Musa and Greater Tunb Islands in the Strait of Hormuz in the Persian Gulf. Ownership of such islands determines control of a strait through which a significant portion of the world's oil supply passes, providing both economic and strategic value.

Intangible Value

Territory does not necessarily have to have tangible value. Rather, territory can also have intangible value such as ethnic, nationalist, or symbolic value (Diehl 1992; Vasquez 1993), which is generally attributed to the territory by the leadership or domestic populace. Territory is "a very substantial material, measurable, and concrete entity," but territory is also "the product and indeed the expression of the psychological features of human groups" (Gottman 1973, 15). In some cases, states claim that territory has what is called "indivisible value," in that the state perceives the territory as indivisible and nonnegotiable, making compromise difficult or unlikely (Goddard 2010; Hassner 2003, 2009; Toft 2003; Walter 2003). In any case, such embedded, intangible value can mean that challenger states are unwilling to compromise or negotiate over claimed ownership of such territories, and therefore disputes are more likely to be enduring. The Argentine claim for the Falkland Islands falls into this category since the islands hold no actual economic, strategic, or ethnic value, nor can they be categorized as having mainland or homeland status, and all the people who live there are British. Yet claims for the island are inherent in the national identity of Argentina. In Plaza de Mayo, directly across from the Presidential Palace in Buenos Aires, there are government-sanctioned banners claiming that the Malvinas will be part of Argentina again someday soon and displays of flags and maps showing the islands as Argentine (Wiegand and Powell forthcoming).

If territory has ethnic value, it means that the disputed territory has people of the same ethnic group as the challenger state living across a border in the target state. In this sense, the territory is valued because it is the home of ethnic kin. The objective is usually irredentism, to unify with a group of people sharing the same ethnic or national background living on the other side of a border. In this case, there must be definitive evidence that co-nationals of the challenger state live within the disputed territory or along the border and that they speak the same language (Huth 1996). Unlike territory with tangible value, territory with ethnic value is important because of its intrinsic, symbolic value (M. Anderson 1996; Knight 1983, 1984; Murphy 1990, 1991; Newman 1999; White 1995). Similarly, Tir (2003) describes intangible value as personal, unsubstitutable, indivisible, which is integral to the national identity.

When disputed territory has intangible value, meaning that the territory itself is valued, division is much more difficult since both states will generally claim that the territory is indivisible. In disputes over territory with ethnic value, division of the disputed territory that results from territorial concessions or settlement provides a different outcome compared to that achieved by settlement of disputes over territory with tangible value. Gains achieved through division of the disputed territory with intangible value are often perceived as equivalent to no gains at all because the value of the territory exists only when it is whole and undivided (Goddard 2010). On the other hand, territory is often perceived as indivisible because the costs of division would damage a state's reputation for future territorial claims (Toft 2003; Walter 2003). It is inherently more difficult to divide specific territory valued for its national symbolism because, by definition, the intrinsic value is a function of the whole territory. For example, the status of Jerusalem is always shelved as a latter issue to deal with in negotiations between Israel and the Palestinians due to the highly symbolic, nationalist, and ethnic value of the city for both sides (Goddard 2010; Hassner 2009). The highly controversial Dome of the Rock or Temple Mount cannot be divided without destroying the value of the disputed territory.

Thus, dividing disputed territory with intangible value would eradicate the intrinsic value of the territory. The only way that decision makers can gain intrinsic value from territory with intangible value is if the whole territory were acquired or defended successfully, providing the winning state with all of the disputed territory. Rational actors are unlikely to select this outcome because one state would lose everything. Therefore, territorial concessions of this type are not as likely. Therefore, attempting settlement is expected to be a much less beneficial strategy for disputes over territory with intangible value because the gains of divided territory are not usually perceived as actual gains.

On the other hand, division of tangibly valued territory, particularly economic, tends to be more feasible due to the fact that states can more easily divide natural resources to be exploited from the disputed territory. Frequent and active attempts to settle the dispute are expected since economic gains from the disputed territory can result only from settlement of the dispute. Without secure and guaranteed access to the natural resources, disputing states are unlikely to attempt exploitation during the dispute. In the few instances in which one state did attempt to exploit natural resources prior to settlement of the dispute, the opposing state responded with some retaliatory move or protest that resulted in the guilty state backing down. Therefore, exploitation generally cannot occur until the dispute is resolved, making settlement attempts more likely for states interested in economic gains from the disputed territory.

Previous Findings on Value of Territory

Predictions about the value of territory and conflict management in past research focus on both tangible and intangible values such as economic, ethnic, and strategic value (Huth 1996; Huth and Allee 2002), and how much combined value territory has (Hensel 2001; Hensel and Mitchell 2005). For example, in a study of Latin American territorial disputes, Hensel (2001) finds that territory with a high salience score is more likely to be the subject of both bilateral negotiations and militarized conflict since more important territory is treated by decision makers with more interest compared to disputed territory with lower value or salience.

Past studies show that tangible value leads to more cooperation and settlement between adversaries and less frequent armed conflict (Rosenau 1967; Mansbach and Vasquez 1981; Vasquez 1993). Specifically, states are more likely to initiate territorial MIDs when the disputed territory has strategic value (Huth 1996; Huth and Allee 2002), and less likely when the territory has significant economic value (Huth 1996). Simmons (2002) finds that arbitration is less likely to occur when the territory has strategic value, suggesting that strategic value makes states less willing to turn over decisions about sovereignty to a third party. Huth and Allee (2002) demonstrate that strategic value makes it more likely for states to attempt settlement negotiations, but less likely to provide territorial concessions to the adversary.

In an analysis of twentieth-century territorial disputes (1950–90), Huth (1996) finds that variation in the value of territory (strategic, economic, or ethnic) influences the likelihood of armed conflict and settlement attempts. Strategically valuable territory is positively correlated with armed conflict and negatively correlated with settlement attempts, while economically valuable territory is negatively correlated with armed conflict and positively correlated with settlement attempts. When the disputed territory has only economic value and no ethnic or strategic value, Huth (1996) demonstrates that settlement is 3.6 times more likely to occur. Another finding is that since 1950, disputes over territory with economic value are much more likely to be settled peacefully than territory with strategic or ethnic value. In fact, there is an increase of 3.6 percent in the probability that the challenger would settle peacefully when significant natural resources are present, compared to decreases in probability if the territory had strategic (–5.5 percent) or ethnic value (–3.6 percent).

Studies about intangible value show that territory with ethnic value is more likely to lead to armed conflict (Mandel 1980; Huth 1996; Woodwell 2004). In an examination of territory that states lost to adversaries in the past, Goertz and Diehl (1992) also find that disputed territory with more intangible value is correlated with militarized conflict. Territory with ethnic value also makes settlement less likely (Huth 1996). Contrary to Huth's findings about ethnic value, Hensel and Mitchell (2005) surprisingly find that at least for Latin American and European states, intangible value like ethnic links, homeland status, and lost autonomy make peaceful settlements more likely. Similarly, Hensel (1996, 2001) and Hensel and Mitchell (2005) show that armed conflict is more likely to occur when disputed territory has a high level of salience, as measured by a combination of both tangible and intangible value, including the presence of a permanent population, valuable resources, strategic value, and ethnic or religious kinsmen. In a study comparing the effect of tangible and intangible values, Hensel and Mitchell (2005) show that militarized conflict is much more likely with intangible value comprising ethnic links, homeland territory, and lost autonomy. Clearly these divergent findings about the effects of territorial value on settlement attempts merit further investigation.

Testing the Value of Territory Explanation

The overall findings of the literature on value of disputed territory indicate that this factor has some influence on the likelihood of dispute strategies regarding armed conflict and resolution attempts. Though there are different findings in the literature, this study uses the hypothesis for the alternative explanation *value of territory* that when disputed territory has ethnic value, strategic value, permanent population, mainland territory status, or homeland status, diplomatic or militarized threats or uses of force should be *more likely* and settlement attempts involving territorial concessions should be *less likely.* Therefore, to test the applicability and validity of the value of territory explanation in explaining variation in territorial dispute management strategies, we should first observe whether the disputed territory has one or several of the values examined in this section—strategic value, economic value, permanent population, homeland or colonial territory, mainland or offshore territory, or ethnic value. I do not include nationalist, symbolic value in this section because this is something I believe is used to mobilize domestic populaces, discussed in the next section. Second, we should see more attempts at settlement and fewer threats or uses of force when the territory has economic value, and fewer settlement attempts and more threats or uses of force when it has ethnic or strategic value. Likewise, when territory is homeland territory or mainland territory, or when it is has a permanent population, settlement attempts should be less likely and threats or uses of force more likely. Lastly, if value matters, we should see disputes with low salience scores or no observable value be enduring since such disputes may lack enough salience for challenger states to actually make any active attempt to deal with the territorial claim, leading to a negative peace.

Value of territory can explain the strategies in a number of enduring territorial disputes, as well as resolved disputes, but not other disputes. In terms of tangible value, the first observation is that 62 percent of the disputes over territory with economic value are settled, which is mainly consistent with previous findings, but not as high as the theory would predict. At the same time, governments are often willing to resolve disputes by giving up economically valuable land, such as Saudi Arabia's willingness to drop claims against oil-rich territories in Kuwait, Qatar, Iraq, and UAE (Walter 2003). Resolution has occurred in 46 percent of the disputes with another tangible value, mainland territory, which provides mixed support for the argument that disputes with this status are more difficult to resolve. Likewise, the number of disputes over territory with strategic value does not support the hypothesis one way or the other since 50 percent of the disputes with strategic value are settled, and the other half are not. There are several territorial disputes that have been successfully settled in which the disputed territory had strategic value. This should have made the disputes less likely to be settled. These disputes include the Sinai Peninsula, returned to Egypt by Israel in 1979 as a result of US mediation; the dispute between Chad and Libya, resolved by the ICJ in 1994; and islands in the strategic Strait of Malacca, disputed by Indonesia and Malaysia and resolved by the ICJ in 2002.

With regard to intangible value, 29 percent of all settled territorial disputes were about territory with ethnic value, which means that not many states involved in this type of dispute were willing to resolve their disputes. This initial finding provides support for the idea that ethnic value makes it less likely that states will settle territorial disputes. The British cession of Hong Kong to China in 1997 and Ireland's withdrawal of its claim for Northern Ireland from the Irish constitution in 1998 are two well-known examples of settled disputes over territory with significant ethnic value for all states involved. Other similar disputes include the settlement of the dispute between Yugoslavia and Italy over Trieste in 1975, the Bakassi Peninsula disputed between Cameroon and Nigeria, resolved by the ICJ in 2002, and several border regions in Eastern Europe in the 1990s. With regard to other intangible values of territory, 64 percent of disputes over territory with permanent populations and 58 percent of homeland disputes were settled, which also provides very limited or mixed support for the explanation of value of territory regarding dispute strategies.

If we look at the values of territory in ongoing disputes, we see some interesting patterns that cast some doubt on the validity of using value of territory to explain territorial dispute strategies and the resulting endurance of disputes. First, only 18 percent of these disputes have strategic value, which is unexpected based on previous literature. This is generally inconsistent with previous findings that settlement of territorial disputes with strategic value is less likely. Of these disputes, 23 percent have no other value. Some of the enduring disputes over territory with strategic value are the Golan Heights disputed between Syria and Israel and Abu Musa and Greater Tunb Islands disputed between Iran and the UAE. The Golan Heights is considered a buffer area for both Syria and Israel. Abu Musa and Greater Tunb Islands, occupied by Iran's military since 1971, are strategically located in the middle of the Persian Gulf.

At the same time, 35 percent of ongoing territorial disputes have economic value, which should provide incentive for states to attempt settlement as a tangible and salient value. Of these disputes, 64 percent have only economic value and no strategic or ethnic value. These disputes, such as the Senkaku/Diaoyu Islands, disputed between China and Japan and Taiwan and Japan, should be easier to resolve since resolution provides economic incentives for the states involved, yet they are not yet settled. Of the seventy-one ongoing disputes, 59 percent are mainland territory, which suggests that status as mainland territories is slightly more common than offshore disputes.

There is a clear correlation and support of previous findings with regard to the intangible value of ethnic links. Ethnicity seems to play a role in the endurance of a good number of territorial disputes, unlike tangible value, since 63 percent of ongoing disputes have only ethnic value. These are disputes like the border dispute between Georgia and Azerbaijan and the enclaves dispute between Bangladesh and India. Most significantly, 96 percent of ongoing disputes are over homeland territory and not colonial or dependent territory. This very high number may be due to the fact that most colonial claims have been resolved. Consistent with previous studies, only 30 percent of unresolved disputes have permanent populations, which indicates that the majority of disputes are about uninhabited territories such as offshore islands or borders in mainland territory, not tracts of inhabited territory.

On the other hand, there are several unresolved disputes that are likely to be enduring specifically because they lack any significant value or salience, making it less likely that the challenger state will threaten or use force or actively seek to pursue settlement. In these cases, it is likely that such low levels of salience or lack of strategic, ethnic, or economic value can explain why challenger states have not made threats or used force, and more importantly why they fail to attempt settlement. It could also be the case that the two disputants have an understanding of sorts so that neither side makes a big deal of the dispute, and it is treated as inactive. These disputes could include the Andean Southern Ice Field disputed between Chile and Argentina; Machias Seal Island and North Rock, disputed between the US and Canada; Bajo Nuevo and Serranilla, occupied by Colombia and claimed by the US, Jamaica, and Nicaragua; Navassa Island, disputed between Haiti and the US; Sapodilla Cays, claimed by Honduras against Belize; and Isla Brasilera, claimed by Uruguay against Brazil.

This overall assessment of the influence of value of territory for settled and unsettled disputes suggests that territorial value cannot sufficiently explain the strategic behavior of challenger states involved in territorial disputes. In addition to its inability to explain the settlement or endurance of a significant number of disputes, there are mixed findings about tangible and intangible value. A further limitation of using value of territory to explain territorial dispute strategies is that there is little variance over time since economic value, strategic value, mainland status, ethnic value, homeland status, and permanent population rarely vary. The only value that does tend to vary is symbolic or nationalist value, when leaders use propaganda to mobilize domestic populaces, discussed below. Unless there are no longer any resources in a territory or if an ethnic population has moved out of a disputed territory, the value will likely stay the same over time, meaning that the predicted behavior based on such value or salience would also remain the same over time. Yet what we observe in real-world disputes is regular shifts in strategies regarding territorial disputes, ranging from settlement attempts, offers of concessions, threats or uses of force, or doing nothing at all. This does not mean that the theories about value of territory are incorrect; on the contrary, it is has been proven that challenger states will choose different dispute strategies depending on the value of territory. At the same time, other theories can add to these explanations about value or salience of territory so that we have a deeper and richer understanding of territorial disputes and varied dispute strategies.

DOMESTIC ACCOUNTABILITY AND MOBILIZATION

Since many resolved and unresolved disputes are not about value of territory, there must be a different explanation for varied dispute strategies and the endurance of territorial disputes. Another potential explanation is that territorial dispute strategies are more or less likely based on domestic factors in the form of domestic costs of settlement (domestic accountability) or benefits of endurance (domestic mobilization), based mainly on the existence of nationalist or symbolic value embedded in the disputed territory by leaders or the people. The domestic accountability explanation postulates that leaders are unwilling to pursue unpopular strategies about territorial disputes due to the risk of potential domestic punishment. This theory rests on the assumption that leaders wish to remain in power and avoid domestic punishment for unpopular policies. The mobilization argument suggests that leaders can use enduring territorial disputes to mobilize public support for the government. If the mobilization is successful, there is less incentive for leaders to consider settlement attempts. This explanation also assumes that leaders wish to remain in power and prefer strong support from the populace or selectorate (those who actually influence political decision making like the military and elite). In both cases, symbolic or nationalist value can help leaders to mobilize or prevent them from making risky decisions about territorial dispute strategies, but it is not necessarily the case that the disputed territory has to have some value. Rather, leaders can easily invent or claim over time how important the disputed territory is to the challenger state to the point that the territory acquires symbolic value.

Domestic Accountability

In terms of the domestic accountability explanation, the decision to attempt settlement of territorial disputes may be due to leaders' fears that they will be punished by the opposition, selectorate, or the public if the leaders offer to concede a territorial claim or ownership to the adversary. For example, ruling political parties of the Japanese government have persevered in their unwillingness to compromise with Russia on the disputed islands of the Northern Territories/Kurile Islands mainly due to fear of punishment by their constituents, as admitted in surveys and interviews of government ministers. Maintaining the Japanese claim has resulted in almost guaranteed domestic support for every Japanese governing political party since 1951, even at the cost of strained Russo-Japanese relations (Kimura and Welch 1998).

Leaders have incentives to avoid policies that will threaten their positions of power and damage their own reputations and those of their political parties, particularly when they are politically unstable (Bueno de Mesquita and Siverson 1995; Bueno de Mesquita, Morrow, Siverson, and Smith 1999; Fearon 1994). Reasons for remaining in power can include personal motivation to hold a leadership position that provides power, attempts to achieve financial gains, and the aspiration to influence policy goals (Huth and Allee 2002). Leaders in both democratic and authoritarian regimes alike are accountable to at least some portion or the majority of the domestic populace since they can be removed from power or public support, legitimacy, or stability can weaken significantly due to unpopular policies or actions taken by leaders. Regardless of how well a regime represents the domestic populace, "every political system attempts to establish and cultivate the belief in its legitimacy in order to have orders obeyed willingly rather than by a threat of force" (Downs and Saunders 1996, 118).

Regarding democratic regimes, numerous studies confirm that foreign policy failure makes leaders susceptible to stronger opposition and removal from power through elections (Buena de Mesquita, Siverson, and Woller 1992; Buena de Mesquita and Siverson 1995; Buena de Mesquita et al. 1999; Downs and Rocke 1994; Fearon 1994; Gelpi and Grieco 2001; Goemans 2000; Ostrom and Simon 1985; Smith 1998). Therefore, policy successes "may help deter political opposition, strengthen a leader's hold on office, and increase the stock of political capital upon which leaders can draw to advance their broader policy agendas" (Huth and Allee 2002, 71). Public opinion literature also indicates that not only are democratic leaders concerned about public opinion of their leadership, but they often pay attention to the opinions of domestic constituents when making both domestic and foreign policy decisions to avoid mass dissatisfaction.[2] In territorial disputes, domestic accountability exists when leaders are vulnerable or susceptible to losing their position due to unpopular policies. Domestic vulnerability can be observed as the existence of strong political opposition to the majority party in a legislature or the closer timing of an upcoming election (Huth and Allee 2002). The more vulnerable democratic leaders are domestically, the less likely they are to engage in strategies that may be unpopular and would result in removal from office in the next elections. As Huth (1996) notes, even though leaders can mobilize using nationalist rhetoric about a territorial dispute, costly or failed attempts at military coercion in the dispute will likely mobilize domestic opposition in the long term.

Though democratic leaders are more susceptible to popular domestic audiences (Fearon 1994), nondemocratic leaders are just as dependent on some degree of domestic support. Authoritarian regimes are also concerned with obtaining and maintaining at least a minimal level of domestic support (Levy and Vikili 1992), even if it does not include the entire populace. Due to the lack of legitimacy of authoritarian regimes, seeking internal unity among key aspects of the domestic populace is probably more important than in democratic regimes. Preventing significant dissatisfaction from potential opponents among powerful elites and high-ranking military officers is particularly important for authoritarian leaders. Guatemala's military leader in 1983, President Efrain Rios Montt, felt this exact pressure when he considered reducing Guatemala's claim from the entire territory of Belize to only the southern province of Toledo. The domestic reaction in Guatemala to Rios Montt's potential withdrawal of Guatemala's claim for all of Belize was quite harsh, leading to the ultimate form of domestic punishment, removal from power. A month after Rios Montt's decision to shift Guatemala's territorial claim, he was overthrown in a coup backed by officers of all three armed services (Wiegand 2005).

Political instability in nondemocratic states like China is measured by Huth and Allee (2002) as high levels of authoritarianism on the Polity IV scale, the recent occurrence of coups, attempts to democratize, and political rebellions involving violence pursued by people outside the military. In territorial disputes, policies that can lead to domestic punishment include offers of territorial concessions by the target state or offers to drop the territorial claim by the challenger state, both of which lead to final settlement. Such policies can lead to domestic punishment because they involve some action that contradicts typical nationalist discourse, which tends to emphasize indivisibility, seeking retribution for an injustice, or unwillingness to compromise to maintain a reputation for resolve. Typical nationalist discourse promises domestic populaces that leaders would never consider dropping the claim or offering any territorial concessions of any kind, emphasizing indivisibility, territorial integrity, and past or potential injustice. By using such discourse, leaders frame the dispute so that any actions taken that contradict the discourse inevitably damage the credibility and reputation of the leaders. Thus, "elites can become trapped in their own rhetoric and choose to pursue risky security strategies rather than jeopardize their rule by not fulfilling popular nationalist demands" (Downs and Saunders 1996, 115).

Domestic punishment is likely to result because populaces do not usually tolerate leaders who have a record of lacking credibility. Leaders who want to stay in power should be particularly concerned with their reputations based on credibility since constituents often use credibility or the potential for credibility as one of the bases for choosing a leader. Domestic punishment can range from a minor drop in public approval for the leader to actual removal from office through election, coup, or forced resignation. Because leaders cannot predict the effect controversial territorial dispute policies might have on a populace, leaders who prefer to remain in power (or who want their political party to remain in power) should be particularly cautious about their policy decisions (Huth and Allee 2002). This means that leaders should be hesitant to engage in any policies that contradict nationalist discourse, including settlement attempts, since such actions will very likely damage their credibility, threaten their reputation, and, more importantly, increase the likelihood of domestic punishment. An important point is that leaders only have to believe that by dropping a claim or offering territorial concessions they would risk domestic punishment. Therefore leaders should be sensitive to policy choices that could damage their political stability and avoid settlement options that contradict previously stated nationalist discourse. Regardless of whether decision makers achieve domestic support through calls for negotiations, provocations, or escalations, settlement, or even some territorial concessions can become costly for the initial decision maker and subsequent decision makers. If they decide to settle and either divide or give up disputed territory that was claimed as an integral part of the homeland, they lose credibility and risk punishment by their constituents and opposition (election, military coup).

Argentina's invasion of the Falkland Islands in 1982 best exemplifies the logic of the domestic accountability explanation. After the military junta received immediate and strong domestic support for the invasion, they realized that their initial decision to withdraw from the islands would lead to fierce domestic opposition, and this realization forced the junta to change its strategy from withdrawal a few days after military occupation to maintaining military occupation of the islands, which provoked a British military response rather than engagement in negotiations, for which the Argentine junta had hoped.[3] Once the invasion occurred, the initial plan of backing down became a nonoption for Argentine decision makers due to the potential of domestic punishment. Never before had the Argentine junta been so popular. The invasion led to a "deep popular mobilization . . . marked by strong feelings shared by the public and an awakening of passions which were to be the driving force behind the junta's decisions during the conflict" (Femenia 1996, 96) and "support for the junta—on that one issue of the Malvinas—had become nothing less than overwhelming" (Melendez 1984, 224). In order to avoid risking domestic punishment with potential riots against the government, the junta later admitted they had little choice but to deliberately shift their strategy and stand firm by keeping the troops on the islands beyond the time they had planned. De-escalating would likely have proven costly for the junta domestically. Thus, they stood firm and maintained a strong level of domestic support. Only when the war ended with full Argentine surrender did the junta finally pay a price, resulting in the forced resignation of General Leopoldo Galtieri.

Previous Findings on Domestic Accountability

Support for the domestic accountability argument is provided by Allee and Huth (2006), Chiozza and Choi (2003), Chiozza and Goemans (2004), Huth (1996), and Huth and Allee (2002). Huth (1996) demonstrates that political leaders in many countries did not give up territorial claims because they risked punishment by the military or opposition groups. Huth and Allee (2002) have several findings about dispute settlement and domestic accountability. First, they demonstrate that as time passes since an election, democratic leaders are less likely to seek negotiations for settlement in order to avoid potential domestic punishment, and that secure authoritarian leaders are more likely to attempt settlement compared to nonsecure authoritarian leaders. Second, they find that leaders are less likely to offer territorial concessions when the disputed territory is valuable and therefore controversial to domestic audiences (Huth and Allee 2002).

Similarly Chiozza and Choi (2003) also show that the willingness to pursue peaceful settlement attempts in territorial disputes is affected by the length of time leaders have served in office. Their findings show that dispute resolution is more likely when new democratic leaders are in power and are thus less likely to be punished since they have just received endorsement from their constituents. With authoritarian leaders, they are more likely to attempt settlement as their time in office grows longer, since they have accumulated political experience in using power and are therefore less constrained by domestic audiences. In a study about international disputes in general, Chiozza and Goemans (2003) find that as the risk of losing office increases, leaders are less likely, not more inclined, to initiate an international crisis. Allee and Huth (2006) confirm that when executives face strong domestic political opposition, leaders are more likely to seek legal dispute resolution (arbitration or adjudication) rather than negotiations or mediation since the latter directly involves decisions by leaders that could be unpopular. Their findings also show that legal dispute resolution is more likely to occur when the disputed territory is more salient to domestic audiences, who would not be pleased with leaders who negotiated away territory on their own initiative.

A different argument about domestic accountability that contradicts most previous findings is offered by Fravel (2008), who argues in the context of Chinese territorial disputes that leaders will pursue territorial concessions in settlement attempts rather than avoid them when they are domestically insecure or unstable. The logic is that when internal threats to the state are present, leaders can trade territorial concessions with neighboring states in exchange for assistance from those states in putting down domestic unrest. Such assistance could include preventing support or safe haven to exiled insurgents or policing a border. Though this theory has only been demonstrated in the context of China, the logic of the theory and its potential applicability demonstrate that the domestic accountability theory is not necessarily universal or definitive since domestic accountability can lead to both avoidance of territorial concessions and seeking such concessions at the same time.

Domestic Mobilization

Domestic mobilization is based on the notion that leaders will discuss the disputed territory in terms of nationalism and patriotism in order to mend their political instability. The significance of gaining territory perceived as a missing part of the homeland can be an effective means of mobilization, if populaces are convinced of the rightful return of lost homeland territory. Governments involved in territorial disputes are likely aware of the ability to mobilize domestically, and many leaders will take advantage of this sentiment by making promises to prevent or right an injustice that will result or already resulted from a change in territorial ownership (Downs and Saunders 1996; James, Park, and Choi 2006). For example, at the time of the January 1995 border conflict fought between Ecuador and Peru, "there were immediate political and military interests involved in the eruption of the dispute at this particular time, due to the declining support for both national presidents . . . these political actors were able to mobilize the population around issues of territory, nationhood and the Amazon in ways which can throw light on the nature of national identities and their relationship with place" (Radcliffe 1998, 273).

Previous Findings on Domestic Mobilization

There is plentiful evidence of governments involved in territorial disputes deliberately attempting to mobilize domestic support behind the disputed territory in order to strengthen their claim or defense by using nationalist discourse. Research about government attempts to mobilize domestic support by using a nationalist discourse has shown that domestic populaces are eager to accept the discourse about defending or claiming territory if it is in the interest of the people (Bonilla 1999; Hensel 2001; Kimura and Welch 1998; Radcliffe 1998). The rally-round-the-flag effect, common when US presidents engage in international crises (Brody 1984; Mueller 1973; Ostrom and Simon 1985; Russett 1990), is easy to implement when territory is threatened or sought after. Feelings about the security of the national territory and borders are often emotionally charged (Radcliffe 1998), so that the domestic populaces immediately support policies to reinforce border regions or disputed territories and threats to use force to defend or acquire territory thought to be rightfully theirs. Support for the argument about domestic mobilization is provided by Huth (1996), who shows that political leaders consistently mobilize the population and key groups such as the military by appealing to nationalism. Tir (2003) argues that when there are ethnic links to disputed territory, the domestic populace will be more likely to reward leaders who acquire such intangibly valued territory, though he finds only mixed results for this argument.

To mobilize successfully using a territorial dispute, leaders can use diplomatic and militarized threats or uses of force to rally the populace or selectorate. By initiating a threat, leaders rally the populace to support the leadership against a potential threat by an adversary, stirring strong nationalist sentiments and defense of the homeland. If leaders are vulnerable due to conditions of political instability, they can therefore use threats or uses of force in territorial disputes to help mobilize support not only for the disputed territory but more importantly for the leadership and government. Domestic mobilization by use of threats or use of force uses the same logic as the diversionary war theory, which argues that leaders will use an international dispute to divert the attention of the public from domestic problems, such as poor economic performance, scandals, or low levels of popular support. Tir (2010) finds support for this supposition by showing that militarized conflict is more likely when leaders experience domestic vulnerability based on a measure of protests, strikes, and riots.

Testing the Domestic Accountability and Mobilization Explanations

To demonstrate that domestic accountability or domestic mobilization is a strong explanation for different strategies in territorial disputes, we should observe conditions of domestic accountability in conjunction with fewer diplomatic or militarized threats or uses of force and fewer settlement attempts through concessions. More specifically, during the months or years when leaders are particularly accountable to the domestic populace or selectorate due to domestic vulnerability, we should observe no diplomatic or militarized threats or uses of force or settlement attempts. For democratic leaders, settlement attempts or diplomatic or military threats or uses of force should be *less likely* when they are closer to an upcoming election or the opposition in the legislature is strong. Authoritarian leaders should likewise be *less likely* to pursue potentially costly strategies of threats or uses of force or settlement attempts involving concessions when a coup has recently occurred, when the Polity IV scores indicate high levels of authoritarianism, during periods of democratization, or when groups outside the military pursue violent rebellions.

For domestic mobilization, we should observe that when the same conditions of political instability exist, making leaders domestically vulnerable, they are *less likely* to attempt settlement but are *more likely* to engage in diplomatic or militarized threats or uses of force. In this case, in order to mobilize effectively, leaders will deliberately engage in some kind of diplomatic or militarized threat or use of force to rally the populace or selectorate to increase domestic support for the leadership. In both cases, it should not matter whether the disputed territory has symbolic or nationalist value, or even ethnic value for the challenger state. As discussed earlier, leaders can easily embed symbolic value onto claimed territory, so this is not a prerequisite to test these explanations. While the two aspects of the theory are the same in regard to attempted settlement, they differ in predictions about threats or uses of force.

The dispute strategies in several disputes can primarily be explained by the existence of symbolic or nationalist value embedded in the territory and use by the leadership to mobilize domestic support. Domestic accountability and mobilization do a good job explaining the strategies of Guatemala's ongoing claim for Belize, Argentina's continued claim against the UK for the Falkland/Malvinas Islands, China's claim for Taiwan, Pakistan's claim for Kashmir and Jammu, South Korea's territorial claim for the Japanese-occupied Takeshima Island/Dokdo Island, the Cuban claim against the US for Guantanamo Bay Naval Base in Cuba, the Atacama Corridor to the sea, which Bolivia lost to Chile and Peru in the War of the Pacific in the 1880s, Gibraltar, a British dependency claimed by Spain, and the Japanese claim to the Kurile Islands/Northern Territories, owned by Russia. In all of these disputes, governments have pursued domestic mobilization using territorial claims, or there have been concerns by leaders to not take risky actions to avoid potential domestic punishment. In these cases, there is little doubt that the disputed territory has strong domestic salience for the populace or selectorate, making it feasible for leaders to mobilize using threats or uses of force. At the same time, such salience and ability to mobilize and achieve domestic gains means that it is not likely that leaders will risk potential domestic punishment through settlement attempts involving territorial concessions. Domestic factors can also partially account for strategies of states in other disputes where domestic accountability or mobilization played a role, but was not the primary factor in explaining the strategies. At the same time, because leaders are able to mobilize using enduring territorial disputes or have to avoid certain strategies due to fear of domestic punishment, these factors do not rule out the feasibility for leaders to also use the disputes to gain bargaining leverage with their adversaries, as discussed in the next chapter.

The theory is able to effectively explain the settlement of several disputes because domestic factors were nonexistent, including the Hawar Islands dispute between Bahrain and Qatar and West Germany's willingness to drop its claims to parts of bordering states including Poland, East Germany, and Czechoslovakia in the early 1970s. In these cases, at the time of final settlement, domestic conditions did not seem to play any role in affecting decisions by leaders to engage in territorial concessions since leaders were not vulnerable to domestic conditions. On the other hand, there are several disputes where domestic factors should have been influential due to vulnerability or instability, but leaders were still willing to settle territorial disputes, including Pakistan's willingness to concede the majority of the Rann of Kutch border region to India in 1968, Argentina's 1977 agreement to an arbitration award in which Chile was awarded sovereignty of the Beagle Channel Islands, Ireland's willingness to drop its claim to Northern Ireland from its constitution in 1998, and the border dispute between Ecuador and Peru in 1998. Just a few years before, Ecuador and Peru had fought in a brief but bloody conflict over their disputed border in the Amazon, which involved significant domestic mobilization (Radcliffe 1998). The willingness of leaders to settle territorial disputes while vulnerable to potential domestic punishment suggests that the theory is unable to explain a number of key disputes that have been settled. Though valuable in accounting for the strategies of challenger states on some occasions in territorial disputes, domestic accountability and mobilization cannot sufficiently explain the variation of dispute strategies in many disputes. This suggests that there is another factor besides domestic mobilization and accountability, and value of territory, that is driving the variance of dispute strategies by challenger states. The next chapter proposes that bargaining leverage is a stronger theory to explain such variation.

CHAPTER THREE

Territorial Disputes as Bargaining Leverage

When a state claims territory that is disputed or belongs to another state, the assumption is that the challenger state wants to change the status quo by acquiring the disputed territory. However, this may not necessarily be true. In most of the cases of peaceful territorial change resulting from settlements from 1815 to 1981, states gave away disputed territory in exchange for economic aid or compensation; political benefits such as peace, diplomatic relations, or political support; or security compensations in the form of military aid or political alliances (Kacowicz 1994). There are several cases where borders have been forcefully and repeatedly moved, such as Alsace-Lorraine and Kashmir and Jammu, which suggests that the transfer of territory is not necessarily the primary objective of the states involved (Tir 2003). The implication is that states do not necessarily dispute over territory because the territory itself has value or salience for the state, even when it is claimed.

It could be that the disputed territory acts as a means to continue domestic mobilization or for other domestic benefits, as discussed in the previous chapter. Another explanation could be that "standing firm in territorial disputes may be useful in maintaining or increasing one's reputation and prestige, and territorial expansion may be considered as an outgrowth of domestic and economic development" (Diehl and Goertz 1988, 104). Walter (2003) argues that governments choose to avoid settlement attempts in domestic-based territorial disputes, not because of the value of territory, but because they are concerned with their reputations in the future. The general logic is that other separatist movements may be encouraged to pursue further territorial concessions granted by the state. This argument is attractive but more difficult to apply to interstate territorial disputes (Wiegand 2011). Another more recent explanation for the endurance of territorial disputes is that they provide benefits at the domestic level for leaders, not in the way that domestic mobilization does, but rather in terms of centralization of authority and military gains. The general argument is that the existence of territorial threats helps to justify large standing armies (Gibler 2010; Gibler and Tir 2010) and more centralized authority in a government (Gibler 2010). A main finding is that parties are less polarized in states with external territorial threats, so that opposition parties support the leader, who is then able to centralize more authority (Gibler 2010). A related argument is that peaceful transfers of territory (settled disputes) are likely to decrease militarization, encouraging liberalization and democratization (Gibler and Tir 2010). The implication is that once a territorial threat is removed, leaders can no longer necessarily justify centralization or military buildup, making the endurance of territorial disputes attractive.

Though logical, this theory of territorial disputes benefiting leaders in terms of government centralization or military buildup can only apply to target states, but not to challenger states. Because target states are the ones experiencing external threats, it is logical that leaders would be able to justify the centralization of government or militarization and buildup of armies due to a threat to the sovereignty of territory from a challenging state. Yet, this study examines the dispute strategies of challenger states that are also able to take advantage of territorial disputes, albeit through interstate relations with their adversaries. In this sense, the theory of external threats benefiting states domestically is complementary to the theory of bargaining leverage that I suggest as a better fit for challenger states. Together, perhaps these theories can sufficiently explain *both* challenger and target state dispute strategies.

The theory of bargaining leverage suggests that challenger states can use territorial disputes as bargaining leverage to gain concessions or compensations in other salient disputed issues. This theory suggests that the salience of territorial disputes is not necessarily because of the disputed territory itself, but because of the ability of challenger states to use territorial disputes as bargaining leverage to influence other salient disputed issues. This argument is somewhat similar to recent findings in the rivalry literature that territorial disputes are not necessarily the cause of armed conflict leading to rivalries, but rather that rivalries sometimes lead to territorial claims and then armed conflict (Rasler and Thompson 2006; Colaresi, Rasler, and Thompson 2007). Similarly, the theory outlined here argues that other salient issues disputed by adversaries influence territorial dispute strategies and, therefore, the lack of settlement and subsequent endurance of territorial disputes. As Tir (2003) notes in a study about peaceful territorial changes: "One could argue that some disputes are actually about nonterritorial issues, but are politically manipulated to appear that way." By avoiding attempted settlement and allowing the endurance of territorial disputes, challenger states can take advantage of their endurance by pursuing diplomatic and militarized threats or limited uses of force and linking such threats to other disputed issues in order to gain bargaining leverage.

An example of territorial disputes being used as bargaining leverage with other disputed issues is Saudi Arabia's deliberate usage of its border dispute with North Yemen. In this case, Saudi troops clashed with Yemeni troops in early 1980 as a form of pressure against North Yemen's proposed merger with South Yemen. Saudi Arabia deliberately provoked North Yemen by initiating force along their border in order to "exert pressure against North Yemen's proposed merger with South Yemen and gravitation towards closer relations with the Soviet Union" (Day 1987, 232). The border clash was therefore Saudi Arabia's way of attempting to compel North Yemen to reconsider unification with South Yemen and Yemeni relations with the Soviets, other issues unrelated to the actual border dispute. In this and many other cases, challenger states like Saudi Arabia will pursue certain dispute strategies, and sometimes even initiate territorial disputes, specifically for the purpose of using the territorial disputes as bargaining leverage, not because the disputed territory is actually so salient to challenger states.

A challenger state can certainly attempt to gain territorial concessions through dispute settlement, but states might also deliberately avoid settlement attempts in order to gain multiple concessions *in other issues* over time. The challenger state may have a stronger incentive to maintain a territorial claim against another state so that settlement of the claim, even in the challenger's favor, is *not* the best outcome. The main premise of this study is that states can benefit from the endurance of a territorial dispute, and therefore they will pursue dispute strategies that best meet their ability to achieve bargaining gains with other disputed issues. The challenger state, the one making the territorial claim, can use the territorial dispute to gain concessions or change the actions or policies of its adversary in other issue areas by linking these other issues to territorial dispute threats. The very endurance of the territorial dispute provides opportunities for the challenger state to use the territorial dispute as bargaining leverage in order to influence other disputed issues. In this chapter, I explain why states are sometimes willing to attempt settlement while at other times they are not, and the conditions that make certain dispute strategies more or less likely. This theory of territorial disputes as bargaining leverage is presented as an alternative to previous research on the value of territory and domestic accountability and mobilization, as well as other findings regarding territorial dispute strategies.

There are many cases of enduring territorial disputes that are linked with other disputed issues. Since 1945, the enduring dispute between Japan and Russia over the Kurile Islands/Northern Territories has prevented the conclusion of a formal peace treaty from World War II. All through the dispute, both states have attempted to use the disputed islands as bargaining leverage in their bilateral relations. Ethiopia can use threats on its border dispute with Eritrea to gain concessions on other issues, particularly access to Eritrea's shipping ports, which landlocked Ethiopia lacks. Iran benefits from its territorial claim against the UAE for Abu Musa Island in the Persian Gulf, since the territorial claim provides Iran with bargaining leverage with regard to shipping lanes (for oil primarily) in a key geostrategic area. South Korea uses territorial claims for the disputed Dokdo/Takeshima Island as bargaining leverage against Japan to gain concessions related to past Japanese aggressions in Korea. In all of these cases and many others, there is little incentive for the challenger states to drop their territorial claims since they can use the territorial claims as bargaining leverage in other disputed issues.

By making diplomatic or militarized threats in a territorial dispute, a challenger state can pursue a strategy of *issue linkage* and *coercive diplomacy* in hopes that the territorial dispute threat will persuade an adversary to seriously reconsider its position on other dispute issues. Issue linkage occurs when a state deliberately links two or more distinct foreign policy issues together, claiming that resolution of one issue cannot occur without resolution of the other issue. Coercive diplomacy is an attempt by one state to compel another state through some type of coercion, threat, or use of force to reconsider or shift its foreign policy on a certain issue. By combining these two foreign policy strategies, the challenger state can use threats in the territorial dispute as bargaining leverage to compel its adversary to shift its policy on other salient issues in which the challenger state lacks bargaining leverage.

Though disputed issues may initially have little or nothing to do with each other, a challenger state can make a diplomatic or militarized threat or limited use of force in the territorial dispute and link the threat to the adversary's compliance with the challenger state's demand about another disputed issue. In this way, the challenger state is able to take advantage of the endurance of a territorial dispute and use it as bargaining leverage to persuade shifts in the foreign policies of its adversary regarding other disputed issues that it otherwise would not be able to influence. It is the combination of coercive diplomacy and issue linkage that makes challenger states unwilling to settle territorial disputes. The endurance of territorial disputes allows challenger states to continue using the disputes as bargaining leverage in other issues, making the maintenance of territorial disputes efficient, with diplomatic and militarized threats or uses of force and avoidance of settlement attempts more attractive dispute strategies than resolution. On the other hand, when other salient disputed issues are resolved or do not exist, incentives for settlement increase, reducing the endurance of territorial disputes.

ISSUE LINKAGE

Though discussed in international law and international relations, the concept of issue linkage is not often considered in international security studies. Issue linkage occurs when a state intentionally links one issue to other initially unrelated foreign policy issues, making the explicit or implicit claim that resolving one issue will affect or be affected by the resolution of another disputed issue. The idea of issue linkage rests on the assumption that there are multiple issue areas within IR about which states agree and disagree, that issue areas such as territorial disputes, trade disputes, human rights, or economic aid can and should each be treated as a separate unit of analysis, and that different issues will affect decisions and outcomes about interstate relations in diverse ways (Diehl 1992; Hensel 2001; Keohane and Nye 1977; Mansbach and Vasquez 1981; Potter 1980; Rosenau 1966). An issue of contention is considered to be "a disputed point or question, the subject of a conflict or controversy" (Randle 1987, 1). In another view, "an issue is what states fight over, not the conditions that led to the choice of military force as the means" (Diehl 1992, 333).

Challenging systems theory and realism, Rosenau (1966, 71) pointed out that "different types of issue-areas elicit different sets of motives on the part of different actors in a political system," and that despite realist leanings in IR, political scientists often unknowingly employed the concept. Keohane and Nye (1977) introduced the idea of issues at stake as part of analysis of IR, followed by Mansbach and Vasquez (1981), who defined and analyzed distinct issues as part of an agenda cycle in IR. Recognizing the differences in issue areas challenges the realist notion that power is the main concern of any state, regardless of the issue (Diehl 1992). Since distinct issues are likely to have distinct characteristics, and states will have different interests regarding such issues, there may be observable variation in relation to the ways in which states behave when certain issues are at stake (Dreyer and Wiegand 2010). Several studies in IR have found that different issues do tend to influence different responses in foreign policy (Mansbach and Vasquez 1981; Rosenau 1966; Zimmerman 1973). A study by Holsti (1991) examines how different issues at stake, including territorial issues, national liberation/creation of a state, commerce/navigation, enforcement of treaty terms, and state/regime survival, have influenced the occurrence of war in different time periods.

The original logic was that different government groups would likely be dealing with different issues in a diverse way and not with one uniform policy. Another argument for focusing on issues in IR is that there are different foreign policy implications depending on the type of issue and level of salience (Hensel 2001). Because diverse issues are valued differently by states, this also means that the degree of salience varies depending on the issue and whether it has low or high salience for states (Diehl 1992; Hensel et al. 2008; Randle 1987). An issue area can be narrow, focusing on something like the eradication of polio, or broad, involving an issue such as international trade, and it can be tangible (resources, immigration, oceans) or intangible (ideology, prestige, national pride).

Recent research on territorial disputes and rivalries in particular has focused more on issues at stake compared to other literature in IR. The literature on territorial disputes is an application of the issues-at-stake genre, in that it separates out territorial disputes from other types of disputes, including regime, policy, and other interstate disputes as identified by the Militarized Interstate Dispute data project. The steps-to-war model and subsequent findings built on the model all use as a premise the idea that issues are distinct, and all expand on the assumption by arguing that leaders of states involved in territorial disputes will act differently than leaders of states involved in other types of disputes (Senese and Vasquez 2003, 2008; Vasquez 1993; Vasquez and Henehan 2001; Vasquez and Valeriano 2008). More explicitly, Hensel (2001) and many subsequent studies are based on a dataset that specifically focuses on issues, mainly territorial, maritime, and river disputes. This dataset, the Issue Correlates of War (ICOW) project, assumes not only that issues are distinct in IR but also that distinct issues have heavily influenced the agenda for research on MIDs and wars, as well as settlement of interstate disputes.[1] In the interstate rivalry literature, scholars have examined territory as a unique issue (referred to as spatial conflict), as well as a positional issue, which is the idea that there is competition near or at the apex of a power hierarchy (Colaresi and Thompson 2005; Colaresi, Rasler, and Thompson 2007; Thompson 1995, 2001). Some key findings in the rivalry literature that focus on issues at stake are that the presence of territorial disputes tends to increase the likelihood of rivalry persistence (Bennett 1998), territorial disputes tend to be at the root of enduring rivalries (Tir and Diehl 2002), and adversarial dyads are more likely to use militarized force when territorial, maritime, or river issues are part of a broader issue rivalry or militarized rivalry (Mitchell and Thies forthcoming).

To claim that two or more issues are linked "implies that somehow, decisions, values, or norms in one area or regime will influence the other" (Leeborn 2002, 16). Sometimes states can link issues substantively, so that issues such as trade and workers' rights logically link together. States can also use issue linkage strategically, with no obvious connection of issue areas (Leeborn 2002, 11). With strategic issue linkage, states can achieve relative bargaining leverage in issue areas where they are relatively weaker. In some cases, strong states will use issue linkage to extend their relative power from one issue area to another, while in other cases, weak states can use issue linkage in an attempt to prevent another state from exercising its power (Keohane and Nye 1977; Leeborn 2002; Oye 1979). Oye (1979, 13) argues that issue linkage results from the diffusion of power in the international system: "The irregularity of the diffusion of power has left many nations with power concentrated on one issue and interests spread across many issues. This distribution of power and interest provides strong impetus to the use of cross-issue linkage, as nations strive to transmit power from an area of strength to secure objectives in areas of weakness." Tollison and Willet (1979) similarly argue that the most successful cases of issue linkage are attempts by one state to extend their dominant bargaining power or leverage in one issue area into other issue areas to achieve maximum advantage. For example, China knows that it has less economic leverage when it comes to influencing Japanese decisions about aid and investment in particular. China also knows that threats of military force provide more bargaining leverage in this area. By shifting the military leverage into an economic issue area, China links the two issues together so it can influence the economic issue using military leverage.

When issue linkage is used, one issue is used as leverage to influence change in another issue, which can be pursued as either a positive inducement of a reward or a negative threat of punishment. Most often, issue linkage is applied to the peaceful resolution of international crises or negotiations on disputed issues

such as trade barriers, fishing treaties, environmental agreements, currency de-
valuation, and so on (Ilke 1964; Keohane and Nye 1977; Mansbach and Vasquez
1981; McGinnis 1986; Oye 1979; Rosenau 1966; Sebenius 1983; Wallace 1976).
In this way, issue linkage is used as a bargaining tool in international negotiations. In negotiations, a state using an issue as positive leverage, also known as
the carrot approach in diplomacy, offers rewards in one issue if the adversary
changes its approach in another issue. By linking issues, states can offer side
payments or concessions in one issue area to achieve change in another distinct
issue area, which provides a better opportunity for dispute resolution (Hoekman 1989). Issue linkage makes agreement between states possible when they
cannot agree on one issue under contention. The "linkage of additional issues
might be required because there is no Pareto-superior agreement that could be
reached on a single issue" (Leeborn 2002, 13). The strategy is basically tit for tat
involving two or more issues—you give me something in one issue area that
you have and I will give you something in another issue area that I have.

Issue linkage is so frequently used in diplomacy that there are many examples
that could be cited. One of the best-known examples of issue linkage used as
positive leverage is President John Kennedy's promise (reward) to the Soviets
to remove US missiles from Turkey, linked to the removal of Soviet missiles
in Cuba, making resolution of the Cuban Missile Crisis possible (C. Morgan
1990). Henry Kissinger's linkage diplomacy with the Soviet Union in the early
1970s as part of the strategy of détente also exemplifies positive leverage and
issue linkage. These linkages were "designed to acquire leverage over the Soviet
Union by publicly committing the United States to a particular *quid pro quo*,"
through offers of concessions in some areas in exchange for acceptable Soviet
behavior in other areas (Dixon 1986, 430).

More recently, the 2008 US decision to drop North Korea from its list of terrorism state sponsors as a result of North Korea's agreement to all nuclear inspection demands is an example of positive leverage and issue linkage. In this
case, North Korea's status as a state sponsor of terrorism was used as leverage or
a concession in order to influence North Korea's willingness to accept weapons
inspections. Critics of this decision to link North Korea's terrorism list status
and the nuclear inspections noted that this strategy was a reward for bad behavior: "With today's action, the administration has given up a critical instrument of leverage. By rewarding North Korea before the regime has carried out
its commitments, we are encouraging this regime to continue its illicit nuclear

program and violate its pledge to no longer provide nuclear assistance to extremist regimes" (CNN.com 2008).

A historic case of positive leverage and issue linkage specifically involving the issue of territorial disputes is the 1846 US offer to the British to draw the Oregon boundary as the British wished it to be in exchange for British support of US attempts to acquire parts of California from Mexico (C. Morgan 1990). Another example is the multiple Soviet attempts from the 1950s to the 1980s to use the disputed Kurile Islands/Northern Territories and fishing rights as concessions in exchange for Japan's cooperation on normalization of Soviet-Japanese relations, reduction of US forces in Japan, and Japanese investment in developing oil and natural gas fields in Siberia (Ueki 1988). Japan's 1972 refusal of the concessions was explained by Prime Minister Sato, who stated, "We do not intend to link the issue of the northern territories with our participation in the development of Siberia" (Gaiduk 2008, 118). The September 1993 negotiation between China and India over their shared border is another case of positive leverage and issue linkage. In these negotiations, China offered a concession to India, "which would have involved trading off NEFA (a small territory near Tibet) to India in exchange for the recognition of Aksai Chin (near Kashmir and Jammu) as Chinese territory" (Chung 2004, 124). In the negotiations, China offered India a concession on one territorial dispute as bargaining leverage for India's policy toward another territorial dispute, but the concession was refused, and the dispute endures to this day.

Coercive Diplomacy

To achieve bargaining leverage using one issue conflict to influence another issue conflict, states will use the strategy of coercive diplomacy, which includes compellence, deterrence, and blackmail, all coercive strategies. The concept of coercive diplomacy is similar to Schelling's (1960) concept of compellence except that coercive diplomacy is used in a defensive way, to get the adversary to stop or change a certain action (F. E. Morgan 2003). The purpose is to persuade an adversary to stop or undo an action already being pursued. The objective could be merely to get the adversary to halt an action, or it could be a demand to reverse course and overturn a decision that has already been made. A state using the strategy of coercive diplomacy (coercer) threatens an adversary in order to get that adversary to halt an action that has already been initiated. In

other words, the adversary has made the first move, and the coercer is responding to that action by issuing a threat to stop the action (Jakobsen 1998).

Schelling (1960, 5) describes compellence as a game of strategy in which the
opponents should focus on the "exploitation of potential force," not the "efficient application of force." Compellence is a strategy of persuasion; it is coercive
bargaining to persuade the adversary to stop or change some action already initiated. The sister strategy of deterrence, compellence strategy is more frequently
used in the post–Cold War era today. During the Cold War, the preoccupation
of security studies with the strategy of deterrence was expected, but this meant
that little theorizing about the strategy of compellence occurred. Though deterrence was the dominant theory through the Cold War era, the strategy did
not provide guidance on how to achieve changes in behavior of the adversary
(Freedman 1998; F. E. Morgan 2003). Hence, policy makers and political scientists came up with the strategy of compellence. Only two major works on compellence strategy were written during this time—Schelling (1966) and George,
Hall, and Simons (1971).

Both compellence and deterrence depend on threats used to persuade an
adversary to behave in a certain way. Schelling (1966) identified deterrence as a
strategy that involves making a threat, then waiting, while compellence involves
an action that has to be taken rather than being a passive strategy like deterrence. The main purpose of deterrence is to prevent an adversary from taking
an action such as the use of nuclear weapons. Deterrence is an attempt to persuade an adversary that the costs or risks of taking a certain course of military
action would outweigh any benefits of taking that action (George and Smoke
1974; Huth and Russett 1984; Snyder 1961). By threatening to use force, the state
applying a strategy of deterrence is attempting to maintain the status quo and
prevent any hostile action by the adversary.

Compellence occurs when the adversary's calculation of costs and benefits
is manipulated by the challenger state. Unlike deterrence, compellence involves
limited use of force or communicating an active threat to get an adversary to
take some action it does not necessarily want to take (Jakobsen 1998). Compellence is a form of strategic coercion (Jakobsen 1998). Freedman (1998, 3) defines
strategic coercion as "the deliberate and purposive use of overt threats to influence another's strategic choices." Strategies of coercion are "a crucial strategy for
international conflict. Through coercive actions some nations force other nations to relinquish values that would otherwise not be relinquished" (Lockhart
1979, 117). One form of compellence is blackmail, which is a threat used to get

the adversary to initiate some action it would prefer not to do. Blackmail entails the coercer attempting to force the adversary into compliance, which means choosing an action that the coercer would prefer (Ellsberg 1959). Coercive diplomacy, coined by George, Hall, and Simons (1971), is a strategy in which one state attempts to persuade the target state to halt an action and return to the status quo situation in favor of the coercer.

The strategy of coercive diplomacy is appealing because it offers a state the opportunity to achieve a foreign policy objective with less cost than use of force, less risk of escalation, and fewer political costs (George 1994). The strategy involves two levels of communication—verbal communication and actions. States can issue explicit verbal warnings, sometimes accompanied by limited military action to signal credibility and resolve of the warning or threat (George 1994). Coercion also involves commitments, where a challenger state communicates a high level of commitment to a certain type of action, and threats, which involve communicating potential application of punishment pursued to induce a change in the target state's actions or attitudes (George, Hall, and Simons 1971; Lockhart 1979; Schelling 1960, 1966; Snyder and Diesing 1977). Commitment can be willingness to defend an ally or, in the case of territorial disputes, dedication to the acquisition of disputed territory. Coercive diplomacy always involves some underlying level of commitment, while the threat can be in the form of communication of a threat or use of force, but it is not necessary for a state to threaten force to successfully pursue the strategy.

To credibly deter a potential attacker, a target must issue a threat in which it signals willingness to use force to defend itself (Huth 1997). Yet, to coerce an adversary to change a certain policy or action, a challenger state must only issue a threat to signal resolve when pursuing a strategy of coercive diplomacy. Strategies of compellence can be coupled with use of force, but such strategies are often used to achieve ends without having to cross the threshold of force (Lockhart 1979). Schelling (1960, 6) argues that the "threat has to be credible to be efficacious, and its credibility may depend on the costs and risks associated with fulfillment for the party making the threat." Because we live in a world of incomplete information, states can only estimate their adversary's level of resolve regarding a disputed issue. For states to be able to signal their resolve more accurately, they must use costly signaling. Costly signaling acts as the mechanism that enables states to update beliefs about their adversaries' resolve. Through a succession of costly signals, opposing states learn about their adversaries' more accurate willingness or resolve to use force in a certain dispute (Fearon 1995; R. Powell 1999; Schelling 1960; Wagner 2000).

To maintain credibility, the threat issued in a costly signal must have a deadline for compliance (Schelling 1966). If no time limit is set, "unwillingness by the coercer to set a deadline for compliance is very likely to be interpreted as a sign of weakness. Opponents will simply not perceive a threat of force as credible unless it is accompanied by a deadline for compliance" (Jakobsen 1998, 29). The failure of the Chinese to compel Vietnam to withdraw from Cambodia in 1979 is an example of this problem, which occurred due to the lack of a time limit and China's wait-and-see approach (Mulvenon 1995). By leaving the demand vague with no time limit, China did not give Vietnam the opportunity to know what would satisfy China's demand for compliance. Any effective use of coercive diplomacy must therefore communicate a time limit for when the adversary should comply. This means that the coercer must issue a threat along with assurances that the threat will be revoked once the target state changes its behavior as demanded by the coercer.

Coercive diplomacy is not a traditional military strategy, but a political strategy that uses just enough of a threat to credibly demonstrate resolve and achieve one's objectives (George 1994). Though coercive diplomacy is often thought of only as militarized threats, it can also be diplomatic, such as threats to withdraw from negotiations, cancellation of negotiations, passage of a law or hostile restatement of territorial claim, or threats to allow the transfer of migrants or refusal to defend a shared border against smuggling. Threats issued in coercive diplomacy can range from a nonviolent break in negotiations to a threat to escalate to warfare. Along the continuum of threats are (in order of intensity) threats of nonviolent breach of existing agreements or breaks in diplomatic relations, threats involving demonstration of force, threats of compulsive settlement by force short of limited invasion, threats of limited armed invasion, and threats of war (Lauren 1994). Threats in breaking off negotiations involve an ultimatum that unless one's own proposal is accepted, negotiations would cease. Other diplomatic threats in coercive diplomacy include the imposition of a time limit in negotiations (threat to walk out), the recall or expelling of diplomats from the opposing state (recall of ambassadors), and the official break of diplomatic relations between the adversaries (Hagstrom 2005). Threats to breach agreements are threats to terminate status quo agreements or treaties. The 1990 threat by Soviet president Mikhail Gorbachev to Lithuania to repeal its declaration of independence or risk termination of trade agreements and the imposition of economic embargoes on oil and gas shipments is a good example of this type of threat (Lauren 1994).

In territorial disputes, these threats occur when the coercer (challenger state) actively confronts the status quo owner of the territory (target state) in a hostile way. As a result of this diplomatic type of confrontation, the level of tension between the two states increases significantly, threatening normal bilateral relations. In many cases, when one state confronts the other through diplomatic conflict, the other state will retaliate in response. Diplomatic confrontations could include official claims or threats to acquire the disputed territory, ratification of laws, international treaties, and constitutions in which the disputed territory is codified as sovereign rather than disputed, refusal to negotiate, and withdrawal from negotiations.

In some circumstances, more credibility is needed than is sufficient in purely diplomatic threats, so limited use of force is threatened. Militarized confrontations are considered as explicit threats to use military force or actual mobilization, deployment, or similar displays of limited military force, all of which signal credibility. The threat or use of force must be overt, explicit, and governmentally sanctioned (Gochman and Maoz 1984). Such threats or uses of force act as costly signals, which help to make the threat credible, compared to merely saying that troops may be mobilized along a border. All of these threats of force are intended to put pressure on the adversary without actual use of military force. Threats of naval force tend to be more effective as a strategy of coercive diplomacy, compared to mobilization of troops along a border, which provides higher levels of risk for escalation. Navies are generally more effective in coercive diplomacy because naval ships "could be moved about more easily than land-based forces, could remain nearby but still be out of sight, and could be used in flexible and incremental ways during diplomatic crises" (Lauren 1994, 32). Such display of naval force, sometimes referred to as gunboat diplomacy, are often effective signals of resolve. Gunboat diplomacy is generally an effective and frequently used type of limited force (Blechman and Kaplan 1978; Lauren 1994; Mandel 1986; Vagts 1956). Analysts refer to such gunboat diplomacy as a tool of political and psychological leverage, not an attempt to use actual force (Mandel 1980).

Threats involving force short of limited invasion mean that a state can use limited force to seize property or impose a blockade, without actually invading the territory. When states use threats of limited armed invasion, the strategy is to threaten actual occupation of certain territory. For example, in March 1970,

Israel threatened to scorch a six-mile stretch of territory in southern Lebanon unless the Lebanese government stopped Arab guerrillas from launching attacks on Israel from across the Lebanese border (Lauren 1994). The choice of threat intensity level used in coercive diplomacy depends primarily on the degree of credibility needed to ensure the threat is persuasive.

Coercive diplomacy is based on threats involving limited uses of force, not full-scale military operations since states use coercive diplomacy "to persuade an opponent to cease aggression rather than to bludgeon him into stopping" (George 1994, 10). Escalation of force is not an objective of coercive diplomacy: "if limited force is used as part of a coercive diplomacy strategy, it is used as a signal intended to convince the opponent that noncompliance is too costly. When coercive diplomacy is successful, the opponent complies without having been defeated militarily first" (Jakobsen 1998, 14). Unlike full-scale war, which limits the adversary to only one choice, coercive diplomacy allows the adversary to choose whether to comply or resist and provides room for bargaining concessions.

If a state has to use full-scale force, this means that coercive diplomacy, the threat to use force unless a state complies with a demand, has failed because the adversary was not successfully intimidated by just the threat. Another distinction between full-scale war and coercive diplomacy is that the objectives are different. The objective of coercive diplomacy is to communicate or signal a threat to the adversary to allow the adversary to make a change, while the objective of full-scale force is to impose compliance directly. Threat of force used as a pretext for war is not coercive diplomacy since the purpose of coercive diplomacy is to avoid war (Jakobsen 1998; Mandel 1980).

The costs of threats or minor uses of force in coercive diplomacy are generally minimal compared to larger uses of force since they typically involve little or no bloodshed, fewer political costs, and less risk of a military escalation. If force is used, coercive diplomacy uses just enough force to demonstrate resolve credibly in order to persuade the adversary to halt its actions. The primary objective of the strategy of coercive diplomacy is therefore to "create in the opponent the expectation of costs of sufficient magnitude to erode his motivation to continue doing what he is doing" (George 1991, 11). The success of the strategy depends on the level of motivation of each side, which is directly tied to how each side perceives the importance of what is at stake in the dispute and the costs they are willing to incur in order to protect their interests. A territorial dispute is the perfect type of dispute with which to apply coercive diplomacy since territory holds such a strong amount of salience for states, particularly the state that holds status quo ownership. The fact that territorial MIDs are more likely to escalate to war compared to disputes over regimes or policy (Vasquez and Henehan 2001) suggests that territory is more salient for some states.

In territorial disputes, coercive diplomacy is sometimes used to persuade the adversary to halt some action it is doing specifically with regard to the disputed territory, without any issue linkage. For example, Thailand mobilized troops along the Thai-Cambodian border in the summer and fall of 2008 to signal Thai resolve about the disputed Preah Vihear Temple on the border. The Thai threat of force was in response to the announcement that Cambodia's application to UNESCO for World Heritage status for the temple was successful. In another case, China deployed ships to the disputed Senkaku/Diaoyu Islands in response to a Japanese decision to recognize a lighthouse erected by a Japanese nationalist activist group. Another example is Qatar's 1986 armed attack of Hawar Island, which was a direct response to Bahrain's attempt to build on the disputed island. The objective of all of these states and their threats of force was to persuade their adversaries to reverse, change, or halt decisions or actions made specifically about the territorial dispute, not involving any issue linkage.

However, it is just as typical for states to use the strategy not to compel the adversary to make a change specifically regarding the territorial dispute, but instead to change action regarding some other disputed issue that has little or nothing to do with the territorial dispute. In these cases, the challenger is using a dual strategy of coercive diplomacy and issue linkage. The combined strategy allows states to use territorial disputes as bargaining leverage in other issues, making the disputes difficult to settle.

THE DUAL STRATEGY OF COERCIVE DIPLOMACY AND ISSUE LINKAGE

Though issue linkage is frequently used to successfully resolve crises or disputes by allowing the exchange of concessions on different issues, the strategy to achieve negative leverage through a threat is used just as frequently, but it is rarely labeled as issue linkage. Negative issue linkage occurs when one state threatens to compel another state to stop a certain action already initiated. The coercer demands of the target some concession on a new issue before resolution of the dispute occurs. Lacy and Niou (2004, 26) note that if the target "does not comply with the coercer's demand, the coercer threatens action on a separate issue, such as restricting trade or failing to renew privileged trading status."

Economic sanctions are the most typical use of negative issue linkage and coercive diplomacy, used to compel adversaries to change a policy on an unrelated but linked issue. Sanctions, "like issue linkage, involve two or more issues. . . . Any incidence of sanctions involves a dispute on at least one issue as well as a conflict over the sanctions" (Lacy and Niou 2004, 26). When sanctions are applied, the sanctions themselves are punishment regarding trade, economic aid, loans, and investment. The intended purpose of the economic sanctions is to get a state to make changes in other issues such as nuclear weapons proliferation, regime change, state sponsorship of terrorism, human rights violations, or a number of other disputed issues that are directly unrelated to trade issues. Therefore, by using economic leverage, states attempt to compel adversaries to shift their activities in the security realm, not the economic realm.

Zeng (2004, 32) notes that "threats to impose sanctions will be more credible if negotiators can tie their own hands with respect to retaliating, link agreement on one issue to another issue area where one has leverage over the partner, offer side payments to foreign governments in order to obtain the acquiescence of those domestic groups opposed to change, and add parties who support one's position to the negotiations."[2] While sanctions are a form of punishment, threats to impose sanctions are a form of coercive diplomacy since the intent is to compel the adversary to halt some action by using a threat. If sanctions are ultimately applied, this means that the coercive diplomacy has failed and the strategy of punishment through compellence is applied (Lacy and Niou 2004, 27).

Though the effectiveness of economic sanctions as a strategy of coercion is debated, there are cases in which the punishment or denial of economic aid or trade compelled a state to shift policies. It is also the case that the actual threat of sanctions, not necessarily the sanctions themselves, put enough pressure on a state to concede (Souva and Montgomery 2010). South Africa's dismantling of the apartheid system of government and Libya's decision to halt sponsorship of terrorism and pay retributions to victims of terrorism are two examples of sanctions being used as negative leverage to compel states to change actions in other issues. Yet the threat of economic sanctions is rarely enough leverage to compel a state to shift its policy regarding another issue like human rights violations or nuclear proliferation. If threats of limited force are used, this makes coercive diplomacy and issue linkage a more effective strategy.

Besides economic sanctions, there are other forms of negative issue linkage. For example, the European Union (EU) "threatens" denial of prospective membership in the organization based on states' compliance with EU demands. Turkey in particular feels the brunt of this conditionality—not only is Turkey's potential EU membership dependent on a halting of human rights abuses, but it is also conditional upon Turkey's resolution of the Cyprus issue. States also use negative issue linkage by using foreign aid to induce compliance among aid recipient states during UN voting (Cia 2005).

The threat to use force in territorial disputes is especially persuasive in influencing the adversary's decisions about other linked issues. In coercive diplomacy, the diplomatic or militarized threat or use of limited force acts as leverage or value that a challenger state can hold over a target state. By pursuing coercive diplomacy with issue linkage, "a bargaining nation must have resources that create options usable for gaining influence over the adversary in the situation at hand if the nation is to expect a successful outcome" (Lockhart 1979, 106). Threats to territory act as this resource. The long-term maintenance of a territorial claim by a challenger state is an ideal form of the commitment aspect of coercion. In this sense, as long as the claim is active, the target state understands the commitment level of the challenger, even more so when actual threats are issued regarding the territorial dispute. By pursuing threats, the challenger state can strengthen its level of commitment to act, as indicated by the threat (Lockhart 1979), and the target should understand that the challenger is resolved about the disputed territory. Such level of resolve and a commitment to the disputed territory makes territorial disputes an ideal means of pursuing coercive diplomacy not merely to achieve ends related to the territorial dispute, but also to other disputed issues with which a challenger state can link to the territorial threat.

Diplomatic threats about the disputed territory are also effective because of the salience of the disputed territory as a national security issue, relative to other issues. The choice of coercive diplomacy in territorial disputes means that a state has chosen to use a threat rather than a reward in order to compel the adversary to make a change on another issue. States can use threats in the form of diplomatic or militarized conflict in the same way that threats of economic sanctions are used, as negative leverage using issue linkage. The purpose of using coercive diplomacy and issue linkage is to give the adversary an opportunity to halt, undo, or change its actions before the challenger state resorts to the use of force. In territorial disputes, challenger states can make a threat about the territorial dispute, whether diplomatic or militarized, and use the threat as bargaining leverage to compel adversaries to make a change on a certain other issue such as a decision to cut economic aid.

China's seizure of the Paracel Islands in the South China Sea in January 1974 from Vietnam, the mobilization of up to 300,000 troops along the Sino-Vietnamese border in 1979, and their continued presence along the border all through the 1980s illustrate the strategy of coercive diplomacy and issue linkage. The seizure of the Paracel Islands was mainly pursued to prevent Vietnam from gaining full control of the islands and therefore to prevent Vietnam—and more importantly its powerful ally the Soviet Union—from gaining influence in the region. By seizing the islands, China was able to extend its maritime control an additional two hundred miles from its mainland, where it could monitor Vietnamese and Soviet naval activity (Burton 1978/79; Chen 1987; Hood 1992; C.-K. Lo 1989).

The objective of the 1979 mobilization and cross-border attack was an attempt to compel Vietnam to withdraw from Cambodia (Japan Defense Agency 1989; Mulvenon 1995; Ross 1988, 1991).[3] Though there are a number of theories to explain China's invasion across the Vietnamese border, "the real cause of the March 1979 border war was Vietnam's invasion of Cambodia in December 1978, an act that greatly provoked the Chinese and drove them to employ a much more aggressive diplomatic strategy" (Mulvenon 1995, 71).[4] A week after the Chinese attack across the border, Deng Xiaoping himself announced the objective of the attack: "to teach them they could not run about as much as they desire," meaning running about Cambodia (Mulvenon 1995, 73). At the postwar negotiations held from April 1979 to March 1980, Vietnam wanted to discuss the issues related directly to the armed conflict and ways to reduce tension at the border. However, in addition to those issues, China wanted to discuss the presence of Vietnamese troops in Cambodia and Laos (Amer 1994).

China continued to maintain its troops along the border all through the 1980s in order to "impose high costs on Vietnam's military venture in Cambodia. The continued presence of Chinese troops along the border compelled Vietnam for a second lesson. Thus, China offered Vietnam reduced border tension and lower defense costs in return for Vietnamese withdrawal from Cambodia" (Ross 1991, 1175). There is little doubt the Chinese mobilization was enacted to continue to pressure Vietnam on the Cambodia issue: "increased Chinese military activities along the border seem to have been linked to Vietnamese offensives in Cambodia" (Amer 1994, 364). When Vietnam finally withdrew from Cambodia in 1988,

China relaxed its anti-Vietnamese rhetoric, withdrew most of its troops from the Sino-Vietnamese border, resumed border trade, and opened negotiations with Vietnam (Ross 1991). According to one analyst, "this evolution indicates that China gradually stopped linking the military evolution in Cambodia to its own policies along the border with Vietnam" (Amer 1994, 364). China used the border dispute with Vietnam as bargaining leverage for the more important issue of Cambodia, not because the border itself was so important to China.

Issue linkage does not have to be a long-term calculated strategy. The strategy can be deliberate or occur as an ad hoc response to an action by the adversary (Dixon 1986). Rather than merely responding to one issue within that issue area, states pursuing issue linkage bring in another disputed issue, linking the two together. By confronting its adversary when circumstances are right, the challenger state signals its resolve, making some threat in the territorial dispute as a form of coercive diplomacy to compel the adversary to change its policy on economic issues, other security issues, or any other salient disputed issue that is exogenous to the territorial dispute.

Though the threat must be overt, the issue linkage is often implicit and not directly communicated to the adversary since this approach would reveal the challenger state's behind-the-scenes intentions of using the threat as bargaining leverage. As Schelling (1966, 73) writes, "compellent threats tend to communicate only the general direction of compliance, and are less likely to be self-limiting, less likely to communicate in the very design of the threat just what, or how much, is demanded." Likewise, Leeborn (2002, 6) notes that "the claimant might not assert that its position on one issue is dependent on the other, but only suggest that for exogenous reasons the two issues ought to be resolved together." What this means is that threats made by challenger states do not necessarily explicitly cite the linked issue in a blatant way, but instead, in an implicit but fairly obvious way. Implicit issue linkages do not mean that they are understated or secret, but rather, they must send a clear signal to the recipient in order to be effective. Schelling (1966) also points out that the tendency of policy makers is to emphasize what the coercer will do if the adversary does not change its behavior rather than focus on what actions of compliance would satisfy the coercer.

China's attack across the Vietnamese border in 1979 also demonstrates implicit demands linked to the militarized confrontation. On the day of the invasion, February 17, the official justification by China for the invasion was "incessant armed provocations and hostile activities" along the border and concern for Chinese expatriates in Vietnam (Mulvenon 1995). The official statement made no mention of China's objective to compel Vietnam to withdraw from Cambodia and failed to set any conditions for Chinese withdrawal from Vietnam if Vietnam complied with the demand. As a result, "Hanoi was left to decipher Chinese ravings about border sovereignty and the meaning of terms like 'self-defense counter attack'" (Mulvenon 1995, 81). Another example of implicit but clearly implied issue linkage is when China accused the Vietnamese of mistreating the minority Hoa people along the disputed border by stating that "behind every anti-Chinese step taken by the Vietnamese authorities is the large shadow of Soviet imperialism" (Rich 2003, 482).

Leaving the demand of compliance somewhat vague allows the challenger state to shift the demand and allows the target state to test the waters to see how much compliance is necessary to avoid the challenger following through on a threat. It could also be the case that policy makers "deliberately choose to be unclear and to keep the enemy guessing either to keep his defenses less prepared or to enhance his anxiety" (Schelling 1966, 75). Sometimes avoiding explicit communication of demands and issuing demands privately is a better strategy, since this provides the target state with the ability not to be embarrassed about compliance (Schelling 1966). The explanation for China's vague message to Vietnam was that it allowed Vietnam to withdraw from Cambodia without losing face (Yee 1980). Yet, Vietnam clearly understood the linkage and received the implied message.

In response to confrontations by the challenger state, the target state can risk use of force and potential occupation of the disputed territory or accede to some or all of the challenger state's demands about another disputed issue. There are certain conditions that will determine whether issue linkage will be successful, meaning that the target state will concede or comply with the demands of the coercer. First, the marginal gain that results from issue linkage must be more beneficial to the states involved than the status quo (Hoekman 1989). This means that challenger states should not attempt to use issue linkage unless the outcome is better than the status quo.

Based on several case studies, George and Simons (1994) concluded that there are several factors that make it more or less likely for coercive diplomacy to succeed so that the target state complies. Five contextual factors matter, including the global strategic environment, the type of provocation, the image of war, whether coercive diplomacy is applied unilaterally or through a coalition, and the isolation of the adversary (George and Simons 1994). Factors that make success more likely are clarity of objective, strength of motivation, asymmetry of motivation, sense of urgency, strong leadership, domestic support, international support, the adversary's fear of unacceptable escalation, and clarity about the precise terms of settlement of the crisis (George and Simons 1994). What is missing from this list is the type of issue about which a threat is being pursued. It would seem rational that states would be more likely to comply with demands of the coercer if the threat is about a salient issue like territory. If the threat is about damage to military bases by air power, for example, this type of threat may not be sufficient to persuade the adversary to comply.

On the other hand, if the threat is about ground troops occupying disputed territory, the adversary—the state that has ownership of the territory already—is more likely to take such a threat seriously. If the adversary does not comply with the coercer's demand to stop some certain action, then the adversary risks escalation and use of force in the actual disputed territory. For issue linkage to work successfully, the states involved in the dispute must place different values on the disputed issues, and the proposed linkages must make conditions more attractive than the status quo (Hoekman 1989). Because states that maintain status quo control of the disputed territory will generally defend their sovereign territory at any cost, signals of threats by challenger states must be taken seriously and be considered high-priority issues. When a challenger state links a territorial dispute to another disputed issue, the target state must seriously consider the challenger state's request for a change in policy on the other issue or risk the challenger state following through on the threat to use force in the territorial dispute. Therefore, the type of issue and the salience of that issue to each state would seem to matter significantly.

Why do target states comply with demands when they know they are being coerced? Pape (1990, 1997, 1998) argues that the cost of punishment or denial must be high enough so that the target is persuaded to halt its actions or risk suffering the costs resulting from a coercer's use of force. Since the defense of territory is considered to be a vital national interest for states, the cost of losing disputed territory would be particularly high for target states. In other words, if the challenger state's threat or punishment does not hurt enough, there is little incentive for the target state to comply with the demands of the coercer. However, if the threat is about something as salient as sovereign territory, compared to other disputed issues, target states are more likely to change a policy on another less salient issue as a concession, in order to prevent the challenger from taking the threatening action. For issue linkage to work successfully, the parties must therefore have different priorities about the linked issues (Pruitt 1981). This means that "the initial issue be more salient than the linkage issue for one party, while the other party sees the additional issue as of greater salience" (C. Morgan 1990, 318). Since the success of issue linkage often depends on the salience or nature of the disputed issues, issue linkage is more likely to succeed if the disputed issue has relative salience (Deutsch 1973; Diehl 1992; Dixon 1986; George 1994; C. Morgan 1990; F. E. Morgan 2003; Pruitt 1981).

Since disputed territory is often *perceived* by states as more salient *compared to other disputed issues,* it is not surprising that a challenger state would be able to use a threat about a territorial dispute as bargaining leverage in another disputed issue.[5] Issue salience refers to "the degree of importance attached to that issue by the actors involved" (Diehl 1992, 334). A territorial dispute is the perfect type of dispute with which to use the strategy of issue linkage particularly since territory holds such a strong amount of salience for the target states. Compared to other disputed issues, territory is often considered to be very important to states due to both tangible and intangible reasons (Hensel 1996; Hensel and Mitchell 2005; Hensel et al. 2008; Vasquez 1993). Even when challenger states do not particularly care for the territory because of its actual value, they can take advantage of the perception that territory is highly salient and use it to gain bargaining leverage from the target state. In this sense, all that matters is the perception that challenger states claim high levels of salience regarding the territorial dispute, so that threats or uses of force are viewed as credible and costly to the target state, enough so that the target state is willing to comply with the demands of the challenger state with regard to other issues linked to the territorial dispute.

The disputed territory is often more important to the target than to the challenger because the target state already maintains control of the territory, and any shift in the status quo could damage a state's reputation and conception of sovereignty. It is generally assumed that territory claimed by a challenger state is by default salient to the target state because a challenge to ownership of territory is a challenge to a state's sovereignty. Target states are more willing to fight for territory and experience fatalities in disputes over territory compared to other disputes (Hensel 1996; Senese 1996). Leaders of states where threats to the territory exist are more willing to sacrifice lives in territorial disputes compared to other types of disputes (Tir and Vasquez 2010). At the same time, the people in states where external threats to territory exist are also more tolerant of greater political autonomy by leaders because homeland territory is challenged (Gibler 2010). It is in target states, where sovereign territory must be defended from challenges to the status quo, where such external threats occur, not in challenger states.

It is easy to acknowledge that "peoples and nations ascribe to their territory a value that is perhaps unequaled or incommensurable, since territory embodies and embraces for them their national sovereignty and identity" (Kacowicz 1994, 7), but it would seem to ring truer in target states where the territory is already controlled and sovereign. For the target state, threats to territory involve active defense, occupation, and control of the land (Gibler and Tir 2010), often making territorial disputes more costly for target states. Though challenger states could perceive salience on claimed territory, there is little doubt that sovereign territory is generally more salient than claimed territory. Therefore, even in cases where territory claimed by a challenger state lacks any actual tangible or intangible value *within issues,* it should be salient to a target state because of the threat to the target state's sovereignty, and this is what makes territory such a salient issue *across issues.*[6]

Another reason why challenger states will use coercive diplomacy and issue linkage in territorial disputes is because states can pursue low-cost threats or uses of force in territorial disputes as a form of compellence that states cannot do in other issue disputes. It is more feasible for states to take actions in territorial disputes than in disputes over regime type, for example, or less salient issues like trade policy. For example, it would be impractical for a state to attempt coercive diplomacy and issue linkage by pursuing regime change by decapitation of a leader in order to link that issue with another dispute issue. Rather, by mobilizing troops to a border or dispatching ships to waters around disputed islands, states are able to send a signal to their adversaries and be taken seriously, all at a relatively low cost.

To prevent risking escalation of force or the potential loss of territory, the target state will generally comply with the demands of the coercer on issues that are less salient, particularly to the target. It is not necessarily the case that the challenger always "wins" the concessions demanded by the use of issue linkage and coercive diplomacy, but if the cost of concessions is low enough for the target, and we assume the challenger's territorial threat is significant enough, the target state should rationally consider paying out demanded concessions to avoid the challenger following through with any threat, particularly militarized actions. If the target state can concede on issues of lower salience, such as increased economic aid to its adversary or changes in policy about fishing rights or illegal migration, the provision of concessions will prevent potential costs and threats regarding the more salient disputed territory. As Randle (1987, 17) argues, "The severity of the conflict depends upon how intensely the parties value the matter at issue." Therefore, the more salient the issue—disputed territory—the more likely that a target state will be willing to suffer costs involved in nonterritorial concessions to satisfy demands of a challenger state regarding other disputed issues.

By giving up some concession to the challenger state, the target state is theoretically able to prevent the challenger from following through on its threats about the disputed territory. As a result, both sides get something—the challenger state receives concessions on another issue, while the territory is safe for the target state, for the mean time. Other factors such as military balance or third-party alliances may play a role in determining whether the target feels threatened enough to give in to demands of the challenger, but in most cases it seems that these factors are not so influential in the end. For example, in the case of China's claim against Japan, regardless of their relative military balance and the promise of US defense of Japan, including the disputed Senkaku Islands, Japanese leaders repeatedly give in to Chinese demands on nonterritorial concessions in order to avoid even considering the potential of armed conflict with China. Even in cases where military balance is drastically uneven, such as Lebanon and Israel, target states like Israel will comply with challenger demands to avoid territorial threats as long as the cost of concessions is relative low and the nonterritorial issue is of relatively low salience, such as the release of Lebanese prisoners in exchange for halted attacks on the disputed Shebaa Farms on the Lebanese-Israeli border.

Therefore, because the challenger's threat is about such a salient issue like territory, the target state will generally provide some concession to the challenger or risk the challenger state following through with the threat or use of force. The challenger state therefore has little incentive to drop its territorial claim as long as other salient disputed issues exist, because it can use threats about the territorial dispute as leverage to gain concessions on other issues from the target state. In the end, though, even when the challenger does not succeed in achieving nonterritorial concessions from the target, it is the attempt that matters, not whether they won concessions or not. States will generally attempt the same strategy or policy approach multiple times regardless of past record, such as with economic sanctions or similar strategies, so it is logical that challenger states in territorial disputes will also continue to attempt issue linkage and coercive diplomacy, maybe upping the ante from diplomatic to militarized. Since territory is assumed to be the most salient issue for target states, such states should be more likely to comply with demands if the cost of nonterritorial concessions is lower than the risk of militarized conflict and potential cost of lost territory.[7]

Testing the Bargaining Leverage Theory

If the theory of territorial disputes as bargaining leverage is valid, we should observe that when other disputed issues exist, challenger states should initiate diplomatic or militarized threats or uses of force, and they should *not* offer or accept territorial concessions to attempt settlement. This means that around the same time that a disputed issue exists, challenger states should first avoid settlement attempts in order to take advantage of the territorial dispute as bargaining leverage; second, challenger states should initiate either diplomatic or militarized threats or uses of force as a means of coercive diplomacy to gain bargaining leverage. We should also observe clear cases of both implicit and explicit issue linkage by the challenger state, linking a particular disputed issue with a territorial dispute.[8] If states claiming territory can successfully compel adversaries to change directions in other issues by threatening diplomatic or militarized provocations in territorial disputes, there is little incentive for these states to drop their territorial claims. This theory should be able to explain the continued initiation of threats or uses of force and the endurance of territorial disputes as long as a territorial claim exists and other disputed issues persist. Under these conditions, challenger states have the opportunity to link threats in a territorial dispute to other disputed issues.

To be effective, the theory must also be able to explain why so many challenger states have not only attempted settlement but also accepted final settlement of their territorial disputes. So how does the theory explain settled disputes? The answer to this question is that we should observe settlement attempts, but not diplomatic or militarized threats or uses of force, under two conditions: when no *salient* disputed issues exist, or when the disputed *salient* issues have been resolved. In the first case, it could be that there were no other salient disputed issues that the challenger state prioritized from which to gain concessions. In any bilateral relationship there are inevitably issues that are regularly disputed, even among close friends like the US and Canada, yet in many cases such disputed issues are not necessarily salient enough to interfere in the dyad's relationship. On the other hand, when disputed issues are perceived as highly salient to the challenger state, such disputed issues will likely interfere in bilateral relations, causing tension or sometimes outright hostility in the dyad.

If there are no other salient issues or these disputed issues have been resolved, there is less incentive to pursue coercive diplomacy and issue linkage. Issue linkage is likely to fail "when the benefits produced by the linkage, are, for at least one actor, not sufficient to overcome the costs involved in bringing the additional issue into the bargaining" (C. Morgan 1990, 320–21). Therefore, if threats about the territorial dispute fail to gain the challenger state concessions or benefits that are larger than the cost of maintaining the dispute, the challenger state is expected not to attempt the strategy of issue linkage and coercive diplomacy. In these cases, other explanations such as value of territory or domestic accountability or mobilization are likely to explain threats or uses of force and lack of settlement attempts. If none of these conditions exist, we are more likely to observe settlement attempts sooner rather than later. For example, the dispute between the Netherlands and Germany over their shared border lasted only five years, from 1955 to 1960. The border area held no economic, strategic, or ethnic value for the Netherlands, the challenger state, domestic mobilization and accountability was a nonissue, and no other salient disputed issues existed between these states at the time. Therefore, it was relatively easy to resolve the territorial dispute, and there was no reason for the Netherlands to persevere in the dispute.

In the case when other disputed issues have been resolved, this means that the target state has given in to demands made by the challenger state in terms of providing concessions, the challenger and target have come to a mutual agreement regarding other disputed issues, or external political conditions have shifted so that the challenger no longer feels the need to demand a shift in policy or action by the target. For example, in the last case, the end of the Cold War, the fall of the Soviet Union, and the shift in regimes in satellite states may have shifted demands of adversaries toward those states. In these circumstances, the cost of maintaining the territorial claim and dispute is higher than maintaining improved relations with the target state since the other more salient issues are resolved. Therefore, even though it seems logical that a challenger state would continue to maintain a territorial dispute as an insurance policy of sorts to use in future disputed issues, the presence of a territorial dispute acts as a thorn in any improved relations on which the challenger and target are working as a result of the resolution of other disputed issues. In the case of the

Sino-Soviet/Russian border, the resolution of much more salient issues such as balance of power, strategic concerns about nuclear weapons deployment, and Soviet/Russian intervention or influence in neighboring states in Asia were all more important to China than the actual border dispute. Once these salient issues were resolved, the Sino-Russian relationship began to improve significantly. If China had continued to pester Russia on the border dispute, the territorial dispute could have threatened the more important overall relationship between the two former adversaries and could have prevented further progress on other more salient disputed issues. Therefore, there appears to be a tipping point where the benefits of resolving the other disputed issues are significant enough that the costs of continuing to pursue the territorial dispute would be too high and possibly detrimental to the benefits of improved bilateral relations.

In either case, if other disputed issues are resolved or dropped, this means that the challenger state does not have incentive to use issue linkage and coercive diplomacy in the territorial dispute since there is no purpose to gain other concessions. If more than one salient disputed issue exists, all of the issues must be resolved before the challenger state can consider no longer pursuing the strategy of issue linkage and coercive diplomacy and can then consider attempting settlement of the territorial dispute. The implication is that challenger states' pursuit of their dispute strategies is determined by the existence of other disputed issues at any given time. In other words, it is not only whether a disputed issue exists, but specifically *when* other disputed issues exist and how states act at that time. A further implication is that states can shift their strategies back and forth depending on the existence of other disputed issues, meaning in some years they will pursue attempted settlement when other issues do not exist or are resolved, and in other years when other disputed issues are present, they can seek diplomatic or militarized threats or uses of force. Thus, even in enduring disputes, challenger states will seek settlement through territorial concessions when other disputed issues are not present, even though they remain unresolved today. Likewise, this also means that in the resolved disputes, there will have been times when challengers were less likely to seek settlement because other disputed issues existed, and vice versa. In the same way, in both resolved and unresolved disputes, threats or uses of force should be more likely when other disputed issues exist, regardless of the fact that a portion of the disputes are eventually resolved and such threats and uses of force are halted (if they ever occurred).

The theory of territorial disputes as bargaining leverage attempts to explain

why many territorial disputes endure and why challenger states are less likely
to attempt settlement of such disputes, while other states have been more likely
to attempt settlement, resulting in successful dispute resolution. Overall, this
theory should be able to explain why a significant number of territorial disputes are enduring while others are resolved, but it is important to acknowledge
that domestic accountability or mobilization theories and value of territory are
likely to explain a number of enduring and settled disputes as well. Together,
these theories should be able to amply explain the dispute strategies of challenger states involved in territorial disputes.

The next chapter outlines the methods used to test the theory of bargaining
leverage and the alternative theories of value of territory and domestic accountability and mobilization. It also provides information about the status of settled
and unsettled territorial disputes in the world today. The subsequent four chapters examine the case studies, starting with China v. Japan in their dispute over
the Senkaku/Diaouyu Islands. While there is support for the alternative theories, the theory of bargaining leverage builds on these previous findings and
provides a stronger explanation for how challenger states strategize regarding
their territorial disputes.

CHAPTER FOUR

Characteristics of Territorial Disputes

Before examining the applicability of the theories to the cases examined, it is important to outline the scope and methods with which these cases were selected and the measurements of the variables examined. In this chapter, I outline the methods used to test the theories and outline the characteristics of the full universe of territorial disputes from 1953 to 2008, including both settled and ongoing disputes. By examining descriptive inferences, we can better understand patterns of strategies in territorial disputes and glean lessons to help prevent such disputes from escalating to armed conflict.

METHODS

To understand the variation in territorial dispute strategies, I test different theories using monthly observations from four case studies that occurred after World War II—three enduring territorial disputes and one settled dispute. The purpose of these cases is to use evidence to test whether support for the theory exists. The reader may find that the evidence presented does not fully falsify the null hypothesis, but as with any qualitative or quantitative study, it is impossible to prove with certainty that such correlations exist. Rather, I attempt to show not only that certain strategies are more likely when certain conditions exist, as quantitative studies do, but also to demonstrate causal mechanisms that make such correlations occur in the real world. This study does not attempt to provide a list of sufficient conditions that affect dispute strategies but to identify the conditions that make certain strategies more or less likely.

Qualitative Research

As gleaned from the literature discussed in chapter 2, there are many in-depth studies of territorial disputes. This book is primarily qualitative, but it attempts to act as a bridge with quantitative studies in that it provides descriptive statistics that quantitative studies can use to better inform the research. In the second part of this chapter, I present useful information and descriptive inferences about all territorial disputes from 1953 to 2008, both settled and unsettled. This section includes tables listing different types of territorial disputes, years of the disputes, and settlement methods, if settled. Such detailed information about the universe of territorial disputes is a necessary and important first step in determining the different dispute strategies used by states in territorial disputes and acts as the starting point for choosing the cases reviewed.

I use case studies here rather than a large-N quantitative study mainly because systematic qualitative analysis provides a means to explore the strategic interaction between actors in the context of specific historical circumstances and allows us to focus more intensely on behaviors *within* disputes and *within* dyads. Such analysis is ideal since "social science research should be both general and specific: it should tell us something about classes of events as well as about specific events at particular places" (King, Keohane, and Verba 1994, 43).[1] Qualitative analysis also allows for rich, in-depth examination of the explanatory variables by providing thick descriptive insight into real-world events.

As with any small-N study, there are limitations to this approach. The most significant limitation is that the theory can be tested for only these four cases and not for the dozens of other enduring territorial disputes. Though ideal, a universal test of all cases is beyond the scope of this study, which focuses on introducing a theory and providing rich descriptions and preliminary testing to demonstrate the feasibility and potential of the theory. However, as with most qualitative studies (Collier and Mahoney 1996), this study does not claim to overgeneralize to all territorial disputes or even most territorial disputes. Rather, the four cases illustrate a likely pattern that must be tested elsewhere. Another limitation is that the use of a smaller sample size means that there are a limited number of variables that can be covered to test alternative explanations, and therefore there may be omitted variable bias. For example, because of the focus on one dyad at a time rather than a cross-sectional study, this research cannot examine the role of alliances or relative military capabilities within the dyad, which change rarely or very little over time. Likewise, it is not feasible to demonstrate which theory actually does a better job of explaining dispute strategies in the entire universe of territorial disputes. Yet, even with these limitations, the benefits are sufficient to pursue this method.

A particular benefit of qualitative analysis in this research is that it provides insight into sequential, causal events that data correlations fail to recognize. Unlike large-N data analysis, which can only show correlations and likelihood of an event or outcome, studying in-depth analyses of cases provides more certainty about a causal claim. For example, data correlation would not recognize that an event that occurred at some undefined point in the past few months causally influenced a dispute strategy months later. Reviewing descriptive materials that explain that this chain of events was indeed causal provides much more reliable evidence to test the theory. Demonstrating the attractiveness of a new theory and its potential for explanatory power helps to set the agenda for future research.

The case studies also provide historic narratives useful for scholars, students, and policy makers studying these particular states and disputes and others who can use such causal stories to help build large datasets. Without such qualitative studies of real-world events, large-N datasets would not exist. Though this book provides in-depth information about just four territorial disputes, this information can serve well in the growing collection of case studies on all territorial disputes and expansion of datasets. As a trained scholar of both quantitative and qualitative research, I framed the case studies in the context of scientific studies, providing not only causal stories but also descriptive statistics and inferences, including tables that list all militarized interstate disputes and attempted settlements in each dispute, as well as linked issues, which indicate causality and correlations. In each case study chapter, I use explicit measurements of the variables to test the theories, just as any quantitative study does, in order to more rigorously demonstrate internal validity of the findings. It is my hope that the cases discussed provide quantitative scholars with a real-world feel for the dynamics that occur with territorial dispute strategies that large-N observations can sometimes miss, while also informing data collection and analysis. Therefore, studies like this one are necessary and critical components of any research agenda, and I hope that this study provides fodder for future studies on territorial disputes.

Case Selection

I chose the four cases covered here from a list that I compiled of all territorial disputes from 1953 to 2008, both settled and unsettled. In addition to collecting information about years of initiation and settlement (if it occurred), duration, the states involved, and regions of the world where the territorial disputes exist(ed), I also gathered information about the type of territory, value of territory, resolution method used in settlements, and divisions of territory if settled. I chose to examine disputes in the second half of the twentieth century for the universe of cases because this time period provided the largest number of dyads due to post–World War II independence gained by states in most of Africa, Asia, and the Middle East. It is also believed to be the most relevant time period to provide lessons to apply to understanding current and future dispute strategies. Altogether, there are 168 territorial disputes, 71 of which are ongoing (68 are enduring) and 97 of which are settled. The information used to compile the data on all territorial disputes came from many sources, including Allcock (1992), Bercovitch (1999), Calvert (2004), multiple years of the Central Intelligence Agency (CIA) World Factbook, Day (1987), Downing (1980), el-Hakim (1979), Huth (1996), Huth and Allee (2002), the Issue Correlates of War (ICOW) dataset (Hensel et al. 2008), the International Court of Justice (ICJ), and thousands of news articles about territorial disputes available from Lexis-Nexis and the International Boundary Research Unit (IBRU) database of news stories.

From this universe of disputes, I then chose four cases to examine in depth: 1) Senkaku/Diaoyu Islands (China v. Japan), 2) Shebaa Farms (Lebanon v. Israel), 3) North African enclaves Ceuta/Sebta and Melilla/Melilia (Morocco v. Spain), and 4) the Sino-Soviet/Russian border (China v. Soviet Union/Russia). The unit of observation is dispute dyad month (a dispute between a pair of states in any given month), with hundreds of monthly observations in each case. This study examines the actual attempts made by challenger states to resolve their territorial disputes through offers of territorial concessions. Therefore, it does not examine only the final settlement, but all attempts to resolve the disputes through concessions. If we studied only final settlements, this would provide a relatively small number of potential observations, yet there are hundreds of observations of offers of territorial concessions in the universe of territorial disputes. Just because an attempted settlement method failed does not mean that no attempt was made at all. It is important to take into account all attempted settlements by challenger states since this indicates a willingness on behalf of the challenger state to consider territorial concessions and final resolution of the dispute.

Settlement attempts can occur several times per year, so examining a dispute dyad year (observation of a dispute between a pair of states in any given year) would miss several observations. Therefore using monthly observations is a more effective unit of analysis. Since I am trying to explain variation of attempted settlement, as well as diplomatic or militarized threats, and not the final settlement of the dispute, there are not just 4 observations, but 1,722 total observations with significant variation in each dyad studied. Examining monthly observations provides for sufficient variation to test the three theories. In this study, although I examine only four territorial disputes, by using a larger number of observations, the theory must be valid in most of those months, not just in the months in which diplomatic or militarized threats or uses of force or settlements occurred. Using monthly observations of all settlement attempts, not just the final and successful attempt, also prevents a selection bias in the cases.

All four cases are enduring, with the shortest dispute currently lasting eleven years (Lebanon v. Israel) and the longest dispute lasting fifty-five years (Morocco v. Spain). The other two disputes have lasted thirty-nine years for China v. Japan and forty-nine years for China v. USSR/Russia. The cases reflect the three major types of territorial disputes: 1) uninhabited islands and territorial waters (the Senkaku/Diaoyu Islands dispute between China and Japan), 2) border disputes (Shebaa Farms between Lebanon and Israel), and 3) inhabited tracts of territory (the North African enclaves Ceuta and Melilla between Morocco and Spain). The fourth case study (the border/territory between China and Russia/Soviet Union) represents a combination of inhabited tracts of territory, a border dispute, and uninhabited islands located in the disputed border rivers. Making distinctions between types of territorial disputes is important since decision makers may make different strategic choices depending on whether the territory is desolate, like a remote border region or an uninhabited faraway island, compared to heavily inhabited homeland, mainland territory, for example. These different types of territory represent different subclasses (George and Bennett 2005) needed to compare the effects of type of territory. Since frontier land along remote borders is typically considered less valuable than homeland or island territories, states are more likely to compromise on such disputes (Fravel 2008).

The main reason for choosing these particular cases is that they exemplify variance of value of territory, domestic accountability and mobilization, and existence of other disputed issues. The cases also reflect different geographic regions of the world, levels of power, economic development, geographic size (ranging from 12 square miles to 130,000 square miles), and types of government. One of the disputes (Lebanon v. Israel) includes a nonstate actor in order to investigate whether the theories apply similarly to nonstate actors engaging in interstate territorial dispute strategies. The variation in the cases also provides a case between two pro-Western states (Morocco v. Spain) and another between communist states (China v. Soviet Union/Russia), cases where leaders are fully authoritarian and others are fully democratic, and states that are great powers and minor players in the international community. Apart from the Sino-Soviet/Russian dispute, the other territorial disputes are lesser known but just as conflictual and important for scholars and policy makers to understand.

The Four Cases

The Senkaku/Diaoyu Islands case, which represents disputed islands and territorial waters, was chosen out of the twenty-nine ongoing island disputes because China and Japan have deep bilateral relations despite their territorial dispute. This factor makes it likely that there would be a number of other disputed issues present to test whether China attempted any issue linkage and coercive diplomacy or attempted settlements. In terms of domestic vulnerability, though there have been infrequent shifts of top leaders in China, there is evidence of the leadership's varied sense of vulnerability from both the military and elite in particular. Chinese territorial nationalism and mobilization is a commonly used tactic in some Chinese territorial disputes. The islands also have varied levels of value for China as the challenger. Besides Taiwan, the Sino-Japanese relationship is arguably the most important issue for Chinese foreign policy.

There are a number of reasons why the endurance of the Sino-Japanese dispute is problematic. From a security standpoint, any dispute that provides China with an opportunity to threaten force against Japan militarily is not good for the stability of the region. Though the apparent intention of the Chinese is not to actually use armed force to take the islands, there is no guarantee that future clashes with Japan will not spiral, inadvertently leading to armed conflict between China and Japan, which would draw the US into the conflict due to its alliance commitments to Japan. Economically, trade and financial relations have been strained in past years due to the dispute. Even with a recent natural gas agreement, it is likely there will continue to be accusations of breaching sovereignty rights, which could negatively affect trade relations.

Of the 21 enduring border disputes, I focus on the Shebaa Farms case for several reasons. First, this case is different than the others in that it includes the actions of a nonstate actor, Hezbollah, acting partly on behalf of the Lebanese government but also for its own objectives. These objectives play a major role in militarized threats against Israel, with the direct approval of the Lebanese government. Studying this case provides a unique insight into how a nonstate actor can use the same strategies as states and demonstrates the applicability of the theory to both states and nonstate actors in the international system. This situation makes for an interesting first-cut test of whether the theory of territorial disputes as bargaining leverage can apply to nonstate actors claiming territory as well. Second, it is a more recently initiated dispute and one that led to the most recent territorial war, in 2006, and is therefore policy relevant. The Shebaa Farms border dispute not only played a role in sparking the 2006 Lebanon War between Hezbollah and Israel, but the disputed land also is located directly along the borders of Lebanon, Israel, and Syria and is considered by Israel as part of the Golan Heights. The existence of this dispute has allowed Hezbollah to continue to justify militant actions in the south of Lebanon, which puts northern Israel at risk. The dispute also allows Hezbollah and Syria to work together to use Shebaa Farms as bargaining leverage for the more important Golan Heights dispute between Syria and Israel and provides further justification for Iranian influence on the regional disputes through the Shi'a group Hezbollah. The dispute is also tied directly to the Israeli-Palestinian conflict since Hezbollah has linked Shebaa Farms to Israeli treatment of Palestinians. Though the Shebaa Farms territory itself is minor, the consequences of the dispute are significant.

This case is also a least likely case and makes it difficult to falsify the null hypothesis since Lebanon (and obviously Hezbollah) and Israel do not have diplomatic relations and therefore have very few other disputed issues that could be linked to the territorial dispute. This case also provides a good test for the domestic accountability and mobilization argument since there is strong public opinion against Israel within Lebanon and among Hezbollah supporters. This suggests that leaders would have to carefully consider any settlement attempts due to potential domestic audience costs. In terms of value, this dispute is interesting because prior to 2000, few Lebanese were aware of Shebaa Farms, but after the Israeli withdrawal from the border region, this dispute immediately became embedded with nationalist value.

The Spanish enclaves of Ceuta/Sebta and Melilla/Melilia in North Africa represent a dispute over inhabited tracts of territory, of which there are 21 enduring disputes. I chose this dispute specifically because it had less extreme values for the explanatory variables. In all the other disputes, there were extreme values for the variables, providing for easier support for or failure of the theories tested. By analyzing a dispute in which the values were more moderate, I was able to test the theory more rigorously. Likewise, the enclaves hold some nationalist value for Moroccans, but not as much compared to the Western Sahara. In terms of domestic vulnerability, though Morocco has had only three kings from 1956 to 2008, several prime ministers have served in office, and other factors such as domestic unrest can indicate domestic vulnerability that could influence dispute strategies toward Spain. There is also evidence of high and low levels of support for the Moroccan government and interelite divisions within Morocco, which is expected to have some influence on dispute strategies.

The enclaves dispute is situated at the Strait of Gibraltar, the access point to the Mediterranean Sea and the "bridge" from Africa to Europe. In the last decade, the dispute has involved an armed conflict in 2002 that required American mediation between Spain and Morocco and, more recently, crises resulting from mass numbers of sub-Saharan African migrants attempting to cross from Morocco into the enclaves to gain European residency. Because of Spain's membership in the EU, this immigration crisis affects not only Spain but also all other EU member states, who by law cannot extradite the migrants to their home countries. Therefore the disputed enclaves act as the doorstep for Europe's African immigration problem. Perhaps the most significant security issue is the fact that the enclaves—Melilla, in particular—are known for Islamic extremism and key locations for jihadist recruitment in Spain. In August 2006, two men in Melilla were arrested on suspicion of carrying out the 2003 Casablanca bombings, and the following month, eleven Islamic extremists were arrested in Ceuta for having links with al-Qaida.

The last case, the territorial dispute between China and the Soviet Union/ Russia, which is now resolved, had significant variation regarding other disputed issues at different time periods. Examining a negative case, a territorial dispute that has been settled, allows for a more rigorous test of the theory and acts as a "hard" case. Unlike the Senkaku/Diaoyu Islands dispute with Japan, in this dispute the territory held significant strategic value for China, which likely affected China's dispute strategies. On the other hand, this dispute is similar to the Senkaku/Diaoyu Islands case in that Chinese decision makers could have been vulnerable to Chinese public opinion regarding the Soviet/Russian border and disputed territory, making this a good test for the domestic accountability theory.[2] Most importantly, China and the Soviet Union/Russia went through periods of close friendship and hostile adversarial relations during the time period studied, providing strong variation for other disputed issues.

In 1969, China and the Soviet Union came close to full-scale war after major armed clashes occurred along their disputed border. For several decades, this dispute not only provided China with an ability to link the border and territorial dispute with other disputed issues as bargaining leverage, but the dispute symbolized the severe tensions between the two major communist powers during the Cold War, which allowed for US détente with China in the 1970s. In 2008, these two major powers settled their longstanding territorial dispute after several decades of hostility and unwillingness to resolve the dispute. The resolution of this territorial dispute has removed a significant barrier in Sino-Russian relations.

Each of these disputes has the potential to be explained by any of the theories, but it appears that the theory of territorial disputes as bargaining leverage can better explain why settlement attempts are less likely and, therefore, why some territorial disputes are enduring, while others are resolved. All of these disputes are located in key strategic and economic areas of the world, making them very policy relevant. The Senkaku/Diaoyu Islands dispute exists between two of the world's major powers and the dominant powers in East Asia, who have a longstanding record of animosity and distrust. The Lebanese-Israeli border dispute not only partly sparked the 2006 Lebanon War between Hezbollah and Israel but also has major ramifications for the greater Arab-Israeli conflict, involving not only Lebanon but also Golan Heights, hotly disputed between Israel and Syria, and the Palestinian-Israeli peace process. The use of the North African enclaves acting as a bridge from Africa to Europe for illegal immigrants into the EU has created major problems for the EU and more specifically for Spain. The Sino-Soviet/Russian dispute involved the only conventional armed conflict that has occurred between two states with nuclear weapons. Until this dispute was resolved, the territorial issue played a major role in tensions between these two major powers, and as a result, it played a key role in US attempts to balance the Soviet Union during the Cold War.

Variables

Though the dependent and independent variables are not always clearly defined in qualitative studies, it is critical to clearly specify how these variables are measured, just as with a quantitative study (George and Bennett 2005). In this study, the primary dependent variable is a peaceful settlement attempt made by the challenger state in any given month measured by an offer of or agreement to a territorial concession. I examine the challenger state rather than the target state because this is the standard used in the literature on territorial disputes, and also because it is the challenger state that is making the territorial claim in an attempt to overturn the status quo. Though the target state could in theory use a territorial dispute as bargaining leverage, challenger states are more likely to do so since they presented the claim, and target states by default would prefer not to deal with the claim or dispute and not change the status quo. There are cases where both states in a dyad make competing territorial claims (directed dyad), where neither state clearly controls the territory. However, in all four cases studied in this book, the challenger state is clearly the challenger with a territorial claim and the target state maintains territorial control as the status quo.

An attempt at peaceful settlement is considered to be when a state engages in negotiations, nonbinding third-party assistance, arbitration, or submission of the dispute to an international court *and* when it makes an offer of or agrees to a territorial concession. The attempt is only counted if it is specifically about the resolution of the territorial dispute, not just a ceasefire or other related issues, meaning that sovereignty and territorial concessions are the focus on the attempted settlement. Some settlement attempts are not intended to settle the dispute, such as procedural or functional negotiations. For example, several negotiations between Argentina and the UK regarding the Falkland/Malvinas Islands dispute have dealt with hydrocarbon exploitation, joint exercises of troops in sea rescue operations in the South Atlantic, and shared attempts to halt poaching by Asian fishing vessels without licenses, among other issues. Yet since 1982, no actual territorial negotiations have occurred between Argentina and the UK. Negotiations between Guatemala and Belize about border security and illegal drug smuggling constitute another example of negotiations not involving settlement attempts. These types of negotiations are procedural, functional, or concerned with issues related to, but not directly addressing, the disputed territory and are not considered substantive attempts at settlement.

To truly understand why some territorial disputes can endure and others do not, it is important to include only settlement attempts that explicitly attempt to resolve territorial disputes. Therefore, to capture the idea that a challenger state is actually attempting to resolve the dispute and not just talking to its adversary, discussion of a territorial concession must be part of the settlement attempt. Without discussion of a territorial concession, the challenger does not necessarily intend to resolve the territorial dispute. Because there is no way to know whether a challenger state that calls for negotiations or engages in border talks is truly willing to consider resolution of the dispute, I do not count such events as attempted settlement if they do not include the offer of a territorial concession.

Peaceful settlement attempts always involve discussions of sovereignty, dropping a territorial claim, or some offer of a territorial concession, such as willingness to accept territorial division. Territorial concessions are usually in the form of territorial exchange, abandonment of a claim, or some other arrangement in which one or both states agree that the formerly disputed territory is no longer disputed. Territorial exchanges most often involve a division of the disputed territory (Kacowicz 1994), but they can also be in the form of the challenger state dropping its claim completely, or the target state turning over all or part of its disputed territory to the challenger. Concessions can be minor or major, but both are considered to be actual attempts to settle a territorial dispute since it is expected that states will attempt to get their adversary to first offer concessions (Huth and Allee 2002), or if they offer concessions, they will start with one that is least costly. To maintain consistency in the literature on territorial disputes, I use a similar measure as Huth and Allee (2002) for territorial concessions. If no concessions are offered, this represents "a very firm and unyielding bargaining position in which state leaders refuse to make any changes in policy," while limited concessions involve a small part of territory, and a major concession involves "many if not all of the territorial demands by the other party" (Huth and Allee 2002, 49). The only difference is that I do not count a settlement attempt through the offer of a concession if it is a nonterritorial concession.

Though settlement strategies are the main dependent variable, I also examine causes of diplomatic or militarized threats or limited uses of force as well because such events play a significant role in the causal mechanism outlined in the theory of territorial disputes as bargaining leverage. Therefore, secondary dependent variables include diplomatic and militarized threats and limited uses of force pursued by the challenger state. Though important to study in general, war and other high-intensity levels of armed conflict are excluded as dependent variables because the focus of this book is the endurance of territorial disputes, an understudied pattern compared to the high level of focus on war and high-intensity armed conflict in so many other excellent studies on territorial disputes. Rather, I examine dispute strategies involving diplomatic threats or militarized threats and limited uses of force because they are expected to be a significant reason why some territorial disputes are enduring and others are not.

In order for the challenger state to achieve bargaining leverage through issue linkage, decision makers must engage in some type of coercive diplomacy or compellence to persuade the target state to shift its position on another disputed issue. Diplomatic or militarized threats or limited uses of force act as a form of coercive diplomacy. Diplomatic threats include threats to withdraw from negotiations, cancellation of negotiations, passage of a law or hostile restatement of territorial claim, or threats that would indirectly inflict costs for the target state, such as allowing the transfer of migrants or refusing to defend a shared border against smuggling. Militarized threats or limited uses of force include any show of potential force such as mobilization of troops, movement of troops near the disputed territory, war games or maneuvers related to the territorial dispute, deployment of ships to disputed waters, or missile launches across disputed waters, using Gochman and Maoz's (1984) definition. Though many studies do not examine diplomatic threats as extensively as militarized threats and uses of force, diplomatic threats play an important role in causing significant bilateral tensions between adversaries and are often the precursor of militarized threats.

The independent variables examined in this book include value of territory and domestic accountability and mobilization of leaders, of which precise measurements were described in chapter 2, and the existence of other disputed issues between adversaries, of which measurement was explained in detail in chapter 3. To understand the strategic behavior of each of the challenger states studied in their respective contexts and to provide information for the independent variables, I read approximately 4,500 news stories from newspapers, radio, television, and Internet sources from the United States (*Newsweek, New York Times*), the UK (British Broadcasting Corporation [BBC] News, *Financial Times, Guardian, Times*), Germany (Deutsche Presse-Agentur), France (Agence France Presse, Radio France Internationale), China (*People's Daily,* Xinhua News Agency, China Central Television), Russia (Russian Information Agency (ITAR/TASS), Lebanon (*Daily Star,* Radio Lebanon, al-Manar Television), Morocco (Maghreb Arab Presse, RTM TV Rabat), Spain (*El Pais, La Razon*), Japan (*Daily Yomiuri,* Kyodo News Service), and other international news agencies.

CHARACTERISTICS OF SETTLED TERRITORIAL DISPUTES

Since 1953, ninety-seven territorial disputes have been resolved and officially settled involving ninety-nine sovereign states. In terms of the type of disputed territory, 24 percent of resolved disputes were over uninhabited islands, 38 percent were over disputed borders, and the remaining 38 percent were about inhabited tracts of territory. An initial observation is that the type of disputed territory does not necessarily matter, particularly whether the territory is inhabited. States will work to resolve territorial disputes regardless of the type of territory. The average duration of these disputes was 32 years, with the longest lasting 176 years and the shortest less than a year. Of the ninety-seven settled disputes, seventy-three were enduring territorial disputes, which by definition lasted 10 years or more. With the large majority of disputes lasting so long, this suggests that not only are territorial disputes difficult to resolve in general, but there are reasons for such endurance.[3]

Geographically, now settled territorial disputes have occurred in every region of the world, with the Middle East having experienced the highest amount of resolved disputes, at 28 percent of the total, followed closely by Africa with 24 percent. Eighteen percent of the resolved disputes were in Asia, 15 percent were in Latin America, 14 percent in Europe, and just one dispute in North America (us-Mexico border). When comparing the number of territorial disputes that are resolved and unresolved, the Middle East and Africa both have a much higher proportion of resolved disputes (four times more for the Middle East and two and a half times more for Africa). The settlement of disputes in Africa is likely to be directly related to the fact that African states have mostly pursued a territorial norm of respecting boundaries laid out by colonial powers, as set out in the 1963 charter agreement and 1964 resolution of the African Union (au), formerly the Organization of African Unity (oau). This norm has been strongly respected, discouraging most African states from pursuing boundary disputes. Nevertheless, a number of African states have been involved in territorial disputes, some resolved through the icj or other means, and others still enduring.

Despite the fact that they are resolved today, these disputes involved a significant amount of armed conflict and wars while they were ongoing. Nine disputes escalated to war, including the 1967 Six-Day War and 1973 Yom Kippur War, fought between Israel and Jordan over their reciprocal territorial claims to Jerusalem and the West Bank, and between Israel and Egypt over the Sinai Peninsula and Gaza Strip, the Football War between Honduras and El Salvador in 1969, the 1978–79 Uganda-Tanzania War, the war between North and South Vietnam, the Vietnam-Cambodia war of the 1980s, the Iran-Iraq War of the 1980s over the border surrounding the Shatt al-Arab Waterway, and the 1991 Gulf War over Iraq's invasion of Kuwait.[4] Armed conflict short of war was even more prevalent in these disputes, with 39 percent experiencing at least one MID short of war.

Most of these settled disputes were resolved through peaceful settlement attempts, but a portion of them were resolved through force, the target ceding territory to the challenger, or the challenger dropping its territorial claim against the target, all listed in table 1. Five of these disputes were resolved through the use of force. In four cases, the challenger state used force to take control of the disputed territory, and the target state accepted the change in status quo: Thailand's takeover of a part of the border with Cambodia, surrounding the Preah Vihear Temple, in 1962 (recently disputed again), Israel's acquisition of Palestinian territories occupied by Jordan until 1967, India's acquisition of the island of Goa from Portugal in 1974, and North Vietnam's reunification with South Vietnam in 1975. In one dispute, Iraq's claim to Kuwait in 1990, coalition forces militarily defeated Iraq on behalf of Kuwait, forcing withdrawal and an end to the claim in 1991.

An additional six disputes were resolved due to the target state willingly and peacefully giving up sovereign rights to the territory, leading to peaceful territorial exchanges, also listed in table 1. Of these disputes, four resulted in bilateral treaties, while the remaining two involved no actual treaty, only an announcement of withdrawal from the territory. In four of the six disputes, the US agreed to withdraw sovereign rights from territory in Nicaragua (Corn Islands), Colombia (Quita Sueno, Roncador, and Serrana), Honduras (Swan Islands), and Panama (Panama Canal), all of which involved bilateral treaties. The other two resolutions of this type involved Spain's decision to withdraw sovereign rights to the Western Sahara in 1975, in effect allowing Morocco to take the territory without any complaint, and France's transfer of sovereignty of several French enclaves to India in 1954. Another ten disputes, listed in table 1, ended because the challenger state dropped its territorial claim against the target state through unilateral pronouncements without any negotiations or other resolution method. These former disputes include Ghana's announcement in 1966 that it would no

Table 1. Territorial disputes settled without resolution methods, 1953–2008

DISPUTED TERRITORY	CHALLENGER–TARGET	YEAR INITIATED	YEAR SETTLED
Use of Force			
Preah Vihear	Thailand-Cambodia/France	1949	1962
Parts of Palestine	Israel-Jordan	1949	1967
Goa, Samao, Diu	India-Portugal	1962	1974
South Vietnam	North Vietnam–South Vietnam	1954	1975
Kuwait	Iraq-Kuwait	1990	1991
Target Ceded Territory to Challenger			
Pondicherry and other enclaves	India-France	1919	1954
Corn Islands	Nicaragua-us	1965	1970
Quita Sueno, Roncador, Serrana	Colombia-us	1890	1972
Swan Islands	Honduras-us	1921	1972
Western Sahara	Morocco-Spain	1956	1975
Canal Zone	Panama-us	1923	1977
Challenger Dropped Territorial Claim			
Border with Guinea	Liberia-France	1958	1958
Border with Ivory Coast	Liberia-France	1960	1960
Sanwi District	Ghana-Ivory Coast	1959	1966
Western Sahara	Mauritania-Spain	1960	1975
Djibouti	Somalia-France	1960	1977
Kagera Salient	Uganda-Tanzania	1974	1979
Part of Kenya	Somalia-Kenya	1960	1981
Border	Malawi-Zambia	1981	1986
Part of Orange Free State, Natal	Lesotho-South Africa	1966	1994
Tromelin Island	Seychelles-France	1976	1997

longer seek the Sanwi District of Ivory Coast and Uganda's official renounce-
ment in 1979 of its claim to the Kagera Salient section of Tanzania. All of these
disputes were in Africa; therefore, it is likely that the norm embedded in the oau
after the end of colonialism to accept borders as they are influenced leaders to
drop claims accordingly.

The remaining seventy-six disputes were resolved through peaceful resolution methods—bilateral negotiations, mediation, arbitration, or adjudication, as listed in table 2. Of these resolved disputes, 62 percent were resolved
through bilateral negotiations in which territorial concessions were exchanged.[5]
Third-party methods including mediation, arbitration, and adjudication have
also been used, but less frequently. Since 1953, mediators have assisted in seven
dispute settlements, an additional seven disputes have been decided by an

Table 2.   Territorial disputes settled through peaceful resolution methods, 1953–2008

DISPUTED TERRITORY	CHALLENGER–TARGET	YEAR INITIATED	YEAR SETTLED
Bilateral Negotiations			
Saar Region	West Germany-France	1955	1956
Caspian Sea islands	USSR-Iran	1922	1957
Islands	Saudi Arabia–UK	1949	1958
Sahara region	Tunisia-Algeria	1959	1959
Border	Netherlands–West Germany	1955	1960
Border	China-Burma	1949	1960
Border	China-Nepal	1949	1961
Border	China-Mongolia	1949	1962
Border	Mexico-US	1895	1963
Eastern Hodh	Mali-Mauritania	1960	1963
Wakhan Salient	China-Afghanistan	1949	1963
Border	China-Pakistan	1949	1963
Lete Island	Benin-Niger	1960	1965
Border	Saudi Arabia–Jordan	1946	1965
Farsi/al-Arabiya Islands	Iran–Saudi Arabia	1949	1968
Rann of Kutch	Pakistan-India	1947	1968
Gadaduma Wells	Ethiopia-Kenya	1945	1970
Western Sahara	Morocco-Mauritania	1957	1970
Bahrain	Iran-UK	1927	1970
Parts of Poland	West Germany–Poland	1955	1970
Northern Epirus	Greece-Albania	1945	1971
East Germany	West Germany–East Germany	1955	1972
Border	Ethiopia-Sudan	1945	1972
Border	Morocco-Algeria	1956	1972
Rio de la Plata border	Argentina-Uruguay	1916	1973
Parts of Sudentenland	West Germany–Czechoslovakia	1955	1973
Buraimi Oasis, Sila, border	Saudi Arabia–UAE	1934	1974
Trieste	Yugoslavia-Italy	1945	1975
Border	Saudi Arabia–Iraq	1922	1981
Border/islands	Vietnam-Cambodia	1954	1985
Buraimi Oasis	Oman–Saudi Arabia	1934	1990
Shatt al-Arab border	Iraq-Iran	1979	1990
Border	Argentina-Chile	1875	1991
South Yemen	North Yemen–South Yemen	1970	1991
Border	Oman-Yemen	1981	1992
Buraimi Oasis	Oman-UAE	1971	1993
Walvis Bay/Penguin Islands	Namibia–South Africa	1990	1994
Border	China-Kazakhstan	1992	1994
Border	Czech-Slovakia	1993	1995
Border	China-Kyrgyzstan	1992	1996
Snake Island	Romania-Ukraine	1995	1997
Kaputa District	Zaire-Zambia	1980	1998

Table 2. (*continued*)

DISPUTED TERRITORY	CHALLENGER–TARGET	YEAR INITIATED	YEAR SETTLED
Bilateral Negotiations			
Border	Estonia-Russia	1992	1999
Border	Togo-Ghana	1960	1999
Islands, border	Saudi Arabia–UK/Kuwait	1922	2000
Border	Saudi Arabia–UK/Yemen	1935	2000
Glorioso Island	Seychelles-France	1976	2001
Border, river islands	China-Russia	1960	2008
Nonbinding Third-Party Mediation			
Kuwait	Iraq-UK	1961	1963
West Berlin	East Germany–West Germany	1948	1971
Shatt al-Arab Waterway	Iraq-Iran	1920	1975
Sinai Peninsula	Egypt-Israel	1967	1979
Beagle Channel Islands	Argentina-Chile	1875	1984
Jerusalem and West Bank	Jordan-Israel	1950	1994
N. Ireland	Ireland-UK	1922	1998
Binding Third-Party Arbitration			
Border	Argentina-Chile	1875	1966
Rann of Kutch	Pakistan-India	1947	1968
Beagle Channel Islands	Argentina-Chile	1875	1977
Border	Egypt-Israel	1982	1988
Border	Argentina-Chile	1875	1995
Border	Ecuador-Peru	1822	1998
Hanish Islands	Eritrea-Yemen	1995	1998
Binding Third-Party Adjudication (ICJ)			
Minquiers/Ecrehos Islands	France-UK	1886	1953
Border enclaves	Netherlands-Belgium	1922	1959
Border	Nicaragua-Honduras	1906	1960
Preah Vihear Temple	Cambodia-Thailand	1954	1962
Beli River Border	Mali–Burkina Faso	1960	1986
Border	El Salvador–Honduras	1899	1992
Azou Strip	Libya-Chad	1973	1994
Chobe River Islands	Botswana-Namibia	1992	1999
Hawar Islands	Qatar-Bahrain	1937	2001
Bekassi Peninsula	Cameroon-Nigeria	1981	2002
Pulau Litigan/Sipadan	Indonesia-Malaysia	1980	2002
Niger River islands	Benin-Niger	1960	2005
Gulf of Fonseca Islands	Honduras–El Salvador	1880	2006
Islands	Nicaragua-Colombia	1969	2007
Pedra Branca Island	Malaysia-Singapore	1980	2008

arbitrator, and the ICJ has successfully adjudicated decisions in fifteen territorial disputes. These settled disputes include borders, uninhabited islands, and inhabited tracts of territory, large and small, suggesting that peaceful settlement is possible with all types of disputed territory. The settled disputes are also in every region of the world, indicating that the geographical region of the world does not necessarily influence the likelihood of settlement.

Of all the territorial disputes settled since 1953, 64 percent have involved division of territory, while the remaining 36 percent involved the challenger or target receiving all of the disputed territory. Division of the territory indicates that both sides gained from settlement, allowing the opportunity of joint economic development of resources, if any exist. Of the successfully divided territories, 70 percent involved fairly equal division of the territory between the challenger and target, resulting in the exchange of relatively equal territorial concessions. In the remaining cases of divided territories, either the target was able to maintain sovereignty over the majority of territory, or the challenger was able to acquire the majority of the disputed territory. In these cases, the state that received the smaller portion of the territory often received nonterritorial concessions in exchange for accepting the smaller portion of territory. Such concessions used in settlement agreements include China's cession of territory to Pakistan in which the reciprocal concession was alliance with Pakistan against India, and Spain's cession of an island to Morocco in exchange for Spanish fishing and other economic rights in the territorial waters surrounding the island. All of the disputes in which territory was divided involved some type of peaceful dispute resolution method.

CHARACTERISTICS OF ENDURING TERRITORIAL DISPUTES

There are currently seventy-one territorial disputes that are unresolved today, involving seventy-nine states, listed in table 3.[6] This means that 41 percent of the world's states are involved in territorial disputes with other states, potentially provoking bilateral, regional, and international tensions. For a territorial dispute to be ongoing, one of two conditions occur: either the states involved have not made any attempt to settle the dispute or settlement attempts have failed. If there is no attempt to settle the dispute, decision makers are effectively choosing to continue their claim for the disputed territory. States have made no resolution attempts in 21 percent of the territorial disputes ongoing today, meaning

Table 3.   Enduring territorial disputes

DISPUTED TERRITORY	CHALLENGER–TARGET	YEAR CLAIM INITIATED
Uninhabited Islands		
Machias Seal Island	US-Canada	1832
Navassa Island	Haiti-US	1857
Bajo Nuevo and Serranilla	US-Colombia	1869
Isla Brasilera	Uruguay-Brazil	1882
Conejo Island	El Salvador–Honduras	1884
Paracel Islands	Taiwan-China	1946
Los Monjes Islands	Colombia-Venezuela	1951
Takeshima Islands	South Korea–Japan	1951
Paracel Islands	Vietnam-China	1954
Spratly Islands	China-Vietnam	1954
Tiran and Sanafir Islands	Saudi Arabia–Egypt	1954
Spratly Islands	Taiwan-China	1956
Spratly Islands	Philippines-China	1956
Isla Suarez/Ilha de Guajara-Mirim	Brazil-Bolivia	1958
Bajo Nuevo and Serranilla	Nicaragua-Colombia	1969
Senkaku Islands	Taiwan-Japan	1969
Abu Musa Islands	Iran-UAE	1971
Corsico Bay Islands	Equitorial Guinea–Gabon	1972
Senkaku Islands	China-Japan	1972
Hans Island	Canada-Denmark	1973
Bassas da India/Europa	Madagascar-France	1973
Spratly Islands	Vietnam-Philippines	1973
Spratly Islands	Malaysia-China	1979
Spratly Islands	Malaysia-Philippines	1979
Unarang Rock	Indonesia-Malaysia	1980
Sapodilla Cays	Honduras-Belize	1981
Matthew & Hunter Islands	Vanuatu-France	1982
Pulau Batek/Fatu	Indonesia–Timor Leste	2002
Border Disputes		
Andean Southern Ice Field	Chile-Argentina	1903
Border	Afghanistan-Pakistan	1947
Border	India-Nepal	1947
Border	China-Vietnam	1954
Wadi Halfa/Hala'ib	Egypt-Sudan	1958
Border/Aksai Chin	India-China	1962
Border with French Guiana	Suriname-France	1975
Border	Suriname-Guyana	1975
Border	China-Bhutan	1975
Border/2 villages	Benin–Burkina Faso	1980
Border/Ban Rom Klao	Thailand-Laos	1984
Border	Georgia-Azerbaijan	1991
Border	Tajikistan-Kyrgyzstan	1992

Table 3. *(continued)*

DISPUTED TERRITORY	CHALLENGER–TARGET	YEAR CLAIM INITIATED
Border Disputes		
Border	Kyrgyzstan-Uzbekistan	1992
Border	Croatia-Slovenia	1993
Drina River Border	Bosnia-Serbia	1995
Border towns	Serbia-Croatia	1991
Border	Eritrea-Ethiopia	1998
Border	Croatia-Bosnia	1999
Shebaa Farms	Lebanon-Israel	2000
Preah Vihear Temple	Thailand-Cambodia	2008
Inhabited Tracts of Territory		
Falkland Islands	Argentina-UK	1833
Belize	Guatemala-UK/Belize	1839
Atacama Corridor	Bolivia-Chile	1884
Kashmir and Jammu	Pakistan-India	1947
S. Korea	N. Korea–South Korea	1948
Taiwan	China-Taiwan	1949
Kurile Islands	Japan-Russia	1951
Ceuta & Melilla	Morocco-Spain	1956
Guantanamo Bay	Cuba-US	1960
Turkish Cyprus	Cyprus-Turkey	1960
Oromo/Ogaden	Somalia-Ethiopia	1960
Sabah	Philippines-Malaysia	1962
2/3 Guyana	Venezuela-Guyana	1962
Gibraltar	Spain-UK	1963
Golan Heights	Syria-Israel	1967
KwaZulu-Natal	Swaziland–South Africa	1968
Enclaves	Bangladesh-India	1971
Mayotte Island	Comoros-France	1975
Tromelin Island	Mauritius-France	1976
Diego Garcia	Mauritius-UK	1980
Kosovo	Serbia-Kosovo	2008

that states involved in 79 percent of the disputes have attempted some form of peaceful resolution method and have thus far failed to resolve the dispute.

The average duration of ongoing territorial disputes is fifty-three years. An overwhelming 96 percent of these disputes are enduring, meaning they have lasted ten or more years. The oldest territorial disputes are between the US and Canada (Machias Seal Island) starting in 1832, and Argentina and the UK (Falkland/Malvinas Islands), beginning in 1833. The three ongoing disputes that are not considered enduring because they have lasted less than ten years are the disagreement between Timor-Leste and Indonesia over their border delimitation, which began in 2002, the dispute over the border surrounding the temple at Preah Vihear, reinitiated by Thailand against Cambodia in 2008, and Serbia's claim for Kosovo since its independence in 2008.

When no settlement attempt occurs, states instead maintain their claims or defense of sovereignty, taking no steps to meet in negotiations, offer concessions, or initiate third-party involvement to resolve the dispute. To maintain territorial claims, states generally issue diplomatic threats about the territory as restatement of the claims. Restatement of the claim or defense of the sovereignty of the disputed territory occurs when a decision maker officially restates the government's position on the disputed territory and usually indicates its resolve to acquire or defend the territory. These statements can serve as reminders of the government's position to the opposing state or as reminders to the people that the government is still interested in the disputed territory. In addition to the seventy-one active territorial disputes, there are also a small number of dormant territorial claims, but these are not actively pursued and are considered "settled" due to the acceptance of the status quo.[7]

In terms of the other dispute strategy available to challenger states, 16 percent of ongoing disputes have escalated to full-scale war, involving three wars between Pakistan and India, the Korean War from 1950 to 1953, the Sino-Indian War of 1962, the 1977 Ogaden War between Somalia and Ethiopia, the 1982 Falklands War, the 1967 Six-Day War, in which Syria lost the Golan Heights to Israel, the Sino-Vietnamese War in 1979, and the wars in former Yugoslavia in the 1990s. More recent are the wars in the Balkans in the 1990s, the war between Eritrea and Ethiopia from 1998 to 2002, and the Lebanese-Israeli border war in the summer of 2006. In addition to these wars, a much larger portion, 46 percent of these disputes, have involved some degree of militarized force short of war.

Of the current territorial disputes, 40 percent are disputes over uninhabited islands, 30 percent are border disputes, and another 30 percent are disputes over inhabited tracts of territory. Like those that have been settled, these numbers suggest that it is not necessarily the fact that the disputed territories are inhabited that makes them difficult to resolve since the majority are actually uninhabited islands. Well-known disputes over uninhabited islands include the Spratly Islands dispute involving China, Vietnam, Malaysia, Taiwan, and the Philippines; the Senkaku/Diaoyu Islands involving China and Japan; and Abu Musa Islands involving Iran and the UAE. Other lesser-known island disputes include Hans Island, a tiny, barren island in the Kennedy Channel between Canada's Ellesmere Island and Greenland, and Conejo Island, disputed between El Salvador and Honduras. Of the twenty-nine enduring territorial disputes over uninhabited islands, none are in Europe, two are in the Middle East, two are in Africa, three are in North America, eight are in Latin America, and the remaining fourteen are in Asia, several of which are the same territories disputed by multiple dyads.

Some of the better-known border disputes include the border between India and China, Shebaa Farms between Lebanon and Israel, and the border between Eritrea and Ethiopia. Of the twenty-one current border disputes, there are five in Europe, two in the Americas, two in the Middle East and North Africa, two in Africa, and ten in Asia. The twenty-one disputes over inhabited territory, which tend to be more salient due to the presence of residents and the effect of a dispute on their lives, include North Korea's claim for South Korea, China's claim for Taiwan, Kashmir and Jammu between Pakistan and India, the Golan Heights between Syria and Israel, and Turkish Cyprus between Turkey and Cyprus. Other disputes over inhabited territory include Gibraltar between Spain and the UK, Guatemala's claim of Belize, the Kurile Islands/Northern Territories between Japan and Russia, and the Falkland/Malvinas Islands between Argentina and the UK. Of the ongoing territorial disputes over inhabited territory, five are in the Americas, three in Europe, five in Africa, two in the Middle East, and six in Asia.

The largest number of ongoing territorial disputes, twenty-nine, occurs in one geographic region of the world, Asia, involving twenty-seven states. Only a handful of Asian states are not involved in territorial disputes: Brunei, Myanmar, Mongolia, Papua New Guinea, Singapore, and Turkmenistan. Of these Asian disputes, a good number involve China. Despite having settled a large number of disputes with neighboring states already, China is still involved in eleven territorial disputes—the highest number of disputes for any state, in five of which it is the challenger. These eleven disputes include Taiwan, the Senkaku/Diaoyu

Islands (Japan), the Spratly Islands (Vietnam, Malaysia, Philippines, Taiwan), the Paracel Islands (Vietnam, Taiwan), Askai Chin region (India), part of the border with Bhutan, and part of the border with Vietnam. Other well-known Asian territorial disputes include North Korea v. South Korea, the Takeshima/ Dokdo Islands (Japan v. South Korea), the Kurile Islands/Northern Territories (Japan v. Russia), Kashmir and Jammu (India v. Pakistan), and the border between Afghanistan and Pakistan. The large number of disputes partly has to do with the fact that there are overlapping claims to several sets of disputed islands by different dyads and a large number of contiguous neighbors.

All of the other geographic regions of the world have much smaller numbers of territorial disputes. Latin America has the next largest number of disputes with fifteen, which include Nicaragua v. Colombia (Bajo Nuevo and Serranilla), Guatemala v. Belize (Belize), Honduras v. Belize (Sapodilla Cays), El Salvador v. Honduras (Conejo Island), Venezuela v. Guyana (two-thirds of Guyana), Suriname v. Guyana (border), Suriname v. French Guiana (border), Jamaica v. Colombia (Bajo Nuevo and Serranilla), us v. Colombia (Bajo Nuevo and Serranilla), Colombia v. Venezuela (Los Monjes Islands), Bolivia v. Chile (Atacama and Antofagasta provinces), Brazil v. Bolivia (Isla Suarez/Ilha de Guajara-Mirim), Chile v. Argentina (Andean Southern Ice Field), Uruguay v. Brazil (Isla Brasilera), and Argentina v. uk (Falkland/Malvinas Islands). Of these disputes, two escalated into full-scale war—the 1982 Falklands/Malvinas War and the 1969 Football War fought between El Salvador and Honduras.

The other territorial disputes in Latin America have spurred a number of clashes, or at least frictions for bilateral relations, between many disputing states. The Latin American disputes are all rooted in disagreements about the status of certain territories after the end of Spanish colonization in the nineteenth century, the end of French and British colonization in the twentieth century, or the validity of certain treaties. For example, Guatemala has maintained its claim that Belize is part of Guatemala based on its conviction that it inherited the territory occupied by Spain upon its independence in 1821 and due to the uk's alleged failure to follow through with an 1859 treaty. Bolivia's claim to a tract of land in Chile that would allow Bolivian access to the sea is based on its claim that the 1884 peace treaty, in which Chile gained a portion of Bolivia's territory, was signed under force and therefore invalid. Bolivia also claims that Chile did not keep up its end of the treaty, also invalidating the treaty, and thus the territorial occupation of the Atacama and Antofagasta provinces, which have been Bolivian.

The nine African territorial disputes today include four disputes against former colonial powers, one against the UK and three against France. These disputes, all of which are island states off the coast of Africa, are Madagascar v. France (Bassas de India and Europa Islands), Mauritius v. France (Tromelin Island), Comoros v. France (Mayotte Island), and Mauritius v. the UK (Diego Garcia). On the continent, the other five disputes include Equatorial Guinea v. Gabon (Corsica Bay Islands), Eritrea v. Ethiopia (border), Somalia v. Ethiopia (Oromo/Ogaden), Benin v. Burkina Faso (border and two villages), and Swaziland v. South Africa (part of KwaZulu-Natal). The almost even split between colonial and homeland disputes suggests that this factor does not make a difference in African territorial disputes.

Though there used to be many more territorial disputes in the Middle East, this number has been reduced due to peaceful settlements or by war. Currently, there are six interstate territorial disputes in this region: Morocco v. Spain (Ceuta/Sebta and Melilla), Sudan v. Egypt (Wadi Halfa/Hala'ib Triangle), Iran v. UAE (Abu Musa, Greater Tunb, and Lesser Tunb Islands), Syria v. Israel (Golan Heights), Lebanon v. Israel (Shebaa Farms), Saudi Arabia v. Egypt (Tiran and Sanifir Islands). The enclaves dispute over Ceuta/Sebta and Melilla/Melilia is based on Morocco's claim to territory in North Africa, surrounded by Morocco, that has belonged to Spain for several centuries. The dispute between Iran and the UAE, initiated in 1971, is not necessarily about the islands themselves, but the legal ownership of waters in the Strait of Hormuz, an area that holds significant geostrategic value due to the fact that currently, 20 percent of the world's oil or 40 percent of all seaborne traded oil passes through the strait from Kuwait, Iraq, Iran, Bahrain, UAE, Saudi Arabia, and Qatar (US Energy Information Administration 2010).

North America has four ongoing territorial disputes, none of which have led to any threats or uses of force. The US is involved in three of these disputes, as the challenger state against Canada (Machias Seal Island), and the other two as a target state challenged by Haiti (Nassava Island) and Cuba (Guantanamo Bay). By far the most famous dispute in North America is about the status of Guantanamo Bay, a territory on the island of Cuba occupied by the US military since a 1903 lease agreement that Cuba's government today claims is void. Due to the ambiguous status of Guantanamo Bay, the US military has used the base as a prisoner camp for the most notorious suspected terrorists and enemy combatants from Iraq and Afghanistan. The other dispute in North America is Canada v. Denmark over Hans Island in the Arctic, a small island roughly equidistant between Canadian territory and Greenland. Though all of the disputes are active, the states involved have not made any active attempts to resolve their differences and end the disputes. Besides the dispute with Cuba, the rest of the states involved in these North American disputes are allies and the disputes are minor, not really affecting bilateral relations.

Despite the relative peace and stability of territorial control through most of Europe in the post–World War II era, a few territorial disputes have arisen due to the breakup of the Soviet Union and Yugoslavia. The eight territorial disputes in Europe today include Spain v. UK (Gibraltar), Cyprus v. Turkey (Northern Cyprus), and Georgia v. Azerbaijan (border), and four that resulted from the Balkan wars of the 1990s: Bosnia v. Serbia (border), Croatia-Slovenia (border), Serbia-Kosovo (Kosovo), and Serbia-Croatia (border). Full-scale armed conflict resulted in three of these disputes: Cyprus (1974), Bosnia (1992–1995), and Kosovo (1998–1999). The dispute over Gibraltar led to significant tensions between Spain and the UK, both members of the EU and NATO, until only a few years ago when restrictions on the border between Spain and Gibraltar were lifted. The island of Cyprus remains divided between Turkish and Greek sections since the war in 1974, requiring a border crossing for residents of both sides and a long-term presence of UN peacekeeping troops in the area.

The seventy-one territorial disputes that exist today are a thorn in the side of some states and a spike in the heart for others. For example, it is extremely unlikely that the US and Canada would ever fight a war or even get involved in some degree of militarized conflict over tiny Machias Seal Island. Yet many other territorial disputes, such as the dispute over Kashmir and Jammu between India and Pakistan, are high stakes and ever threatening for the states involved, the people living in or near the disputed territories, other states in the region, and potentially the world due to their nuclear status. Since territorial disputes are the number one cause of interstate war, it is imperative to understand the factors that make threats or uses of force and settlement strategies more or less likely. The next chapters examine the effectiveness in the theories examined in this book to explain such endurance and potential uses of force.

CHAPTER FIVE

The Senkaku/Diaoyu Islands Dispute

For almost four decades the People's Republic of China (PRC) and the Republic of China (ROC) have disputed Japan's sovereignty over several small rocky islands in the East China Sea, called Senkaku in Japanese and Diaoyu (or Diaoyutai in Taiwan) in Chinese.[1] Since the dispute began, the PRC, hereafter referred to as China, has regularly made diplomatic and militarized threats about the disputed islands. In September 2005, China deployed five naval ships in the vicinity of the disputed waters, including a guided missile destroyer with its guns pointed at a Japanese P3-C surveillance aircraft (Valencia 2005). In the past few years, a number of clashes have occurred between government-backed Chinese activists attempting to land on the islands and the Japanese military, creating political tension for both states. The sinking in June 2008 of a Taiwanese fishing boat involving the Japanese coast guard in the vicinity of the islands led not only to major tensions between Taiwan and Japan, but also to serious concern expressed by China.

More recently, Tokyo issued a white paper about China's "more provocative and overconfident" efforts to secure ownership of the islands based on the sightings in March and April 2010 of sixteen Chinese military vessels, including a destroyer and submarine, passing near Japanese islands (*Economist* 2010). In September 2010, the two states clashed over the Japanese arrest of a Chinese fisherman found in waters near the islands. China's main concern diplomatically was that allowing a Chinese national to be tried in Japan would tacitly signal Chinese acceptance that the disputed islands are, in fact, Japanese (*Pan Orient News* 2010). The diplomatic incident drew the US, as an ally of Japan, into the dispute, with concerns about growing friction with China. The flare-up even led Secretary of State Hillary Clinton to declare that what happens in the East China Sea is in the national interest of the US (McCabe 2010). Regarding the tensions the disputed islands have caused for this dyad, one China-Japan scholar notes, "since the beginning of the 21st century, the political and security environment has changed considerably, which makes a solution of the disputes [in the East China Sea] simultaneously more difficult and more urgent" (Drifte 2008b, 4).

There is no indication that Japan will cede the islands to China by choice, nor is it likely that China will take the islands by force, provoking war against Japan and, therefore, the US, as Japan's ally. Until the islands dispute is peacefully settled, this contentious issue will continue to provide China with opportunities to confront Japan in an antagonistic way with a host of outstanding issues still unresolved—Japan's official position on government visits to the Yasukuni Shrine, textbook portrayals of Japan's occupation of China, Japan's support for Taiwan, and its continued defense agreement with the US, including the contentious missile defense shield. Though tensions have decreased, these other issues and the continued existence of the territorial dispute itself will continue to put pressure on bilateral relations. For example, just a week after a historic joint gas agreement was signed in 2008, China lodged an official protest at the Japanese Embassy in Beijing about an aerial inspection of the disputed islands by several Japanese Diet members (*Straits Times* 2008).

Despite the joint gas development agreement signed in June 2008, China continues to claim sovereignty of the islands. Sovereignty has not been on the table at any negotiations between China and Japan. Since island disputes are relatively cheap for China to maintain (Fravel 2008), there is no rush for China to resolve the dispute, unless conditions change that make it more likely. Up to this point, Chinese-Japanese negotiations and the June 2008 agreement have only focused on joint development of natural gas resources in waters stretching across what Japan claims as the median line and have not included any development of oil or gas resources in the disputed zone.[2] After the June 2008 agreement, both states immediately assured their peoples that neither had abandoned their territorial positions and claims on the Senkaku/Diaoyu Islands.

There are a number of reasons why the endurance of this dispute is problematic and worthy of study. First, though the dispute has not escalated to war, there is no guarantee that future clashes will not spiral, inadvertently leading to armed conflict between China and Japan. As Suganuma (2000, 151) noted, "If there is a flash point to ignite a third Sino-Japanese War, it will be the ownership of the Diaoyu Islands in the East China Sea." Just five years ago Japan prepared detailed military plans for a potential Chinese attack on the islands, and

the US has offered military support to help Japan defend the islands if necessary. In December 2010, the US and Japan engaged in a naval exercise in the East
China Sea, partly as a signal to China of their resolve regarding potential future
threats from China. China's substantial expansion of its military, though primarily aimed at Taiwan, is also in response to the US-Japanese missile defense
shield and increasing assertiveness of the Japanese military. Japan's heightened
sense of security has only provoked China into expanding its own militarization as a demonstration of a security dilemma. Although bilateral relations
are officially friendlier since the May 2008 friendship agreement (the fourth
of its kind since 1972) and June 2008 gas agreement, the reality is that the dispute could turn for the worse with the dire competition and dependence for
energy resources in the region, therefore affecting economic, political, and security dominance in Asia. A number of scholars (Blanchard 2000; Chiu 1996/
97; Nathan and Ross 1997; Valencia 2000) have referred to the islands dispute
as "one of the most burning matters in Sino-Japanese relations and even in East
Asian politics at large" (Hagstrom 2005, 160). Studying China's strategy in this
dispute can also provide insight into China's strategy in the South China Sea
disputes (Spratly Islands and Paracel Islands) as well. Therefore, the international community should continue to keep an eye on this seemingly minor territorial dispute, which could, in fact, turn into a time bomb.

Second, economic relations have been strained in past years due to the dispute, and even with the natural gas agreement, it is likely there will continue
to be accusations of breaching sovereignty rights, which could negatively affect
trade relations. With Japan as China's largest trading partner and China as Japan's second largest trading partner, both states are exceedingly interdependent
on each other economically. In 2007, total trade between China and Japan was
$236 billion (Miks 2008). China has relied on more than $30 billion in official
development assistance from Japan in the past few decades as well. Japanese
investment in China is in the hundreds of billions, and Chinese investment in
Japanese equity funds is in the tens of billions.

With such economic interdependence and the potential for negative consequences affecting their economic relationship, China and Japan cannot afford
to allow a militarized territorial dispute to interfere. However, until the dispute
is settled, it continues to influence all bilateral relations. In 2005, oil drilling
close to each state's exclusive economic zones (EEZs) led to official protests, resulting in the boycott of Japanese goods in China and the cancellation of Japanese contracts. Even with the natural gas deal, the likelihood of future disagree-

ments is high when it comes to who gets how much and where drilling should occur. The two states have yet to mutually agree on the exact locations for joint development, the ratio of investment by each state, or the distribution of profits, which could all spark future economic disagreements (*MCOT English News* 2008).

Third, the very existence of an enduring territorial dispute between China and Japan could potentially threaten the recently warmed bilateral relations between the two states, especially since the sovereignty of the islands was set aside as an issue of discussion in the May 2008 agreement. During a press conference announcing the joint gas development agreement in June 2008, Japanese foreign minister Masahiko Komura noted that even with the joint gas agreement, "Japan and China have different stands, and the talks [on their rapprochement] will be very long," referring to the disputed islands (Fesyun 2008). Likewise, Chinese vice foreign minister Wu Dawei defended the agreement to the Chinese public, confirming that China had not abandoned its sovereignty claim for the islands. Besides Taiwan, Sino-Japanese relations are arguably the most important issue for Chinese foreign policy.

It is not surprising that China continues to press its claim for sovereignty of the islands since the area around the islands is suspected to have massive oil resources, similar to the disputed Spratly Islands in the South China Sea (Curtin 2005; J. H. Lee 2002; Suganuma 2000). Access to further oil resources is a critical priority for the Chinese government due to its increasing modernization programs and soaring economic growth. However, despite Japan's proposal for joint development of the oil resources if China drops its claim, China refuses to drop the territorial claim.[3] One possibility is that China is waiting for Japan to offer more regarding the development of oil resources, but China has made no attempt to negotiate on this point. Since it is unlikely that the territorial status quo will change, why then does China continue to press its territorial claim and provoke Japan with regularity? What explains China's strategy regarding its territorial dispute with Japan?

This chapter examines how China applies issue linkage and coercive diplomacy as a strategy in this territorial dispute, and provides reasons for why this strategy explains the persistence of the dispute compared to the value of territory or domestic factors. Value of territory cannot explain Chinese unwillingness to resolve the dispute and use of threats or force, considering the significant economic value from which both China and Japan could benefit. Domestic mobilization and accountability play some role in influencing Chinese dispute strategies. Yet, as the evidence demonstrates, it is China's use of the islands dispute as bargaining leverage to gain concessions from Japan on other disputed issues that has most influenced its dispute strategies.

THE ISLANDS

The Diaoyu/Senkaku Island chain, referred to in English as the Pinnacle Islands, comprises eight small, uninhabited, barren islands. The islands are located approximately 120 nautical miles west of Fukien Province in China and about midway between Taiwan and islands in the Japanese Ryukyu Island chain, which includes Okinawa. The largest island is no greater than two miles in length and less than a mile in width.

There is historic evidence of the islands being used as early as 1372 by Chinese fishermen as shelter, by sea captains as nautical reference points, and as part of the coastal defense system during the Ming dynasty (1368–1644) and Qing dynasty (1644–1911), events that play a significant role in China's claim (Blanchard 2000; Hagstrom 2005; H. Shaw 1999; Suganuma 2000). The Japanese first annexed the islands as part of the Ryukyu Kingdom in 1879. It is believed that Chinese Empress Dowager Cixi gave the islands to a Chinese businessman in 1893, though the Japanese had claimed them.

Japan officially acquired the islands as surrounding islands of Formosa (Taiwan) in the Treaty of Shimonoseki after the Sino-Japanese War of 1895, incorporating the islands as part of the Okinawa Prefecture. This is an important point since the islands are directly related to China's claim for Taiwan. Prior to that time, the Chinese had been aware of the islands and considered them Chinese for centuries, but as is the case with China's other claims for disputed islands, they never effectively controlled or occupied them, lacking the ability to project naval power near the islands (Fravel 2008). Japan claims the islands were *terra nullis,* nonoccupied, but China claims they were historically part of Chinese territory.

In 1953, as a result of the 1951 San Francisco Peace Treaty after World War II, the disputed islands were put under US military administration as part of the Ryukyu Islands. The complex dispute over the Senkaku/Diaoyu Islands was sparked in 1968 due to the discovery of massive oil deposits under and near the islands. The discovered oil deposits resulted from a November 1967 cooperative agreement between Taiwan, South Korea, and the Philippines to survey the East China Sea and the Yellow Sea (Chiu 1999).[4] A May 1969 report publishing

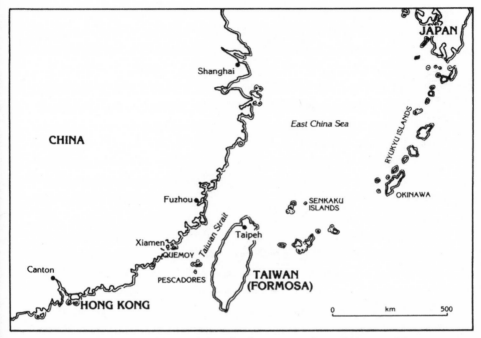

Figure 1. The location of the Senkaku Islands. From *Border and Territorial Disputes,* 4th edition, Peter Calvert, ed., London: John Harper Publishing, 2004.

the findings of seismic surveys conducted in October and November 1968 reported that the continental shelf in that region may "have one of the most prolific oil and gas reservoirs in the world," comparable to the Persian Gulf area (Chiu 1999, 4). The report also cited that the most favorable area was the two hundred thousand square kilometers surrounding the Senkaku/Diaoyu Islands. The Japanese announced that the survey led the government "to believe the area is worth prospecting for oil resources" (Suganuma 2000, 130–31). By May 1969, even before the Japanese survey, 4,000 applications for drilling rights had been filed with the regional Ryukyu government of Okinawa Prefecture; by September 1970, the number of applications was up to 25,000 (Suganuma 2000).

Until the oil deposits were discovered in 1968, there was little if any interest in the islands shown by China, Japan, or Taiwan. Negotiations to revert the islands back to Japan from US administration started soon after the Japanese realized the potential for oil resources. On October 23, 1970, Taiwan also showed interest in potential oil revenue and, as a result, made an official claim of sovereignty over the disputed islands (Chiu 1999; Stuckey 1975).[5] Once China started showing signs of interest, the Japanese government decided to suspend any attempted development of the oil deposits around the islands (Suganuma 2000). According to analysts, the "intention was to prevent the oil dispute from affecting the détente between the People's Republic of China and the US; Japan had no choice but to go along" (Suganuma 2000, 133). Both Japan and the US were in the midst of approaching China to normalize relations, and China had just developed hydrogen and nuclear bombs, shifting the geopolitical status of the region (Chiu 1999).

From May 1969, when the report about oil discovery in the East China Sea was published, to late 1970, China had been "strangely silent" about both the discovery of oil deposits and sovereignty over the Senkaku/Diaoyu Islands (Suganuma 2000, 132). A formal, territorial claim by China was not actually made until December 30, 1971, six months after the US and Japan had signed the reversion treaty. In the official claim for the islands, included as part of its greater claim to Taiwan, the Foreign Ministry office claimed usurped ownership. The assertion was that the islands had been part of China's territory since the fifteenth century, that "gross encroachment upon China's territorial integrity and sovereignty" had occurred, and that the "Chinese people absolutely will not tolerate this" (Chiu 1999, 9–11). The statement also announced that the islands "have been an inalienable part of Chinese territory since ancient times," and the acts of Japan and Taiwan in particular "cannot in the least alter the sovereignty of the PRC over her territory" (Chiu 1999, 11). Another aspect of the claim is that the islands have a geological connection to China and not Japan since the deep continental shelf of the East China Sea lies between the disputed islands and the Ryukyu Island chain of Japan (Hagstrom 2005).

The US turned over administrative rights of the islands to Japan on May 15, 1972, as accorded by the Okinawa Reversion Treaty signed June 17, 1971. Since 1972, Japan has had effective control over the islands, with regular monitoring by the Japanese Maritime Safety Agency (MSA). The Japanese reaction to China's territorial claim over the islands, issued by the Foreign Ministry office on March 8, 1972, was that having "thus ascertained carefully that the islands were not only uninhabited, but without any trace of control by China ... the Senkaku islands have been consistently a part of Japan's territory of Nansei Shoto" (Chiu 1999, 11). Japan bases its claim on the principle of discovery and effective control and occupation, which is generally recognized in international law as determining ownership rather than historic claims. China refutes the legality of the Japanese ownership of the islands since 1895 due to the unfair circumstances in which Japan acquired the islands when China lost Formosa (Taiwan) and islands "appertaining or belonging to" Formosa, understood by Japan as including the Pinnacle Islands, to Japan in the Treaty of Shimonoseki.

DISPUTE STRATEGIES

The main Chinese strategy in this dispute since 1971 has been to delay any resolution of the dispute by not only avoiding any territorial concessions but also avoiding any negotiations over sovereignty in general. China's strategy to postpone any settlement is simply a strategy "to bide time and to avoid damaging China's relations with Japan" (Fravel 2008, 271). Despite the 2008 agreement of joint natural gas development in parts of the East China Sea, there have never been any negotiations to attempt to settle the territorial dispute and ownership of the surrounding waters. The status quo remains just as it was in 1971; Japan maintains occupation of the islands, claiming there is no territorial dispute, while China claims the islands as part of its national sovereignty.

Overall, China confronted Japan on eighteen occasions from 1971 to 2008, fourteen of which were militarized threats and four of which were diplomatic threats, listed in table 4.[6] These threats or uses of force occurred in 4 percent of the observed months of the dispute and 24 percent of the dispute years observed. The most strained years for Sino-Japanese relations, based on the frequency of diplomatic and military confrontations, were 1996, 2004, and 2005. Prior to 1978, neither China nor Japan had taken any action on the dispute, instead maintaining their claims of sovereignty without pressing the issue. Of the eighteen diplomatic and militarized threats or uses of force, 88 percent were linked to some other disputed issue, providing initial strong support for the theory of territorial disputes as bargaining leverage.

The first crisis in the dispute occurred in April 1978, a few weeks after the Japanese Diet linked sovereignty of the Senkaku/Diaoyu Islands to an important issue for China, Japan's signature of the Sino-Japanese Peace and Friendship Treaty (PFT), designed to balance a mutual adversary, the Union of Soviet Socialist Republics (USSR). China retaliated by approving the deployment of Chinese fishing boats, some led by People's Liberation Army (PLA) officers, around the islands. The incident led to tense bilateral relations for some time. The following year, in April 1979, the Chinese authorized sixty Chinese fishing boats to sail to the waters close to the islands. It was not until October 1990 that China again pursued action in the territorial dispute when the Chinese

Table 4. Chinese diplomatic and militarized confrontations, 1971–2008

DATE	TYPE	CHINESE ACTION	LINKED ISSUE
April 1978	Militarized	Armed fishing vessels surrounded islands with support of government	Peace and Friendship Treaty negotiations with Japan
October 1990	Diplomatic	Foreign Ministry demands Japan give up control of islands	Potential SDF deployment to Gulf War
December 1991	Militarized	Armed ship fired warning shots at Japanese fishing ships near islands	China claimed act was an accident, no issue linkage
February 1992	Diplomatic	Territorial Waters Law passed	Potential SDF deployment to UN peacekeeping operations
August 1995	Militarized	Two fighter planes flew in airspace near islands	Japanese economic sanctions
July 1996	Militarized	Two submarines deployed to islands	UN Convention on the Law of the Sea took effect in Japan, affecting islands; US-Japan security alliance renewal; Japanese economic sanctions
September 1996	Militarized	Warships dispatched to waters around islands; joint air force, navy, army maneuvers done; mock blockade of island chain	US-Japan security alliance renewal; Japanese economic sanctions
October 1996	Militarized	Navy conducted military surveillance around islands	US-Japan security alliance renewal; Japanese economic sanctions
November 1996	Diplomatic	Official claim of sovereignty made to UN	US-Japan security alliance renewal; Japanese economic sanctions
May 1999	Militarized	Naval warships dispatched to waters surrounding islands	Japanese bill reaffirming US-Japan security alliance
July 1999	Militarized	Naval drills conducted near islands	Japanese bill reaffirming US-Japan security alliance
July 2004	Militarized	Naval ship conducts research in disputed waters; training, intelligence gathering in Japanese waters	No stated issue linkage; Japan announced it would begin its own oil exploration
October 2004	Militarized	Naval ships in disputed waters	US-Japan talks held on security alliance; Japan hosts multilateral maritime exercises; Japan reveals missile defense plan
November 2004	Militarized	Nuclear Han class submarine deployed to disputed waters	Japanese SDF reveal military scenarios against China
February 2005	Militarized	Two destroyers deployed to disputed waters	US & Japan declare Taiwan is mutual security concern; renewed US-Japanese security agreement

Table 4.　*(continued)*

DATE	TYPE	CHINESE ACTION	LINKED ISSUE
April 2005	Diplomatic	Government approved violence against Japanese government and businesses in China protesting Japanese ownership of Diaoyu Islands	New "whitewashed" history textbooks issued in Japan; Japan actively bid for seat on UN Security Council
September 2005	Militarized	Five naval ships deployed to disputed waters; spy planes collected data on Japanese military vessels; military established special naval reserve fleet for East China Sea	To influence upcoming talks on territorial dispute; Koizumi's insistence of right to visit Yasukuni Shrine
October 2005	Diplomatic	China cancelled talks on territorial dispute and visit by Japanese foreign minister	Japanese prime minister Koizumi visited Yasukuni Shrine for fifth time

Foreign Ministry officially restated its territorial claim on the islands in protest of a September 29 decision by Japan to officially recognize a lighthouse on the islands built in 1978 by a Japanese nationalist group. In December 1991, the first militarized use of force since 1978 occurred when armed Chinese ships fired warning shots at Japanese fishing ships in the vicinity of the islands. Just a few months later, in February 1992, at the twenty-fourth meeting of the Standing Committee of the National People's Congress, the top legislative body in China, lawmakers adopted the Territorial Waters Law, which included a claim to sovereignty over the disputed islands (Suganuma 2000). Besides stipulating the islands as Chinese, the law also asserted the right of the military to expel by force foreign ships that violated territorial waters around the islands, allowing the PLA to chase ships out to international waters. The next incident occurred in August 1995 when Chinese decision makers chose to escalate the dispute by dispatching two Chinese fighter planes near the islands, coming close to violating Japanese airspace. Japan responded by sending two Japanese F-4 fighter planes to the islands and radioing the Chinese planes that they might have flown into Japanese airspace.

The summer and fall of 1996 involved several diplomatic and militarized threats by China, including the dispatching of two armed submarines to the islands. On July 14, 1996, Japan ratified the UN Convention on the Law of the

Sea (UNCLOS), to go into effect July 20, which meant that Japan would enforce its control of its EEZ, including the disputed islands. In support of the Japanese law, a Japanese nationalist group rebuilt a lighthouse on one of the disputed islands and requested approval on July 25 from the government for the light-house to be recognized as an official beacon. Days after the UNCLOS territorial waters law went into effect and the Japanese government considered the re-quest by the nationalist group, China filed an official protest stating that it was deeply concerned that the act violated Chinese sovereignty, accused the Japa-nese government of reviving Japanese militarism, and urged Japan to take ef-fective measures. At the same time, China sent two submarines to the waters around the islands.

On September 9, members of a Japanese nationalist group returned to one of the disputed islands to conduct repairs to the lighthouse and reapplied for recognition as an official beacon the next day. On September 10, the Chinese government demanded that Japan remove the lighthouse, with Chinese Foreign Ministry spokesman Shen Guofang "warning that bilateral ties will be seriously harmed if Japan does not take appropriate action." Shen threatened that if the Japanese government did not take effective measures to reign in the nationalist group, which infringed on China's sovereignty, "it would be bound to cause se-rious damage to Sino-Japanese relations" (Kyodo News Service 1996c). The next day, the PLA issued a report, stating that the use of armed force against Japan would become inevitable if the problem were not solved diplomatically (Kopnov 1996). Two days later, on September 13–14, China conducted large-scale mili-tary maneuvers involving joint army, air force, and navy exercises, conducted off China's northeastern coast. The exercises involved mock blockades and land-ings on a group of unidentified islands off the northeastern coast of Liaoning Province.

A few years later, in May 1999, China pursued the largest threat of force when Chinese leaders dispatched twelve warships, including a 1,700-ton frigate within seventy miles of the disputed islands, inside of Japan's EEZ but outside its territorial waters. The first of several confrontations in 2004 occurred in late March, when government-backed Chinese activists landed on the islands for the first time ever. On March 24, several Chinese ships entered the waters near the islands. The Japanese Coast Guard turned away the majority of activists, but seven skirted around the coast guard, landing on one of the islands. Within hours, the Japanese arrested them and took them to Okinawa Prefecture for prosecution. China reacted strongly to the arrests, demanding immediate and unconditional release of the seven arrested Chinese on what they claimed was Chinese territory.

A new crisis arose regarding the islands in October 2004, this time due to the deployment of four armed Chinese navy ships to the waters near the disputed islands. Two weeks later, on November 10, the deployment of a Chinese nuclear Han class submarine in waters claimed by Japan continued to cause friction in bilateral tensions. The Japan Maritime Self-Defense Forces (SDF) tracked the submarine with P-3C patrol planes, two destroyers, and a number of helicopters until the submarine left Japanese waters. This was only the second time in postwar Japan's history that the SDF has triggered a naval security alert. The most recent incident involved five Chinese naval ships sent to the disputed waters in September 2005, including missile-equipped destroyers and frigates, spy planes sent to gather intelligence on Japanese maritime vessels, and the announcement of the establishment of a special naval reserve fleet specifically for use in the East China Sea.

VALUE OF TERRITORY

How well does the value of the disputed islands explain the endurance of this territorial dispute and the decisions made by China regarding threats and uses of force and settlement attempts? Past research would predict that the strategic and ethnic value of the disputed territory makes it less likely for China to attempt settlement, while economic value makes it more likely for China to attempt settlement (Huth 1996; Huth and Allee 2002). Other research would predict that higher salience overall would make attempted settlement, mainly bilateral negotiations, and nonbinding third-party intervention more likely (Hensel 2001). On the salience scale ranging from 1 to 12 with 12 being the most valuable, the Senkaku/Diaouyu Islands have a score of 7 (Hensel and Mitchell 2005). This score suggests that the value of the islands should make it just slightly more likely for China to attempt settlement of the dispute, but this has not happened.

Examining the specific types of value, both tangible and intangible, can somewhat help to explain the lack of settlement. In terms of tangible value, first, the islands are hundreds of miles from China and are therefore clearly offshore islands. There is no permanent population on the islands—except goats—and the islands are not particularly inhabitable. With regard to strategic value, there is no real benefit for China to hold the islands. Though China is making an apparent effort to expand its naval power eastward and form a "string of pearls" as a perimeter around East Asia (Mazza 2010), owning these tiny islands would not particularly help the effort, as the islands are just north of Taiwan, a much bigger prize claimed by China. Since the islands lack any ethnic or strategic value, the dispute should be more likely to be resolved with China willing to offer concessions. Yet, there has been no attempt by China or Japan to resolve the dispute since it began in 1971, let alone any offers of territorial concessions or willingness to drop the claim.

While there is no strategic value, there is enormous economic value. The islands themselves lack any real value since they are mostly barren and rocky and could not really support habitation. The only historic economic gain from the islands, albeit minor, was the collection of bird guano for the use of fertilizer in the early part of the twentieth century. Yet, sovereignty of the islands could provide access to 20,750 square nautical miles and all resources in that area, which include rich marine resources and oil deposits, so there is significant economic value (S. Lee 2002). An early estimate of potential oil deposits was 7.5 billion barrels (Stuckey 1975). A 2005 estimate of oil resources in the East China Sea is 100 to 200 billion barrels, enough to provide energy sources to either state for fifty to eighty years (Curtin 2005).

Both China and Japan are beginning to benefit from natural gas resources in the East China Sea despite the endurance of the territorial dispute. In the past few years, China has been building natural gas platforms and pipelines in Chinese waters in the East China Sea and is already reaping the benefits. In June 2008, after a dozen rounds of negotiations over a two-year period, China and Japan signed an agreement to jointly develop natural gas resources in areas that crossed the median line of the disputed waters, but the agreement did not involve any of the disputed waters near the islands. According to the terms of the agreement, Japan is able to invest in and claim proportional profits from Chinese gas fields already set up, so both states benefit. This major breakthrough indicates that economic gains from the East China Sea are not necessarily conditional on the resolution of the territorial dispute.

Until China and Japan are willing to take the risk to invest heavily in the disputed waters for potential joint development, neither state will be able to make individual gains from the gas and oil resources. It would only be worthwhile if the benefits outweighed the costs with certainty, and currently they do not. Even when the joint gas agreement was announced in June 2008 to the public, officials in both states immediately assured their people that neither state had abandoned their territorial positions and claims on the Senkaku/ Diaoyu Islands. These statements indicate that there is something beyond the alleged economic value of the territory that drives the endurance of the dispute and that economic value is not a sufficient explanation. Most importantly, since economic value is the only actual value of the islands, it should make settlement attempts more likely, but clearly this has not been the case. Therefore, economic value does not appear to influence Chinese dispute strategies.

With regard to intangible value, there is no ethnic value since Chinese people never lived on the islands and do not currently live on the islands. Furthermore, Chinese leaders have never made any reference to any ethnic links in their territorial claims for the islands. Though the islands are not colonial territory, they cannot be claimed as homeland territory either since China has never had effective control of the islands. On the other hand, there is some degree of nationalist or symbolic value embedded in the islands. According to one China specialist, "it is the symbolic significance of these islands, rather than any rights to natural resources which may be conferred by establishing control and ownership, that lies at the heart of the dispute" (Deans 2000, 120). Other specialists argue that even if oil resources did not exist, China would not give up one inch of what is considered its territory, pointing out that the symbolic value "far outweighs the commercial value the islands may hold" (H. Shaw 1999, 5). Chinese decision makers have consistently stated that the islands have "always been part of the Chinese territory and China has indisputable sovereignty over the islands" and that "a great number of historical facts have proven the Diaoyu Islands belong to China" (Kyodo News Service 1990b). A related view is that with "historical grievances and indivisible sovereignty, it seems that the limits of diplomacy have truly been reached, at least with this dispute" (Chung 1998, 161), and that either state "could not risk breaking valuable economic ties or jeopardizing regional security over what were essentially small matters of more emotional than material value" (Chung 1998, 163). At the same time, there is not as much symbolic value compared to some of China's other past and present territorial disputes, particularly Taiwan. Though the intangibility argument is attractive, and it is certainly applicable to other territorial disputes, neither state has ever had any permanent population on these uninhabitable islands, and there is little evidence of leaders actually talking about indivisibility or symbolic value. Rather, only historic, legal claims have been used. It is also not clear how much of this is from efforts to use the islands, along with other territorial claims, to mobilize the domestic populace, discussed below. Therefore, intangible value does not play much if any role in explaining China's unwillingness to consider settlement.

Limitations of the Value of Territory Explanation

If economic value made settlement attempts more likely, then there should have at least been some attempts to resolve the disputes so that China and Japan could benefit from the significant oil resources located near the disputed islands. Strategic and ethnic value are lacking, the territory does have economic value, there is no permanent population, the territory is not part of the homeland, and it is an offshore territory; all of these factors should have made it more likely for China to engage in dispute resolution attempts through the offer of territorial concessions or willingness to drop the claim. The fact that China has been unwilling to propose sovereignty negotiations or any other resolution method with Japan indicates that something other than the value of the disputed islands and surrounding waters is driving the dispute. Therefore, this explanation is insufficient in explaining the lack of settlement attempts, continued diplomatic and militarized threats and uses of force, and the overall endurance of the dispute.

DOMESTIC ACCOUNTABILITY AND MOBILIZATION

The domestic accountability and mobilization explanations would predict either that Chinese leaders would use the territorial dispute to mobilize domestic support, providing incentive to delay settlement and instead mobilize using threats or uses of force, or that they would not attempt settlement because of the fear of some degree of domestic punishment, not through elections but through public opinion and reputation of the Chinese Communist Party (CCP). Throughout the time period examined, China has been an authoritarian regime with Polity IV scores ranging from −8 at the worst and −7 at the best, with −10 being the most authoritarian and 10 the most democratic. The only shift in Polity score occurred at the end of the Cultural Revolution in 1976, when China moved from a −8 to a −7, but this could hardly be considered democratization. The accountability argument asserts that the more domestic insecurity, in the form of coup attempts, regime instability, strong authoritarianism, or phases of democratization, the less likely it is for China to make attempts to resolve the dispute with Japan. The theory is consistent with China's lack of concessions since none were ever offered, but this also means that even when domestic security existed within China's government, concessions were still not made. Therefore, since there was variation of domestic government stability, but there was no variation in concessions, the theory cannot effectively explain China's strategy in the dispute. Since China never attempted settlement or offered territorial concessions to Japan, there is no way to know with certainty whether domestic punishment would arise in China.

In terms of threats or uses of force, though, the domestic accountability theory would predict that at times of domestic unrest, such threats or uses of force would be unlikely. This aspect of the theory is consistent with the evidence in that most of the threats and uses of force were initiated by China in the mid- to late 1990s, during a time of relative domestic stability in the years after the Tiananmen Square incident of 1989. Not only was democratization shut down during this time, but under Jiang Zemin, China was politically more stable than it had ever been since the end of the Qing dynasty. Though consistent, it is difficult to falsify this explanation since there is only a lack of domestic unrest and no clear indication that Chinese officials made their decisions based on calculations about the lack of domestic unrest. Rather, what is more likely is that they took advantage of opportunities to gain bargaining leverage and even used some provocations to mobilize domestic support for the government.

The domestic mobilization argument is a stronger alternative explanation for China's continued claim for the islands and regular confrontations with Japan based on the role of territorial nationalism in China. The rhetoric about the Senkaku/Diaoyu Islands is present in China, but it does not play a major role in domestic mobilization as one would expect based on China's emphasis on territorial nationalism. As one China expert wisely points out: "nationalism in Northeast Asia and arguments over the islands must not be taken at face value. Rather, the domestic considerations which drive the dispute and motivate nationalist groups . . . must be understood. The governments concerned find themselves obliged to take a hardline approach because of domestic pressures and the implications of other issues," but both states "have taken care to downplay the dispute because of the wider significance of their wider political and economic ties" (Deans 2000: 128–29).

When the PRC was established in 1949, the new government worked hard to maintain control over territories inherited from the Qing dynasty by successfully defeating independence movements and, more recently, by reclaiming sovereignty over Hong Kong and Macau (Baogang 2004). The Chinese government has used the call for reunification with Taiwan as a means to promote unity and domestic mobilization of the people, yet with other territorial disputes including the Senkaku/Diaoyu Islands, the Chinese government has used the islands dispute to mobilize domestic support only to some degree.

Rhetorically, hardliners in the Chinese government have always cited the significance of territory and territorial nationalism. At the same time, moderate, reformist Chinese decision makers have been hesitant to use the dispute to mobilize domestic support and have not been as concerned about domestic punishment in the form of major criticism and weakening legitimacy of the CCP, as demonstrated in the October 1990 incident. These decision makers have tended to downplay tension around the dispute with Japan in order to prevent damage to bilateral economic relations and also to prevent the anti-Japanese demonstrations from becoming anti-government sentiment. Thus, even when hardliner Chinese officials escalated the dispute in order to mobilize domestic support, more moderate decision makers almost always won out and de-escalated the dispute, even at the expense of domestic criticism. Therefore, even with so much rhetoric, territorial nationalism has not played a major role in influencing China's stance on its territorial dispute with Japan. Despite the claim that the islands hold nationalist significance, Chinese government officials have rarely used the East China Sea dispute to mobilize domestic support.

Though not many, there are a few instances of clear domestic mobilization using the Senkaku/Diaoyu Islands dispute. The most prominent case occurred in the crisis of 1996. In this incident, "the PRC's approach was fuelled by arguments over domestic policy and the politics of succession" (Deans 2000, 122). Initially, Chinese decision makers utilized the escalated tension to mobilize domestic support, but to a limited degree. CCP and army newspapers adopted an anti-Japanese tone in the weeks before and after the anniversary of the Japanese invasion on September 18, 1931, of the Manchurian Province of China in order to "circumvent criticisms by local and overseas Chinese of its alleged 'softness' toward" the dispute (Chung 1998, 148). As long as anti-Japanese rhetoric remained in the Party newspapers, "it could in no way weaken the nationalist credentials of any or all of the current Chinese leaders hoping to inherit the mantle of the late strongman Deng" (Chung 1998, 151–52). Prime Minister Li Peng "beat the nationalist drum" in an address to the nation "that carried a specific warning to Japan over an emotional territorial dispute in the East China Sea" (Deutsche-Presse Agentur 1996b). The tone of Li's speech reflected growing nationalist trends in China and provoked both nationalist appeal and anti-Japanese sentiment among the general populace.

In September and October 1996, groups of academics, former soldiers, activists, and businessmen sent letters to the Central Military Commission and President Jiang Zemin urging stronger action against Japan in regard to the disputed islands. They requested that the military take action to demolish all structures built on one of the islands by the Japanese right-wing group. For several weeks, the Chinese government benefited from the escalation by achieving a high level of domestic support not only among the masses but, more importantly, from the military and civilian elite, a part of the selectorate, who influenced the ruling decision makers. Chinese leaders stood firm for several weeks, making the incident the longest-lasting clash in the dispute.

Eventually, Chinese decision makers backed down and discouraged anti-Japanese sentiment, as they had in the October 1990 crisis, for two reasons. Despite attempts by some decision makers to continue domestic mobilization, "dominant voices in the CCP were at pains to play it down" (Deans 2000, 123). First, decision makers were concerned about preventing damaging economic relations with Japan, which could have threatened economic performance in China. Since economic performance has been a cornerstone in providing legitimacy to the CCP, the loss of economic aid from Japan could have been very damaging. Secondly, decision makers were growing increasingly concerned with competition from nonstate actors within China who were promoting their own version of Chinese nationalism, particularly in the form of popular books such as the bestsellers *China Can Say No* and *China Can Still Say No,* referring to China's ability to say no to other states, and student Internet activism (Gries 2004). Decision makers fearful of losing control over the nationalist agenda also feared that "anti-Japanese demonstrations could snowball into a larger, possibly destabilizing, movement critical of the CCP" (Deans 2000, 123). As a result, the CCP attempted to suppress the competing nationalist movement by promoting a circular, which emphasized that "patriotic actions require guidance" and announced that the public could not organize without guidance and permission from the CCP (Gries 2004, 124).

More recently, the Chinese government took advantage of domestic outrage directed at Japan and mobilized domestically. In this case though, the government did not instigate the anti-Japanese sentiment, but merely rode the wave of mobilization started by private anti-Japan groups. In April 2005, the largest anti-Japanese protests in communist China's history occurred all across the country against Japanese ownership of the disputed islands and other disputed issues. The Chinese government approved and choreographed the large-scale protests, involving tens of thousands of people nationwide in Beijing, Guangzhou, Chengdu, Shenzhen, and other cities. In a country where protests and demonstrations are forbidden, any protests that do occur must by default be approved by the government. The anti-Japan protests, which began at the beginning of April, lasted for several weeks and led to violent attacks on the Japanese embassy and Japanese-owned businesses, prompting Japan to condemn the attacks and call for the Chinese government to reign in the protesters. The primary organizers of the protests were the same activist groups that had sponsored several of the government-backed attempted landings on the disputed islands (e.g., China Federation to Protect the Diaoyu Islands). Protected by hundreds of police, an explicit sign of approval from the Chinese government, protesters focused primarily on the territorial dispute by holding banners calling for Japan's withdrawal from the disputed islands and a return of East China Sea resources to China. Other issues were brought up at the protests as well.

The massive protests, which primarily focused on the disputed islands, successfully led to a shift in Japan's attitude toward its historical record. On April 23, at a meeting of Asian and African leaders in Jakarta, Koizumi made an official apology about Japan's wartime atrocities, one of only a handful since the war ended: "Japan squarely faces these facts of history in a spirit of humility . . . and with feelings of deep remorse and heartfelt apology engraved in mind" (Lloyd 2005, 48). The Chinese government reacted to the apology by reigning in the protesters, shutting down anti-Japanese websites, and organizing public lectures in cities where protests were held to emphasize the need for good relations with Japan. The Chinese partially won this round, though Koizumi would later visit Yasukuni Shrine again in October 2005. This incident demonstrates China's ability to use territorial disputes to mobilize domestically, but as noted earlier, it cannot be fully attributed to the Chinese government since nonstate actors instigated the protests. This incident also demonstrates the unwillingness of the Chinese government to allow anti-Japanese sentiment to continue for too long.

Limitations of the Domestic Accountability and Mobilization Arguments

As noted in the September and October 1996 incident, Chinese officials have often downplayed escalatory incidents used to signal resolve to Japan in order to prevent too much anti-Japanese sentiment. This is not surprising based on the context of Chinese domestic politics: "anti-Japanese sentiment and its mobilization in the PRC are complex and multifaceted, and need to be viewed in the light of elite struggle amongst the Chinese leadership" (Deans 2000, 122). For example, in the October 1990 incident, Chinese officials did exactly the opposite of what was expected by not giving into domestic pressure regarding Japanese recognition of a lighthouse on one of the disputed islands. In response to the Chinese backing down and not pressuring Japan, the Chinese domestic populace rose up behind the government and called for strong reactions against Japan when the lighthouse was recognized. Despite this domestic pressure and the likelihood of domestic punishment in the form of decreasing legitimacy, Chinese decision makers chose to downplay the incident and "abandon its strident rhetoric in order to avoid damage to Sino-Japanese economic ties and to maintain domestic stability" (Downs and Saunders 1998, 126). The Chinese explanation was that they "felt protests over claims . . . would adversely affect Sino-Japanese ties" (Kyodo News Service 1990a). This decision resulted in vigorous public criticism by the domestic populace, which led to a negative impact on the legitimacy of the regime (Downs and Saunders 1998). Though downplaying the incident "improved China's international position and preserved its economic ties with Japan, the failure to back up its nationalistic rhetoric with action angered many Chinese, who regarded Beijing's reactive posture as evidence that the Chinese leaders did not actually support the patriotic sentiments they promoted" (Downs and Saunders 1998, 132).

The CCP was criticized for pursuing an accommodating approach to the dispute in order to guarantee the resumption of Japanese and international loans that had been sanctioned due to the 1989 treatment of student protestors. China was in a difficult position in which standing firm on the territorial dispute would likely have negatively influenced Japanese decisions about the loan package and its influence on other states. If China had continued seeking an aggressive strategy during the escalation, it "would threaten economic ties with Japan and Japanese diplomatic support, which was critical in persuading the Group of Seven to support the resumption of multilateral lending to China" (Downs and Saunders 1998, 132).

The domestic criticism that resulted "highlighted the contradictions between the Chinese leadership's nationalist claims and its passive actions during the dispute" (Downs and Saunders 1998, 132). Prime Minister Li Peng in particular was criticized for "begging for Japanese loans" while also banning anti-

Japanese protests about the territorial dispute. China found itself between a rock and a hard place, being forced to choose protecting economic aid from Japan over domestic mobilization and legitimacy. In the end, China agreed with Japan to de-escalate the tension caused by the territorial dispute and risked domestic accountability in exchange for cooperation on much needed economic aid. Clearly, bilateral relations with Japan trumped gains of domestic support, even at the cost of losing domestic legitimacy. In this incident, the Chinese government was criticized not for offering concessions or for escalating the dispute by using risky threats or uses of force, but instead for de-escalating the crisis in order to improve relations with Japan. This incident therefore demonstrates how domestic accountability can work, but not in the way that the theory predicts. Likewise, it is not clear that the Chinese government was domestically vulnerable at the time since it was a year and a half after the Tiananmen incident. Another example is the February 1992 incident, when China passed the Territorial Waters Law claiming the islands and threatening to use force against Japanese ships in the territorial waters. In this case, as with the 1990 incident, the Chinese government downplayed the law and "tried to nip domestic upheaval in the bud" regarding anti-Japanese sentiment (Hagstrom 2005, 175).

Due to divisions within Chinese leadership, some decision makers have focused more on relations with Japan and mobilization of nationalism, while others have not. The first likely reason for the government's lack of effort to use the disputed islands for mobilization is the concern by Chinese officials that too much nationalist sentiment might turn into anti-government sentiment, leading to protests and possible revolt. Since anti-Japanese statements could get out of control and provoke domestic resentment against the CCP, such domestic mobilization is generally prevented (Fravel 2008). The general strategy of the CCP has been to allow anti-Japanese protests, which divert political frustrations toward Japan rather than the government, but then to call them off soon afterward in order to prevent them from spiraling into anti-government protests. As Gries (2004, 125) notes, since "popular nationalism can threaten the Party's legitimacy, it is an increasingly significant constraint on China's Japan policy." Even though Chinese decision makers "may also wish to inculcate and galvanize nationalistic feelings or exploit xenophobic tensions as diversion from economic management, ethnic conflicts, or other problems," they must take into consideration the possibility that they "may lose control of nationalist sentiments," a situation that Chinese leaders do not want to face (Chung 1998, 159). In several diplomatic and military conflicts with Japan, the CCP was willing to incur "significant damage to its nationalist credentials" in order to prevent the territorial dispute from harming bilateral relations with Japan and threatening the elite's hold on power, as discussed earlier (Downs and Saunders 1998, 117). Thus, government officials mobilized domestic support only to the point where the government appeared like it was defending homeland territory, but not enough to provoke the masses into nationalist demonstrations that might threaten the tight control the ruling elite have over the masses.

A second problem with the domestic accountability and mobilization arguments is that Chinese leaders have actually compromised on numerous occasions specifically when domestic unrest or insecurity was at its highest within China. Fravel (2005, 2007, 2008) argues that Chinese leaders actually used territorial concessions and compromises deliberately to squelch domestic insecurity such as popular uprisings so that neighboring states could assist Chinese leaders to maintain stability of borders, where ethnic unrest was likely to occur. China's territorial compromises with Burma, Nepal, and India in the 1960s all involved these states' assistance in dealing with stabilizing borders with Tibet.

A third reason that domestic accountability cannot justifiably explain China's dispute strategies is that economic performance often supersedes territorial nationalism in China, at least in the past two decades, meaning that despite rhetoric to the contrary, Chinese officials are ultimately more concerned about economic success than territorial nationalism. Though there is an immense appeal to territorial nationalism in China, there is also a competing agenda, that of economic performance. With the gradual decline of the legitimacy of Marxist, Leninist, and Maoist ideology in the 1980s and 1990s, the CCP implemented major economic reforms, causing widespread employment, corruption, and periodic spells of high inflation. As a result, the CCP turned to gaining legitimacy via both economic performance and territorial nationalism. China, therefore, has been balancing a fine line, appealing to nationalism with territorial disputes, but then reassuring other states that the CCP wants to cooperate economically with them. The key factor is that forced to choose one over the other, Chinese leaders have often chosen to protect bilateral relations, especially with economic partner Japan, rather than attempting to mobilize domestic gains or satisfy domestic demands (Downs and Saunders 1998, 122). The frequent suspensions of anti-Japanese protests by the Chinese government illustrate China's concern to not allow nationalism to affect bilateral relations with Japan. Although nationalism has been a significant aspect of Chinese government rule in the past few decades, the "intention was to fill the gap in the national psyche that had previously been occupied by socialism, not to encourage provocative gestures of public demonstrations which might scare away China's biggest creditor nation" (Chung 2004, 50). Because of these reasons and the lack of strong evidence demonstrating significant domestic accountability or mobilization, these explanations are insufficient in explaining China's dispute strategies.

BARGAINING LEVERAGE

Since the late 1970s China has used the territorial dispute to achieve bargaining leverage in other issues disputed with Japan, such as economic aid, trade agreements, potential Japanese troop deployment, or Japan's treatment of historic events regarding China. The vast majority of the threats against Japan, 83 percent, occurred around the same time period when China and Japan were disputing other issues. Of the three times when China used coercive diplomacy, but not issue linkage, the confrontation was pursued half the time to gain leverage directly in the territorial dispute. These preliminary findings provide initial support for the argument that China's confrontations with Japan in the territorial dispute have been linked to other disputed issues happening around the same time. By making threats in the territorial dispute, China has used the dual strategy of issue linkage and coercive diplomacy. Combining these two foreign policy strategies, China has been able to take advantage of the endurance of the territorial dispute and use it to gain concessions or shifts in Japanese foreign policies regarding other disputed issues. China pursues the strategy of coercive diplomacy to pressure Japan to reconsider a policy on an unrelated but linked issue. China is able to use the territorial dispute to gain bargaining leverage when deemed necessary. By confronting Japan in response to some Japanese action, China signals its resolve, threatening to use force in the islands dispute if Japan does not change its policy on economic issues, other security issues, or any other disputed issue that is exogenous to the islands dispute.

The Sino-Japanese relationship is too complex and multifaceted to be discussed in much detail here, but it important to understand that because of historic events and present-day interdependence between the two states, and because they are competitors for the status of regional power of Asia, there are many issues that China and Japan could dispute and have disputed. Pan (2007, 85) argues, "the dispute over the Diaoyu/Senkaku Islands is not the only problem dividing China and Japan and since it is frequently interlocked with other Sino-Japanese disputes such as historical issues, [the] Yasukuni Shrine visit issue, and textbook issue, to name a few, the dispute either serves as a source igniting Sino-Japanese confrontations, or becomes a result deriving from other troubles in Sino-Japanese relations." The asymmetrical relationship the two states maintain means that their "friendship and cooperation" is often disturbed by friction and distrust, causing difficult problems for overall bilateral relations (Ijiri 1996). I argue that a major reason why China has not attempted settlement of the territorial dispute and why it has pursued both diplomatic and militarized threats and uses of force is because it has been able to efficiently use the dispute as bargaining leverage when other disputed issues with Japan existed.

This dual strategy entails China first confronting Japan through diplomatic or militarized conflict regarding the territorial dispute and threatening to take further action if Japan does not make a change or reconsider its stance on other disputed issues. In this way, China links two or more distinct issues, using the threat of action in the territorial dispute to compel Japan to change its behavior or policy on other disputed issues. China knows that Japan values the disputed territory, so China expects that Japan will give in to its coercive diplomacy strategy and change its policies, especially since China holds a strategic advantage over Japan (Dutton 2007). To avoid escalation of Chinese threats, Japan almost always gives in on other disputed issues or at least registers China's dissatisfaction with the other issues.

The Senkaku/Diaoyu Islands dispute, like many international disputes, is a classic illustration of a pawn used by both China and Japan, but primarily by China, in an attempt to score points in the broader competition for whether China or Japan will be the dominant Asian power in the twenty-first century. Both China and Japan have used the territorial dispute as a pawn in this competition, but as the one who could threaten Japan's status quo ownership of the islands, China has been able to use the territorial dispute much more frequently to gain concessions from Japan.

Though it is difficult to accurately predict the foreign policy actions of the Chinese government, analysis of Chinese confrontations of Japan from 1972 to 2008 provides solid insight into which issues are most likely to cause China to use the strategy of issue linkage and coercive diplomacy, listed in table 5. By far the most significant issue linked to the territorial dispute is renewals, talks, or realignments of the us-Japanese security agreement, followed by Japan's treatment of wartime atrocities (issuance of textbooks, visits by Prime Ministers to the Yasukuni Shrine), and Japanese decisions to cut aid or place economic sanctions on China. sdf troop deployment is the next biggest issue, followed

Table 5.   Japanese issues linked by China to the territorial dispute

DISPUTED ISSUE	NUMBER OF LINKAGES
US-Japan security agreement	8
Wartime atrocities and visits to Yasukuni Shrine	5
Economic sanctions, foreign aid cut	5
SDF troop deployment	4
General Japanese military plans (missile defense shield)	3
Bilateral talks upcoming (other issues)	2
UN Security Council bid	1

by general Japanese military plans (missile defense shield), upcoming bilateral talks (on other issues), and Japan's bid for a permanent seat on the UN Security Council. Though some of these disputed issues, such as visits to the Yasukuni Shrine, may seem minor or not so salient compared to a territorial dispute or other major issues, the important point is that the Chinese government feels they are salient enough to pursue coercive diplomacy and issue linkage. What this information tells us is that China is most likely to use the strategy of coercive diplomacy and issue linkage to protest US-Japan security arrangements, but also to attempt concessions regarding Japan's wartime atrocities in China. The latter issue is not so surprising, considering that through a gentleman's agreement, Japan has offered China billions in official development assistance in lieu of monetary retribution for the war. The following discussion of incidents provides strong support for the idea that Chinese decision makers have pursued a strategy of issue linkage and coercive diplomacy to gain leverage on other issues, and therefore China has had little incentive to settle the territorial dispute.

Peace and Friendship Treaty Negotiations and the 1970s

The first use of Chinese issue linkage and coercive diplomacy occurred when the friendship treaty negotiations (PFT) meant to balance the Soviet Union started on February 17, 1978. Not much progress had been made by April 7, when antitreaty Diet members met with Foreign Minister Sonoda to get him to "pressure the Chinese government into conceding sovereignty over the Senkakus, in exchange for agreeing to an 'anti-hegemony' clause" in the proposed treaty (Chung 1998, 136). Chinese decision makers had been observing Japanese domestic politics during this period, aware of the repercussions for treaty negotiations. The common perception among many Chinese decision makers was that Japanese decision makers were dragging their heels and that Japanese prime minister Takeo Fukada was both stalling and wooing his opponents at the same time in an attempt to gain domestic support. The Chinese reaction to delay tactics by Japan ranged from impatience to outright criticism, which was the dominant perception, led by PLA chief of staff Teng Hsiaop'ing.

The Chinese chose to respond to Japan's moves by threatening to use force in the islands dispute. On April 12, just five days after Japan made the issue linkage of the territorial dispute and the treaty official, approximately eighty Chinese fishing boats, half of which were armed with machine guns, encircled the disputed islands. The fishing boats were either under the naval command of the PLA or had approval from the Politburo. The hostile action effectively ended treaty negotiations. The deployment was "in truth a visible and forceful demonstration by China that it would not let the Japanese claim over the disputed islands go unchallenged, or allow their territorial integrity to be compromised by the need for a peace treaty" (Chung 2004, 37).

China's first objective was to use the escalatory behavior to signal resolve of its sovereignty claim toward Japan and other states. Specifically in regard to the dispute with Japan, "Peking wanted to dramatize to the Japanese before any treaties were signed that Tiaoyutai [Diaoyu] is Chinese" (Mathews 1978, A20). China's other major objective was to link the disputed territory to the treaty negotiations, just as Japan had done. By confronting Japan in the territorial dispute, Chinese decision makers signaled to Japan to stop delay tactics and move forward with negotiations for the treaty. China's use of force to improve its bargaining leverage was evident in several ways. China "deliberately arranged an incident at that time near the Tiao Yu archipelago, as the Senkaku islands are called in Japan. Peking's design had two purposes: firstly, to further its claim to this territory and secondly, to exert pressure on Tokyo so as to make it speed up the signing of the Japanese-Chinese treaty" (BBC 1979a). Although Japanese lawmakers had made the first move in linking the disputed territory to the treaty negotiations, "the Chinese felt that some physical, not simply verbal, reaction was needed to demonstrate their annoyance with the Japanese Government for not keeping the issue quashed and embarrassing Chinese leaders in the process" (Tretiak 1978, 1242). Thus, the Chinese confrontation was not used to enter into conflict but to compel Japan on another disputed issue by pushing

the state into conclusive treaty negotiations. Apparently the Chinese government had adopted a strategy initiated by Japan, one that would come back to
haunt Japan on many occasions in the future.

On April 15, three days after China retaliated by threatening force against
Japan, Chinese vice premier Di Biao began to de-escalate the incident by announcing that it was a fortuitous incident that would not happen again. According to one analyst, it "would have been very poor diplomacy for the Chinese to admit that Chinese boats had virtually attacked islands claimed by the
Japanese" (Tretiak 1978, 1243). It is believed that Chinese officials milked the
crisis with Japan to the extent that they could, then de-escalated to save face
and continue negotiations on the friendship treaty. China's escalation was not
to provoke Japan to the point where it would never sign the treaty, but rather to
prod Japanese decision makers into making progress on the treaty negotiations.
Thus, de-escalation was a logical move in order to save face and get Japanese
decision makers to move on the treaty negotiations. It was also logical since
China's objective was not to change the status quo of the islands, but to signal
resolve for bargaining, particularly with regard to the treaty negotiations.

By April 17, all of the Chinese boats had moved out of Japanese waters, but
approximately 140 boats remained in waters thirty to thirty-eight kilometers
northeast of the islands, right outside Japanese territorial waters, and 10 boats
returned to Japanese territorial waters on April 18 to maintain some resolve. As
a result, Japanese foreign minister Sonoda was soon able to announce that the
incident was over, and treaty negotiations would go ahead. The Chinese "explanation" of the incident had been enough to save face for both sides, allowing
treaty talks to go forward without having to resolve the territorial dispute. Two
weeks later, on April 29, Fukada welcomed a statement made by Liao Cheng-
chih, which stated that China would prevent future conflict with Chinese fishing vessels. By the end of April, both states agreed to shelve the territorial dispute in order to proceed with the negotiations over the PFT on May 27, 1978,
resulting in the signing of the treaty on August 23, 1978. Deng's "skillful use of
economic incentives and exploitation of the Soviet bogeyman" worked to resolve the stalled treaty negotiations, by "asserting his country's claims to the
Diaoyu Islands so visibly and forcefully" (Chung 2004, 40).

Though Japan had initially linked the territorial dispute with the PFT, China
took advantage of the situation, deployed the armed fishing boats to signal
China's resolve on its claim to the islands, and used the deployment to pressure
the Japanese to go ahead with the treaty negotiations. The plan worked; Japan

backed down on the demand to discuss sovereignty, letting the Chinese continue to maintain their territorial claim at the same time the PFT was signed by both states. As one analyst reported,

> Deng understood the basis of "synergy," which is to exploit joint gains or mutual benefits in international bargaining, through the creation of coalitions favoring cooperation in both China and Japan. In this case, joint gains or mutual benefits in bargaining over the PFT involved an increase in trade and investment between China and Japan, an expansion of the Chinese market to Japanese economic penetration, an external validation of Deng's "open-door" policy by a powerful neighboring Asian country, and the creation of an informal front against possible military moves from the Soviet Union. (Chung 2004, 39)

The 1978 use of force by China indicates that Chinese leaders considered issue linkage and coercive diplomacy to be an effective strategy, one they would continue to use again the following year, then not again until 1990. In April 1979, when China authorized, really meaning "ordered," sixty Chinese fishing ships to the waters around the disputed islands, it appears that Chinese leaders were again linking the islands dispute with other issues, this time because "the hegemonists in Peking have been irritated by Japan's unwillingness to give unconditional support to their hegemonist foreign policy and its refusal to conduct trade with China on unequal and disadvantageous terms" (Tsvetov 1979). The timing of the incident was clearly not coincidental. Just a week before, at a meeting with a Japanese delegation, Liao Chengzhi, a high-ranking Chinese official, had strongly accused Japan of losing interest in improving bilateral relations with China and urged that Japan reconsider showing more of an effort with Sino-Japanese relations. Apparently, "Peking seems to be feeling that verbal pressure is not enough. That is why it is taking this current action in the Senkaku Islands area. By doing so, Peking intends to warn Japan that it too cannot escape China's 'punitive action' if it insists on behaving obstinately against China" (Tsvetov 1979). It appears that Japan did not respond to the attempted coercion and increase its amount of foreign aid to China at that time. Just a few months later, Chinese leaders appear to have shifted strategies; at a meeting with Zenko Suzuki of Japan in June 1979, Deng Xiaoping mentioned the disputed islands, but with a reserved and "deliberately conciliatory tone" (Moscow Home Service 1979). The strategy seems to have been that China would pressure Japan as a reminder that they could exert pressure if necessary, followed by a conciliatory approach. In this case, during the meeting with Suzuki, Deng was attempting to get Japan to sign several treaties regarding scientific, technological, and industrial cooperation, in addition to Japanese loans (Moscow Home Service 1979).

Positive Bilateral Relations in the 1980s

Besides sending ships to the disputed waters in 1979, China did not pursue any other diplomatic or militarized threats against Japan until 1990. Rather, during the 1980s, China kept its word to Deng Xiaoping's proposal in 1978 to shelve the issue of sovereignty and territorial rights for future generations by not mentioning the dispute, nor pursuing diplomatic or militarized threats or uses of force. In fact, from 1978 to 1982 China proposed to Japan to consider joint development of offshore oil and natural gas resources in the waters around the islands. A series of talks regarding the possibility of joint development of hydrocarbon resources in the East China Sea occurred until the talks were halted due to the building of a lighthouse by a Japanese right-wing group and an eventual fear by China that the presence of oil rigs would influence future sovereignty claims (Chung 1998). In 1983, Deng reiterated China's suggestion that the islands dispute be shelved for a future generation to resolve (Suganuma 2000).

There are two major reasons why China did not pursue issue linkage and coercive diplomacy during the 1980s. In the early 1980s, China and Japan enjoyed relatively normal relations with no real upsets. In March 1984 during a visit of Japanese prime minister Yasuhiro Nakasone to China, the Japanese ambassador to China declared that Sino-Japanese relations were "in the best condition ever" (Ijiri 1996, 69). In the years after Mao's death and the gradual shifts in economic planning by Deng Xiaoping, Japan pursued a relatively friendly approach toward China, particularly through financial aid. China became the largest recipient of development assistance from Japan in the early 1980s. The Japanese sought a policy of economic development of China mainly to maintain political stability and avoid economic collapse, since a weakened China might use its military might to attain economic wealth, affecting regional neighbors adversely, particularly Japan. From 1981 to 1996, China's economy benefited from a significant amount of Japanese yen loans, a symbol of growing Sino-Japanese cooperation (Kyodo News Service 1996d). Although the territorial dispute caused some degree of tension between the two states, during this time both states were able to recognize their respective significance to each other. Until the Tiananmen Square incident in 1989, a salient disputed issue, few other disputed issues arose between China and Japan. At that time, Japan and other major states in the international community placed economic sanctions on China in response to the major human rights abuses and casualties that resulted from PLA actions in June 1989.

Another major factor for the lack of Chinese provocation in the dispute during this time was the de facto strategic alliance between the US, China, and Japan that was in essence a means to balance against their mutual adversary, the Soviet Union (Chung 1998). Basically, Chinese leaders realized that their larger adversary was the Soviet Union, due to several factors including their own territorial dispute over their massive shared border, Soviet support for Vietnam's intervention in Cambodia, Soviet deployment of troops to Mongolia along the Chinese border, and the Soviet invasion of Afghanistan, all issues of which China severely disapproved since these actions suggested Soviet encroachment on China (discussed at length in chapter 8). Because of the strategic necessity to balance against the Soviets, Chinese leaders had little choice but to open détente, first with the US and later with Japan. This ease of relations with Japan would shift drastically in the 1990s, when Sino-Russian relations had significantly improved and China no longer depended on Japan to help balance the Soviet Union. Most importantly, this shift allowed China to be more selective about concerns regarding Japanese actions toward China, all of which led to a significant number of Chinese provocations in their territorial dispute and a shift away from Deng's promise to set aside the dispute for future generations.

The theory does not perfectly explain China's strategies in the 1980s since there were a few occasions in July through September 1982 when Chinese leaders expressed concern about Japanese history textbooks and statements by Japanese officials denying wartime atrocities in China (Ijiri 1996; D. Yang 2002). Also, in August 1984, China complained about Japanese prime minister Nakasone's visit to a war shrine where war criminals were buried (Ijiri 1996). Yet Chinese leaders did not apply issue linkage and coercive diplomacy to these issues. It is likely but also a supposition that economic incentives from China were important enough during this time period that Chinese leaders were unwilling to press Japan too hard on these other issues, unlike in future years. Though China and Japan are more economically interdependent today, it was much more of a unilateral dependence of China on Japan in the early 1980s. At that time, the Chinese perceived Japanese trade, investment, and technology flows as "critical elements in its modernization programme, while Japan sees enormous commercial opportunities and a means to influence the stability and direction of change in China" (Shambaugh 1996, 90). As one analyst best summed up Sino-Japanese relations at that time, "Even though harsh in criticism of Japan, the Chinese government has always emphasized the importance of Sino-Japanese friendship, even if their words may sometimes sound hollow" (D. Yang 2002, 25). It is also possible that China was busy focusing on its adversary, the Soviet Union, which was extremely busy through the 1980s until 1987 with coercive diplomacy and issue linkage (see chapter 8). Yet, even without issue linkage to the territorial dispute, by the later 1980s there was already a long-standing pattern of China criticizing Japan about a particular policy with which it was displeased and Japan making concessions to China in order to avoid immediate friction (Ijiri 1996). This pattern suggests that Chinese decision makers were familiar with Japanese decisions to provide concessions in order to avoid further tensions with China; therefore, a strategy of issue linkage and coercive diplomacy would be useful to pursue when other disputed issues arose.

By the late 1980s, as China reconciled with the Soviet Union in its own territorial dispute due to the reduction of other disputed issues (see chapter 8), the tide began to turn for Sino-Japanese relations. In early to mid-1987, "events took a particularly nasty turn" when Deng announced he was greatly dissatisfied with an increase in Japanese defense spending, among other disputed issues (D. Yang 2002). As one China specialist noted, "1987 also witnessed the most serious tensions in Sino-Japanese relations in five years" (Whiting 1989, 149). In January 1987, Japan announced it was lifting its ceiling on defense expenditures by 1 percent, causing concern for China. In August 1987, Japan had released its Defense White Paper, outlining the increase in defense spending. Then over the next few months, China was irate as a result of a Japanese court ruling that acknowledged Taiwanese ownership of a Kyoto dormitory (Ijiri 1996; Whiting 1989). In the summer of 1988, relations continued to sour when China brought up a number of issues under contention. China was exceptionally critical of Japan for failing to purchase enough Chinese products and make enough foreign direct investment compared to Hong Kong and the US; the Chinese were concerned about Japan's growing military budget; and China was particularly angry about remarks made by right-wing Japanese politicians who played down Japanese aggression against China in World War II. However, no coercive diplomacy or issue linkage with the territorial dispute was pursued. Only in 1990 would such a strategy become a regular strategy for the Chinese. My best assessment for China's lack of issue linkage and coercive diplomacy is that China was heavily focused on using coercive diplomacy and issue linkage with the Soviet Union until the late 1980s, a strategy that it would halt with Russia in the 1990s but continue with regularity with Japan, and it was hesitant to demand too much from Japan during a time when it still was balancing the Soviet Union with the help of Japan and the US.

Growing Tensions in the 1990s

A significant shift occurred in the early 1990s in Sino-Japanese bilateral relations, partly due to the fall of the Soviet Union and partly due to China's fast economic and military growth during this time, worsening already tense relations. A Japanese analyst noted that "by the mid-1990s, with China's dramatic increase in productive capacity, on one hand, and its military modernization and buildup, on the other, China emerged as a competitor and threat to Japan" (Katada 2001, 52). Relations began to particularly cool off after 1992, and by 1995 and 1996, the worst political frictions since World War II were occurring, mainly due to the disappearance of the common enemy of the Soviet Union, which forced China and Japan to redefine their strategic relationship (Xide 2002). The first disputed issue that arose during this period was China's frustration in 1990 with Japan's consideration to send SDF troops to the Middle East to participate in the Gulf War. In the fall of 1990, the Japanese Diet began heated debates about the possible deployment of SDF troops to the Gulf through the Gulf Cooperation Bill. China's reaction to the news of potential Japanese deployment to Iraq, which would break a forty-five-year ban on sending Japanese troops abroad, was not surprising: "naturally they [the Chinese] are very sensitive to Japan's sending troops overseas" (China Central Television 1990). At the same time, the Japanese MSA decided to officially recognize a lighthouse erected by a Japanese national group on one of the islands in 1978.

These decisions led to the issuance of a diplomatic threat to Japan regarding the islands dispute in October 1990. The Chinese Foreign Ministry immediately announced its grave dissatisfaction about Japanese proposals to send SDF troops to the Middle East and explicitly linked the issue with the territorial dispute by strongly demanding that Japan halt all unilateral actions on the disputed islands (Kristof 1990).[7] Chinese Vice Foreign Minister Qi Huaiyan held an emergency meeting with the Japanese ambassador, making "stern representations on the Diaoyudao [Senkaku Islands] issue. He also made clear China's stand on the question of the Japanese government dispatching troops abroad" (China Central Television 1990). On October 25, a Chinese Foreign Ministry spokeswoman issued an implicit threat regarding Japan's choice about the light-house application: "We have always held that China and Japan should place their overall interests above everything else and handle the Diaoyu Islands is-sues prudently, thus preventing it from affecting bilateral relations . . . if the Jap-anese side fails to do that, it undoubtedly will bring an unfavorable effect on the relations between the two countries" (Suganuma 2000, 141).

Even Japanese leaders acknowledged the issue linkage when Prime Minister Toshiki Kaifu promised to "act prudently" in response to the lighthouse appli-cation, a statement that, according to scholars studying Sino-Japanese relations, "demonstrated Japan's desire to prevent the issue from escalating and sought to reassure China that the pending Diet bill authorizing deployment of Japa-nese forces for United Nations peacekeeping missions did not represent a resur-gence of Japanese militarism" (Downs and Saunders 1998, 129). By linking the disputed islands with the protest of troop deployment, China was able to com-pel Japan to reconsider this decision: "China, mindful of history, is unhappy at the idea that Japanese troops, albeit in small numbers and as noncombatants, may soon be going to the Gulf. The Diaoyutai islands provide an easy way to express that unhappiness and embarrass Mr. Toshiki Kaifu and his government in Japan" (*Economist* 1990, 37).

The Chinese strategy of issue linkage was to threaten Japan so much about the islands that it would provoke Japan to deploy the SDF to patrol the islands; then China and other Asian states could claim that Japan's actions in the islands dis-pute further demonstrated Japan's alleged growing militarism shown by planned deployment of SDF troops to the Middle East. An editorial in the *Straits Times,* an English newspaper in Singapore, noted how "the dispute [over the islands] might make Asians skeptical of Prime Minister Toshiki Kaifu's proposal to send Japan's Self-Defense-Forces to the Persian Gulf. A bellicose Japanese attitude in the matter would, in fact, be counterproductive for Tokyo. In such a situation, military assertiveness over the islands might complicate Japan's efforts to assure its Asian neighbors that its intentions [to deploy troops to the Middle East] are good" (*Straits Times* 1990).

The Chinese decision to threaten Japan diplomatically rather than threaten military force near the islands was an intentional decision by practical decision makers who were also concerned about the resumption of Japanese loans and the end of economic sanctions placed on China by Japan, among other states, as a result of the Tiananmen Square incident the year before. A week after hostilities had escalated due to the war of words between China and Japan over the islands, the Chinese attempted to de-escalate the tensions by calling for negotiations. On October 27, the Chinese vice foreign minister suggested that the two governments hold talks as soon as possible regarding joint exploitation of marine resources (including oil) in the area and the opening of fishing resources in waters near the islands. Though Japan rejected the proposal, both governments agreed to "quietly drop the dispute and avoid further provocative actions" (Downs and Saunders 1998, 130). If China had sought an aggressive strategy during the escalation, it "would [have] threaten[ed] economic ties with Japan and Japanese diplomatic support, which was critical in persuading the Group of Seven to support the resumption of multilateral lending to China" (Downs and Saunders 1998, 132).

The two-stage issue linkage plan worked for China. By making a hostile restatement of its territorial claim, China was able not only to warn Japan of its dissatisfaction with the Japanese government's recognition of the lighthouse, but also to compel Japan to reconsider the deployment of SDF troops to the Middle East. By backing down a week later and proposing negotiations, China then signaled to Japan that it was not so hostile after all and would be accommodating to receive much needed economic loans again. After the de-escalation of tensions, Japanese decision makers responded by announcing that they would not be sending SDF troops to the islands and they would resume loans to China. Within three weeks, Japanese prime minister Kaifu announced that the government would not recognize the lighthouse as an official beacon, promising that there were no plans to dispatch Japanese military ships to the islands (H. Shaw 1999; Downs and Saunders 1998). According to China scholars Downs and Saunders (1998, 129), "Kaifu's statement demonstrated Japan's desire to prevent the issue from escalating *and* sought to reassure China that the pending Diet bill authorizing deployment of Japanese forces for United Nations peacekeeping missions did not represent a resurgence of Japanese militarism." The statement was a direct response to China's initial issue linkage of the lighthouse issue on the disputed islands and the SDF troop deployment. Though implicit, Japan recognized the intended issue linkage and responded accordingly.

Because of domestic opposition and to prevent provoking China, Japan scrapped plans to send SDF transport planes to the Gulf as planned, instead sending minesweepers for cleanup of the Gulf in April 1991. There is little doubt that the resumption of economic aid to China was directly linked to China's

willingness to back down off the islands dispute and reign in anti-Japanese protests in China. Thus, the "perceived linkage between the CCP's accommodating posture toward the Diaoyu dispute and resumption of Japanese loans highlighted the contradictions between the Chinese leadership's nationalist claims
and its passive actions during the dispute" (Downs and Saunders 1998, 131).
The Chinese media criticized Prime Minister Li Peng for "begging for Japanese
loans" while the CCP banned anti-Japanese protests and backed off the Diaoyu
Islands claim (Ping 1990). In the end, Japan ended up backing down on the
lighthouse issue and the troops issue and resuming economic aid to China the
following week when a formal agreement was signed on November 3. By 1991,
full restoration of Sino-Japanese relations occurred, and a ban on ministerial
visits was lifted, resulting in an August 1991 visit to China by Japanese prime
minister Toshiki Kaifu, the first G-7 state leader to visit China after the Tiananmen incident in 1989 (Shambaugh 1996).

The next use of coercive diplomacy was in the form of a diplomatic threat
when the Chinese National People's Congress Standing Committee passed the
Territorial Waters Law in February 1992, claiming that the PLA could use force
against any ships in the waters around the islands. The passage of the law in effect acted as a diplomatic form of an official threat of force and an "important
departure from the position that 'the issue' be shelved" (Hagstrom 2005, 166).
Military leaders and conservatives from the general headquarters of the military, the navy, the Guangzhou military region, and Shanxi and Hainan provinces had pushed for the law because they believed it "would give the initiative
to China in future negotiations over the Diaoyu Islands with Japan and underlined the importance of these islands strategically and economically" (Suganuma 2000, 230). According to military sources, "by making clear Beijing's position, China can grasp the initiative in future negotiations with Japan" (Kyodo
News Service 1992). Proponents believed that Japan had broken a verbal agreement from 1978 to leave the islands alone (based on Deng's call to shelve the dispute), but instead Japan had been effectively controlling the islands. Thus, the
law was intended to signal to Japan China's resolve in standing firm with regard
to its claim to sovereignty and its willingness to use force to defend the disputed
islands. The move did indeed provoke Japan. Besides Japan's immediate reaction to the law by reaffirmation of Japanese sovereignty, Japan also enacted its
own maritime law in July 1996, when the Japanese Diet ratified UNCLOS, claiming its own two-hundred-mile EEZ around the islands (Chung 1998). Japanese
decision makers admitted at the time that the Japanese law had been directly in-

fluenced by China's 1992 territorial waters law. Both moves solidified each state's respective claim to sovereignty over the islands, strengthening their bargaining reputations in regard to resolve. It appears that no other issues were linked to this use of coercive diplomacy and that the action was only to signal resolve to Japan regarding the dispute.

The following two years, it appears that there were no other disputed issues, nor any use of coercive diplomacy and issue linkage. In early 1993, Chinese premier Jiang Zemin visited Japan, which indicated that "a distinct warming in relations was evident during the term of [Japanese] Prime Minister Hoso-kawa" (Shambaugh 1996, 87). The following year, in March 1994, Hosokawa visited China, where he apologized for Japan's wartime atrocities against China, a major symbolic gesture of friendship. Yet, by the summer of 1995, another disputed issue arose causing tensions in Sino-Japanese relations. The next use of coercive diplomacy in the territorial dispute occurred in August 1995, when two Chinese fighter planes flew near the islands and came close to violating Japanese air space. The show of force had one clear purpose: to pressure the Japanese government to reconsider a threat to cut grants to China in protest of nuclear tests that had occurred on several occasions that year. Though the amount of actual aid was not that large, it was the symbolic gesture of the uni-lateral threat by Japan to cut aid that mattered to China (Katada 2001). In May and again on August 17, 1995, China conducted a series of nuclear tests, which "further added to the negative impact created by China's rising military budget and territorial claims" (Drifte 2002, 56). Rather than just issuing a formal pro-test, Japan engaged in its own form of coercive diplomacy and issue linkage, but in this case, between Chinese nuclear testing, a salient issue to Japan, and Japa-nese grant aid to China. After the first test in May, Japan issued a threat to cut the grant aid. Then after the second testing in August, Japanese leaders made a decision just two weeks later to cut the grant aid to China, specifically threaten-ing not to reinitiate the aid until Chinese leaders foreswore further nuclear test-ing. The Japanese decision "shocked the Chinese government" (Katada 2001, 47). On August 24, a week after the nuclear tests and further Japanese threats to impose a form of aid sanctions, China attempted to use coercive diplomacy by threatening force in the islands dispute to pressure Japan to back off its threat of cutting the aid when it sent several Sukhoi 27 fighter planes to fly near the islands. The Japanese responded by sending two Japanese F-4 fighter planes to the islands and radioing the Chinese planes that they may have flown into Japa-nese airspace. The Chinese planes responded by turning around thirty to forty kilometers from the islands and returning to China. Less than a week later, on August 30, Japan announced its decision to impose the aid sanctions. This was a clear instance of implicit issue linkage in which Chinese decision makers used a threat regarding the territorial dispute in an attempt to influence the outcome of another disputed issue and compel Japan to reconsider cutting its grant program. In this case, the issue linkage did not work since Japan did cut grant aid and did not reinitiate the aid until the spring of 1997. Apparently, for Japan, China's nuclear testing was more salient of an issue than the threat to the islands and following through on the second threat to cut grant aid was more important as a signal to China of Japan's disapproval of the nuclear testing.

The following year, several disputed issues arose that provided an opportunity for China to seek bargaining leverage using the islands dispute. From July to October 1996, tensions between China and Japan were higher than during any other time of the dispute. In addition to China's dissatisfaction with the conditionality that resulted from the nuclear testing and Japan's aid sanctions against China, other issues of dispute arose. When China dispatched two submarines to the islands on July 24 in response to activities pursued by a Japanese nationalist group, according to analysts at the US-based *Defense News* (Soh 1996), it was just days after the Japanese UNCLOS territorial waters law, which included the islands, went into effect on July 20, and the same time that the Japanese right-wing nationalist group was applying for official government approval of the lighthouse erected on July 14 (H. Shaw 1999).

Though China's threat of force was a direct response to Japanese provocation in the territorial dispute, China linked the tensions in the territorial dispute to other issues of concern. Chinese Foreign Ministry spokesman Shen Guofang made a statement in August at a press conference that explicitly linked the territorial waters dispute with other disputed issues. According to Shen, a planned visit by Japanese prime minister Ryutaro Hashimoto and five cabinet members to the Yasukuni Shrine in late July, along with the claim of some Japanese politicians that the 1937 capture of Nanking was a hoax, were the events that provoked China to respond in the islands dispute. At the press conference, Shen noted, "All these [events] added up to giving a green light to these actions. . . . Japan has failed to arrive at what is a right understanding of history. The Japanese government therefore should have a sober-minded perspective and clear understanding as regards this issue. Otherwise Sino-Japanese relations would be seriously affected" (Associated Press 1996).

Admitting issue linkage, Shen also noted that "the recent words and actions of some Japanese right-wing groups and other people are not accidental and directly related to the attitude of the Japanese government," citing the government visits to the shrine specifically (Kyodo News Service 1996a). The Chinese reaction to Japan's move regarding the UNCLOS territorial waters law and the approval of the lighthouse on the islands was therefore not only about the UNCLOS law and recognition of the lighthouse built by the Japanese nationalists, but it also demonstrated China's greater concern for actions by the Japanese that signaled a lack of regret with regard to historic Japanese aggression toward China. By simultaneously threatening Japan with China's claim for the islands and deploying the submarines, China was able to use the territorial dispute as leverage in an attempt to compel the Japanese to reconsider its attitude toward Japan's historic role in China. Though never explicitly mentioned in the issue linkage at the time (it would later be mentioned in September), China's frustrations with Japan were also partially because of a white paper issued by Japan's National Defense Agency in late July, during the territorial waters crisis, which stated that Japan should watch China with caution due to its promotion of nuclear weapons, modernization of its air force and navy, and an annual 10 percent increase in its defense budget in the past eight years (Chung 1998).

The tensions continued through September, with China sending maritime exploration ships to the waters near the disputed islands, ignoring warnings by the Japanese MSA in early September. This action was followed by a verbal warning to Japan on September 10 that bilateral issues would be greatly damaged if Japan took no action. Then a second exploration ship was sent to the disputed waters on September 11, and an actual threat of force occurred on September 12 when the Chinese navy sent patrol boats to remain on duty around the islands. The military also drew up plans to use force if it became necessary and the dispute could not be resolved through diplomatic means (Kopnov 1996). China also threatened that the dispute would escalate if Japan did not take action to reign in the Japanese nationalists and reconsider actions and policies regarding several other disputed issues. Though Japan responded the next day with a plea to China to appeal for calm in dealing with the dispute, and the Japanese foreign minister instructed maritime authorities not to recognize the nationalists' lighthouse as an official navigational beacon, China nevertheless was dissatisfied with this concession on the territorial issue and continued to escalate the crisis by holding exercises involving large-scale maneuvers and mock blockades and landings on the islands on September 13 and 14, and again on September 18, the sixty-fifth anniversary of the Japanese invasion of northeastern China (Deutsche Presse-Agentur 1996a). These were done "in an apparent warning to Japan over a disputed island chain in the East China Sea" (Agence France Presse 1996a).

The Chinese government's strategy of warnings to Japan was made evident by a report on the naval exercises "on the same page as a Foreign Ministry warning to Tokyo over the islands" in the national newspaper *China Daily* (Deutsche Presse-Agentur 1996a). An unnamed Western diplomat in Beijing noted that "the side-by-side reports were no coincidence, even if the Chinese general did not mention the islands. There is no threat as such, but a clear signal that says 'you know what we think'" (Deutsche Presse-Agentur 1996a). In terms of issue linkage, during the crisis there was strong suspicion within Japanese diplomatic circles that China's confrontations were done to try to compel or persuade Japan to reconsider a number of other disputed issues including the economic sanctions placed on China for nuclear weapons testing, compel Hashimoto to halt visits to the Yasukuni Shrine, and reconsider its recently updated security agreement with the US. The Japanese understanding of China's attempt at issue linkage was clear: "Behind the rising criticism against Japan is China's distrust of Prime Minister Ryutaro Hashimoto, who visited the controversial Yasukuni Shrine for the war dead in July. . . . As a result, the recent criticism of Japan is a more serious matter that many Japanese may believe" (Sasajima and Mori 1996, 3). As a Japanese analyst wrote, "By applying pressure this way, Beijing hopes Japan will reconsider its plans to cut economic aid to China, and ease its criticism of China's military buildup and nuclear testing program" (Sasajima 1996, 7). The best evidence of issue linkage is the Japanese understanding of China's intentions: the Japanese government "fears that Beijing is accusing Japan of considering the ownership [of the islands] issue *in connection with* Prime Minister Ryutaro Hashimoto's visit to Yasukuni Shrine and the reaffirmation of the Japan-US security treaty" (*Daily Yomiuri* 1996).

Diplomatic talks to discuss the economic sanctions and general bilateral relations had been scheduled for September 24 in New York between Chinese foreign minister Qian Qichen and Japanese foreign minister Yukihiko Ikeda. The intention of both the Japanese nationalist group and the Chinese government was to use the dispute to influence the talks and the other issues at hand. On the day of the talks, at a press conference in Beijing, Shen made the linkage of the islands dispute and the talks about other issues more explicit when he announced, "When Vice Premier Qian (Qichen) meets with Foreign Minister Yukihiko Ikeda in New York, Japan should be clear that the Diaoyu Islands are an inseparable part of Chinese territory" (Kyodo News Service 1996b). Shen also made the linkage of the islands dispute and the Japan-us security treaty more explicit. Shen announced: "We hope the Japanese government can adopt a sensible attitude concerning this question [on the islands dispute]. From a historical perspective, what constitutes a threat of war in our region, I'm afraid, is no other country than Japan" (Kyodo News Service 1996b). According to Japanese analysts, "Shen was referring to an agreement between Japan and the United States last week on expanding defense ties to cover joint operations in regional crises (Kyodo News Service 1996b). At the bilateral talks themselves, Qian explicitly linked the Japanese inaction on reigning in the nationalist group and its lighthouse on the islands and China's territorial claim for the islands with regret over Hashimoto's visit to the war shrine and the renewal of the Japan-us defense security agreement, which China warned would cause anxiety if it was expanded (*Jiji Press* 1996).

Since China clearly lacked economic leverage, it instead used its military leverage by threatening force near the disputed islands in an attempt to influence Japanese economic policy. The issue linkage and coercive diplomacy used by China was successful overall. Japan's response to Qian's issue linkage at the bilateral talks held in New York was that Hashimoto would drop his plan to visit the shrine the following month and that the us joint declaration did not assume any third country as a threat (Agence France Presse 1996b). Ikeda also promised that the Japanese government would not approve the application of the nationalist group to make the disputed lighthouse an official navigational beacon (Chung 1998). Though the foreign ministers discussed the islands dispute at length during the meeting, they avoided any discussion of sovereignty. After the talks, a Japanese editorial in the conservative *Sankei* newspaper concluded that "the Chinese strategy against Japan has been outstandingly effective" and "the result would appear to be what the Chinese side has been seeking [concessions]. The Japanese government should draw lessons from such cunningness" (Agence France Presse 1996c). On November 25, Hashimoto and Chinese president Jiang Zemin agreed to repair bilateral relations and resume Japanese economic aid to China, with Jiang suggesting to shelve the territorial dispute again.

In May 1999, China once more used the dispute in a military confrontation in an attempt to compel Japan to reconsider aspects of the Japan-us security agreement by dispatching twelve Chinese warships to the islands immediately before the passage of a bill in Japan to implement the revised Japan-us Guidelines for Defense Cooperation. According to political analysts in Japan, "this incident is regarded to be an act of deterrence *in connection with the bills*" (BBC News 1999). Though the coercive diplomacy did not lead to a reconsideration of the defense guidelines, the Chinese were still successful in using the islands dispute deployment to signal to Japan China's discontent with the guidelines and to remind Japan of its military capabilities if need be. Even though China was willing to threaten force, they were also reluctant to use force to actually attempt to acquire the islands partly due to the Japanese-American bilateral security agreement (Drifte 2002).

Chinese-Japanese Bilateral Relations during Koizumi's Presidency in the 2000s

From 2001 to 2006, bilateral relations between China and Japan, led by nationalist prime minister Junichiro Koizumi, became heavily strained, mainly due to Koizumi's visits to the Yasukuni War Shrine and repeated dismissals of Chinese demands to halt such visits. In addition to the broadened rift between China and Japan over Koizumi's visits to the shrine, several other issues were disputed, making conditions ripe for Chinese issue linkage and coercive diplomacy and unwillingness to consider settlement of the dispute. After a number of controversial visits of Koizumi and other top-ranking government officials to the Yasukuni Shrine, Chinese leaders made a decision to link the visits, along with several other disputed issues, to the territorial dispute through issue linkage and coercive diplomacy, starting in early 2004.

The year 2004 was by far the most difficult year for Chinese-Japanese relations in recent history. The islands dispute was used by China on a number of occasions as bargaining leverage to influence other disputed issues. Chinese endorsement of activists attempting to land on the islands in March 2004 and the cancellation of bilateral talks scheduled a few days later about UNCLOS and maritime research in the East China Sea were the first of several forms of coercive diplomacy. The Japanese press interpreted the cancellation of the talks due to "growing concern that China's anger at Japan's detention of the seven activists could affect the bilateral diplomatic schedule, *including those not directly linked to the territorial dispute*" (Kyodo News Service 2004a; emphasis added).

The diplomatic provocation came at an ideal time to put pressure on Japan. Not only were talks scheduled on the East China Sea on March 30 and 31, but Japanese foreign minister Yoriko Kawaguchi was scheduled to visit Beijing April 3–4 for high-level bilateral talks. Prime Minister Koizumi admitted in a statement to the press that he was concerned that the arrest of the Chinese activists would have a negative effect on bilateral relations. The Chinese practically admitted the protest about the arrests was being used to put pressure on Japan. Vice Foreign Minister Dai Bingguo lodged an official protest to the Japanese ambassador the day after the arrests, demanding that Japan recognize how serious the issue over the arrested Chinese citizens was and warned that "this issue could be complicated and intensified to jeopardize Sino-Japanese relations. The serious outcomes from this would have to be borne by Japan" (Xinhua News Agency 2004a). This was followed by an official statement by Chinese Ambassador Wu Dawei to the Japanese Ministry of Foreign Affairs in Tokyo, in which Wu stated, "Should Japan cling obstinately to its own course and continue its moves to deteriorate China-Japan relations, Japan will be responsible for all consequences arising thereupon" (Xinhua News Agency 2004b).

At the April 3 meeting in Beijing between Kawaguchi and Chinese premier Wen Jiabao, Wen linked a number of bilateral issues together, including the territorial dispute, by reiterating the Chinese claim to the islands, urging Japanese leaders to halt visits to the Yasukuni Shrine, and indicating that continued visits not only hurt the feelings of the Chinese people but could also damage future bilateral relations overall. The Chinese government had not invited Koizumi to visit China since October 2001 because of his repeated visits to the shrine, despite Chinese objections. A Japanese editorial reacted by recognizing China's attempted issue linkage: "Beijing should stop trying to exploit the Yasukuni issue," and "making the Yasukuni visit a diplomatic issue, China is trying to use it as a bargaining chip in its dealings with Japan" (*Daily Yomiuri* 2004). Yet, it appears that the shrine visits were the key issue and that China was exploiting its territorial claim to link to the shrine visits, not the other way around.

Other troublesome issues, all related to China's fear of rising nationalism in Japan, were linked to the territorial dispute issue. Other issues cited at the meetings included Japan's support of Taiwanese independence, the dispatching of SDF troops in a noncombat mission to Iraq, and Koizumi's attempt to change Article 9 in the Japanese constitution (Faiola 2004). All of these issues were of great concern to China, particularly Japan's stance on Taiwan, which China considered as interference in a domestic issue. The Chinese government–approved landing of activists on the islands served not just as a signal to Japan about China's resolve in claiming the islands but also as a way to compel Japan to seriously reconsider a number of issues. Japan received the warnings on these other issues at the bilateral talks with Wen.

Another use of coercive diplomacy and issue linkage occurred in October 2004 when China dispatched four armed naval ships to the islands. The threat of force took place just weeks before bilateral talks were held in Beijing to discuss China's ongoing natural gas exploration in the East China Sea. There is little doubt the Chinese were signaling resolve to Japan partially to influence the talks. The talks, which lasted much longer than anticipated, ended in stalemate. Besides signaling resolve on the islands dispute, there were several reasons for the military confrontation by China. The first issue was ongoing talks on US military realignment in Japan and the two states' security alliance. On the day after the East China Sea talks were being held in Beijing, a senior-ranking Chinese military official, General Xiong Guangkai, met with Japanese vice minister Takemasa Moriya at the Japanese Defense Agency (JDA) in Tokyo, warning Japan to be cautious and judicious in its decisions about the role of the US military in the region. Moriya acknowledged China's implicit issue linkage and responded by protesting that Chinese navy ships had repeatedly entered Japan's EEZ area around the disputed islands without prior notice. Xiong also protested Japan's hosting of multilateral maritime exercises, which started the same day, involving Japan, the US, Australia, France, and eighteen other observer states. Finally, Xiong also expressed that China was opposed to Japan's development of a missile defense plan, which could destabilize the strategic balance in the region (BBC News 2004).

Only two weeks later, another incident occurred when a Chinese nuclear Han class submarine was sent to the waters near the islands. Just two days prior, on November 8, the JDA had announced three military scenarios to deal with China, indicating a strong warning to China that it was considered a serious threat to Japan. The first scenario dealt directly with the disputed islands and a potential Chinese attack on the islands by military force; the second scenario dealt with Chinese military occupation of marine gas fields in the East China Sea; the third scenario was a response to a Chinese attack on parts of Japan in a potential conflict over Taiwan, in order to prevent US forces in Japan from aiding Taiwan. The JDA report noted that while China was "cautious about using military force to solve international issues . . . it is likely that the Chinese Communist Party will go its own way to secure its sovereignty and territory as well as expand its interests in the sea" (Kin 2004). The Chinese Foreign Ministry responded to the report on November 9 by rejecting Japan's claims that China was a military threat. The next day, the Chinese submarine was found in Japanese waters. That same day, China's state-run media rebuffed the JDA report, calling it "full of imagination" and "clearly provocative," claiming that the report "is an attempt by Japan to intervene in the settlement of the Taiwan question and domestically legalize their claim of sovereignty over the Diaoyu Islands and territory in the East China Sea" (Kyodo News Service 2004b). According to Japanese military analysts, the foray of the Chinese submarine was perceived as a Chinese signal to project its growing naval power relative to Japan (T. Johnson 2005). For example, Hisahiko Okazaki, a Japanese security analyst, stated after the crisis that "China had artificially rekindled public hostility towards Tokyo," using the territorial dispute threat, in order to influence Japan's nationalist agenda (McCurry and Watts 2004, 14).

In April 2005, China again used issue linkage and coercive diplomacy, this time in more of an indirect way, by endorsing violent attacks on Japanese businesses in China and massive protests about the Diaoyu/Senkaku Islands. These were done in reaction to a decision by Tokyo to allow Japanese companies to explore for natural gas in disputed waters, which China called a serious provocation. The first of the other issues was the issuance of new Japanese history textbooks by the Japanese Ministry of Education that were said to whitewash Japan's wartime atrocities in China. The second reason for the protests was Japan's active bid for a permanent seat on the UN Security Council, prompting Chinese protesters to call for opposition to such a move and 27 million people to sign an online petition in China opposing the move. In the midst of the protests, Chinese premier Wen made the issue linkage explicit by calling on Japan to admit its wartime atrocities in China and reconsider its bid for a permanent seat on the UN Security Council. In his speech, Wen warned that the protests in China should make Japan reconsider its decision to seek the UN Security Council seat. This all occurred in the days right before the Japanese foreign minister was scheduled to visit Beijing. Meanwhile, amid all of these other issues, both states were skeptical of each other's military ambitions.

Just a few months later, another event occurred that provoked China to use issue linkage and diplomatic and militarized coercive diplomacy. To officially protest another visit by Koizumi to the Yasukuni Shrine in October 2005, China cancelled a visit by Japan's foreign minister and talks that were set to discuss potential joint exploration of natural gas reserves in disputed waters. In the weeks before, at the same time maritime border consultations were ongoing, China issued a threat of force by deploying five naval ships to the islands. The Chinese Foreign Ministry justified the establishment of the special naval reserve fleet as a right to protect China's territorial sovereignty (BBC News 2005; Drifte 2008a).

China-Japan relations scholar Reinhard Drifte (2008b) argues that the military threats were primarily aimed at influencing the upcoming talks on the territorial dispute and potential joint exploration of natural gas resources in the disputed waters, but it was also used to signal strong discontent at Koizumi's continued insistence that he had the right to visit the Yasukuni Shrine.

Japanese officials and politicians responded by protesting China's strategy of issue linkage and coercive diplomacy—what they called China's gunboat diplomacy tactic. The head of the Liberal Democratic Party (LDP) parliamentary group on marine resources criticized the Chinese strategy of coercive diplomacy and issue linkage: "The Chinese side has used military power to leverage their political situation. The squadron was an attack squadron [five naval ships deployed in September] and its purpose was quite clear—to strengthen against the Japanese position. This is really an unfortunate development, for it could lead to the kind of vicious cycle that descends into military conflict" (*Economist* 2005). Retired US Navy rear admiral Eric McVadon, a former military attaché in Beijing, agreed that the Chinese were using the ship deployment as a means to gain leverage: "They were saying to the Japanese, 'We used to be inferior to you. Now we have to be taken seriously'" (Carly and Kashiwagi 2006). Then just a week later, Koizumi visited the Yasukuni Shrine, enflaming China further, leading to the cancellation of talks on the territorial waters. The tit-for-tat actions of each state demonstrate the attempts by both states to provoke the other in their larger relationship by using the territorial dispute in attempts to gain leverage. As the claimant state that could take control of the islands away from Japan, China was able to signal its frustrations and attempt to compel change in policy and actions by using the territorial dispute threats as bargaining leverage.

Reduced Tensions

After Koizumi left office as Japanese prime minister in September 2006, replaced by Shinzo Abe and then Yasuo Fukada in September 2007, Sino-Japanese relations improved significantly, allowing the two states to work toward the May 2008 friendship treaty and June 2008 joint natural gas agreement in the East China Sea. Under Abe, Japan sought to mend its relations with China, with Abe visiting China as his first official trip (traditionally it was to the US), which led to an agreement to accelerate talks on the dispute in the East China Sea. Talks that led to the June 2008 joint gas development agreement began in December 2006. Chinese premier Wen followed suit by visiting Japan in April 2007 as part of the thawing between the two states. In June 2008, the two states agreed to the "Principled Consensus on the East China Sea Issue," in which they agreed to joint exploration and development of oil and maritime resources in the waters outside the disputed waters near the islands. This level of cooperation was unprecedented, though it has put the islands dispute on the back burner. This implies that the two states will not seek to resolve the actual territorial dispute anytime immediately. At the same time, if China is satisfied with its level of cooperation with Japan on other issues, China may no longer have the need to continue its claim for the islands if it cannot use the dispute to gain bargaining leverage against Japan.

In the dozen or so talks held to negotiate the joint gas development agreement, China was careful to insist it would *not* work toward settling the actual territorial dispute. A China expert from the International Crisis Group's East Asia program notes: "the Chinese have been proceeding with a more pragmatic approach because they want to continue their economic growth. But the Senkaku Islands issue has not been resolved, and the problem could actually deepen" (Miks 2007, 5). Though the recent thawing of Sino-Japanese relations has made observers more optimistic, the existence of the territorial dispute will continue to act as a thorn for China and Japan.

There was some concern that Sino-Japanese relations would not be so positive when Taro Aso came into power in Japan in September 2008. This concern was due to Aso's record of tough talk on Japan's wartime history, shrine visits, and determination to make Japan a stronger state, yet that was not the case. Japan's next prime minister, Yukio Hatoyama, continued to work toward improving Sino-Japanese relations, promising not to visit the controversial war shrines, promoting an East Asian community, modeled after the EU, with the idea that China and Japan would essentially share the leadership, and specifically attempting to persuade China's leadership to break a deadlock over the agreement on joint oil exploration in the East China Sea made in June 2008 (*Japan Times Online* 2010a). China, however, was wary of Hatoyama's plan for the East Asian community, particularly due to their longstanding adversarial relationship and China's intention to be the most powerful state in the region. None of this will come to fruition, though, since Hatoyama resigned due to a controversy over US military bases in Okinawa and was replaced by Naoto Kan in June 2010.

As a result of the reduced tensions, Chinese confrontations of Japan stopped after 2006. However, since 2008, there have been a number of incidents, including the deployment of Chinese warships entering Japanese waters on the way to the Pacific Ocean, Chinese submarines running on the surface, Chinese coast guard ships patrolling near the islands, and fighter plane dogfights in 2009 when two Chinese J10A fighter planes chased three Japanese F2 fighter planes in the area of the disputed islands (*Surface Forces* 2010). Most recently, a unilateral announcement by Japan to explore the East China Sea for seabed resources and rare metals has riled China (*Japan Times Online* 2010b), which could provoke Chinese leaders to shift gears on cooperation with Japan in the East China Sea. The latest clash over the arrest of a fishing captain and the planned US-Japanese joint maneuvers in 2010 has created the largest rift in Sino-Japanese relations since 2004, threatening to put a hold on further talks related to the 2008 plans for natural gas exploration and exploitation.

CONCLUSIONS

Despite the agreement by China and Japan to jointly develop natural gas re-sources in waters outside of the disputed zone in 2008, China continues to press its territorial claim of the Senkaku/Diaoyu Islands. China's confrontations with Japan were only partially a result of promoting Chinese nationalism through domestic mobilization, while it appears that the overall lack of Chinese at-tempts at sovereignty negotiations or other dispute resolution methods was not due to domestic accountability since there was no variation in this strategy. In terms of value of territory, ownership of the islands provides the owner with ac-cess to what is suspected to be an immense amount of economic resources in the waters around the islands. Though Japan has implied willingness to divide maritime resources with China, Chinese leaders have been unwilling to offer or accept territorial concessions or drop the territorial claim. Even without the other types of value such as homeland territory, permanent population, strate-gic value, or ethnic value, all of which make territory more valuable, China has not once attempted to discuss territorial concessions. At the same time, China has issued diplomatic and militarized threats and uses of force on several oc-casions against Japan, which are generally correlated with ethnic or strategic value or more salient territory. Yet, economic value should make the dispute more tenable to compromise and settlement, which has not happened in this dispute.

Though no Chinese leader would likely admit it, the conclusion of this study is that even if China can benefit eventually from the economic gains from oil deposits near the islands, the Chinese government does not necessarily want to settle the dispute anytime in the near future. Over the years, different Chinese leaders have been able to effectively use the Senkaku/Diaoyu Islands dispute as bargaining leverage against Japan to compel it to reconsider other disputed issues through the use of issue linkage and coercive diplomacy. This should not be surprising since "Chinese policymakers have prioritized economic development and modernization over sovereignty" (Hagstrom 2005, 161). By using the territorial dispute as bargaining leverage, China has been able to effectively compel Japan to shift its policies or actions on economic issues, as well as culturally sensitive issues such as leaders' visits to the Yasukuni War Shrine and security concerns like the Japan-us security pact and the potential use of Japanese troops in foreign conflicts. The vast majority of the instances of coercive diplomacy were linked by the Chinese government to other disputed issues. By threatening Japan diplomatically at times, but mostly through militarized threats of force, the Chinese government has been able to link the territorial dispute with other disputed issues to compel a change in Japan's policies or actions regarding the other disputed issues. The findings of this study have demonstrated that on many occasions Chinese leaders have applied the dual strategy of issue linkage and coercive diplomacy and have succeeded, therefore benefiting from the strategy and the endurance of the territorial dispute.

China's current strategy to negotiate with Japan over joint development of natural gas and oil resources outside the disputed zone seems to be the most rational strategy it can take in the dispute. Rather than dropping its territorial claim, China continues to maintain its claim for sovereignty, while at the same time benefiting from joint development of natural gas resources. By maintaining the territorial claim, China also sustains its ability to confront Japan through diplomatic and militarized conflict when other disputed issues arise. In this way, China can benefit from both joint development of some natural gas resources and simultaneously benefit from using a strategy of issue linkage and coercive diplomacy to signal resolve and achieve bargaining leverage in other disputed issue areas if they arise.

Since the maintenance of the territorial claim has low costs for China, there seems to be little incentive for China to drop its territorial claim unless Chinese leaders decide that relations have improved significantly enough that there are no longer any other disputed issues with Japan that are significant enough to link to the territorial dispute. Continued improved relations may depend on the potential of a joint economic community shared by China and Japan. Based on the findings of this research, the likelihood of China dropping its territorial claim and ending its diplomatic and militarized confrontations of Japan is relatively feasible if bilateral relations continue to improve. Since bilateral relations have improved significantly in the past few years, China may be willing to attempt settlement since the benefit of coercive diplomacy and issue linkage has limited, if any, purpose now. In this way, the costs of maintaining the territorial claim and diplomatic or militarized conflict with Japan may become higher than the benefits of using the islands dispute to gain bargaining leverage in other disputed issues with Japan. At the same time, it may be more feasible for China to not attempt settlement and continue the status quo in which both states jointly benefit from exploitation of oil resources near the islands without any Chinese confrontations. In this case, both sides, but particularly China, could save face. However, since China has continued some recent confrontations, such an arrangement may not be feasible. Until Chinese leaders come to the conclusion that there are no longer any significant disputed issues with Japan and, more importantly, that the likelihood of other disputed issues is significantly reduced now that bilateral relations have improved so much, it is likely that the dispute will continue to endure. Unfortunately for Japan, Chinese leaders will continue to maintain some degree of leverage until the dispute is resolved in finality.

CHAPTER SIX

The Shebaa Farms Border Dispute

The Lebanese-Israeli border is one of the most militarized and conflict-prone borders in the world. "Inhabited by Syrians, occupied by Israelis, and claimed by Lebanese," the hotly disputed Shebaa Farms "form the centerpiece of one of the Middle East's most intractable border disputes" (Butcher 2005, 12). For two states that lack diplomatic relations (Lebanon does not recognize the state of Israel), they have many regular interactions, not by choice but because of their proximity and contiguity. Though the border between Lebanon and Israel was determined in the 1949 armistice agreement at the end of the first Arab-Israeli war, Israel's 1978 invasion into Lebanon and the twenty-two-year occupation of south Lebanon provided the conditions for Lebanon—and the militant group Hezbollah—to claim territory and demand liberation of the occupied sovereign territory. Israel thought all territorial claims would be settled once its military withdrew from south Lebanon in the summer of 2000. However, the Lebanese government and Hezbollah leaders immediately claimed that a small piece of territory, Shebaa Farms, was Lebanese territory that Israel still occupied. Despite a decision by the UN that the disputed territory is actually Syrian territory occupied by Israel as part of the Golan Heights, Lebanon has continued to press the territorial claim, allowing the nonstate actor Hezbollah to engage in threats and uses of force against Israel. Since 2000, there have been numerous armed clashes on the border near Shebaa Farms pursued by Hezbollah, one of which escalated into the Israeli war against the group in the summer of 2006.

This territorial dispute shares many common features with other disputes, but the major difference here is that a nonstate actor, the militant group Hezbollah, has acted as the major player in the dispute, not the Lebanese government. Though the Lebanese government is the official claimant and challenger to Israel's occupation of the Shebaa Farms territory, and the UN has asserted that the territory is Syrian, neither Lebanon nor Syria has pursued threats or uses of armed conflict in the dispute. Rather, in the earlier years of the dispute, which began only in the summer of 2000, the Lebanese government allowed Hezbollah to pressure Israel on the border dispute instead of involving its own army in a potentially dangerous clash with the Middle East's strongest military. The Syrian government has not made any separate claim to Shebaa Farms apart from its larger claim of the Golan Heights, occupied by Israel since the summer of 1967. Instead, Syria has supported the actions of Hezbollah, through financial, political, and military support. In this way, Syria has been able to use Hezbollah to pressure Israel without the Syrian military having to confront the Israeli military directly. Syria is therefore involved because of its backing of Hezbollah, but also because the UN claims that the Shebaa Farms is part of the Israeli-occupied Syrian Golan Heights, a much larger and significant territorial dispute.

Unlike the other disputes studied in this book, the Shebaa Farms dispute is complicated because it involves actions and decisions by three major players—the Lebanese government, the official claimant and challenger state; Hezbollah, a nonstate actor that acted as the major player in the dispute; and Syria, which influences Lebanese politics and is the rightful claimant state according to the UN. The dispute is not just a dispute between Lebanon and Israel. Therefore, this chapter is different in that in addition to examining why the Lebanese government has not attempted settlement of this dispute, it also studies why Hezbollah pursued threats and uses of force in the territorial dispute. This chapter provides a test for whether the theory of bargaining leverage and the alternative explanations for territorial dispute strategies still hold for nonstate actors who pursue threats and uses of force.

Though Lebanon issued a number of diplomatic threats to Israel regarding the disputed territory, it has been Hezbollah that engaged in threats and uses of force against Israel, with clear support from the Lebanese government until 2006. Since the end of the 2006 war, there has been no militarized action on the border, with the Lebanese Army stepping up and taking control of the border area, and Hezbollah stepping back and refraining from threats and uses of force. The question here is why Hezbollah as a nonstate actor pursued numerous threats and uses of force and why the Lebanese government has continued to press the territorial claim and not attempted settlement of the dispute. A review of the interactions between Hezbollah and the Israeli army, the Lebanese claim, domestic factors in Lebanon, and the value of the disputed territory all suggest that Hezbollah pursued threats and uses of force in order to gain bargaining leverage in other disputed issues and that the Lebanese government has deliberately avoided attempted settlement to allow for such bargaining gains. Though indirect, it seems that the Lebanese government was unwilling during the first half of the dispute years to consider any attempted settlements through territorial concessions while Hezbollah was actively engaging the Israeli military since several of Hezbollah's goals mirrored goals of the Lebanese government. Therefore, the Lebanese government had little incentive to attempt settlement since both actors, as well as Syria, were benefiting from the ongoing territorial dispute. Throughout the dispute, major factions in the Lebanese government have pursued policies that were pro-Syrian, making it likely that Lebanese decisions on Shebaa Farms were linked to Syria's preferences as well.

Until the Shebaa Farms dispute is resolved, it will continue to remain a thorn for Israel and a weapon for Lebanon, Syria, and Hezbollah. In a 1985 book on the Lebanese-Israeli border, one scholar noted that the frontier problems, "if not adequately addressed by an adequate Lebanese-Israeli arrangement, can be expected to arise again" (Hof 1985, 2). A quarter century later, the disputed border continues to spell trouble for Lebanon, Syria, and Israel. The consequences of this dispute are enormous. In 2001, Timur Goksel, former United Nations Interim Forces in Lebanon (UNIFIL) officer and expert on south Lebanon stated that the dispute was "a very dangerous situation. The Shebaa Farms is definitely a potential ignition point. Escalation is very possible" (Blanford 2001b, 8). Five years later in July 2006, war erupted between Hezbollah and Israel, resulting in the deaths of almost a thousand Lebanese civilians and dozens of Israeli civilians. Thousands more Lebanese and hundreds of Israelis were injured. The damage to property in Lebanon and northern Israel was extensive, costing hundreds of millions dollars. Additionally, the existence of the dispute continues to allow Hezbollah a justification for its armed movement against Israel along the border and reason not to disarm, as required by UN Resolution 1701. In recent years, the US and Israel have recognized the Shebaa Farms dispute "as a potential key to stabilizing the last frontline in the Arab-Israeli conflict" (Blanford 2008, 6). An Israeli scholar who has studied Shebaa Farms agrees: "Even problems that are viewed as micro-level conflicts have, in some cases, macro implications for the security of the region. The Shebaa farms controversy is one such case" (A. Kaufman 2004, 37). The little town of Ghajar, which is split between Lebanon and the Israeli-occupied Golan Heights, and Shebaa Farms could be considered "the epicenter of one of the world's most dangerous strategic games" (Radin 2002). Negotiations on Ghajar are ongoing, but no attempts have been made to settle the Shebaa Farms dispute.

SHEBAA FARMS

The Shebaa Farms territory is a twelve-square-mile area made up of fourteen farms at the southwestern foothills of Mount Hermon. The fact that this dispute is over such a tiny parcel of territory and that such militarized conflict has occurred as a result of this dispute suggests that either the territory is valuable, no matter the size, or that states and nonstate actors can use even the smallest amount of disputed territory to gain bargaining leverage or domestic mobilization. The disputed territory, which is only about 5.5 miles long and 1.5 miles wide, is nestled between the Lebanese town of Shebaa and the Israeli-occupied Syrian Golan Heights. Ten of the farms are no longer inhabited since the residents fled to Lebanese villages when they were expelled from their homes by Israel occupation in 1967. Lebanese residents of the four other farms currently live under Israeli occupation. Israel considers the residents as Syrians, though they claim Lebanese nationality (Fisk 2000). The area around Shebaa Farms is historically best known as the site where Abraham received his divine covenant from God as written in the Old Testament (Mitnick and Blanford 2006).

During the Ottoman Empire, Lebanese families owned the farms, but there was no need to identify with a larger entity like Palestine, Lebanon, or Syria, none of which were yet states. It was only at the end of World War I, when the British and French took over the former Ottoman territories in the Levant region, that the idea of a border dividing these three territories into states came about. Shebaa Farms fell right along the British- and French-drawn border; some maps showed it in Lebanon, while most maps showed it in Syria despite the Lebanese ownership of the farms. The eventual division of Lebanon and Palestine began its course in the Sykes-Picot Agreement of 1916, in which the French and British determined the division of the Ottoman Empire's territorial possessions. The border lines determined by Sykes-Picot shifted slightly by 1918 when the French and British created actual military occupation zones. After several years of negotiations, the border was officially set as part of the Anglo-French convention of March 1923, taking its final form in April 1924. As Hof notes, "the presumably simple process of drawing a line between two territorially insignificant states, had, in fact, been an extraordinarily ardu-

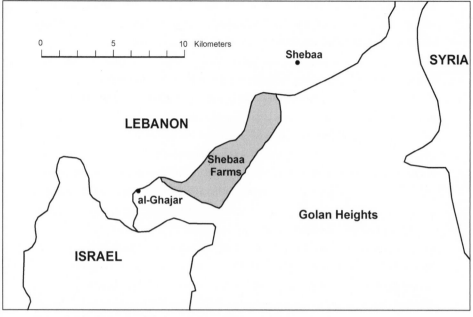

Figure 2. The location of Shebaa Farms. Map by Jie Tian.

ous endeavor involving the machinations of two major actors and their clients"
(Hof 1985, 3).

The border that evolved out of the negotiations resulted from a compromise between the British, pressured by Zionists to extend the territory of Palestine northward, and the French, pressured by Lebanese Christian nationalists to extend the territory of Lebanon southward. The 1920 compromise called
for the boundary to be set just a few miles north of the Sykes-Picot line, but to
turn north in the eastern part of the boundary, in order to include the north-
ernmost Jewish settlements and the Hula Valley (Hof 1985).[1] In December 1920,
the British accepted the French proposal for the Lebanon-Palestine boundary
in entirety, which led to the creation of a commission that would demarcate the
actual boundary. The demarcation agreement, signed in February 1922, was ratified in March 1923. However, the final agreement "left subject to possible rene-
gotiation" a short part of the border between Metulla and Banias, "half of which
was part of the Palestine-Lebanon boundary and half of which divided Palestine and Syria." According to the agreement, "The British Government shall
be free to reopen the question of readjusting the frontier between Banias and

Metallah on such terms as may be agreed between the two mandatory Powers with a view of making the north road between these two villages the final frontier" (Hof 1985, 13–14).

In the years between the 1923 border demarcation and the 1949 armistice agreement between Lebanon and the newly created state of Israel, the residents of the farms considered themselves to be a part of Lebanon, paying taxes to the Lebanese government, even though French maps showed the farms to be located in Syria. Residents conducted legal and administrative affairs in Lebanese cities, not Syrian cities. Though this practice was recognized by French officers in the area, no actions were taken to resolve the discrepancy surrounding Shebaa Farms (A. Kaufman 2004). Because the French controlled both Syria and Lebanon, the mandate government did not take an official position on the confusion of the exact border around Shebaa Farms. In March 1949, at the end of the first Arab-Israeli war, a General Armistice Agreement was signed by Lebanon and Israel, leaving the two states in a technical state of war, but declaring the armistice as the penultimate step toward peace. Israeli troops withdrew from parts of south Lebanon that they had occupied during the war, pulling back to the Armistice Demarcation Line, which mirrored the 1923 international boundary between Lebanon and Palestine (Hof 1985). Syria claims to have ceded the farms to Lebanon in the 1950s, but the agreement was never formally ratified, so there is no legal evidence of this territorial cession. Because of a lack of Lebanese political rule in the farms, Syria took administrative control for the residents, which continued until the 1967 Arab-Israeli war (A. Kaufman 2004).

Further confusion about the actual border arose as a result of the June 1967 Arab-Israeli war, when Israel occupied the Syrian Golan Heights, which purportedly included the Shebaa Farms area. Regarding Lebanon, Israel claimed the 1949 armistice agreement to be null and void due to Arab aggression. Despite the lack of hostilities between Lebanon and Israel in the war, Israel claimed that Lebanon was a legal participant in the war. The real reason was likely because Israel could not claim the armistice agreements, which included practically the same language, invalid with Syria, Egypt, and Jordan, but not Lebanon (Hof 1985).

After the 1967 war, south Lebanon became a launching ground for Palestinian insurgents and terrorists to conduct cross-border attacks on Israeli soldiers and civilians. By the late 1970s, Israel's patience had been tried, and it was ready to take the offensive to go after the Palestinians in the south of Lebanon.

In a military campaign called Litani Operation, Israel launched an invasion of Lebanon on March 14, 1978, involving eight thousand Israeli soldiers marching north to the Litani River in south Lebanon. The invasion was strongly condemned by the international community due to the thousands of Lebanese civilians killed and injured and Israel's disregard for Lebanon's sovereignty. The UN Security Council adopted Resolution 425, calling for the immediate and full withdrawal of Israeli forces from Lebanon and the reestablishment of Lebanese control over *all Lebanese territory*. By June 1978, Israeli forces had withdrawn, leaving the UNIFIL to maintain peace at the border.

The more severe and longer-term invasion of Lebanon occurred in June 1982. Initially called Operation Pines, the campaign was later labeled Peace for the Galilee Operation and eventually became known in Israel as the Lebanon War. As in 1978, Israel's invasion of Lebanon was retaliation for Palestinian attacks, but this time Israel sought destruction of the Palestine Liberation Organization (PLO) in Beirut, so Israeli forces went all the way to the capital. By January 1985, Israel decided to withdraw most of its forces to the Lebanese-Israeli border, creating what Israel labeled a security zone in the south of Lebanon. As one scholar notes, "The holding of the Security Zone became the basis of Israel's security policy in Lebanon up to the final withdrawal in May 2000. This gave birth to a host of problems: for one thing, Israel never officially laid out the principles of its security doctrine regarding the Security Zone, and the area's borders were never properly charted" (Blum 2007, 197). Additionally, Israel denied its status as an occupying force, claiming its military was present in the south of Lebanon for defensive reasons only.

From 1992 to 2000, Hezbollah's militia had primarily fought Israeli ground troops in the occupied area of south Lebanon and launched rocket attacks into northern Israel, claimed as retaliation for Israeli attacks in Lebanon. When Israel finally withdrew in May 2000, Hezbollah claimed victory and was praised all throughout Lebanon for defeating the Israeli occupation of south Lebanon. Hezbollah's victorious status was difficult to deny: "Israel pulled out of southern Lebanon without conditions mainly because of the repeated blows it suffered from Hizballah. No Arab army had ever achieved such a victory—forcing Israel out of Arab territory unconditionally, without having to comply with Israeli demands for a settlement or a peace treaty" (Zisser 2006, 89). The liberation of the security zone immediately became the justification and motivation for an armed resistance against Israel, which would last until May 2000, when Israel withdrew from south Lebanon. That same month, Lebanon and Syria (and unofficially Hezbollah) refused to acknowledge that Resolution 425 had been implemented, meaning that Israel had not yet withdrawn from all occupied Lebanese territory. Lebanon rejected the UN demarcation of the official Lebanese-Israeli border, called the Blue Line, claiming that a small piece of territory, Shebaa Farms, was Lebanese and still occupied by Israel.

DISPUTE STRATEGIES

Between May 2000 and December 2008, Lebanon and Hezbollah confronted Israel on twenty-seven occasions, listed in table 6.[2] The Lebanese government confronted Israel diplomatically three times, relying on Hezbollah to act on their behalf as a proxy army using limited military force in the remaining twenty-four threats and uses of force. Hezbollah's militarized threats involved the use of antiaircraft missiles aimed at Israeli military aircraft, ground operations that had directly targeted Israeli soldiers at their bases or during patrol in the disputed territory, including capturing them as bargaining chips to use in negotiations for the release of Lebanese prisoners in Israel, and rocket attacks on Israeli military bases in northern Israel. From 2000 to 2006, Hezbollah fighters fought Israeli ground troops and the Israeli-sponsored South Lebanese Army (SLA), consisting of Lebanese working for the Israeli military, and launched rocket attacks into the occupied area of south Lebanon and occasionally into northern Israel. Throughout the resistance against the Israeli occupation of south Lebanon, Hezbollah officials openly admitted to having coordinated very closely with Syria (Norton 2000). Hezbollah continued its resistance against Israel by taking over control of south Lebanon after the Israeli withdrawal and working towards acquiring the disputed Shebaa Farms territory.

The dispute was born just weeks before the Israeli withdrawal from the south of Lebanon in May 2000, when the Lebanese government issued an official claim for Shebaa Farms on May 4, backed immediately by the Syrian government. In an overnight mission, the Israeli military pulled out of Lebanon for good on May 24, 2000. Israel's decision to withdraw from the security zone in south Lebanon resulted from a pledge in 1999 by the new Israeli Labour leader Ehud Barak to withdraw Israeli troops from Lebanon. As part of this decision, Barak approached Syria to discuss a potential peace agreement, which would lead to a parallel agreement with Lebanon, since Syria still heavily influenced Lebanese politics. Syria rejected Israeli negotiations with Lebanon "until progress on its own negotiation with Israel secured the Golan Heights" (Blum 2007,

Table 6.   Lebanese and Hezbollah diplomatic and militarized confrontations, 2000–2008

DATE	TYPE	LEBANESE/HEZBOLLAH ACTION	LINKED ISSUE
May 2000	Diplomatic	Official claim of sovereignty made to United Nations by Lebanon	Pressure Arab-Israel peace process; demand for Israel to release Lebanese prisoners
May 2000	Militarized	Hezbollah attacked Israeli army post in Shebaa Farms	Justification for continuation of armed resistance movement against Israel
October 2000	Militarized	Hezbollah attacked Israeli army post; captured 3 Israeli soldiers	Pressure for Israel to release Lebanese prisoners; assist Palestinians in renewed uprising; retaliation for Israeli killing of 12-year-old Palestinian boy in Gaza Strip
November 2000	Militarized	Hezbollah attacked Israeli soldiers using roadside bombs; 1 Israeli soldier killed and 2 others injured	Support of Palestinians in 2-month revolt against Israel
February 2001	Militarized	Hezbollah killed 1 Israeli soldier in border ambush	Ninth anniversary of Israeli assassination of Hezbollah leader Sheikh Abbas al-Moussawi
April 2001	Militarized	Hezbollah attacked Israeli army post; 1 Israeli soldier killed	Support for Palestinians in Gaza Strip and West Bank; Syrian pressure on Israel to withdraw from Golan Heights
May 2001	Militarized	Hezbollah attacked Israeli army post	Syrian pressure on Israel to withdraw from Golan Heights
July 2001	Militarized	Hezbollah attacked Israeli army post	Pressure for Israel to release Lebanese prisoners
October 2001	Militarized	Hezbollah attacked Israeli army post	Pressure for Israel to release Lebanese prisoners
April 2002	Militarized	Hezbollah attacked Israeli army posts; 4 Israeli soldiers wounded	Support of Palestinian *intifada* in West Bank; attempt to distract Israeli from West Bank military operations; pressure Israel to halt reconnaissance flights over Lebanon
August 2002	Militarized	Hezbollah attacked Israeli army posts	Pressure for Israel to release Lebanese prisoners
January 2003	Militarized	Hezbollah attacked Israeli army posts	Pressure for Israel to release Lebanese prisoners
August 2003	Militarized	Hezbollah attacked Israeli army posts	Retaliation for Israeli car-bombing assassination of Hezbollah security official in Beirut, Lebanon
October 2003	Militarized	Hezbollah attacked Israeli army posts	Retaliation for Israeli air strikes on alleged training camps for Palestinian militants in Syria

Table 6. (*continued*)

DATE	TYPE	LEBANESE/HEZBOLLAH ACTION	LINKED ISSUE
January 2004	Militarized	Hezbollah fired missile at Israeli bulldozer; 1 Israeli soldier killed	No issue linkage stated; Israeli bulldozer inadvertently crossed border into Lebanese territory
March 2004	Militarized	Hezbollah attacked IDF posts	Retaliation for Israeli assassination of senior official of Hamas in Gaza
May 2004	Militarized	Hezbollah attacked Israeli troops patrolling border and Israeli army posts	Pressure negotiations for prisoner exchange between Lebanon and Israel
June 2004	Militarized	Hezbollah attacked Israeli army posts	No issue linkage stated
July 2004	Militarized	Exchange of fire across border; 2 Israeli soldiers killed	No issue linkage stated
May 2005	Militarized	Hezbollah attacked Israeli army posts	No issue linkage stated
June 2005	Militarized	Hezbollah attacked Israeli army posts; 1 Israeli soldier killed	Hezbollah attempt to kidnap Israeli soldiers to use as bargaining chips for release of Lebanese prisoners
November 2005	Militarized	Hezbollah attacked IDF post; 1 Israeli soldier killed	Hezbollah attempt to kidnap Israeli soldiers
February 2006	Militarized	Hezbollah attacked Israeli army posts	Hezbollah attempt to kidnap Israeli soldiers; retaliation for Israeli killing of 17-year-old Lebanese shepherd found in Shebaa Farms
May 2006	Militarized	Hezbollah attacked Israeli army posts	Hezbollah attempt to kidnap Israeli soldiers; retaliation for car-bombing assassination of Palestinian Islamic Jihad official in Sidon, Lebanon
July 2006	Militarized	Hezbollah attacked Israeli army posts; Hezbollah seized 2 Israeli soldiers and killed 9 others	Kidnapping of Israeli soldiers to use as bargaining chips for release of Lebanese prisoners
October 2006	Diplomatic	Lebanese government threatened to resume military campaign using Hezbollah to liberate Shebaa Farms	Pressure Israel to demine cluster bombs, halt Israeli violations of Lebanese airspace, and release Lebanese prisoners
July 2007	Diplomatic	Official claim of sovereignty by Lebanon	Pressure Israel to demine cluster bombs, halt Israeli violations of Lebanese airspace, and release Lebanese prisoners

200). Despite Syria's refusal to allow Lebanon to negotiate a peace agreement with Israel, Barak made a unilateral decision to withdraw the Israeli troops by June 2000, "partly to lean on Syria, which saw a unilateral Israeli withdrawal as a threat to its future capacity to conduct its proxy war in Lebanon" (Blum 2007, 200). In March 2000, the Israeli cabinet approved Barak's proposal to withdraw from Lebanon, preferably through an agreement with Lebanon, otherwise unilaterally. Lebanon responded by stating that it would only negotiate with Israel if Israel also withdrew from the Syrian Golan Heights, helped to solve the problem of the more than three hundred thousand Palestinian refugees located in Lebanon, and agreed to fully withdraw from the south of Lebanon, including Shebaa Farms, which were claimed by Lebanon on May 4, weeks before the actual withdrawal occurred (Prados 2001).

After the last Israeli soldier left the south of Lebanon on May 24, 2000, negotiations between Syria, Israel, and Lebanon were conducted by the UN to determine whether Israel had complied with the requirements of Resolution 425. The Lebanese government immediately confronted Israel diplomatically by issuing an official claim to the UN, stating that Israel's withdrawal was incomplete from Shebaa Farms, and therefore Resolution 425 was not met. Weeks before the Israeli withdrawal, on May 4, the Lebanese government issued a letter to UN secretary general Kofi Annan, requesting that the implementation of Resolution 425 required a withdrawal to the 1923 borders, including a withdrawal from Shebaa Farms. Ironically, the Lebanese chose to use a bargaining method used by Israel with the Palestinians in their territorial negotiations. Just as the Palestinians thought that they had achieved statehood as a result of the Oslo agreement, Israel produced detailed geographical proposals and modification, which almost completely halted the peace process (Fisk 2000). Lebanon came up with detailed geographical maps and documents in an attempt to prove that Israel had to withdraw from Shebaa Farms to comply with Resolution 425.

In a letter to Kofi Annan, supplemented with historic maps and documents, Lebanese prime minister Selim Hoss wrote: "It is clear and unequivocal that the farms of Shebaa are Lebanese. An Israeli pullout from these farms is an integral part of the application of Resolution 425, if not it would be incomplete" (Deutsche Presse-Agentur 2000b). After weeks of studying historic maps and documents, the UN demarcation team declared that the Shebaa Farms was Syrian territory, currently occupied by Israel as part of the Golan Heights. Despite Lebanese claims for Shebaa Farms, Annan announced to the Security Council on June 16, 2000, that Israel had effectively withdrawn to the line of withdrawal, as demarcated by the UN, meaning that Israel had complied with the resolution (UN Security Council 2001). Both Lebanon and Syria officially rejected the UN decision, arguing that Israel's withdrawal was incomplete in the area of Shebaa Farms and claiming the right to use all means possible, including force, against Israeli forces occupying the disputed territory (Prados 2001).

In addition to the official Lebanese government claim and Syrian support of the claim, the group Hezbollah backs the territorial claim almost to the point that it seems like Lebanon is backing Hezbollah's claim. Though Hezbollah is technically a nonstate actor, the group has acted at different times as a proxy army for the Lebanese government in its attempt to liberate Shebaa Farms from Israeli occupation. Not only did the Lebanese government endorse Hezbollah's role in pushing Israel out of Lebanon, but the Lebanese Armed Forces avoided going into the south of Lebanon until after the 2006 war, instead allowing Hezbollah to do their work for them. After the Israeli withdrawal in 2000, the Lebanese government deployed a small mixed force of only about a thousand military and police units to isolated parts of the south of Lebanon, allowing Hezbollah to take over and effectively control the remainder of the former Israeli security zone (Prados 2001). Former Lebanese defense minister Khalil Hrawi explained concisely the role of Hezbollah in Shebaa Farms: "They don't tell us and we don't know. The resistance can take action that a government can't. Our government does not want to look like it is doing something not accepted by law" (Schneider 2001, A13).

When asked in 2001 whether he should try to disarm Hezbollah, former prime minister Rafiq Hariri answered: "When we have peace, everybody will do their part. We in Lebanon are afraid of Israel. We are a small country. We don't have enough means to defend ourselves. . . . During the occupation, they [Hezbollah] were an important part of resisting the occupation. But I know that someday peace will come" (Weymouth 2001, B1). At the same time, when asked about whether he agreed with Hezbollah's claim on Shebaa Farms, Hariri responded by stating: "This is not the theory of Hezbollah; this is the theory of the Lebanese government. We believe it is Lebanese territory for sure" (Weymouth 2001, B1), indicating that Hezbollah was merely backing an already official claim by the Lebanese government. More recently, in the summer of 2006 when the war began, Lebanese prime minister Fouad Siniora officially described Hezbollah as a resistance movement rather than a militia, exempting the group from UN Security Council Resolution 1559, which requires all militias in Lebanon to disarm. Former senior UN official in South Lebanon Timur Goksel noted in 2006, "Hizbullah is part of the government and they have now put the government in a very awkward position" (Halpern and Blanford 2006, 1).

Hezbollah's backing of the Lebanese claim for Shebaa Farms is considered a major part of its resistance movement against Israel. Nawwaf al-Musawi, the official in charge of international relations in Hezbollah, stated most clearly Hezbollah's objective in Shebaa Farms:

> the resistance's task is primarily to continue working toward the liberation of Lebanese land that remains under occupation. Its second task is to defend Lebanon's sovereignty, land, and rights as was done when the resistance defended Lebanon's right to regain part of its waters in the al-Wazzani River. Its third task, as long as the Arab-Israeli conflict persists and as long as Lebanon is part of the comprehensive Arab identity, Hezbollah will adhere to its obligation and play its role within the framework of this conflict. Being part of Lebanon, Hezbollah is playing its role in this conflict. This is thus the three-pronged task of the resistance after the Israeli defeat. The course of operations in the Shab'a region must be understood in light of this three-pronged mission. (al-Haruji 2003)

After the withdrawal of the Israeli military from the south of Lebanon in 2000, Hezbollah focused on the liberation of Shebaa Farms, the release of Lebanese prisoners in Israel, and the potential future aggression of Israel against Lebanon. The Lebanese government officially endorsed Hezbollah's continued resistance against Israeli occupation of south Lebanon, recognizing it as a national resistance, not just representing Hezbollah's aspirations. Hezbollah was not only allowed to pursue guerilla activities in south Lebanon, but it was openly and officially supported as a legitimate organization pursuing what is perceived by the Lebanese government as a legitimate resistance to Israeli occupation of Shebaa Farms. As early as 1992, after the Taif Accords ended the Lebanese civil war, the Lebanese government had officially agreed to the idea that Hezbollah could continue its armed resistance against Israeli occupation of south Lebanon, and this endorsement continued until 2006. As Nawwaf al-Musawi noted in a 2003 interview, it is the Lebanese government that made the initial claim against Israel for Shebaa Farms. Al-Musawi also pointed out that the government "repeatedly announced the legitimacy of the right of resistance in working to retrieve that land" (al-Haruji 2003). Syrian officials also legitimated Hezbollah's continued resistance movement against Israel along the border region of the three states. Thus, initially it was both Syria's increasing political influence in Lebanon and Lebanese government approval that enabled Hezbollah to continue its resistance movement.

The first use of force by Hezbollah in the Shebaa Farms dispute occurred on May 22, 2000, two days before the Israeli withdrawal from the south of Lebanon, when Hezbollah attacked an Israeli army post in Shebaa Farms. The next attack occurred less than five months later on October 7, 2000, when Hezbollah guerillas captured three Israeli soldiers by attacking Israeli army posts with Katyusha rockets. Israel retaliated by threatening decisive action, with gunships shelling areas in south Lebanon, wounding ten Lebanese civilians. The crisis escalated to some degree when Israel deployed large numbers of troops and armaments to the northern border and Israeli flights over Beirut increased, leading to the Lebanese Army being put on full alert. Lebanese Speaker of the Parliament, Nabih Berri, stated in response to the Hezbollah attack: "Israel alone is responsible for the safety of its soldiers, not Lebanon or Syria. . . . The soldiers in question were on land that is not theirs and among people who are being oppressed, killed, displaced, and threatened" (Schneider 2000).

The third Hezbollah attack occurred the following month, in November 2000, when Hezbollah attacked the Israeli army using roadside bombs. In that attack, one Israeli soldier was killed and two others were injured. In retaliation, Israeli planes and artillery units shelled a border village and other targets in south Lebanon. In the year 2001, Hezbollah launched six attacks on Israeli army posts in the Shebaa Farms territory. The first attack was in February 2001 when Hezbollah fighters killed an Israeli soldier in an ambush along the border. After an April 2001 Hezbollah attack, resulting in the death of an Israeli soldier, the Israeli Air Force struck a Syrian radar station in Lebanon, killing four Syrian soldiers. The following month, in May 2001, Hezbollah again conducted an attack in Shebaa Farms, striking an Israeli army post. Two similar attacks occurred in July and October 2001, leading to retaliation by the Israeli army against Hezbollah.

In April 2002, over a two-week period, Hezbollah began daily mortar and rocket attacks on Israel Defense Forces (IDF) posts in Shebaa Farms, with four Israeli soldiers wounded. The attacks led to Israel responding with air strikes in Lebanon. Other attacks on Israeli army posts in Shebaa Farms occurred in August 2002 and January 2003. Later in August 2003, Hezbollah fired artillery at Israeli troops in Shebaa Farms, leading to Israeli fighter planes firing missiles at Hezbollah targets and Israeli helicopters flying missions over southern

Lebanon. As with the August strike, in October 2003, Hezbollah fired mortar shells and rockets at IDF positions in Shebaa Farms. The next Hezbollah attack in Shebaa Farms occurred in January 2004 when Hezbollah fired a missile at an Israeli bulldozer that crossed into Lebanese territory. In March and June 2004, Hezbollah attacked Israeli army posts in Shebaa Farms, and in May 2004, Hezbollah attacked Israeli troops patrolling the border, as well Israeli army posts. Tensions were ratcheted when in July 2004, an exchange of fire occurred across the disputed border, and two Israeli soldiers were killed. The following year in 2005, three attacks on Israeli army posts occurred, in May, June, and November. In the May incident, there were no casualties, but in the June incident, one Hezbollah fighter and one Israeli soldier were killed. In the November incident, three Hezbollah fighters and one Israeli soldier were killed. In 2006, Hezbollah attacked Israeli army posts in Shebaa Farms and elsewhere along the border on three occasions, in February, May, and July. It was the last attack, in July 2006 that led to the deaths of nine Israeli soldiers and provoked the massive Israeli offense against Hezbollah, leading to the 2006 war.

Israel's response to the abduction of two Israeli soldiers by Hezbollah was a full military offensive involving some seven thousand aerial bombings and missile strikes by Israel all over Lebanon, and a full-scale ground invasion of south Lebanon. Hezbollah retaliated by striking northern Israel with thousands of rocket strikes. Later evidence showed that Israel had been planning such an attack and that the abduction provided the perfect justification. In the thirty-four-day war, casualties included over a thousand Lebanese civilians, forty-two Israeli civilians, and dozens of Hezbollah fighters and IDF soldiers (Human Rights Watch 2007).[3] Israel's intention was to wipe out Hezbollah once and for all. Not only did the mission fail, but the war was a stalemate, and Hezbollah regrouped after the war and strengthened in size. The Winograd Commission in Israel, which investigated how Israel conducted the war, was strongly critical of the Israeli government. Since the summer of 2006, no further militarized threats or uses of force have been pursued by Hezbollah. Only the Lebanese government has pursued diplomatic threats since then.

VALUE OF TERRITORY

With regard to tangible value, the farms have no real economic value, especially since most of them are no longer inhabited or used by farmers. Prior to 1967, residents of the Lebanese town of Shebaa farmed in the disputed territory, and after Israeli occupation in 1967, Israel allowed Lebanese residents to harvest olives in the area every two years. Later, parts of the farms became a winter resort for Israelis (Prados 2001). There is no oil, water, or any other natural resource that makes the territory economically valuable. The territory itself is mostly arid and rocky terrain with limited arable land that was used in the past primarily for cattle to graze, olive groves, and growing lentils and wheat.

On the other hand, there is strategic value to some degree. The value of Shebaa Farms is indeed strategically important, not to Lebanon but to Israel. The Middle East's largest military observation post was built by Israel on the farms (Deutsche Presse-Agentur 2000a). For Lebanon, the strategic value was rooted in Hezbollah's ability to launch most of its attacks on the Israeli military from 2000 to 2006 in the Shebaa Farms area. Yet ownership of the territory by Lebanon would not provide any additional strategic value since Shebaa Farms is only a small portion of the Lebanese border that Hezbollah forces can use to attack Israel, making it less strategically significant.

Other tangible values would be mainland territory and a permanent population. Shebaa Farms is part of a mainland and not made up of offshore islands. There is a fairly permanent population, but it is very small, made up of only a handful of families that could easily be relocated. In terms of intangible value, despite claims by Lebanon and Hezbollah that the Shebaa Farms are valuable and part of the Lebanese homeland, besides the few Lebanese families living in the disputed territory, there are no strong ethnic links to the territory. More significantly, as discussed in the next section, there are limited nationalist and symbolic links to the territory in Lebanon.

Limitations of the Value of Territory Explanation

Since there is no economic value, this might explain the lack of incentive to attempt settlement, as previous studies have found. Yet the lack of economic value does not explain the frequent threats and uses of force. Therefore, it cannot be economic value that drives dispute strategies with regard to Shebaa Farms. The value of territory theory would predict that it is the strategic value of Shebaa Farms that makes the territory so valuable, therefore making Lebanon less likely to attempt settlement with Israel and more likely for Hezbollah to pursue threats and uses of force. Yet, without strategic value for Lebanon and Hezbollah, it cannot be strategic value that is driving dispute strategies. Therefore, the endurance of the Shebaa Farms territorial dispute cannot be explained by Lebanon's aspiration for territorial acquisition based on economic or strategic value. Since the territory lacks both tangible and intangible value, it is difficult to use these factors to explain dispute strategies.

DOMESTIC ACCOUNTABILITY AND MOBILIZATION

The domestic accountability theory would predict that in the years Lebanon was authoritarian, Lebanese leaders were unwilling to attempt settlement of the dispute in periods of democratization, domestic unrest, when levels of high authoritarianism existed, or recently after a coup. In the years Lebanon was a democracy, we should witness limited attempts at settlement the sooner an election is to be held and when the opposition in the Parliament is strong. In both cases, the idea is that such settlement would likely involve territorial concessions of land perceived as Lebanese given over to Israel, an arch enemy of Lebanon. Such concessions would lead to major dissatisfaction among the Lebanese public, who would then punish their leaders by demanding new elections or conducting massive protests, like those conducted in 2005 to 2008.

The domestic mobilization theory would predict that the Lebanese government would use the dispute to mobilize the domestic populace during times of domestic unrest and instability. Because Hezbollah is a nonstate actor, it is difficult to make certain predictions about Hezbollah's accountability to and mobilization of its constituents. However, since Hezbollah is a political party and therefore a political actor that wishes to remain in power, it would seem that Hezbollah would also be concerned with domestic accountability and mobilization with regard to its strategies in the Shebaa Farms dispute.

Lebanon is a mixed-type regime with some aspects of democracy and some aspects of authoritarianism. Though it is an electoral democracy and holds regular elections, there is some question as to the validity of the elections, and the same major clans and families are represented as candidates on party lists. Because of the weak consociational system, there are frequent disagreements within the government, leading to political crises, some of which led to civil war, others that have led to standstills, such as the 2007–8 crisis when there was no Lebanese president. The Polity IV score during the years of 2005–8 was 7, meaning that Lebanon was primarily democratic. Prior to 2005, Lebanon could be categorized as a transitional democracy, but under tight Syrian control.[4] Until the Syrian withdrawal of Lebanon in 2005, elections were tightly monitored and approved by the Syrian government, and the first democratic elections in Lebanon were held only in 2005. During the years of the dispute, there were no coup attempts, but there was domestic unrest, mainly in the first few months of 2002, when the Lebanese economy was falling apart, and in 2005, when millions of people marched in the Cedar Revolution to demand withdrawal of the Syrian military. In early 2002, during the economic crisis, there is evidence that Hezbollah did show some degree of restraint in the territorial dispute in order to avoid domestic accountability (Zisser 2006). A period of democratization also occurred in 2005. After democratization, elections were held in 2005, and the opposition has been strong since then. In the June 2009 elections, Hezbollah's bloc won fifty-seven seats, almost 45 percent of the total seats in the Parliament, making the bloc, the March 8 Alliance, just barely the opposition. Despite the variation in domestic factors, the Lebanese government has made no attempts at any time, regardless of domestic factors, to settle the dispute, nor to mobilize the public using the dispute.

Before the summer of 2000, Shebaa Farms was an unknown piece of territory for the Lebanese. During the Israeli occupation of Shebaa Farms in 1967, no mention was made in Lebanese newspapers (A. Kaufman 2002). According to Adib Farha, a former aide to Lebanese prime minister Fouad Siniora, "most Lebanese had never heard of it until Hizbullah brought it up in 2000" (Mitnick and Blanford 2006, 10). Since 2000, the disputed territory has been used for domestic mobilization to some degree, mainly by Hezbollah, but not the Lebanese government. A 2004 public opinion poll covering a sample of Lebanese from various religious sects and regions found that 70 percent of the population supported Hezbollah's continued resistance in Shebaa Farms (Beirut Research and Information Centre 2004). So the potential for Hezbollah's use of the disputed territory for mobilization purposes did exist at some point, primarily in the elections of 2000, when Hezbollah gained more seats in the Parliament as a result of riding the wave of success it was awarded after the Israeli withdrawal from south Lebanon. However, Hezbollah also pursued a use of force in May 2000 during the withdrawal, just a few months before an upcoming election in which it was participating, when they should have been least expected to do so due to domestic accountability. Since Hezbollah is not a state actor, it is difficult to accurately know whether upcoming elections influenced Hezbollah's decision to pursue a use of force against Israel.

Yet, when the war began in the summer of 2006, most Lebanese were furious that Hezbollah had dragged Lebanon into a war against Israel. Hezbollah did receive some public support for their fighting against the IDF, but it was short-lived. A public opinion poll taken at the end of July 2006 during the war reported that the majority of the Lebanese public, including Sunni Muslims, Christians, and Druze, supported Hezbollah's actions taken against Israel. Overall, 87 percent of the Lebanese population supported Hezbollah's actions, while 70 percent supported the initial capture of the Israeli soldiers. Among the different religious sects, 80 percent of Christians, 89 per cent of Sunnis, and 80 percent of Druze supported Hezbollah's actions against Israel (Beirut Research and Information Centre 2006). By the time Resolution 1701 was passed by the UN Security Council, calling for the disarmament of Hezbollah and Lebanese army control of southern Lebanon, the Lebanese public was primarily in favor of the resolution. Hezbollah could therefore attempt to mobilize only its own supporters using Shebaa Farms, not the general public. On the contrary, there was some degree of accountability to deal with rather than effective mobilization. Hezbollah sought other means to mobilize its constituents domestically after 2006, mainly with regard to improved conditions, infrastructure, and other domestic issues.

Limitations of the Domestic Accountability and Mobilization Explanations

Overall, though there was significant variation in domestic factors regarding unrest, democratization, timing of elections, and a strong opposition in the Parliament, there has been no variation in Lebanese attempts to settle the dispute. Hezbollah, as a political party, was able to mobilize domestic support to some degree using the Shebaa Farms dispute, but not enough that mobilization would be the driving factor in its dispute strategies and decisions to threaten and use force against Israel. Since neither the Lebanese government nor Hezbollah could consistently use the Shebaa Farms dispute to mobilize domestic support, domestic accountability cannot explain the endurance of the dispute. At the same time, domestic accountability likely played an influential role in Hezbollah's halting of militant attacks in Shebaa Farms and elsewhere along the border since Hezbollah was so severely criticized for provoking the 2006 war, leading to mass destruction and significant deaths of noncombatants in Lebanon.

BARGAINING LEVERAGE

By pursuing a strategy of coercive diplomacy and issue linkage, both the Lebanese government and Hezbollah, with the support of the government, have made diplomatic and militarized threats about Shebaa Farms on numerous occasions since the summer of 2000. By using a nonstate actor, Hezbollah, as a proxy army of sorts, the Lebanese government has been able to avoid using its own armed forces to engage Israel. Hezbollah, condoned by the Lebanese government, was happy to confront Israel militarily until the war in 2006, primarily because the group has its own objectives with regard to other issues disputed with Israel. There are many issues that the government and Hezbollah link to the Shebaa Farms dispute, listed in table 7, but mainly they involve releases of Lebanese prisoners, support for the Palestinian cause, justification for Hezbollah's continued armament, Hezbollah's objective to challenge Israel's security overall, and the Israeli occupation of the Syrian Golan Heights. Asher Kaufman (2004, 37) notes that many issues are involved, writing, "Issues such as border formation in the region, inter-Arab relations and the dynamics of the Arab-Israeli conflict, are all manifest in this small piece of land." One observer perfectly summed up the use of Shebaa Farms as bargaining leverage:

> While the issue at first seemed an example of diplomatic hair-splitting, it has since proved useful to the Arab side. For Syria, it means Hezbollah can still be used to keep the Israelis off balance; *for Lebanon, it provides a way to apply pressure over other issues,* like the return of Lebanese prisoners still held in Israeli jails. For Hezbollah, it is a reason to keep its militia armed and active, providing a ready new goal for a resistance movement that otherwise has nothing left to resist. (Schneider 2001, A13; emphasis added)

In 75 percent of the confrontations pursued by the Lebanese government or Hezbollah, the actors linked the Shebaa Farms dispute with other disputed issues, most of them being explicit linkages. The vast majority of confrontations were linked to demands for Israel to release Lebanese prisoners detained in Israel. The next most frequently linked issue was Hezbollah retaliations for killing Palestinians and Lebanese guerillas, terrorists, or civilians. Support for the Palestinian *intifada* in the West Bank and Gaza Strip was the next most commonly cited issue linked to confrontations in Shebaa Farms. Other issues that were linked included Syrian pressure on Israel to withdraw from the Golan Heights, Hezbollah's justification of its continued armed resistance movement against Israel, influence over the greater Arab-Israeli peace process, pressuring Israel to halt violations of Lebanese waters and airspace, and pressuring Israel to demine cluster bombs dropped in the 2006 war.

Table 7. Israeli issues linked by Hezbollah/Lebanon to the territorial dispute

DISPUTED ISSUE	NUMBER OF LINKAGES
Pressure on Israel to release Lebanese or Palestinian prisoners from Israeli jails	12
Retaliation for assassinations/killings of Lebanese or Palestinians by Israel	6
Hezbollah support for Palestinian *intifada*	4
Pressure on Israel to halt violations of air space and Lebanese waters	3
Syrian pressure on Israel to withdraw from the Golan Heights	2
Pressure on Israel to provide maps for demining of cluster bombs	2
Justification of Hezbollah's continued armed resistance movement	1

Israeli Withdrawal from South Lebanon, 2000

The first official Lebanese use of coercive diplomacy and issue linkage coincided with the Israeli withdrawal from south Lebanon and Lebanon's official territorial claim for Shebaa Farms. To symbolize the claim, the Lebanese parliament held a historic session in southern Lebanon a week after the Israeli withdrawal. At the parliament meeting, Prime Minister Hoss called for the release of all Lebanese prisoners from Israeli jails and emphasized that all Lebanese territories should be returned to Lebanon, including Shebaa Farms. Additionally, it is believed that the official claim was pursued to allow Hezbollah to put pressure on Israel regarding other disputed issues, a move that the Lebanese military was unwilling and unable to do. Some analysts have argued that Syria persuaded Hezbollah to press the claim for Lebanon in order to pressure the Israeli military to withdraw from the Golan Heights (Prados 2001).

As a result, the Lebanese claim provided Hezbollah and Syria with the justification they needed to continue the resistance movement against Israel and a continuing dispute to use as bargaining leverage against Israel. Immediately after the Israeli withdrawal and deployment of Hezbollah in the south of Lebanon, an Israeli military source told foreign journalists that Syria had manufactured the territorial claim on Shebaa Farms to provide a pretext for Hezbollah to continue to "bleed" Israel (Reeves 2000, 15). The Israeli view is that the dispute was a fabrication invented for Hezbollah to continue its armed resistance (A. Kaufman 2004). Gidi Grinstein, president of the Reut Institute, a Tel Aviv think tank, likewise argued that since the 2000 Israeli withdrawal from south Lebanon, because Lebanon and Hezbollah have lacked a legitimate reason for resistance against Israel, Shebaa Farms has acted as "a symptom of this phenomenon" (Mitnick and Blanford 2006, 10).

For years, Israeli occupation of the south of Lebanon provided Hezbollah's resistance movement with international and domestic legitimacy, but once Israel withdrew from Lebanon in the summer of 2000, the resistance movement lacked a clear justification. In fact, it is important to note that contrary to assumptions, Hezbollah was not particularly pleased with the Israeli decision to withdraw from the south of Lebanon in 2000. Rather, Hezbollah worked hard to prevent Israel from withdrawing from the security zone since "Hizballah thrived on Israel's occupying presence, which allowed the organization to preserve its dual façade: that of a moderate movement within Lebanon and a militant, radical army vis-à-vis the outside world. Hizballah was not happy, then, with Israel's willingness to pull out, even though it effectively exploited these sentiments for its own purposes" (Zisser 2006, 94). This suggests not only that the acquisition of Shebaa Farms was not truly a real goal for Hezbollah, but also that they were using the Israeli occupation of Lebanese territory in the south as a justification for their continued resistance movement in the name of other disputed issues, mainly the Palestinian cause.

Besides domestic pressure, Israel's other intention for withdrawing from south Lebanon was to prevent Syria and Hezbollah from using the occupation of Lebanese territory to put pressure on Israel. Barak himself had argued to skeptical Israeli military leaders that a unilateral withdrawal from south Lebanon would create "an invisible wall of delegitimacy" for Hezbollah, which would prevent future Hezbollah attacks. According to Barak's predictions, the withdrawal would also remove the primary justification for the Syrian army's occupation in Lebanon (Harel and Issacharoff 2008, 22).

In order to prevent Hezbollah and Syria from having any further justifications for their actions, Israel would have to fully comply with Resolution 425, so Barak insisted on a full Israel withdrawal from "every single inch of Lebanese soil" (Harel and Issacharoff 2008, 22). One scholar clearly explains the Israeli perspective:

> No longer could Syria use Hizbollah to militarily pressure Israel with impunity. Nor could Syria any longer hope to wrest concessions from Israel during peace talks. Most importantly, Tel Aviv appeared not only to be pulling the rug of legitimacy out from under Syrian feet in Lebanon, but also to be severing any future connection between Lebanon's and Syria's peace negotiations

tracks. Why should Syria keep its supposedly protective heavy military presence in Lebanon when Israel's military threat to the sovereignty of the country no longer existed? Why should the Lebanese track remain wedded to that of Syria? Suddenly, the configuration of the Israeli-Syrian conflict appeared to change at the expense of Syria's role. Out of this fluid situation, a new one emerged centering on Shebaa Farms. (Rabil 2003)

Therefore, the Lebanese territorial claim for Shebaa Farms was primarily made by the pro-Syrian Lebanese government on behalf of Hezbollah and Syria so they could justify Hezbollah's continued militant resistance against Israel and the presence of Syrian troops in Lebanon. Therefore, it appears that, at first, "Hizballah needed a reason to continue the conflict with Israel that would not alienate it from the rest of the Lebanese population. The territorial ambiguity around the area of the Shebaa Farms appeared to be a perfect choice for this purpose" (A. Kaufman 2002, 579). This was the first of three diplomatic moves by the Lebanese government to pressure Israel on other disputed issues. After this first move, Lebanon allowed Hezbollah to take the reins with regard to the territorial dispute. However, it is unlikely that the Lebanese government explicitly knew in advance about all the dispute strategies pursued by Hezbollah, meaning that Hezbollah was acting independently of official Lebanese decision making.[5]

On May 22, as a signal to Israel of Hezbollah's interest in Shebaa Farms, two days before Israel started withdrawal from south Lebanon, Hezbollah pursued its first use of limited force in an attack on an Israeli army post in Shebaa Farms, which was perceived as "a preview of the future," the first attack in the area in more than a decade (Hockstader 2000, A1). In a statement claiming the attack, Hassan Nasrallah demanded that Israel also leave Shebaa Farms. Though not linked to other disputed issues explicitly, Hezbollah's intention was clear— it wished to use the Shebaa Farms dispute to justify its continued resistance movement against Israel, a movement based not on the territorial dispute but on other disputed issues with Israel.

Hezbollah's Early Kidnapping Strategy, 2000

In addition to providing a justification for continued armed resistance, Hezbollah began to use militarized confrontations in Shebaa Farms as bargaining leverage to influence Israeli decisions about the detention of Lebanese and Palestinian prisoners in Israel. Though calm around Shebaa Farms persisted for some time after the Israeli withdrawal in May 2000, this only lasted four and a half months. The first evident move to kidnap Israeli soldiers in Shebaa Farms to use as bargaining leverage to pressure Israel into releasing Lebanese prisoners occurred in early October 2000. Hezbollah attacked an Israeli army post in Shebaa Farms with the intention of kidnapping Israeli soldiers to use as bargaining chips. By keeping Israeli soldiers hostage, Hezbollah gauged that Israel would be willing to negotiate the release of Lebanese and Palestinian prisoners. Though Hezbollah announced that it was willing to negotiate the release of the Israeli soldiers in return for Lebanese prisoners in Israel, it turned out that the three Israeli soldiers had actually been killed during the kidnapping attempt.

Hezbollah explicitly admitted on the Hezbollah-run television station al-Manar that the main objectives of the October 2000 military operation were to liberate the Shebaa Farms, pressure Israel to free Lebanese detained in Israeli prisons, and support the Palestinian *intifada,* which had just been renewed in September 2000 (Deutsche Presse-Agentur 2000c). Secretary General Nasrallah announced on al-Manar the night of the attack: "The aim of this operation is human. It is to secure the release of prisoners and detainees in Israeli jails, but I will not go into details" (Kifner 2000, A16). Sheikh Naim Qassem, Hezbollah commander of south Lebanon, was quoted as saying: "We decided to capture a group of Israeli soldiers to exchange them with detainees in Israeli prisons. This is a very suitable opportunity because of the intifada and to confirm the importance of Shebaa Farms as occupied Lebanese territory" (Kifner 2000, A16). In another statement, they reiterated their intention, "that it would seek to trade its three new captives for about a dozen Lebanese held in Israeli jails, including two guerrilla leaders" (Sontag 2000, 1). According to Hezbollah leaders and military experts, though the primary goal of the attack was the abduction of the Israeli soldiers to pressure Israel to release the nineteen Lebanese prisoners, in addition it "was a well planned operation intended to coincide with the outburst of Palestinian protests over control of a Jerusalem site sacred to both Muslims and Jews" (Kifner 2000, A16).

In the fall of 2000, nineteen important Lebanese prisoners were still detained in Israeli prisons, including some prominent Hezbollah leaders, held by Israel as bargaining chips for information on three Israeli soldiers missing since the 1980s, including Ron Arad, an airman whose plane crashed in Lebanon in 1987 (Kifner 2000).[6] Israel's desire for the return of the bodies of the captured Israeli soldiers had become a major national objective for Israel, and it was no secret that Lebanese prisoners were being held by Israel as bargaining chips (Hirst 2000), meaning that Israel itself was pursuing its own issue linkage and coercive diplomacy. Hezbollah knew that Israel would consider the bargaining ploy based on past experience. Despite Israel's claim that, as a policy, it does not negotiate with terrorists, Israel and Hezbollah had indirectly negotiated the release of prisoners in exchange for the remains of Israeli soldiers on several occasions: September to December 1991, July 1996, June 1998, and December 1999 (Associated Press 1991; CNN.com 2004; Dakroub 1998; Radio Lebanon 1996, 1999; Schweid 1991). After the abduction, Hezbollah claimed that they had given ample warnings about their intentions and had repeatedly promised that their armed resistance against Israel would not be complete until full Israeli withdrawal from Shebaa Farms (Hirst 2000). Nizar Hamzeh, a Hezbollah specialist, noted that soon after the October 2000 abductions, "Hezbollah laid its cards on the table immediately about what it wants" (Morris 2008, B1). Though denouncing the use of force, even a UN representative of Secretary General Kofi Annan, Rolf Knutsson, called on Lebanon and Israel to release their respective prisoners unconditionally and without delay (Deutsche Presse-Agentur 2000c), so it was clearly a key issue under contention and one that was not an extraordinary request by Hezbollah. As a result of the hostage taking, international mediators including the UN, US, Russia, and Germany, began working hard to organize a prisoner exchange.

Though the Lebanese government was careful to clarify that they were not involved in the kidnapping, government officials did suggest that an immediate solution to the problem would be to have an exchange of prisoners, indicating that their goal was the same as that of Hezbollah. The week after the abduction occurred, President Emile Lahoud requested Arab summit countries to support Lebanon's official claim on Shebaa Farms, simultaneously calling for the Arab summit countries to support the release of all Lebanese detainees in Israel (Xinhua News Agency 2000). By December 2000, negotiations began between Hezbollah and Israel through a German mediator to exchange the prisoners. It would take three years to achieve success in the negotiations, with the prisoner exchange finally occurring in January 2004. Hezbollah turned over the bodies of the three Israeli soldiers abducted in October 2000 and businessman Elhanen Tannenbaum, who had also been abducted by Hezbollah sometime in 2001. In exchange, Israel turned over twenty-one Lebanese prisoners to Lebanon, including two top militia leaders, and the remains of sixty Lebanese fighters. As part of the deal, Israel also freed more than four hundred Palestinians to return to their homes in the West Bank and Gaza Strip (Ephron 2004). President Emile Lahoud and Prime Minister Rafiq Hariri, as well as dozens of ministers of Parliament, were at Beirut Airport to welcome the released Lebanese prisoners (Fisk 2004), again demonstrating the parallel interests of the Lebanese government and Hezbollah with regard to the disputed issue of Lebanese prisoners held in Israel.

Though a secondary objective, the October 2000 attack was also justified by Hezbollah leaders as demonstrating support for the Palestinian cause. The timing of the Israeli withdrawal from the south of Lebanon and the start of the second *intifada* was ideal for Hezbollah: "The dilemma facing Hizballah in the wake of Israel's pullout from southern Lebanon was resolved with the outbreak of the Al-Aqsa Intifadah in October 2000. As violence swept the Palestinian territories, Hizballah, to the surprise of many, renewed its armed struggle against Israel" (Zisser 2006, 89). The timing of its second use of force was therefore not coincidental, but rather carefully planned by Hezbollah. Hezbollah's support of the Palestinians is rooted in the objectives of the group's mission statement, the Open Letter, published in 1985. Since publishing the Open Letter, Hezbollah leaders have continued to call for the destruction of Israel as a Jewish state, viewed as the oppressor of their fellow Palestinian brothers and occupier of the holy city of Jerusalem, and the creation of a state inclusive of Palestinians and particularly Muslims (Hezbollah Central Press Office 1985). According to Sheikh Atallah Ibrahim of Hezbollah, head of Hezbollah's special information unit and official responsible for detainees and prisoners in Israel, as stated in a June 2000 interview with the author,

> Hezbollah has an ideology—Israel was the enemy and will remain the enemy always because it is written in the Quran. In the beginning, God talked about these people, but not that they were to occupy Palestine. They came out of nowhere into Palestine and stole the land. . . . The only way to negate Israel is for them to leave Palestine . . . it's not good enough until they leave completely. (Ibrahim 2000)

In regard to the October 2000 attack specifically, Hezbollah officials claimed that "the kidnapping was deliberately timed to coincide with and encourage the Palestinians' own intifada" and symbolized the killing of a twelve-year-old Palestinian boy, who was shot in the Gaza Strip the previous week (Hirst 2000, 6A). During the prisoner exchange negotiations, Sheikh Qassem asserted that the abduction of the Israeli soldiers "was planned before the outbreak of the

Palestinian uprising but executed after its eruption to dramatize Hezbollah's support of the Palestinians" (Xinhua News Agency 2001). Therefore, the October 2000 attack was clearly linked to several other issues, not just an attempt to influence Israeli decisions about Shebaa Farms. Issues linked to the attack in Shebaa Farms were support of the Palestinian *intifada,* retaliation for the killing of a Palestinian boy in Gaza, and kidnapping of Israeli soldiers to use as bargaining chips to pressure Israel to release Lebanese prisoners. Support for the Palestinians was also the primary objective of a November 2000 attack in Shebaa Farms, in which Hezbollah killed an Israeli soldier and injured two others. Hezbollah leaders announced in a statement that the bombing was "intended to spur the Palestinians to step up their two month old revolt against Israeli occupation on the eve of the Muslim fast month of Ramadan" (Gozani 2000). A senior Israeli cabinet member admitted that he saw a linkage of the incident and the ongoing Palestinian-Israeli conflict (Gozani 2000).

Retaliation and Resistance, 2001–2004

According to Hezbollah, the next attack that occurred in February 2001 was scheduled to coincide with the ninth anniversary of Israel's assassination of Hezbollah leader Sheikh Abbas al-Moussawi (*Sunday Telegraph* [Sydney] 2001, 52). Assuming that Israel would not react with a heavy military response since it would be difficult to come up with a legitimate *casus belli,* Hezbollah continued its attacks. Only after Ariel Sharon became prime minister of Israel in April 2001 did Israel start reacting militarily. Despite the Israeli military reaction, Hezbollah still continued the attacks, partly since Syria could not retaliate without risking war with Israel, but Hezbollah could act on its behalf (Zisser 2006). As with all of the other attacks since May 2000, the purpose of the April 2001 attack was not an attempt to seize territory in the Shebaa Farms area but to use the dispute as bargaining leverage by linking the territorial dispute with other issues and using coercive diplomacy. After the attack, Hezbollah announced three motives for its continued resistance: to demand the complete liberation of south Lebanon, specifically citing Shebaa Farms, to act as a model for the Palestinian *intifada,* and to serve Iran and Syria as sponsors, so that they could use the dispute as bargaining leverage against Israel (Hirst 2001).

The next attack in May 2001 was noted by Hezbollah as occurring on the fortieth day after the anniversary of Imam Hussein's death at the battle of Karbala, which eventually led to the split between Sunni and Shi'a Islam (Fisk 2001, 13).

On a wider scale, analysts believe the attack was further pressure on behalf of Syria, "in what is widely viewed as a bid to squeeze concessions from Israel over the return of the Golan Heights to Syria'" (Blanford 2001b, 8). Two other attacks followed in 2001: one in July and one in October. In both cases, Hezbollah cited the objectives of releasing Lebanese prisoners in Israeli jails and retaliating for Israeli attacks on the Syrian radar position in Riyaq as the motives for their sporadic military attacks in Shebaa Farms. According to Hassan Ezzieddine, a member of Hezbollah's political council, "We look at the two issues [Shebaa Farms and Lebanese prisoners] through the same telescope. The Israeli entity perpetrates aggressions in both cases. What we are doing is responding to this aggression. That's why the resistance will continue achieving its goals in liberating the detainees and recovering the occupied land" (Blanford 2001a, 8). Yet again, Hezbollah pursued a militant attack specifically as a form of coercive diplomacy and issue linkage, mainly on behalf of Syrian and Lebanese interests. It later was revealed that Syria had, in fact, provided missiles to Hezbollah to retaliate against Israel on its behalf in the July attack (Zisser 2006).

The next set of attacks in April 2002 were directly linked to another disputed issue with Israel; they occurred right after Israel had engaged in Operation Defensive Shield, a campaign that attempted to destroy terrorist infrastructure in the West Bank starting in March, leading to widespread attacks on refugee camps, private homes, and other locations. The Hezbollah attack occurred for two reasons; first, Hezbollah was able to signal support for the Palestinian *intifada* in the West Bank and, second, the attacks were an attempt to distract the IDF from the West Bank military operations (Edwards 2002; Zisser 2006). Zisser (2006, 102) points out: "It may be, however, that Hizballah did not really seek to cause a direct all-out confrontation, but rather that it saw a window of opportunity that had been opened by events in the Palestinian territories and tried to exploit it in full."

In the two weeks before the April 2002 attacks, Sheikh Nasrallah warned on numerous occasions that Hezbollah would open a second front if the situation in the Palestinian territories worsened, directly linking an imminent Shebaa Farms attack with the Palestinian *intifada* (Blanford 2002a). After the attack, Nasrallah admitted that Hezbollah fighters were "getting ready for direct military intervention from Lebanon" to assist the Palestinian *intifada* (Blanford 2002b). He also explicitly noted that the military campaign had a dual purpose: "These military operations carried out in the Shebaa Farms aim to liberate the land. We are also trying to convey a message to Israel that we are acting in solidarity with the Palestinians" (Taylor 2002, 8). Deputy Secretary General Qassem similarly stated: "Our method is hit and run; we strike at specific targets in specific circumstances. As for our current operations, you should note that we stepped up our struggle in response to the events in Palestine [Operation Defensive Shield]. We have made clear that these were warning signals for Israel and are meant to express our solidarity with the Palestinians" (Radio Nur 2002). Hezbollah also called on Arab states to support the Palestinians against the Israeli military force being applied in the West Bank, but promised that Hezbollah would only attack the Shebaa Farms area. Nasrallah also linked another issue, demanding that Israel halt all reconnaissance flights over Lebanon (Zisser 2006).

Two attacks on IDF posts in Shebaa Farms that occurred in August and October 2003 were both pursued as retaliations for Israeli killings. In a statement faxed to news agencies in Beirut, Hezbollah stated that the purpose of the August 2003 shelling was in retaliation for the assassination of a Hezbollah security official whose car was bombed in southern Beirut the week before (J. W. Anderson 2003). According to Hezbollah sources, the October 2003 attack was pursued in retaliation for an Israeli air strike on alleged training camps for Palestinians within Syria, another disputed issue linked to actions in the Shebaa Farms dispute.

Hezbollah's Second Kidnapping Strategy, 2004–2006

The next attack in May 2004 was linked directly to the prisoner exchange negotiations. The attack was specifically scheduled to put pressure on Israel at a time when Israeli officials had spoken of progress in the German-mediated negotiations for another prisoner exchange. This time Hezbollah was hoping to secure the release of Sami Kantar, a Lebanese citizen, in exchange for information on downed airman Ron Arad (*Weekend Australian* 2004). Between May 2004 and June 2005, Hezbollah initiated three other attacks, but no other issues were directly linked by Hezbollah. Only in June 2005 did Hezbollah admit that it had been strategizing for the past year about using attacks in the Shebaa Farms to kidnap Israeli soldiers to use as bargaining chips, in hopes of exchanging them for Lebanese detainees in Israeli jails.

Because the October 2000 Hezbollah kidnapping of the two Israeli soldiers in Shebaa Farms led to them successfully being used as bargaining chips to release Lebanese prisoners in 2004, Nasrallah knew that the strategy of issue linkage and coercive diplomacy worked. As a result, "the prisoner issue became almost an obsession with Nasrallah, and he brought it up at every opportunity" (Harel and Issacharoff 2008, 57). During the campaign leading up to the May 2005 parliamentary elections in Lebanon, Nasrallah used the prisoner issue to mobilize domestic support for Hezbollah. According to a former Israeli intelligence chief, Nasrallah thought that Hezbollah could "kidnap a soldier, force Israel to attack, and respond with Katyusha fire—thus proving his indispensability as the defender of Lebanon" (Harel and Issacharoff 2008).

The revised strategy to use the Shebaa Farms dispute to kidnap Israeli soldiers to be used as bargaining leverage for the release of Lebanese prisoners was put into practice for the first time in June 2005. Video footage made by Hezbollah forces and found by an Israeli paratroop unit in Shebaa Farms in late June 2005 indicated that Hezbollah was planning to abduct Israeli soldiers in the disputed area. The attack consisted of a Hezbollah attack on two IDF posts with mortar shelling and an attempted infiltration of a base in a mountainous area of Shebaa Farms. According to the IDF, three Hezbollah special forces members were identified in Shebaa Farms and chased by the IDF. One was killed and two escaped, with Hezbollah forces conducting a heavy bombardment of IDF posts in Shebaa Farms as a cover for the escape (Blanford 2005). Over the next year, Hezbollah forces made three other attempts to infiltrate Shebaa Farms and kidnap soldiers, but all were thwarted (Harel and Issacharoff 2008).

In late November 2005, dozens of Hezbollah special forces crossed into Shebaa Farms with the intent to kidnap Israeli soldiers. The attack on an IDF army post was thwarted due to Israeli intelligence, which allowed the IDF to ambush the Hezbollah forces, killing three Hezbollah fighters (Wilson 2005). At the funeral of the three Hezbollah fighters, Nasrallah announced that it was the duty and right of Hezbollah to kidnap Israeli soldiers (Harel and Issacharoff 2008). Israeli forces thwarted another Hezbollah attack in February 2006 pursued with the same intention to kidnap soldiers. That attack had been in retaliation for the killing of a seventeen-year-old Lebanese shepherd who had been found in Shebaa Farms. Hezbollah decided to take advantage of the opportunity to avenge the shepherd's death so they could attempt a kidnapping (Macleod 2006). In an April speech commemorating the anniversary of Samir Kantar's detention in Israel, Nasrallah specifically pledged to obtain Kantar's release by kidnapping Israeli soldiers to exchange for him and stated that the kidnapping would take place very soon (Achcar 2007).[7]

In late May 2006, another opportunity allowed Hezbollah to allegedly justify an attack in Shebaa Farms in an attempt to kidnap Israeli soldiers. This time Hezbollah claimed that the attack was retaliation for the car-bombing assassination of a Palestinian Islamic Jihad official in Sidon (Lebanon) (*Press* 2006). According to findings of Israel's Winograd Commission on the War in Lebanon, "The next abduction was just a matter of time and it was doubtful if it could be avoided" (*Winograd Commission* 2008). Their reasoning was justified; at a June 8 meeting with other political leaders in Beirut, Nasrallah announced that Hezbollah would have to take Israeli soldiers as prisoners in order to use them as bargaining chips for the release of Lebanese prisoners in Israel (Harel and Issacharoff 2008).

2006 Lebanon War

Just a few weeks after the May 2006 kidnapping attempt, Hezbollah leadership was inspired by the Palestinian kidnapping of an Israeli soldier, Gilad Shalit, in the Gaza Strip in late June. He had been kidnapped to use as a bargaining chip to release Palestinian prisoners (Achcar 2007). According to Israeli military sources, "the abduction in Gaza could stimulate the appetite of Hezbollah, and Hassan Nasrallah might be tempted to grab the reigns of the struggle from the Palestinians" (Harel and Issacharoff 2008, 10). As a result of this analysis, the Israeli army was put on high alert along the northern border with Lebanon. Two weeks later, after no action on the border, the alert level was reduced (Harel and Issacharoff 2008). On July 12, 2006, Hezbollah forces took advantage of this reduced alert period to cross the border, not in Shebaa Farms as expected, but elsewhere along the border. Hezbollah attacked two Hummers on border patrol, killing nine Israeli soldiers and kidnapping two soldiers, Ehud Goldwasser and Eldad Regev, provoking the second Lebanon War.[8]

The timing was well intended. Syria and Iran had hoped that an offer by Hamas and Palestinian prime minister Imail Haniyeh to release the Israeli soldier captured in Gaza in exchange for a release of minors, females, and elderly Palestinian prisoners and an end to the Israeli offensive in Gaza and the West Bank would force Israel to be humbled in having to deal with Hamas. When Israel rejected the offer, Iran approached Hezbollah to increase pressure on the Israeli government to negotiate an exchange of Lebanese and Palestinian prisoners held in Israeli jails (Jansen 2006). Less than an hour after the attack, Hezbollah television, al-Manar, announced the kidnapping and then reminded the viewers that the organization had kept its promise to free Lebanese prisoners, specifically naming Samir Kuntar, whose release was rejected in the 2004 prisoner exchange.

Press statements were full of stated intentions to pursue a new comprehensive prisoner exchange with Israel. At a press conference in Beirut later that day, Hezbollah was even more explicit in its issue linkage when Nasrallah reported that "the captured soldiers are in a safe place far from here. The only way of returning them is through indirect negotiations for a prisoner exchange. . . . We've been saying for a year that we'd kidnap Israeli soldiers. . . . From the beginning of the year, we've placed the capture of soldiers at the top of our priorities in order to bring about the release of Palestinian and Lebanese prisoners" (Nasrallah 2006). In another statement Nasrallah announced that Israel's military assault would not return the soldiers to Israel; only through indirect negotiations and a trade would they be returned (Henderson 2006).

Though Hezbollah's intention had been to use the kidnapping as bargaining leverage to gain the release of Lebanese prisoners from Israel, unlike in past occasions when Israel did not respond with much force, Israeli leaders decided this time to respond with full force. Hezbollah had underestimated Israel's response, thinking that Israel would respond with a few aerial bombings and rocket attacks across the border and then start indirect negotiations for the prisoner exchange. Though Israel had perceived Hezbollah as "merely a nuisance along its northern border" in the past, in the years prior to the war Israeli assessments were that the militant group had "turned into a serious strategic threat, one as great as that posed by Syria, Iraq, and Iran, and that a new conflict with Hizballah, if it takes place, would be an existential war" (Zisser 2006, 87). After the war ended, Nasrallah admitted that Hezbollah had grossly underestimated Israel's response to the kidnappings: "In the history of wars, it never happened that a state launches a war against another state for a few apprehended soldiers and a few killed. Now if you ask me if I had known that this abduction would lead to a war of such a dimension with one percent probability, well, we would certainly not have done it, for human, moral, military, social, security, and political reasons" (Achcar 2007, 33).

The war ended on August 14, 2006 with a ceasefire, declared in UN Security Council Resolution 1701. The resolution, negotiated between the US and France, included a reference to Shebaa Farms due to the demands of the Lebanese government, the first diplomatic threat taken on Shebaa Farms since the summer of 2000. Lebanon had demanded that any resolution ending the war also include a call for Shebaa Farms to be transferred to UN jurisdiction, in addition to demanding that the disarmament of Hezbollah not be discussed in the resolution. The French ambassador to the UN noted: "I was very rigid on the Shaba'a matter. Obviously Siniora wouldn't agree to a solution unless it included a reference to this issue, but Bolton [US ambassador to the UN] wanted to expunge the Farms from the draft" (Harel and Issacharoff 2008, 202, 205). In the actual resolution, the Lebanese side partially got its way with reference to Shebaa Farms included. In addition to cessation of armed force, the resolution requested that the secretary general's office develop proposals within thirty days to finish delineating the border between Lebanon and Israel, including Shebaa Farms (UN Security Council Resolution 1701 2006).

Postwar Relations

Since August 2006, the entire border area including Shebaa Farms has been quiet. Both sides agreed to maintain a truce, and Hezbollah has kept its word thus far. Lebanese army forces moved into the south of Lebanon along with UN peacekeeping forces in the area around Shebaa Farms to keep the peace with relative success. A year after the war, in July 2007, Lebanese Prime Minister Siniora issued another diplomatic threat by restating the official claim for Shebaa Farms and noting that the Lebanese government was still working to reclaim the territory through Resolution 1701. In addition to Shebaa Farms, Siniora made a direct linkage with other issues disputed with Israel: "The Shebaa Farm, the demining of cluster bombs, the release of Lebanese detainees in Israeli prisons, in addition to putting an end to daily Israeli violations of our land, air, and waters, are among the main objectives of the government" (*Daily Star* 2007). Most important is the fact that the Lebanese government has made no attempt to resolve the territorial dispute through territorial concessions.

Even though the initial abduction of the Israeli soldiers provoked a devastating war, Hezbollah's initial strategy of issue linkage and coercive diplomacy eventually worked. Toward the end of the war, during ongoing negotiations for a ceasefire, the Lebanese government was adamant that the Lebanese prisoners be released in exchange for the Israeli soldiers, as Hezbollah demanded. Israel rejected this proposal at that time, but negotiations continued until an actual prisoner exchange took place in July 2008 (*New Zealand Herald 2008*. Israel's cabinet voted twenty-two to three in favor of a deal to exchange the bodies of the two Israeli soldiers abducted in July 2006 and the remains of soldiers killed in the 2006 war for the release of Samir Kantar, four other Lebanese prisoners, and the bodies of dozens of Hezbollah fighters. Despite the fact that Kantar served three decades in an Israeli jail for the murder of two men and two children in northern Israel, the return of Samir Kantar to Lebanon was widely celebrated, not just by Hezbollah but by the Lebanese government, much to the dismay of Israel. Yet again, Hezbollah declared a victory, and the Lebanese government partook in the celebrations. Hezbollah's objective of freeing the highly symbolic Samir Kantar was a major success for the group and for Lebanon, only further proving that using issue linkage and coercive diplomacy was a useful strategy. Now that Kantar and senior Hezbollah officials have been released, it is unlikely that Hezbollah will plan future attacks to kidnap Israeli soldiers since there are no major Lebanese prisoners to exchange. If such plans are made, they will likely be to pressure Israel on Palestinian prisoners or more generally in support of the Palestinian cause.

There are three major reasons why Hezbollah halted attacks after August 2006 and why they are unlikely to engage in even minor uses of force along the border in the near future. First, Hezbollah achieved its main objective of gaining the release of Lebanese prisoners, including high-level prisoners, through issue linkage and coercive diplomacy. Despite the major costs of the war, Hezbollah's capture of the two Israeli soldiers in July 2006 led directly to prisoner exchange negotiations, resulting in the release of the last Lebanese prisoners Hezbollah demanded by 2008. The halting of attacks is therefore due partially to the fact that Hezbollah, and the Lebanese government indirectly, mainly achieved its goal regarding the release of Lebanese prisoners. Second, with regard to support for the Palestinians, the second *intifada,* which had begun in September 2000, began to wane by 2005, when Hamas announced it was running as a political party in the January 2006 Palestinian Legislative Council elections. Once Hamas won power in the elections and then took power in the Gaza Strip after interfighting with Fatah in 2007, Hezbollah apparently did not need to play a primary role in assisting the Palestinians since Hamas seemed to be handling the situation fine on its own terms.

A third reason for the halting of attacks appears to be due to domestic accountability, since it was so severely punished, along with the state of Lebanon, in the 2006 war. The reduction in Hezbollah attacks in the Shebaa Farms dispute is likely because of the massive Israeli retaliation that occurred in the 2006 war, making the attacks very costly, as well as leading to the forced pullback from the border area and the replacement of Hezbollah with the Lebanese Army. In this way, the cost of future attacks became too high for Hezbollah as a dispute strategy, to the point that the attacks could provoke the Israeli army to retaliate harshly, a cost that is higher than any benefit of releasing minor Lebanese prisoners, releasing Palestinian prisoners, or providing support for the Palestinians cause. What is likely to happen is that Hezbollah will continue to work politically in public and militarily underground, preparing for other means to pressure Israel, such as support for militant Palestinian groups and infiltration of the Israeli military and government. Hezbollah is working to rebuild its supply of armaments, however, which indicates that the organization has not given up its option of using force against Israel in the future if other disputed issues arise.

CONCLUSIONS

In June 2008, US secretary of state Condoleezza Rice announced that it was time to find a solution to the Shebaa Farms dispute according to Resolution 1701. In a visit to Beirut, she promised to press UN secretary general Ban Ki-Moon to lend his good offices to resolve the dispute over sovereignty. Rice also stopped in Israel to apply pressure on the government to consider a settlement with Lebanon. Rice described the potential solution to the Shebaa Farms dispute as a catalyst for solving larger problems in the region (Bronner and Worth 2008). French president Nicolas Sarkozy also discussed the Shebaa Farms issue with Israeli officials during a visit to Israel the same month. A French official suggested that "since the adoption of Resolution 1701, Israel has been systematically refusing the settlement Lebanon suggested and the Security Council adopted, since it is refusing to give Hezbollah a political victory" (*Daily Star* 2008).

As a result of US and French pressure, Israel offered to start peace talks with Lebanon, stating that all issues would be negotiable, including Shebaa Farms. Lebanese prime minister Siniora rejected the offer, stating, "there's no room for bilateral negotiations between Lebanon and Israel. The Lebanese position is unchanged" (Witte 2008). He reiterated Lebanon's opposition to peace talks unless Israel first returned Shebaa Farms, as well as Lebanese prisoners in Israeli jails, and provide maps showing mines and cluster bombs from the 2006 war. Hezbollah also criticized the offer as an Israeli attempt to disarm Hezbollah. Justifying its continued call for Shebaa Farms and its militarized resistance movement, Hezbollah sources claimed, "as long as part of the Lebanese homeland is occupied, it needs its weapons because the national army is weak" (Bronner and Worth 2008, 6).

The implication of Lebanon's rejection of the peace talks is that Lebanon is not willing to give up the ability to use the Shebaa Farms territorial dispute as bargaining leverage in other issues disputed with Israel. Meanwhile, Israeli officials worry that if Israel gives up Shebaa Farms, Hezbollah will just find another reason to keep its arms. At the same time, Hezbollah has kept its agreement to the 2006 ceasefire and has not pursued any militant attacks in the past five years. Even if the Lebanese government was willing to negotiate with Israel in peace talks, it is highly unlikely that Hezbollah would be satisfied with the results of any such talks. Shortly after the June 2008 offer of peace talks, Deputy Secretary General Sheikh Naim Qassem stated on Hezbollah's television station, al-Manar:

> Let the Farms be liberated first. In fact, we have been clear. If the Farms are liberated to the last inch, whether through diplomacy or resistance, then this would be an Israeli escape. We would be happy if all of the Shebaa Farms region is liberated. If they liberate it inch after inch, we would celebrate every liberated inch at a time. If they put it under UN care, we will bless this move, but we will also tell the United Nations that this would not be complete liberation unless the region is back to Lebanese sovereignty. Liberate the Shebaa Farms and we will sit down and discuss a defensive strategy and we will all become a resistance that works for Lebanon's interest. (al-Manar Television 2008)

Even though Hezbollah and the majority government in Lebanon experienced significant tensions in 2007 and 2008 and Syrian influence on Lebanese politics has been reduced, Hezbollah's influence on the Lebanese government is still highly considerable. The government has little choice about Hezbollah's continued armament. Hezbollah is stronger and more effective and has more resolve than the Lebanese army, and the government knows this. As a result, the Lebanese government will likely continue to give Hezbollah the ability to have strong influence in Lebanese foreign policy, especially with regard to Israel. Because Hezbollah is part of the Lebanese government and shares a coalition with several major parties, the group not only has strong influence in the government but also shares similar goals with the rest of the government with regard to Israel. As a result, regardless of the fact that the current majority coalition disagrees with Hezbollah's coalition on the degree of Syrian influence in Lebanon, both sides agree on the continued claim of Shebaa Farms since they share similar goals.

Based on the findings of this research, the assessment is that Hezbollah is not likely to engage in further threats or uses of force against Israel anytime in the near future, but at the same time, the Lebanese government should be unwilling to resolve the dispute, leading to an enduring territorial dispute between Lebanon and Israel. As discussed earlier, the Lebanese-Israeli border dispute seems to have little prospect for resolution as long as the Lebanese government maintains other disputed issues with Israel, including more than three hundred thousand Palestinian refugees in Lebanon, Israeli flights over Lebanese airspace, the need for maps for demining in the south of Lebanon, and for some pro-Syrian parties in the government support for Syria regarding the Golan Heights. As one scholar writes, "its interrelatedness with the Israeli-Syrian and even the Israeli-Palestinian conflict has made it impossible to resolve in isolation. Despite Israeli consideration of withdrawing from Shebaa Farms, there is little likelihood of a dispute settlement that would allow the Lebanese-Israeli border to be peaceful. All efforts to reach a peace agreement or even a more-limited cease-fire arrangement have failed" (Blum 2007, 225). Since Lebanon and Israel never officially signed a peace treaty after 1949, the likelihood of an agreement about Shebaa Farms is just as unlikely. As long as the state of Lebanon can continue to provide even minor pressure on Israel through its claim for Shebaa Farms, the Lebanese government has no incentive to drop its territorial claim.

CHAPTER SEVEN

The Ceuta/Sebta and Melilla/Melilia Enclaves Dispute

Since 1956, when Morocco gained independence from France, it has officially maintained a territorial claim against Spain for two enclaves in North
Africa, Ceuta (Sebta in Arabic) and Melilla (Melilia in Arabic), the Plazas de
Sobrania (Chafarinas Islands in Arabic), and the Penones (Rocks) of Alhucema
and Velez de la Gomera off the coast of North Africa. Though Moroccan officials have declared that Morocco's territorial integrity will not be complete until
the enclaves are returned and that settlement of the dispute is their main objective, evidence indicates that this is not necessarily the case. Over the years, there
have been few actual settlement attempts by Morocco, none involving territorial concessions, and no attempts to negotiate by Spain. Rather, Moroccan officials have regularly reignited Morocco's claim to the enclaves but have failed to
follow through with any active attempts to settle the dispute.

Since 1956, the three ruling kings of Morocco (King Mohammed V, King
Hassan II, and King Mohammed VI) have rarely made active attempts to change
the status quo by attempting peaceful dispute resolution methods or by using
force to settle the dispute once and for all. Rather, critics often pointed to King
Hassan's apparent ambivalence and lack of resolve regarding the enclaves, a reputation that King Mohammed VI was determined to change once he gained
power in 1999. In his forty-three years of rule, King Hassan's lack of action
on the claim beyond the rhetoric was viewed as a sign of weakness by both
Spain and opposition groups within Morocco. Until his death in July 1999, King
Hassan and other Moroccan officials occasionally pressed territorial claims for
the enclaves through rhetorical statements about Moroccan territorial integrity. The Spanish government responded by stringently refusing any dialogue,
and the Moroccan government always dropped the issue for some time. King
Hassan's rhetoric was also perceived as cheap talk and mostly ignored by the

Spanish government. Some say this was an embarrassment for Morocco, indicating that King Hassan was never really resolved to gain the territory as he let the matter drop with regularity. In July 2002, King Mohammed VI, the successor to the Moroccan throne, suddenly switched Morocco's strategy of inaction and provoked Spain by occupying one of the disputed islands near the enclaves. In reaction, Spain deployed seventy-five Special Forces soldiers, seven helicopters, four combat aircraft, and five warships in the operation to reacquire the island and take the Moroccan troops present on the island as prisoners for a short time (BBC News 2002). Though the US successfully de-escalated the crisis, it served as a strong reminder to Spain that Morocco's territorial claim was a problem that could not be ignored. Yet since 2002, King Mohammed has not actively attempted settlement either, following in the footsteps of his father.

Spain's objective is to maintain the status quo. Spanish officials have been adamant about maintaining sovereignty over the enclaves and have been unwilling to consider negotiations at all. As the target state, Spain claims that Morocco has no legitimate grounds for the territorial claim and treats it as a nuisance. At the same time, Spanish officials have recognized the potential threat that Morocco could incite, and thus they have pursued a strategy of appeasement on numerous occasions to keep Morocco at bay. Through appeasement, Spain has given in to several demands by Morocco that have resulted from Moroccan issue linkage of the territorial dispute and other disputed issues such as fishing rights and illegal immigration of Moroccans to Spain. This chapter examines all Moroccan dispute strategies against Spain from 1956 to 2008 and demonstrates that value of territory and domestic accountability and mobilization cannot explain Moroccan dispute strategies, while the theory of territorial disputes as bargaining leverage can. Overall, the evidence indicates that Moroccan leaders have effectively used the enclaves dispute to pressure Spain on a number of disputed issues unrelated to the enclaves. Unless Moroccan leaders decide there is no need for further linkage, the dispute is likely to endure.

THE ENCLAVES

Morocco's claim to the enclaves includes Ceuta and Melilla, as well as surrounding islands. Ceuta, located opposite of Gibraltar and only 18.5 miles from the Spanish mainland, has an area of about 7 square miles and shares a land border with Morocco that is about 5 miles in length. Melilla, located 311 miles east of Ceuta and closer to Tangiers, has an area of 4.5 square miles and a land border

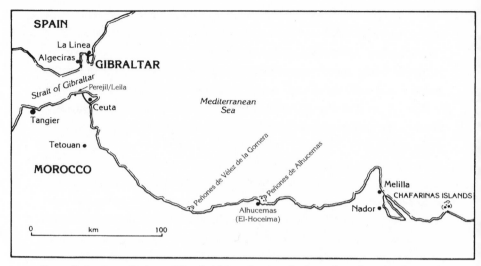

Figure 3. Southern Spain and North Africa, showing the Spanish enclaves on the north Moroccan coast. From *Border and Territorial Disputes,* 4th edition, Peter Calvert, ed., London: John Harper Publishing, 2004.

with Morocco of 7.5 miles (Allcock 1992). Ceuta has a population of approximately 76,600 people, and Melilla has a population of approximately 69,440 people, most of whom are Spanish (BBC News 2009). Melilla has experienced greater Moroccan influence compared to Ceuta due to its farther location from Spain (Solsten and Meditz 1988). In each enclave, there are between six to seven thousand Spanish troops stationed at any given time (Gold 2000).

Spain has effectively occupied Melilla since 1497 and Ceuta since 1580, along with the Chafarinas Islands, annexed in 1848, the Rock of Velez since 1508, and the Rock of Alhucema since 1673, which are all small islands located near the enclaves (Allcock 1992). When Spain joined the European Community (EC) in 1986, the two enclaves also joined the EC by default, since they are considered part of Spain and European territory (Solsten and Meditz 1988). However, despite Spain's membership in the North Atlantic Treaty Organization (NATO) since 1982, the North African enclaves are not covered by the NATO charter (Gold 2005). Spain conquered Melilla in 1497 when the rulers of Spain, Ferdinand and Isabelle, sent the Duke of Medina Sidonia to conquer the territory that now encompasses the enclave. The objective was for Spain to have a watch point for potential Muslim invaders attempting to cross the straits to Spain (Tarvainen

1997). Prior to that, Melilla had been part of the kingdom of Fez and acted as a frontier town.

The enclaves historically fell under the control of various Muslim caliphates since the eighth century AD (Rézette 1976). Ceuta was first taken by European powers in 1415 when Portugal seized the point of land from the local Berber population. The primary objective to acquire Ceuta was to further promote Christianity in the area and expel Muslims. In 1580, Portugal united with the Spanish kingdom, and all Portuguese settlements became Spanish territories, so Ceuta came under Spanish autonomy under King Philip II. When Spain and Portugal divided in 1640, the inhabitants of Ceuta voted to remain Spanish (Ellman 1985), and Ceuta became reincorporated as part of the kingdom of Castille in 1668. Since then, Ceuta has been ruled by Spain, and as declared in its 1978 constitution, it forms part of Spain's national territory.

On many occasions in the late seventeenth and eighteenth centuries, local Moroccan rulers attempted to oust Spain from Ceuta—from 1694 to 1720, from 1727 to 1728, in 1732, and from 1790 to 1791—and from Melilla in the years from 1694 to 1696 and from 1774 to 1775. The Spanish persevered, however, maintaining control of the enclaves. Moroccan rulers not only attempted to use force in the past but also signed a number of treaties with Spanish rulers regarding the enclaves. The first treaty was signed in May 1767 by Spanish King Charles II and Moroccan Sultan Mohamed bin Abdullah, in which the Sultan guaranteed the safety of Christians in the enclaves and promised not to lay claim to the enclaves. A March 1799 treaty signed by King Charles IV and Sultan Moulay Slimane renewed the 1767 treaty, which was followed by another treaty in 1782, which set the boundaries of Ceuta. Further treaties in May 1845, August 1859, and June 1862 confirmed the boundaries of Ceuta and Melilla, providing for the extension of the borders around both enclaves for defense purposes and expanded Spanish access to fishing rights in the strait. A brief conflict occurred in 1859–60 regarding reparations for damage inflicted on Ceuta by Rif tribesmen, resulting in an April 1860 treaty recognizing the "full possession and sovereignty" of Spain. Another treaty signed in 1911 confirmed the boundaries of the two enclaves determined by previous treaties (Calvert 2004). Until 1956, when the newly independent Morocco made its official claim for the enclaves, the only other action regarding the enclaves was in 1893 when Rif tribesmen attacked the Spanish population in Melilla. In response, the Spanish army descended on Morocco, and in response to that move, as one analyst noted, the Sultan of Morocco "settled the problem by paying an indemnity of 4 million douras (650,000 British pounds) to Spain and successfully avoided another intervention. What else could the Moroccan Sultan do to preserve the integrity of his empire?" (Hamboyan 1968).

Morocco's claim is based on the ideas that the enclaves and islands make up a natural part of Morocco's territory as part of North Africa and not Europe, that Spain's control of the enclaves and surrounding islands is anachronistic, representing European colonial control of territory in North Africa, and that turning over the enclaves is a natural conclusion to previous Spanish cession of other territories to Morocco, mainly the island of Ifni in 1969 and the Spanish (Western) Sahara in 1979 (Calvert 2004). Technically, Morocco also claims the Canary Islands but has never actively pursued this claim. The UN list of colonized territories does not include the enclaves since the Spanish have effectively occupied the towns for a significant amount of time prior to the independence of Morocco in 1956 (del Pino 1983).

DISPUTE STRATEGIES

Since 1956, Moroccan leaders have regularly reignited Morocco's claim to the enclaves but failed to follow through with any active attempts to settle the dispute. They never made any active attempts to offer territorial concessions and never came close to dropping the territorial claim for the enclaves. What could arguably be attempts at settlement have instead been reassertions of the territorial claim framed in calls for joint commissions to examine Morocco's claim to sovereignty. None of these actions can be classified as attempts to settle through territorial concessions. The lack of any real attempt by Morocco to change the status quo suggests a lack of interest in actual settlement of the dispute, even if Moroccan leaders would never explicitly admit this. The Moroccan approach to the dispute was best summed up by Moroccan interior minister Driss Basri in 1998 when he announced that Morocco "shall wait for as long as it takes for things to get back to normal, without aggression, hatred or polemics, and in the most civilized way possible" (BBC News 1998a).

Between 1956 and 2008 Morocco issued thirty-six diplomatic threats and two militarized threats, as shown in table 8.[1] Unlike the other territorial disputes studied in this book, almost all of Morocco's threats fall at the far extreme of minor diplomatic threats, mainly as reassertions of the claim meant to deliberately provoke the Spanish government. The reason these actions are considered diplomatic threats is because this is how Spain has perceived them. The

Table 8. Moroccan diplomatic and militarized confrontations, 1956–2008

DATE	TYPE	MOROCCAN ACTION	REASON FOR ACTION
March 1961	Diplomatic	Official claim for enclaves issued; imposition of transit restrictions	Ascension of King Hassan II to Moroccan throne
June 1962	Diplomatic	Reassertion of claim; territorial waters law passed	No reasons given
January 1975	Diplomatic	Reassertion of claim made to UN Decolonization Committee	No reasons given
June 1975	Militarized	Clash of Spanish and Moroccan troops	Response to arrests of 400 Moroccans suspected of bombs that exploded in enclaves
November 1975	Diplomatic	Reassertion of claim	Spanish claim for Gibraltar
November 1978	Diplomatic	Reassertion of claim	Spanish recognition of Polisario Front
May 1979	Diplomatic	Reassertion of claim	Spanish support for Polisario Front
December 1980	Diplomatic	Reassertion of claim	Spanish support for Polisario Front
November 1982	Diplomatic	Reassertion of claim	Spanish protest about US-Moroccan military relations
February 1983	Diplomatic	Arab Union approved Moroccan motion demanding return of enclaves to Morocco	Spanish negotiations on Gibraltar
August 1984	Diplomatic	Reassertion of claim	Libyan-Moroccan military treaty
November 1984	Diplomatic	Reassertion of claim	Spanish negotiations on Gibraltar
February 1985	Diplomatic	Reassertion of claim	British-Spanish treaty on status of Gibraltar
July 1985	Diplomatic	Resolution passed calling for "liberation" of enclaves	Libyan-Moroccan federation
March 1986	Diplomatic	Reassertion of claim	Spanish claim for Gibraltar
June 1986	Diplomatic	Reassertion of claim	Spanish claim for Gibraltar
January 1987	Diplomatic	Reassertion of claim; call for joint commission	Treatment of Muslim minorities in enclaves
March 1987	Diplomatic	Reassertion of claim	26th anniversary of ascension to throne
July 1987	Diplomatic	Reassertion of claim	Expiration of fishing agreement between EU and Morocco
October 1988	Diplomatic	Reassertion of claim at UN General Assembly	Spanish support for Algerian motion for the Western Sahara referendum
March 1994	Diplomatic	Reassertion of claim	Autonomy of enclaves; Spanish support of referendum in the Western Sahara

Table 8. (*continued*)

DATE	TYPE	MOROCCAN ACTION	REASON FOR ACTION
April 1994	Diplomatic	Reassertion of claim	Autonomy of enclaves; Spanish support of referendum in the Western Sahara
September 1994	Diplomatic	Reassertion of claim	Autonomy of enclaves
March 1995	Diplomatic	Reassertion of claim	Autonomy of enclaves; expiration of fishing agreement between EU and Morocco
April 1995	Diplomatic	Reassertion of claim	Expiration of fishing agreement between EU and Morocco
September 1995	Diplomatic	Reassertion of claim at UN General Assembly	Fishing rights negotiations
September 1997	Diplomatic	Reassertion of claim at UN General Assembly	Spanish celebration of 500th anniversary of Melilla
April 1998	Diplomatic	Reassertion of claim	Impending visit of Spanish prime minister to Morocco
April 1999	Diplomatic	Reassertion of claim	Return of Hong Kong and Macau to China; expiration of fishing agreement between EU and Morocco
May 1999	Diplomatic	Reassertion of claim	Expiration of fishing agreement between EU and Morocco
August 1999	Diplomatic	Reassertion of claim	Fishing negotiations between EU and Morocco
December 1999	Diplomatic	Reassertion of claim	Return of Macau from Portugal to China
January 2000	Diplomatic	Reassertion of claim	Spanish prime minister's visit to Melilla
May 2000	Diplomatic	Reassertion of claim	Illegal immigration issue
October/November 2001	Diplomatic	Reassertion of claim	Illegal immigration issue; Spanish backing of Polisario Front; Spanish fishing rights
July 2002	Militarized	Military occupation of Perejil/Leila Island; ambassador recalled	Spanish-Gibraltar negotiations; Spanish support of the Western Sahara referendum
October 2005	Diplomatic	Threat not to defend enclaves' borders	Spanish/EU economic aid to Morocco
November 2007	Diplomatic	Reassertion of claim; ambassador recalled; cancellation of meeting of prime ministers	Protest of royal Spanish visit to enclaves

inconvenience of the repeated territorial claims over the years has had a clear effect on Spanish decision making regarding the enclaves and its relations with Morocco.

Though Morocco's claim for the enclaves became official in 1956 when it gained independence from France, the first attempt to press its claims did not occur until 1961 when Morocco, under the new leadership of King Hassan, called on the UN to recognize its rights to the enclaves. In March 1961, the newly crowned King Hassan reasserted Morocco's territorial claim as part of his claim for Morocco's territorial integrity, including the Western Sahara, occupied by Spain until 1975. As a result of the claim, Spain reinforced the borders around the enclaves. The next diplomatic threat occurred in June 1962 when Morocco reasserted its territorial claim and extended its territorial waters from six to ten nautical miles, affecting access by Spanish fishing boats. Spain reacted by sending warships to escort its fishing boats into the territorial waters around the enclaves and set up a reinforcement of military garrisons in the enclaves (Calvert 2004).

No other action was taken by Morocco until January 1975, when Morocco reasserted its claim by making a formal request to the UN Decolonization Committee to press Spain to cede the enclaves to Morocco. Spain interpreted this move as a diplomatic threat and condemned the action as "a threat to Spain's national unity and territorial integrity" (Calvert 2004, 54). A few months later, in June 1975 Spanish and Moroccan troops clashed at the borders of the enclaves after a series of bombs exploded in Ceuta and Melilla, and four hundred Moroccans were arrested as suspects. Morocco responded to the arrests with a complaint to the UN secretary general about Spanish violations of human rights, causing increased tensions between the two states (Calvert 2004). Later in the year, in November 1975 after King Juan Carlos ascended the throne in Spain upon the death of General Francisco Franco, King Hassan issued a threat stating that if Spain were to acquire Gibraltar, then Morocco would have to acquire Ceuta and Melilla since "no power can permit Spain to possess both keys to the same straits" (Calvert 2004, 54). A group calling itself the Moroccan Patriotic Front bombed several locations in Ceuta and Melilla in 1978 and 1979, but there was no evidence of the Moroccan government's involvement (Allcock 1992). The Moroccan government reasserted its claim to the enclaves again in November 1978, May 1979, December 1980, and December 1982. In February 1983, representatives from fourteen states comprising the members of the Arab Parliamentary Union met in Rabat to back a Moroccan motion to call on Spain to immediately negotiate sovereignty of the enclaves. Further assertions to the territorial claim were issued in August and November 1984, February and July 1985, and March and June 1986. In July 1985, a Libyan-Moroccan Parliament, which resulted from a treaty agreement signed in August 1984 to set up a federation, voted on a resolution to "liberate" the Moroccan territories of Ceuta and Melilla.

The next action taken in the dispute occurred in January 1987 when King Hassan proposed a joint commission or think tank to King Juan Carlos of Spain, made up of Spanish and Moroccan representatives, to discuss the disputed sovereignty of the islands and make proposals on settlement (which is very different from offering concessions). The very next day, Spain rejected the proposal, claiming that "Spain continued to regard Ceuta and Melilla as Spanish and there were therefore no grounds for forming a consultative commission" (D. White 1987b, 2). During a speech in March 1987 celebrating his twenty-sixth year on the throne, King Hassan again reasserted the territorial claim explicitly citing Ceuta and Melilla as Moroccan towns (Gold 2000). In July 1987 Morocco again reasserted its claim to the enclaves. The following year, in October 1988, Moroccan prime minister Abdellatif Filali addressed the UN General Assembly, calling for Moroccan sovereignty over the enclaves.

In the mid- to late 1990s, Moroccan officials reasserted the claim and restated their request for a joint commission to review the status of the enclaves, and each time, Spanish officials rejected the proposals. In March and April 1994, Morocco reasserted its territorial claim, followed by a call in September 1994 at a UN General Assembly meeting by Moroccan prime minister Abdellatif Filali for the creation of a joint commission to examine Morocco's claim to sovereignty, which Spain promptly rejected. The following year, in March 1995, Morocco pressured Spain on the enclaves after King Hassan approved the creation of a new Moroccan government led by Prime Minister Filali. Filali's first address to the parliament included clear references about territorial integrity, not only regarding the Western Sahara but also Morocco's claim to the enclaves. The following month, in April 1995, at the Inter-Parliamentary Union meeting held in Madrid, vice president of the Moroccan Parliament Abdelawahed Radi took advantage of the international forum to reiterate Morocco's claim to the enclaves, which Spain considered an insult (Gold 2000). Another claim was reasserted in September 1995 at a UN General Assembly meeting. Two years later, Morocco again reasserted its claim in September 1997 at the UN General Assembly meeting, followed by another claim in April 1998, just prior to a scheduled bilateral summit.

In April, May, and August 1999, Prime Minister Filali repeated the proposal to create a joint commission, which Spain again rejected. Since then, no attempts at settlement have been made by King Mohammed VI. Despite Moroccan claims to want to settle the dispute, this meager set of calls to negotiate does not indicate an active interest in final settlement when compared to actions taken by actors in other territorial disputes. More importantly, none of the actions involved any offers of territorial concessions in the form of dropping the territorial claim. In August 1999, just three weeks after King Mohammed took power in Morocco after his father's death and just prior to Spanish prime minister José María Aznar's visit to Rabat, Moroccan prime minister Abderrahmane Youssoufi reasserted Morocco's claim, indicating that "Morocco is about to drop its softly-softly approach on the issue" (Tremlett 1995, 13). Youssoufi justified the renewed territorial claims, stating, "Morocco is entering the 21st century under the leadership of a contemporary king, and that it is time for Sebta and Melilia to have a new situation and to prepare Spanish public opinion for this matter" (ArabicNews.com 1999). The Spanish government responded two days later, stating that the "situation of the two pockets [enclaves] is determined in the constitution and therefore there is nothing to be changed," adding that Aznar's visit to Rabat would not involve discussions on the enclaves (ArabicNews.com 1999). Morocco again pressured Spain in December 1999 and October/November 2001 to turn over the enclaves.

In July 2002, Morocco and Spain engaged in minimal use of force in a ten-day crisis that threatened to escalate and that ended due to third-party mediation by the us, un, Arab League, and other organizations. The crisis began when the Moroccan government sent six soldiers to the tiny, rocky, barren, and uninhabited island known in Morocco as Leila, two hundred meters (650 feet) off the northern coast of Morocco less than a mile from the enclave of Ceuta. Within hours the Spanish government sent a diplomatic letter to Rabat, claiming that Morocco had threatened Spanish sovereignty over the island known in Spain as Perejil ("parsley" in English), demanding immediate withdrawal of the Moroccan troops. Morocco responded by refusing to remove the troops from territory they claimed was sovereign Moroccan territory. At the same time, the Spanish government began sending warships to the waters surrounding the island, as well as to the enclaves. Six days after the dispute began, the Spanish military placed twenty-eight Special Forces soldiers on the island, replacing the Moroccan flag with its own flag and taking the six Moroccan soldiers as prisoners (they were repatriated within hours). Over the next few days, more Spanish soldiers were placed on the island, gradually reaching a total of seventy-five soldiers. On July 20, through third-party mediation, both parties agreed to resolve the crisis, demilitarize the island, and meet in September to formalize bilateral relations. Since the 2002 crisis occurred, Morocco has only pressured Spain on the enclaves on two other occasions, one in October 2005 when Morocco threatened not to defend the Moroccan side of the borders of the enclaves, and the other in November 2007 when a claim was issued and a meeting of prime ministers was cancelled.

VALUE OF TERRITORY

For Morocco, the enclaves have fairly limited tangible value. First, they are part of the mainland and not offshore islands, which could be considered a tangible value to Morocco. They do have a permanent population, but the population is Spanish, not Moroccan. This means that for Spain, permanent population matters a lot, but not necessarily for Morocco. Unlike Gibraltar, another disputed piece of land that juts out into the Strait of Gibraltar at the entrance to the Mediterranean Sea (claimed by Spain and owned by the UK), the enclaves of Ceuta and Melilla have no real strategic value for Morocco. This lack of strategic value is because Morocco already controls miles of coastline along the strait that are equally, if not more strategically, significant. A primary point is that neither state has claimed ownership of the enclaves for strategic reasons.

Similarly, the enclaves have relatively little economic value. Ceuta is a port for petroleum products and passengers, while Melilla is a port for iron ore and fishing. Morocco claims that because it did not have access to the ports of Ceuta and Melilla, it was forced to build new ports for trade and passengers in Tangier and Nador (Calvert 2004). This means that the enclaves historically had value before those latter ports were built, but now that these newer ports exist, gaining those in Ceuta and Melilla would not return the investment for building the ports at Tangier and Nador. If anything, money laundering, drug smuggling, illegal immigration from North Africa and sub-Saharan Africa, and growing tensions between Muslim and Christian Spaniards cause many problems for the enclaves' governments. There are no natural resources to be exploited either. The only economic value that the enclaves provide is from tax-free trade, selling fuel supplies to passing ships, small-scale industries, sardines, and anchovies, as well as greater access to fishing rights in the territorial waters around the enclaves and islands, none of which are of significant value. There has also been little investment in the enclaves by Madrid due to their unstable status (Chehabi 1985).

In terms of intangible value, the territory could be considered homeland territory since geographically the enclaves are surrounded by Moroccan homeland territory. However, the enclaves have not been part of Moroccan territory since the sixteenth century, so there is definitely no historic attachment. There is no real ethnic value either. Though some Moroccans do live in the enclaves, they are recent immigrants who moved there by choice to work and who make up a small minority of the population. There is some degree of intangible value as nationalist, symbolic value, but this exists only because the Moroccan government inspired and promoted such value to use for domestic mobilization purposes, and it is not something the people initially perceived.

Limitations of the Value of Territory Explanation

If value of territory is a suitable explanation for the endurance of this dispute, the theory would predict that the dispute should be easier to resolve since the territory is lacking in value. Since the permanent population is not Moroccan, but Spanish, this should also make it more feasible for Morocco to drop its claim without concern about any ethnic minorities in the enclaves. In addition, the territory has no real economic value for Morocco either, making it less likely to for Morocco to settle the dispute in order to realize economic gains. Since the enclaves lack any tangible or intangible value besides the limited nationalist value promoted by the government, value of territory is not the major incentive that drives Morocco's strategy in the dispute. The territorial gains that could be achieved by settling the dispute are not significant enough to provide incentives for Morocco to attempt settlement with Spain. It may be that the lack of value means that the Moroccan government has another incentive for trying to acquire the enclaves. It is not clear why Morocco continues to press its claim on occasion or even proffer a claim to the enclaves in the first place. In either case, the theory of territorial value cannot explain why there have been no real attempts to settle this territorial dispute or why Morocco continues to pursue diplomatic threats on occasion.

DOMESTIC ACCOUNTABILITY AND MOBILIZATION

As early as 1956, following independence from France, "historically conscious Moroccan nationalists earnestly sought Morocco's territorial unity. The reintegration of all Moroccan territories was a necessity and an immediate goal for the nation. The Moroccan border issue was reopened with full vigor and wide implications. Independent Morocco was now ready to pursue and defend her territorial claims, fully convinced of their legitimacy" (Hamboyan 1968, 126). After the Spanish government turned over the enclave of Tarfaya in 1958, Spain announced it was not willing to turn over any other Spanish enclaves in North Africa, and it has stood by this claim to this day. For Morocco, "it was inconceivable that her historically legitimate entitlement could ever be abandoned. National aspirations would never permit demise of these claims" (Hamboyan 1968, 128). However, though the Moroccan government has always claimed that "this is an issue that enjoys sweeping national consensus" (BBC News 1998b), there is little evidence of strong, nationwide public support for the recovery of the enclaves, especially when compared to feelings about the Western Sahara.

A clear case of domestic accountability for Moroccan officials with regard to the enclaves occurred in September 1997 when Spain celebrated the five-hundredth anniversary of Spanish sovereignty over Melilla. The Spanish celebration provoked widespread protests in Morocco. Representatives of the nationalist party Istiqlal called the celebrations "an aggression against Morocco," and Moroccan newspapers described Spanish occupation of Melilla as "500 years of abuse" (Deutsche Presse-Agentur 1997a). The four main opposition groups in Morocco also held a meeting to protest the celebrations in Melilla. As a result of the domestic pressure, Moroccan officials pressured Spanish officials to downplay the celebration, which Spain did by having King Juan Carlos stay at home rather than visit the enclaves during the festivities.

In this way, Moroccan officials satisfied the Moroccan public and opposition groups and were able to prevent domestic punishment. At the same time, though, Morocco's leadership was hesitant to allow protests to get out of hand and potentially hurt cooperative bilateral relations with Spain. King Hassan requested that the protests be minimized, asking trade unions and political parties to keep their members from protesting against the celebrations. Interior Minister Driss Basri also requested that political parties announce a communiqué to halt protests; "Basri's coded message was that the anti-Spanish protests should not get out of hand and damage the relations between Spain and Morocco," according to analysts in Rabat (Deutsche Presse-Agentur 1997b). The call to downplay the protests could have had something to do with the fact that Spain was preparing to approve lines of credit worth $60 million in December 1997 (*Info-Prod Research* 1997). Moroccan officials did not attempt settlement during this time, but as noted earlier, they did not seek settlement at any other time either, so it is unlikely that domestic vulnerability played a role in influencing the choice of dispute strategy.

There is only limited evidence of Moroccan officials attempting to mobilize domestic support by taking action in the territorial dispute. Moroccan officials have occasionally rallied the public around rhetoric of territorial integrity, but it is unlikely that actions were taken regarding the territorial dispute in order to achieve domestic gains. Analysts wondered when King Hassan was still living if he would use force in the enclaves in order to mobilize domestic support. For example, one analyst wrote in 1985, "if the throne of Morocco's King Hassan were seriously endangered at some point in the not too distant future, it is possible that he would resort to the old trick of uniting the nation behind him by ordering an invasion of Ceuta, Melilla, and the three 'plazas menores'" (Chehabi 1985, 222). King Hassan did cite the claim to the enclaves on occasion in speeches given to the nation, such as in March 1987, when he cited the enclaves on the twenty-sixth anniversary of his ascension to the throne.

There was some speculation that the 2002 invasion of Perejil/Leila Island was an attempt by King Mohammed to divert attention from such domestic issues as corruption and socioeconomic pressures. Just the month before, a major trade union had sponsored a general strike in several major cities in Morocco (Maghreb Arab Presse 2002a). A September 2002 poll taken just prior to new parliamentary elections by Maroc 2020, a Casablanca-based nongovernmental organization, showed that the approval rating for the government's performance on reform and social and economic development was 41 percent.

Yet, the poll also showed that the territorial dispute with Spain failed to appear in any of the lists of urgent, moderate, and lesser-priority issues. Instead, unemployment, fighting poverty, dealing with illiteracy, education reform, access to housing, and other basic needs were the issues cited (Maroc 2020 2002). More important is that King Mohammed would have been taking a risky move to use the Perejil/Leila Island incident to mobilize domestic support since at the time of the invasion, most Moroccans had never even heard of the island. Though there were Moroccan protests (involving about four hundred people) against Spain for its military reaction against the Moroccan troops on Leila

Island (Maghreb Arabe Presse 2002b), it is not clear that such anti-Spanish protests translated into pro-Moroccan government and led to domestic mobilization. Even if this were the case, it is highly unlikely that Morocco pursued such a risky military confrontation with Spain to divert attention from a trade union general strike or a relatively decent (41 percent support) amount of domestic support for the government. Therefore, it appears that domestic mobilization was not the driving factor.

Where the Moroccan government has used threats and force to mobilize domestic support is in the Western Sahara, not the Spanish enclaves. The Western Sahara, known as the Southern Provinces in Morocco, has held much more prominence for the people and government of Morocco compared to the enclaves and thus would be the more likely candidate for diversionary force or domestic mobilization. The Moroccan government has used the Western Sahara as a means to distract domestic attention, and it is the only policy issue that unites all political parties in Morocco (Zunes 2002), while the enclaves do not hold such sway among the populace or the selectorate.

Limitations of the Domestic Accountability and Mobilization Explanations

If the domestic accountability and mobilization explanation is to be able to explain Morocco's dispute strategies, first there must be evidence of variation regarding domestic insecurity or unrest. On a variety of occasions, there has been some degree of domestic insecurity for the government. Morocco has been an authoritarian regime since 1956, with limited features of democracy in regard to competition between political parties and a bicameral parliament with more autonomy since King Mohammed II took power in 1999. However, Morocco's Polity IV democracy/autocracy score has ranged from -9 at worst to -3 at best, with 10 being the most democratic and -10 being the most authoritarian. If we look at the years in which Morocco was experiencing some degree of democratization, as measured by an increase in the Polity IV score (1961, 1963, 1977, 1992, 1998), in most of these years the Moroccan leadership pursued no strategies with regard to the enclaves dispute. Yet in 1961, Morocco made its first diplomatic threat when it provoked Spain by taking the claim to the UN. The domestic accountability explanation predicts that during these years Morocco would have been less likely to pursue threats or uses of force or settlement attempts, which is mostly consistent with Morocco's actual record. At the same time, Morocco did not pursue either dispute strategy in most of the years when democratization, high levels of authoritarianism, or other domestic insecurity was lacking, meaning there was little variation.

There were two coup attempts made on King Hassan, one in 1971 and one in 1972, and no action with regard to the enclaves dispute was pursued in the subsequent years until 1975, Yet, this had been the case since 1956, as noted earlier. So again, threats or uses of force and settlement attempts were just as unlikely during or in subsequent years when no coup attempt had occurred. Morocco's leaders should also have been least likely to pursue either dispute strategy during years when Morocco had high levels of authoritarianism (1965 to 1991). This is mainly consistent with the record since in most of those years, Morocco did not pursue attempted settlement or threats or uses of force. However, during this same time, Morocco's government did issue eight diplomatic threats against Spain, which is inconsistent with the theory. There is also no variation in the months and years when protests aimed at the government occurred—in June 1981, January 1984, January 1990, October 1998, April 1999, October 1999, and June 2002 (BBC 1990; *Financial Times* 1998; Kamm 1984; Maghreb Arabe Presse 1999c, 1999b, 2002a, 2002b; and *New York Times* 1981)—and in years when there were no protests, another limitation for the explanation.

Even when King Hassan was extremely vulnerable due to coup attempts, significant criticism from opposition leaders, and domestic unrest caused by high unemployment, corruption, and lack of economic reform, he never threatened or used force in the enclaves to mobilize domestic support. Overall, with the lack of variation and the lack of evidence supporting the explanations, domestic accountability and mobilization do not seem to be able to explain the strategies of Morocco in the enclaves dispute.

Bargaining Leverage

Though Moroccan decision makers have declared that Morocco's territorial integrity will not be complete until the enclaves are returned to Morocco, and thus settlement of the dispute is their main objective, Morocco's dispute strategies suggest that this is not necessarily the case. It would be one thing if Spain had refused to agree to Spanish negotiations over sovereignty, but Morocco has made no offers of territorial concessions and no serious attempts to discuss sovereignty with Spain. Therefore, though it is difficult to say that Morocco is not interested in settling due to lack of resolution attempts, and because it has never actually made a true attempt to settle the dispute, it is not clear that Morocco's only intention is to acquire the enclaves. Even if the main objective is indeed to settle the dispute, Morocco has nevertheless taken advantage of the enduring dispute by making bargaining gains from Spain that it probably could not have otherwise achieved.

Evidence indicates that Moroccan officials have effectively used the territorial dispute and threat to the Spanish-controlled enclaves as bargaining leverage in negotiations with Spain over other disputed issues. Of the thirty-eight threats issued, 58 percent involved issue linkage and coercive diplomacy over several different disputed issues, mainly Spanish support for the Polisario Front and referenda in the Western Sahara, allowing the Sahrawi people a choice of self-determination, Spanish fishing rights in Moroccan waters, and immigration issues. Another 16 percent were linked directly to British-Spanish negotiations or Spain's claim to Gibraltar, which Morocco has been keen to point out was for the same reasons that Morocco claims the enclaves. The remaining threats occurred due to Spanish actions specifically regarding the enclaves, such as the five-hundredth anniversary celebration of Melilla in 1997, the Spanish king's visit to the enclaves in 2007, and autonomy statutes providing Ceuta and Melilla with more political rights, or for other random reasons, discussed below. The number of times other disputed issues were linked by Morocco is listed in table 9.

Besides the dispute over the enclaves and islands in the north of Morocco, Moroccan-Spanish relations have been strained for decades for a multitude of reasons: Spanish support for the independence movement in the Western Sahara, historic antagonism between Morocco's Muslims and Spain's Catholics, illegal Moroccan immigrants living in Spain and their negative treatment by Spaniards, an illicit drug trade across the Strait of Gibraltar, and fishing disputes over access to waters off the coast of Morocco and between the Western Sahara and the Canary Islands. Though relations have improved due to bilateral aid agreements and increased trade in particular, "in the sphere of diplomatic relations between the two countries there is no doubt that the territorial dispute over Ceuta and Melilla has exercised an important influence, and *the issue is raised whenever Morocco finds it opportune to do so*" (Gold 2000, 5; emphasis added). As the challenger state, Morocco has made significant bargaining gains on other disputed issues with Spain by taking advantage of the territorial dispute. As the weaker and poorer state, Morocco has been limited in its ability to bargain hard with Spain and the EU, but the dispute over the enclaves, always a subtle and sometimes provocative reminder that Morocco can

Table 9.   Spanish issues linked by Morocco to territorial dispute

DISPUTED ISSUE	NUMBER OF LINKAGES
Spanish fishing rights in Moroccan waters	8
Spanish support for Polisario or referenda in Western Sahara	7
Spanish negotiations with the UK over Gibraltar	6
Illegal immigration issue	2
Spanish-EU economic aid to Morocco	1
Spanish protest of joint US-Moroccan military exercises	1

threaten Spain, has provided Morocco with a means to even out the playing field to some degree.

In response to Moroccan diplomatic threats about the enclaves, Spain can risk further Moroccan action in regard to the enclaves or accede to some or all of Morocco's demands about other disputed issues. Because Spain will assumedly defend its sovereign territory (as demonstrated in the 2002 crisis described later in the chapter), a threat by Morocco is taken seriously and is considered by the Spanish government to be a high priority. Therefore, when Morocco links the territorial dispute to another disputed issue, Spain seriously considers Morocco's demand for a policy change on the other issue. Morocco knows that Spain values the disputed territory, so Morocco expects that Spain will give in to its strategy and change its policies.

Why would Spain comply with Moroccan demands when it knows it is being coerced? Since the defense of territory is considered to be a vital national interest for states, the cost of losing territory is particularly high. While territory is the most salient issue in international relations and the issue most likely to cause armed conflict (Goertz and Diehl 1992; Huth 1996; Vasquez 1993), it is not surprising that Spain would treat the territorial threats seriously. To prevent further Moroccan actions regarding the enclaves, Spain will generally comply with Moroccan demands on issues that are less salient to Spain, but more salient to Morocco (such as the Western Sahara). Since the threat is about something as salient as sovereign territory, Spain is more likely to change a policy on another less salient issue as a concession, in order to prevent Morocco from taking actions in the much more important enclaves.

Because territorial control is ultimately more salient to Spain than payments for fishing rights or support for independence of the Western Sahara, Morocco's strategy of issue linkage and coercive diplomacy is generally successful. For the most part, Spain has reacted to Morocco's coercive diplomacy and issue linkage by providing nonterritorial concessions on other disputed issues such as fishing rights and downplaying provocations regarding the enclaves. In this way, both sides benefit; Morocco gets concessions in other issues that are minor to Spain but major for Morocco, and Spain gets to protect its sovereignty. As long as other disputed issues exist, and Morocco continues to assert its territorial claim, Morocco has the opportunity to link threats in the enclaves dispute to other issues disputed with Spain. What makes the endurance of the dispute attractive to Morocco is its ability to use the dispute as bargaining leverage in other disputed issues, providing little or no incentive for Morocco to drop its territorial claim for the enclaves unless other disputed issues with Spain are resolved.

There are two primary areas in which Morocco has made bargaining gains from Spain and, by extension, the EU. The first area involves Spanish support for independence of the Western Sahara, a position to which Morocco is fiercely opposed. Since 1975, Morocco has been embattled in a fierce clash over the Western Sahara against the Polisario Front, a group representing the Saharawi people and seeking independence from Morocco, which has received political support from Spain on and off throughout the dispute. The second area is other disputed bilateral issues between Spain and Morocco, most importantly fishing rights of Spanish trawlers off the coast of Morocco and illegal immigration of Moroccans to Spain. These two issues have ignited significant tensions between the two states on numerous occasions, and as shown in the evidence, Morocco has used the dispute over the enclaves to apply pressure on Spain in both issue areas. As a result, Morocco has gained higher financial contributions for fishing rights from Spain and has been able to get Spain to agree to fairer immigration policies and laws applicable to Moroccans.

From 1956 to 1961, during the reign of King Mohammed V, Spanish-Moroccan relations were positive due to Spanish leader General Francisco Franco's support for Spanish independence, so no territorial claims for the enclaves were made by the first king. When King Hassan came into power in 1961, part of his new leadership included a reassertion of Morocco's right to territorial integrity, including the claim to the enclaves and surrounding islands, along with the island of Ifni, returned by Spain in 1969, and Spanish (Western) Sahara, under Spanish occupation until 1975. There appear to be no other reasons for the reassertion except the change in leadership in Morocco and the decision by the king to reassert broad territorial claims. The next reassertion occurred the following year in June 1962 as part of the announcement of a Moroccan territorial waters law, claiming the enclaves and surrounding islands, with no explicit reasons provided by the Moroccan government. No other diplomatic or militarized threats or uses of force occurred for the remainder of the 1960s. This is likely due to the fact that Moroccan-Spanish relations improved significantly as a result of two meetings in 1963 and 1965, when General Franco met with King Hassan to discuss the status of Gibraltar, the island of Ifni, returned to Morocco through the involvement of the UN Decolonization Committee in 1969, and the Spanish Sahara. No discussion of the enclaves or other disputed islands occurred, allowing for improved relations on other issues. The next diplomatic threat was not issued until January 1975, when Morocco took its claim to the UN Decolonization Committee. It is not clear why King Hassan decided to reassert Morocco's claim to the enclaves at this time, but no issue linkage occurred. Likewise, the June 1975 incident when Moroccan and Spanish troops confronted each other at the borders of the enclaves was not a means of issue linkage, but instead a direct response to the arrest of four hundred Moroccans suspected of involvement in bombings that occurred in the enclaves.

Spain's Position on the Western Sahara, 1975–2008

The first use of issue linkage and coercive diplomacy by Morocco as bargaining leverage against Spain was Morocco's explicit linkage of the dispute in the Western Sahara with the dispute over the enclaves in November 1975, in what turned out to be an effective attempt to achieve bargaining gains from Spain. At the same time that the annexation took place in November 1975, King Hassan reasserted Morocco's claim to the enclaves, reminding Spain that the Western Sahara was not the only piece of Spanish territory it wanted. In response to a reference made by King Juan Carlos in his ascension speech after General Franco's death about Spain's wish to acquire Gibraltar, King Hassan announced a few days later that "no power can permit Spain to possess both keys to the same straits" (Rézette 1976, 164).

Morocco's involvement in the Western Sahara and the constant battle with the Polisario Front has indirectly involved Spain since 1975.[2] The dispute between the Polisario Front and Morocco began in 1975 when Spain ceded the territory to Morocco and Mauritania. In 1974, due to international pressure on Spain to cede rights to the then Spanish Sahara, General Franco made arrangements with the Polisario Front, formed in 1973, and Algeria to safeguard Spain's economic interests in the region, and agreed to hold to a UN supervised referendum in the Saharan territory. Morocco and Mauritania protested this move and took the case to the ICJ, yet before a decision had been declared, Morocco and Mauritania arranged a secret agreement to divide the territory between them. Despite the court's rejection of Morocco's and Mauritania's appeals, the two states annexed the territory in October 1975, when King Hassan led the famous Green March, in which hundreds of thousands of Moroccan civilians peacefully occupied the disputed territory carrying nothing but copies of the Koran (Downing 1980). Just a week before General Franco's death in 1975, the weakening leader agreed to hand over the Spanish Sahara to Morocco and Mauritania equally, without any regard for the wishes of the inhabitants of the territory (*Economist* 1978).

The Polisario Front fought a guerilla war against the Moroccan military until September 1991 when the UN arranged a ceasefire. Since then Moroccan leaders have promised referenda on the status of the territory, but such referenda have been delayed for years and have yet to take place despite multiple attempts by the special envoy to the UN on the Western Sahara, James Baker. On numerous occasions, King Hassan and King Mohamed have claimed that securing the Western Sahara as Moroccan territory has been the most significant national interest of the state. Regardless of the rhetoric about territorial integrity, there is strong evidence that the Moroccan people and even the opposition strongly support the government and its military campaign in the Western Sahara: "Hassan has woven the cause into his country's social fabric so well that it is even a rallying cry for Moroccan opposition leaders" (Burns 1995).

Although Morocco claims that both the Western Sahara and the enclaves are significant parts of the mother country, there is little doubt that the more significant territory is the Western Sahara, and not the enclaves. The Western Sahara is the "most pressing foreign policy issue for the Moroccan government," since it has invested so much financial, human, diplomatic, and militarized investment into a territory that makes up one third of the country's size (Zunes 2002, 291). Morocco's major military investments amounting to billions of dollars invested in the Western Sahara attest to this assertion. Estimates from 2007 are that half of Morocco's entire military budget is spent on security of the disputed territory, totaling about $5 billion a year. Over the past thirty years, it is estimated that Morocco spent over $2.4 billion on infrastructure in the region and an additional $870 million from 2004 to 2008. There is little doubt that the amount spent in the Western Sahara "has come at the expense of the development of other regions, many of which suffer from poverty and insufficient state investment" (International Crisis Group 2007). From 1975 to 1987, during the guerilla war waged by the Polisario Front, Moroccan troops numbered 149,000 in the Western Sahara, with losses of an estimated 7,000 Moroccan soldiers. Today, about 130,000 Moroccan soldiers are stationed in the disputed territory (Immigration and Refugee Board of Canada 2000).

Despite the heavy cost of maintaining control of the Western Sahara for Morocco, the economic value of the territory apparently makes it worthwhile. The primary value of the territory is based on rich high-grade phosphate deposits, which has been one of Morocco's most significant exports (CIA 2008; Downing 1980). Morocco is a leading producer of phosphate, a major ingredient of fertilizer, controlling two-thirds of the world's phosphate output. Multiple states worldwide depend on Moroccan exports of phosphate from the Western Sahara. Ownership of the territory also provides rich fishing grounds off the coast of the Western Sahara and potential oil deposits (CIA 2008; Guy 2004). In 2001, Morocco signed oil exploration contracts with several oil companies to explore off the coast of the Western Sahara. Yet since then oil exploration by TotalFinElf, Kerr-McGee, Wessex, and other European oil companies has been halted due to pressure from EU-based ethical investment firms (Guy 2004).

Because of Spain's past occupation of the Western Sahara and its continued support for a referendum for the Sahrawi people, the issue of Spain's support for the Western Sahara has become a long-standing disputed issue causing tension between Spain and Morocco. Spain's military assistance to the Polisario Front on occasion and economic aid to the Saharawi people has not helped either (Gillespie 1999). In response to the diplomatic threat for the enclaves issued by Morocco in November 1975, Spain requested that Morocco back off the claim in exchange for Spanish support for annexation of the Western Sahara. Not only did Spain not interfere, but it signed a Tripartite Treaty with Morocco and Mauritania to cede the partitioned territory to them. What is significant is that this agreement included major concessions by the parties involved, including "fishing concessions [for Spain], a Moroccan promise not to press for the return of the Mediterranean enclaves, and economic guarantees" (Downing 1980, 63). In other words, Moroccan officials agreed to back off from their claim to the enclaves as a concession to get Spain to cede more important territory to Morocco, the Western Sahara. Without the claim to the enclaves, a nuisance for Spain, Morocco would not have had as much bargaining leverage. The very promise to back off the enclaves in exchange for Spanish support of

Morocco's annexation of the Western Sahara strongly suggests that the Sahara was much more salient as territory for Morocco. Therefore, this first use of issue linkage was a combination of negative and positive issue linkage and coercive diplomacy.

During the next few years, Spain found itself in a difficult position regarding the Western Sahara and its relationship with Morocco. Though Spain had sided with Morocco on its claim for the territory, it also had to concern itself with Algeria, Morocco's adversary due to a former territorial dispute with that state, and because of Algeria's military support of the Polisario Front. At that time, Spain depended heavily on Algerian oil and gas exports and was attempting to persuade Algeria not to support the independence movement in the Spanish Canary Islands. At the same time, Spain was keenly aware of Morocco's potential threat regarding the enclaves and therefore knew that it could not withdraw full support for Morocco in the Western Sahara. In October 1978, Spain switched from a pro-Moroccan stance to recognizing the Polisario Front, followed by an open backing of the group once Mauritania withdrew from the Western Sahara in May 1979. The recognition was risky: "Spain's position in the western Saharan tangle is particularly delicate: it needs to keep its relationship sweet with both Algeria and Morocco. . . . But Spain's two enclaves on Morocco's Mediterranean coast, Ceuta and Melilla, dictate a gentle line with King Hassan" (*Economist* 1978, 82). Yet, recognition and support for the Polisario Front was pursued mainly to appease Algeria in order to improve Spanish relations with Algeria because it provides a significant amount of oil and gas to Spain. Two weeks after the October 1978 recognition, King Hassan reasserted the claim to both the Western Sahara and the enclaves in an implicit warning to Spain to back off its support of the Polisario Front (Associated Press 1978).

In May 1979, not only did Spain announce the switch in its policy toward the Western Sahara issue, but Spanish prime minister Adolfo Suárez traveled to Algeria to discuss economic relations and, while there, met directly with the leaders of the Polisario Front, a slap in the face to Morocco. At the meeting, Suárez announced that the "Western Saharans have a right to decide their own future, and the international community must see that they are allowed to exercise it" (*Economist* 1979, 76). Spanish officials predicted that the move would provoke Morocco, but they nevertheless considered the action worthwhile in order to appease Algeria. Suárez also predicted potential issue linkage and coercive diplomacy by Morocco when he told officials in his Union of the Democratic Centre (UCD) party from Ceuta and Melilla that it was possible Morocco could reassert its claim "in connection with the attitude adopted by the Spanish Government on the question of the Sahara following Adolfo Suárez's visit to Algiers. . . . It could not be avoided if, from an opportunist stand, Morocco were to try to take advantage of the situation to bring up the question of Ceuta and Melilla again" (BBC News 1979c). Since then, Spanish support for the Polisario Front and the referendum for self-determination for the Saharawi people has acted as a continual thorn, another disputed issue, for Moroccan-Spanish relations (Gillespie 1999; Gold 2000).

Just five days after Suárez visited Algiers to meet with the Polisario Front, Moroccan officials condemned Spanish support for the Polisario Front, and the Moroccan Chamber of Deputies unanimously approved a statement claiming that "the sovereignty over the Moroccan Kingdom over its restored provinces cannot be affected either by pressure or conspiracies hatched in Algeria at the expense of our holy national cause," and that "the unity of the Moroccan Kingdom cannot be complete without all its usurped lands being restored to it, foremost of which are Melilla and Couta and their dependent islands" (BBC News 1979b). Morocco had been passive about its claim for the enclaves for some time, but provoked by Spain's explicit support of the Polisario, "in retaliation, Morocco has stirred up once more the issue of the Mediterranean enclaves and reopened the fishing dispute" with Spain (Downing 1980, 63), in order to remind Spain of its bargaining leverage regarding the enclaves. This direct linkage between the Western Sahara dispute and the dispute over the enclaves clearly indicates issue linkage, since Spain's support of the Polisario directly influenced the strategy of Moroccan officials regarding the enclaves. Spain's reaction to Morocco's issue linkage of the enclaves and the Western Sahara was to denounce Moroccan claims of the enclaves and announce that "the official position was that the subject was not only not negotiable but also not open to discussion" (BBC News 1979c).

A year and a half later, in December 1980, Spanish officials provoked Morocco by officially recognizing the Polisario and "strongly endorsed the right of the people of the contested Western Sahara to self-determination" (*Facts on File World News* 1980, 995). Ironically, the Spanish move was done as a form of issue linkage in order to arrange for the release of thirty-six Spanish fishermen who had been captured by Polisario guerrillas off the coast of the Western Sahara. The Moroccan reaction was to again link the enclaves to the Western Sahara dispute. Over the next decades, Morocco would use the enclaves dispute again and again in order to put pressure on Spain to back off from supporting the

Polisario and the idea of a referendum to decide whether the Saharawi people preferred independence from Morocco.

The 1980s continued to witness tense relations on occasion between Morocco and Spain due to Spanish support for the Polisario. Yet another disputed issue, fishing rights, arose during this time, adding to the friction. According to the theory of territorial disputes as bargaining leverage, there should have been continued uses of coercive diplomacy and issue linkage, which there were. The first disputed issue to arise since 1980 was a dispute in November 1982 over a Spanish protest regarding joint US-Moroccan military exercises. In early November, the US Marines announced that they were about to start joint practice landings on the Moroccan coast in a location close to the enclaves, a move that led to an official Spanish protest by the new socialist government led by Prime Minister Felipe González, who promised in his campaign to negotiate a base agreement with the US (Hoffman 1982). In response to Spain's protest, Morocco pursued issue linkage and coercive diplomacy by reasserting its claim just ten days after another official Spanish protest about joint US-Moroccan military exercises in December. A few months later, in February 1983, the Arab Parliamentary Union unanimously voted to back a Moroccan claim for the enclaves, which they apparently pursued because of ongoing negotiations between Spain and the UK on Gibraltar. In response to the claim, Prime Minister González "appealed to Spaniards to keep calm" regarding the enclaves issue, "directly linked by Morocco to Spain's claim to sovereignty over Gibraltar" (D. White 1983, 2). Just three days after the Arab Parliamentary Union vote, the director general of the Spanish military ordered air and naval exercises near the enclaves. Though the director general claimed the exercises were part of a regular rotation of military units, the commandant general of Melilla made it clear that the exercises were a warning to Morocco and the Arab Parliamentary Union to back off the claim for the enclaves since the vote had "aroused a certain indignation and rejection among the public" in Spain (BBC News 1983c). With tensions ratcheted, González basically admitted the military exercises served as a warning to Morocco when he asserted, "We are in condition to defend Ceuta and Melilla, which are, without doubt, Spanish cities" (Martinez-Soler 1983, 4).

In this case, Morocco took advantage of the negotiations over Gibraltar to push Spain regarding the enclaves. Morocco did not explicitly link any other disputed issues. However, it appears that in the midst of the crisis, Moroccan officials realized they could potentially use issue linkage and coercive diplomacy with the enclaves to pressure Spain on fishing rights payments. In the previous year, Morocco had regularly renegotiated fishing rights agreements for Spanish fishing boats to have access to Moroccan waters. In early March, Spain and Morocco had begun new negotiations on trade and a fishing rights agreement, the main topic of the talks. By April, Spanish media reports noted that "there are storms looming over fisheries relations between Spain and Morocco" since Morocco had extended a security zone off the coast of the Western Sahara where Spanish fishing was prohibited and had seized three Spanish boats in the zone (BBC News 1983d). This time, the move involved issue linkage of fishing rights negotiations with the Spanish position on the Western Sahara. Spanish officials, who protested against the security zone, realized that they could not negotiate a new fisheries agreement with Morocco, "for to negotiate in regard to the waters of the former Western Sahara would imply Spanish recognition of Moroccan sovereignty over that territory," which Morocco hoped would result through the issue linkage (BBC News 1983a). Though Spain did not officially recognize Moroccan sovereignty in the Western Sahara, by August 1983 Morocco and Spain had agreed to sign a new fisheries agreement with Morocco gaining significant financial concessions and a reduction in Spanish fishing boats of 40 percent (Xinhua News Agency 1983). The Polisario definitely perceived the agreement as a shift in Spain's position when the deputy secretary general of the Polisario Front called the agreement "an act of treachery towards the Saharan people," asking Spain to pressure Morocco on the future of the former Spanish colony (BBC News 1983b). It appears that Moroccan officials realized how they could link a territorial issue with the fishing rights, a move they would later use with the enclaves, reversing the linkage in order to make bargaining gains on fishing rights.

The next reassertion of Morocco's territorial claim to the enclaves occurred in August 1984, not accompanied by any issue linkage, but only because King Hassan felt emboldened by a new military treaty with Libya, a move that caused concern for Spain and its hold on the enclaves (*Economist* 1984). In February 1985, King Hassan again took advantage of Spanish negotiations with Gibraltar (which resulted due to Spain's entry into the EC) and demanded the return of the enclaves to Morocco. A few months later, in July 1985, the Libyan-Moroccan Parliament of the newly created federation passed a resolution in its first session calling for "the liberation of the Moroccan territories of Ceuta and Melilla which are still under colonial rule" (Gold 2000, 6), though no issue linkage was evident.

Fishing Rights Negotiations and the Immigration Issue, 1987–2008

In addition to the Western Sahara issue, Morocco has also frequently used the enclaves dispute as bargaining leverage to gain payments by Spain for fishing rights off the coast of Morocco and as an immigration dispute, starting as early as 1987. In January 1987 King Hassan took advantage of a visit to Morocco by the Spanish minister of the interior, Jose Barrionuevo, and requested that a message be given to King Juan Carlos calling for a joint commission, or think-tank as he called it, to discuss sovereignty of the enclaves. Despite Spain's refusal to consider the creation of such a commission, Moroccan officials continued to press for their claim throughout the year, and yet again "the Spanish government found that the temperature between Madrid and Rabat had been raised by the Moroccan sovereign seizing opportunity to exploit an apparently routine visit by a Spanish minister" (Gold 2000, 8).

The timing of the proposed commission, perceived by Spanish officials as a claim for the enclaves, as evidenced by a February 1987 speech by Prime Minister González referring to the enclaves in his State of the Nation, was not random. The claim was not targeted just as acquisition of the enclaves, but also as a means to make bargaining gains on other disputed issues, immigration issues and Spanish fishing rights in Moroccan waters. Part of the reason why Barrionuevo had come to Morocco for talks was due to violent clashes in Melilla that occurred from January 31 to February 2 involving the Spanish civil guard, flown in from Spain, and the minority Muslim population seeking improved rights denied to them in a 1985 Spanish immigration law. As a result of these clashes and the subsequent talks, King Hassan linked the claim to the enclaves with the treatment of Muslim minorities, demanding improved rights on their behalf.

Another issue that arose was the impending expiration of an agreement allowing access for Spanish fishermen in Moroccan-controlled waters that had been signed by Spain and Morocco in 1983, due to expire in July 1987. At stake was access of seven hundred Spanish fishing vessels to Moroccan waters off the coast of the Western Sahara, one of the world's richest fishing grounds, in exchange for which Spain had paid Morocco $500 million in aid (Ellman 1987b). First, King Hassan decided to let the four-year agreement expire without renewing it or promising negotiations any time in the near future as a bargaining ploy. This decision was detrimental to Spain's fishing fleet, one of the largest in the world, comprising about 28,000 fishermen, because the Spanish fishing fleet catch 70 percent of its yield outside of Spain's territorial waters (Percival 1995).

The issue linkage was deliberate and well timed: "By mid-June 1987 it was clear that Morocco was preparing a new offensive to set up bilateral negotiations with Spain on the future of Ceuta and Melilla. The offensive was to coincide with the visit to Rabat by the Spanish foreign minister, Francisco Fernandez Ordonez, on July 3 and 4 and aimed to use as a lever the expiry of the four-year fisheries agreement between Morocco and Spain on July 31 and its replacement by an agreement between Rabat and Brussels" (Gold 2000, 10). Morocco pursued bargaining leverage by making a "linkage between the fishing pact and its negotiations on a new commercial agreement" and the enclaves (D. White 1987a, 2). At the same time, the government called for a meeting to discuss the "non-traumatic return of Ceuta and Melilla to Moroccan sovereignty" (Gold 2000, 10). Spain got the message loud and clear since Spanish officials were concerned "that the fisheries issue, which affects some 700 Spanish vessels and could become a big social issue in the south, will also be used as leverage in the Spanish enclave question, given the importance which is being attached in Morocco to the King's latest initiative" (D. White 1987a, 2). Yet, Moroccan officials intended to make gains on the fisheries agreement, as well as a related issue regarding the export of Moroccan goods into the EC, not the enclaves. Rather, the "king has practiced subtle linkage between fishing rights and the enclaves to the dismay of Spanish officials who had hoped that entry into the EEC would prevent this" (Ellman 1987b). Hence, Morocco's pressure on Spain for discussions on the enclaves made the Spanish foreign minister's trip to Rabat to deal with the two issues "particularly delicate because of Spain's anxiety to maintain access to Moroccan-controlled fishing waters" (D. White 1987a, 2).

In essence, King Hassan "put considerable pressure on the Madrid Government recently, and has linked the fishing rights issue to the future of the two Spanish enclaves in northern Morocco, Ceuta and Mililla" (Ellman 1987a). The efforts by King Hassan to link the two disputes were done "to squeeze as high a price as possible from Spain in exchange for allowing its vessels to continue to fish in Moroccan waters" (Ellman 1987b). Spain sent representatives to attempt to negotiate with Morocco by offering concessions of transit rights for Moroccan agricultural products to the EC and an offer from the EC for additional funding for an extension of the agreement. Such concessions were equivalent to bargaining gains that Morocco was seeking by using the enclaves as a bargaining chip. More importantly, after extensive talks, the EC agreed on behalf of Spain to provide Morocco with $95 million in exchange for an extension of the fishing rights accord until November 1987. Without its threat to take action on the enclaves, Morocco would have lacked bargaining leverage, which would have made demanding further concessions from Spain on the fisheries issue more difficult.

Two other issues arose in 1988 that created bilateral tensions. The first occurred in February 1988 when the EC ordered that visas would be required for Moroccan citizens (and other North African citizens) to enter Spain, an order that Morocco opposed due to the large number of Moroccans traveling, living, and working in Spain. Even though the order was issued by the EC, Spain bore the brunt of Moroccan frustration since it was cited as the country of entry in the order. The new immigration law was particularly provocative to Morocco since it required visas to enter Ceuta and Melilla, which were considered Moroccan towns (López García, Planet, and Ramírez 1996). Though this immigration issue provided an opportunity for Morocco to use the enclaves to pressure Spain, Morocco did not pursue issue linkage and coercive diplomacy. It is possible that Moroccan leaders felt that since the order was issued by the EC and not directly by Spain, issue linkage and coercive diplomacy would not be an effective strategy. A few months later, partly to appease local parties in the enclaves, the Spanish government announced a bill allowing for further political autonomy of the enclaves. In order to avoid the wrath of Morocco and potential issue linkage and coercive diplomacy, Spain agreed to the largest credit package ever issued to Morocco in the amount of $830 million over a five-year period "to sweeten the pill" (Gold 2000, 12).

Later in the year, though, in October 1988, Morocco pursued a diplomatic threat when Moroccan foreign minister Abdellatif Filali addressed the UN General Assembly, insisting on Moroccan sovereignty of the enclaves. The action was not explicitly linked to any other issue, but it is likely not coincidental that the threat was issued at the same time that Spain offered support for an Algerian motion at the UN to hold a referendum in the Western Sahara (Hernando de Larramendi 1992). Morocco had withheld any demand for the enclaves in an address to the UN for the previous ten years due to its focus on the Western Sahara issue and its wish to avoid confrontation with the UN regarding the issue of self-determination of the Western Sahara. Yet prior to the address to the General Assembly, Morocco had agreed to a peace plan with the Polisario Front, which "allowed Morocco to break its silence at the UN on the issue of the enclaves" (Gold 2000, 13). As a result of the Spanish support for the Polisario Front, Morocco postponed the first visit of King Hassan to Spain, which had been scheduled for November 1988. The combined postponement of the king's visit and the official diplomatic threat regarding the enclaves served as warnings to Spain that Morocco was displeased with its support for Algeria's proposal for a referendum in the Western Sahara.

Over the next few years, the Western Sahara issue remained on the backburner as a disputed issue between Spain and Morocco, but Spain did not pursue any active support of the Polisario or a referendum in the Western Sahara, suggesting that Morocco would not pursue issue linkage and coercive diplomacy and would not avoid seeking settlement attempts through territorial concessions. Morocco's strategies from 1989 to 1993 support the predictions of the theory. The first few years of the 1990s did not witness any coercive diplomacy and issue linkage due to overall improved relations. It is believed that though the official Spanish policy was "not one of appeasing Rabat at any price in order to avoid conflict over Ceuta and Melilla," Spanish leaders made a strong effort to improve relations with Morocco in order to "pre-empt anticipated Moroccan territorial pressures" (Gillespie 1999, 54). There were numerous attempts at improved relations during this time period. First, King Hassan made an official visit to Spain in September 1989, where the two kings signed agreements on mutual investments, military cooperation, and the feasibility of a tunnel linking the two states, avoiding discussion of the enclaves. The following year, Spanish prime minister González visited Morocco, suggesting the significance of good relations for Spain. Even in early 1991 when a portion of Moroccan society argued that Morocco's claim to the enclaves was similar to Saddam Hussein's claim to Kuwait based on territorial integrity, King Hassan not only sided with the Western coalition but also specifically avoided any link with the enclaves so as to avoid tension with Spain (Gold 2000).

In July 1991, King Juan Carlos of Spain visited Morocco to agree to a treaty of Friendship, Good Neighborliness and Cooperation, which dealt with many unresolved disputed issues including development, international law, respect for sovereignty, human rights, and nonintervention in domestic affairs (Hernando de Larramendi and Nunez Villaverde 1996). This was in the middle of a five-year credit deal in which Spain was providing $800 million to Morocco in aid, demonstrating relatively positive Moroccan-Spanish relations (Gold 2000). The following year, King Hassan made no reference to its claim for the enclaves, despite a January 1992 European Parliament decision to link Morocco's human rights record to a decision to postpone the ratification of the fourth protocol of the EC-Morocco Cooperation Agreement, which affected $600 million in European aid to Morocco from 1993 to 1996 (G. W. White 1996). Likewise, in the summer of 1992, when a large number of illegal immigrants attempted to enter Spain, causing problems for the country, King Hassan did not use issue linkage and coercive diplomacy because Spain was actively advocating on behalf of Morocco in an attempt to persuade other European states to provide aid to Morocco. In response to Spain's good offices, Morocco actually agreed to the extension of a European fishing agreement for another two months as a goodwill gesture, allowing for 650 Spanish fishing vessels in Moroccan waters, in exchange for 310 million ECU (European Currency Unit)(Gold 2000). Because of this positive relationship and the lack of overt Spanish support for the Polisario Front, there apparently was no need for Moroccan issue linkage and coercive diplomacy.

By late 1993, after a Spanish election, new issues began to arise, including Spanish threats to freeze quotas on Moroccan produce, the expulsion of Moroccans with false documents, and, most importantly, an upcoming planned referendum in the Western Sahara, which forced Spain to take a position. During the second half of 1993 and into early 1994, the Spanish government also moved forward on its plans for the autonomous status of the enclaves, which directly provoked Morocco. This planned status for the enclaves and Spanish support for the referendum in the Western Sahara provoked Morocco to link the two issues in March 1994. On the first of the month, the Moroccan crown prince visited Madrid to pressure Spain to withdraw support for the Polisario and instead "gain the Spanish government's support for the report to be submitted soon by the UN Secretary General about developments in the peace process in Western Sahara" (Algerian Radio 1994). Just three days after the crown prince's visit to Spain, King Hassan made a speech assessing the status of the enclaves, in which he stated that the Moroccan right to the enclaves was inalienable, and the solution to the dispute "could not wait any longer" (Radio Exterior de España Servicio Mundial 1994). The statement was perceived by the Spanish government as a veiled threat, which Morocco presumably intended it to be.

The understanding in Spain was that "this tough line was being taken partly because of the impending autonomy statues, but also in response to further initiatives by the nationalist party Istiqal, and in the context of imminent activity in the UN over the promised referendum in Western Sahara" (Gold 2000, 18). By restating Morocco's claim to the enclaves just days after a request for Spain to support Morocco in the Western Sahara, King Hassan was able to link the two disputes and use the enclaves, not only to warn Spain about the decision to grant further autonomy in the enclaves, but to pressure Spain on its position in the Western Sahara dispute. After Prime Minister José María Aznar visited Rabat in late March to discuss soured Spanish-Moroccan relations and the Moroccan Parliament pressed the territorial claim, King Hassan again reiterated the need to return the enclaves to Morocco on April 9. Later that year, another reassertion of the territorial claim was issued to Spain in September 1994, this time directly as an offense against a plan by Parliament to pass a statute to further the autonomous status of the enclaves (Percebal 1994).

In March and April 1995, the fishing rights issue arose again, and Moroccan officials made another attempt to link the enclaves dispute with Spanish fishing rights in Moroccan waters. As in 1987, Moroccan officials used the enclaves dispute to make gains on the fisheries issue. This time Moroccan officials insisted on a fishing ban for two months out of each year so that fish stocks could recover. As a result, Morocco insisted that the EU fleet of mostly Spanish vessels limit the level of their normal catch by 50 percent in order to conserve stocks. The EU had paid Morocco $490 million for fishing rights for a three-year contract from 1992 to 1995 and another $41 million for research, training, and infrastructure repairs at ports in Morocco (Percival 1995). Unlike in 1987, when Spain was willing to grant other concessions to Morocco in order to ensure fishing rights to its fishermen, Spain rejected the terms for the proposed new fishing agreement between the EU and Morocco, meaning that Morocco's bargaining leverage with the enclaves was not taken as seriously. Instead of giving in to Moroccan demands, Spain agreed to pay up to $16 million per month to approximately seven thousand Spanish fishermen who were out of work as a result of the disagreement (Tremlett 1995). Despite seven attempts to reach consensus between April and August 1995, no progress was made due to both Spain's refusal to reduce fishing rations and Morocco's insistence on the reductions. By August, Spanish officials were warning that "it will reconsider its ties with Morocco" and that "it would be difficult to cooperate with Morocco in other areas if a new agreement on fishing rights cannot be reached" (Xinhua News Agency 1995). Despite Spain's refusal to compromise, Morocco continued to stand firm, determined to maintain its bargaining leverage. Later in the year, in September 1995, Moroccan prime minister Abdellatif Filali gave a speech at the UN General Assembly calling for Morocco's territorial right to the enclaves (Gold 2000), perhaps as a reminder to Spain of the ongoing issue linkage with the fishing rights negotiations.

By October 1995, progress had been made in negotiations, and the only disagreement was over a subsequent demand by Morocco that fish caught by EU vessels be unloaded at Moroccan ports (*Middle East Economic Digest* 1995). The following month, Morocco succeeded in gaining further concessions in the fisheries dispute when the EU and Morocco signed a new four-year agreement to allow 477 mostly Spanish fishing vessels to fish in Moroccan waters in exchange for $650 million (Damis 1998). Under the agreement, EU fishermen had to reduce their rations and unload them in Moroccan ports (Islam 1995). Not only was Morocco successful in achieving its objectives in the negotiations, but it was also able to secure significant concessions including 350 million ECUs to be distributed over three years and EU trade concessions, which allowed Morocco to export increased quantities of citrus fruit, tomatoes, and cut flowers to the EU (Islam 1995). Again, Morocco was able to effectively gain bargaining leverage on other bilateral issues by linking the enclaves dispute to the fishing dispute with Spain and the EU.

After the fishing rights agreement was signed, relations over the next few years were relatively good, and no other disputed issue arose on which Morocco could make gains with the enclaves threat. At what would be Spanish prime minister González's last visit to Morocco in February 1996, Morocco did not press its territorial claim since the purpose of the visit was to continue improving relations, mainly by Spain considering writing off part of Morocco's $2 billion debt and issuing further credits in the amount of $1.2 billion to Morocco over the following years (Tremlett 1996). In addition, the fishing agreement treaty was signed by the Council of Ministers of the EU later in the month, so there was no reason to pursue issue linkage. Finally, Morocco also suspected that there would be a change in government as a result of impending Spanish elections, which there was, and the timing for a demand on the enclaves would be poor (Gold 2000). No other action was taken by Morocco regarding the enclaves in the initial period of newly elected Spanish prime minister José María Aznar. Aznar appeared to recognize the significance of Morocco to Spain by making Rabat his first official visit outside of Spain in May 1996, where he made no reference to the "Spanishness" of the enclaves as he had during the election (Xinhua News Agency 1996). Bilateral cooperation continued into 1997, with Morocco agreeing in December 1996 to the readmission of sixty-five illegal African immigrants from the enclaves (Radio France Internationale 1996).

However, the following year, in September 1997, tensions arose when the Spanish government held celebrations for the five-hundredth anniversary of Melilla. Morocco was clearly provoked, with King Hassan calling the celebration an act of aggression and demanding that Spain downplay the anniversary,

which they did since neither King Juan Carlos nor Vice Premier Francisco Al-
verez Cascos attended (Deutsche Presse-Agentur 1997a). The following week,
Moroccan prime minister Abdellatif Filali brought up Morocco's territorial
claim to the enclaves again at a UN General Assembly meeting, calling the enclaves Moroccan towns under Spanish occupation, yet no further action was
taken until April 1998 due to continued bilateral cooperation on illegal immigration, countering drug smuggling, civil protection, and technical assistance
(RTM TV Rabat 1998).

In April 1998, the new Moroccan prime minister Abderrahmane Youssoufi
cited the enclaves in an address to the Moroccan Parliament just a week before
a bilateral summit between Youssoufi and Aznar. It is suspected that Youssoufi
brought up the enclaves not for issue linkage in this case, but to act as a reminder of the territorial claim just prior to a bilateral meeting with Spain. The
result of the meeting was to further bilateral cooperation on regional and international issues, stability in the Mediterranean region, economic development,
and bilateral loans from Spain (Kingdom of Morocco Radio 1998).

Despite the relatively good bilateral relations, in April and May 1999, Morocco
made another official claim for the enclaves, linking the claims to another round
of fisheries negotiations. As in 1987 and 1995, Moroccan officials linked the dispute over the enclaves with the fisheries issue in hopes of Morocco attaining
bargaining gains in the form of concessions. It was no coincidence that tensions
had been rising between Morocco and Spain due to Morocco's announcement
that same month that Morocco would not renew the current fishing agreement
that was due to expire at the end of November 1999. Moroccan officials claimed
that EU fishermen, predominantly Spanish, overfished the stocks and that parts
of the 1995 agreement were not respected (*Moneyclips* 1999). Morocco was also
seeking concessions on another issue involving 27,000 Moroccans having access
to seasonal work in Spain in exchange for access to fishing stocks in Moroccan
waters. At a meeting between the new King Mohammed VI and Spanish prime
minister Jose Aznar in August 1999, the two leaders discussed EU fishing rights,
particularly Morocco's decision to let the current agreement expire. Negotiations
on fishing rights were set for September, but Morocco promised that its bargaining stance would not weaken. No progress was made in those or future negotiations, and by December the agreement lapsed.

Other reassertions of the territorial claim were issued in August 1999 with
perfect timing. Not only had local elections in Ceuta and Melilla just led to political chaos, a time that Morocco thought suitable to press its claim, but Aznar

was planning to visit Morocco for a bilateral meeting the following week (Tremlett 1999). At the meeting, Aznar and King Mohammed discussed the fishing rights negotiations, brought up by Aznar, and the enclaves dispute, brought up by King Mohammed (Deutsche Presse-Agentur 1999). It is not clear if King Mohammed explicitly linked the two issues. The other claims were issued in April 1999, then again in December 1999, citing the parallel of Morocco's claims and the end of Portuguese colonial rule of Macau and China's gain of territory (Maghreb Arabe Presse 1999a). As one newspaper editorial stated, "the end of the Portuguese colonial rule of Macau was an opportunity to remind Spain of the need to reconsider its colonial rule of the two Moroccan towns of Ceuta and Melilla which have been waiting for so long to be freed from occupation" (Maghreb Arabe Presse 1999a). In the later cases, though issue linkage occurred, it did not involve other disputed issues, and the enclaves were not used as bargaining leverage. An additional claim was issued in January 2000 specifically as a counter to Aznar's first visit to Melilla, where he issued a statement about the Spanish status of the enclave (Agence France Presse 2000).

In June 2000, Moroccan officials reiterated their refusal to allow EU fishing vessels into Moroccan waters, continuing the deadlock on fishing rights. In December 2000, Spain delimited the maritime boundary of the Canary Islands without consulting Morocco first. Analysts believed "this decision could be linked to the atmosphere which surrounds the Moroccan-EU fisheries talks" (BBC News 2000b). Fishing negotiations continued to fail and the deadlock over EU fishing rights increased tension between the two states. Spain refused to give in to Moroccan demands because "an acceptance of Morocco's conditions would set a bad precedent," indicating its concern for its bargaining reputation (*Financial Times* 2001, 54). By April 2001, both parties ceased ongoing negotiations, mainly due to strong resolve by both sides, but also due to Spain's refusal to give any further concessions to Morocco.

In addition to the fishing rights dispute and failed negotiations, which continued into 2001, two additional bilateral disputes between Spain and Morocco came to the forefront. The first occurred when Spain called on Morocco to step up its efforts to halt organized rings that allowed for illegal immigrants to cross the strait into Spain, blaming Morocco for not taking enough action to halt such movements. At the same time, Morocco was complaining about the expulsion of undocumented immigrants from Spain. In May 2000, Moroccan officials complained to Spanish officials about the poor treatment of Moroccan migrant workers in Spain, hoping that Aznar would address the concern. At a meeting that occurred the same month when Aznar visited Morocco, Prime Minister Abderrahmane Youssoufi raised the issue of the enclaves, reiterating Morocco's claim yet again, this time describing the Spanish-occupied enclaves as dangerous for illegal immigration and Morocco's economy. According to one observer of Spanish-Moroccan relations, "Youssoufi's intervention regarding the enclaves hardly came as a surprise, but there is no doubt that he was more interested in the measures being taken by Spain to protect Moroccan migrant workers, control illegal immigration and assist with his country's underdeveloped northern region than he was with any action relating specifically to the enclaves" (Gold 2000, 30).

By early 2001, Spanish authorities had increased arrests of illegal immigrants significantly. In the first eight months of the year, approximately 8,500 illegal Moroccan immigrants had been arrested in Spain (Agence France Presse 2001a). Relations had worsened significantly by April 2001, not only because of the immigration issue, but also because Spain was threatening retaliation against Morocco for its refusal to renew the fishing agreement, which had led to the unemployment of 25,000 Spanish fishermen (Deutsche Presse-Agentur 2001). By September, bilateral relations had deteriorated significantly due to the exchange of accusations about illegal immigrants to the point that the daily *El Pais* claimed that "all of Spain's problems have their origins in Morocco," which King Mohammed rebuffed (*El Pais* 2001b, 3) and that "the level and tone of the dispute is rising dangerously" (*El Pais* 2001a). In the midst of the immigration crisis, Morocco ceased ongoing negotiations over Spanish fishing rights as well.

In addition to the immigration issue and the fishing rights deadlock, another influential factor was Spain's decision not to support a French proposal to the UN that would favor Morocco's position in the Western Sahara (Giles 2001). In what Moroccan officials called "the straw that broke the camel's back," after more than two years of tension due to disputes over fishing rights and immigration, tensions worsened because of Spain's refusal to back the French proposal (BBC News 2001). Earlier in the year, in March 2001, talks had occurred between Spanish members of Parliament and the president of the Saharan National Council Parliament, provoking Morocco. Spain had also refused to give in to Moroccan demands to support the proposal favoring Morocco's position on the Western Sahara. As a result of the accumulated disputed issues, Morocco withdrew its ambassador from Madrid at the end of October 2001 and postponed a summit meeting scheduled for December 2001 (*El Pais* 2001d). Moroccan foreign minister Mohamed Benaissa made a direct link between the enclaves dispute and the reasons for withdrawing the ambassador. Accusing Spain of taking an aggressive stance regarding bilateral relations, Benaissa simultaneously reiterated Morocco's claim to Ceuta and Melilla, calling them occupied cities and questioning Spain's sovereignty. According to a Spanish news daily, the Moroccan minister of foreign affairs was "particularly critical of the conduct of Spain regarding matters over which the two countries have been most divided in recent years, and also questioned the Spanish sovereignty of Ceuta and Melilla" (*El Mundo* 2001).

Two weeks later, in November 2001, Morocco restated its claim to the enclaves, directly linking Spain's support for a referendum in the Western Sahara. In the statement, government officials noted that "Morocco has demanded the support of Spain in seeking a quick and definitive solution to the question of Western Saharan autonomy within the Moroccan kingdom" and called for the end of Spanish occupation of Ceuta and Melilla since it was anachronistic (*El Pais* 2001c, 27). Moroccan officials had made a direct link between its pressure on Spain to support the Moroccan position on the Western Sahara and the enclaves. Later in the month, relations worsened when four Moroccan journalists were sent home and not allowed to cover a protest in Seville demanding independence of the Western Sahara (Agence France Presse 2001b), and Moroccan authorities seized a Spanish fishing boat (ABC.es 2001). Despite the pressure put on Spain and the attempt to show resolve by reminding Spain of Morocco's claim to the enclaves, Spanish officials continued to support the idea of a referendum so that the people of the Western Sahara could decide their own future.

The second and only other threat of militarized force by Morocco against Spain occurred in July 2002 when Morocco claimed that it had the right to conduct military surveillance on its sovereign territory and occupied the island of Leila/Perejil. Shortly after the ten-day crisis, Moroccan secretary of foreign affairs and cooperation Taieb Fassi Firhi made a direct link between the Leila/Perejil Island incident, Moroccan claims for the enclaves, and other disputed issues. Calling for a frank discussion of "all the subjects that disturb the relations between both countries," he specifically cited territorial claims in the Western Sahara, the fishing area around the Spanish Canary Islands, and clandestine immigration from Morocco to Spain (*El Pais* 2002; Sanz and Egurbide 2002). As a commentator noted, "the real reasons why Mohammed VI ordered the comical invasion of Parsley" became evident to Spanish officials only after the crisis was defused (Hamilos 2002).

The Moroccan government placed troops on the island claiming to use them for surveillance, but it appears they were placed there to test the waters of a Spanish reaction, as in a wait-and-see approach to coercive diplomacy. More importantly, it is likely that the Moroccan government chose to provoke Spain using subtle military action in order to send a message that they were serious about their territorial claims against Spain. It is likely that they estimated a military reaction by Spain, at least in terms of sending warships to protect the enclaves, even though they claimed to be shocked and called the military action an act of war and disproportionate considering how minor the dispute is, and that Morocco was devoted to diplomatic channels rather than using its force in the dispute.

In the end, the Moroccan government succeeded in linking the crisis with the enclaves dispute, the Western Sahara, and other disputed issues. As a result of the bargaining leverage, it seems that

> Morocco might just have gained a rare upper hand.... Yesterday's talks in Rabat were seen by many as a political trap into which Spain had foolishly placed its foot. Knowing that his troops would easily be repelled, but that the resulting fracas would turn the world spotlight on to Morocco's grievances, Mohammed VI was prepared to accept a minor humiliation over Parsley Island. Whether he wins the diplomatic victories over Ceuta, Melilla, the Canary Islands and the Western Sahara remains to be seen, but he is obviously quite happy to play a waiting game. Spain, on the other hand, can ill-afford to be drawn into a diplomatic spat with an impoverished Muslim nation that, no matter what the plans of its king, wants little more than modernisation and a fair crack of the whip. (Hamilos 2002)

For Morocco, the postcrisis talks provided a jumping point from which other more important and pressing issues concerning Morocco could be discussed with Spain, particularly the thorny issue of the Western Sahara and the territorial waters around the Canary Islands, which are full of fish and more recently were linked to potential oil exploration. For several months prior to the crisis, many other disputed issues had been building up:

> What one witnessed was the accumulation of disputes to which there was no concerted problem-solving response. The crisis did not begin on 1 July; there had been various incidents and points of tension over the preceding year. Some examples of unsettled disputes are the suspension of the fishing agreement between the EU and Morocco, the obstacles placed by Spain where

agriculture is concerned; the divergences over Western Sahara and over the control of illegal migrants, with the Spanish government actually proposing economic sanctions against their countries of origin, in other words, primarily against Morocco. To this list one has to add that for Moroccans it is not acceptable to see progress in the resolution of the Gibraltar issue without similar progress over the issue of Ceuta and Melilla. (de Vasconçelos 2002)

In February 2002, Spain had announced in a royal decree that it would authorize oil drilling in the waters between the Spanish-owned Canary Islands and the Moroccan coast. The Moroccan government had immediately protested the move, claiming it threatened Moroccan sovereignty. With regard to the Western Sahara issue, Spain had returned to its original position on the Western Sahara, arguing again that the Saharawi people should be provided the choice of self-determination. As a Spanish think tank report noted, "The choice of Spain as a non-permanent member of the Security Council, just when the Council is about to decide on the final statute for the territory [Western Sahara] is undoubtedly uncomfortable for the Moroccan government, though it officiously maintains that Spain no longer matters" (del Pino 2002). Therefore the timing of the threat of force was not coincidental, while Spain was voting on a Security Council resolution regarding a referendum in the Western Sahara. Even though it was never admitted explicitly, it is pretty clear that the Leila incident had not been the main focus of Morocco's crisis with Spain; rather the focus was these other pressing issues with Spain. Morocco used the crisis to signal resolve to Spain, not only on the enclaves dispute, but also with regard to the disputes over fishing rights, Spanish oil drilling, illegal immigrants, and general relations between the two states. To some degree, one could say that Morocco succeeded in its use of issue linkage and coercive diplomacy; no referendum occurred in the Western Sahara, no economic sanctions were placed on Morocco for the issue of illegal immigration to Spain and the EU, and it would take another three years of negotiations before Morocco agreed to a certain amount of concessions for Spanish fishing rights in Moroccan waters.

Moroccan-Spanish Relations under Zapatero, 2004–2008

After the Spanish election of a socialist government under the leadership of Jose Luis Rodriguez Zapatero in 2004, Spanish-Moroccan relations improved significantly. This ease of relations was primarily due to Zapatero's policy of providing Morocco with concessions, which Morocco was happy to take in exchange for improved relations. During Zapatero's tenure in office, Spain and Morocco cooperated on several ventures, including joint peacekeeping forces deployed to Haiti in 2004, joint cooperation in the fight against Islamic terrorism, joint border patrols of the enclaves to prevent illegal immigration from sub-Saharan Africa to Europe, and Spanish assistance to improve Morocco's relations with other EU states (McLean 2006). In May 2005, to signal better relations, Spain sold Morocco M-6 tanks on the condition they were not positioned near Ceuta and Melilla.[3] The deal was made possible in the context of Zapatero's attempt to normalize bilateral relations with Morocco and Morocco's pledge to limit its territorial claim on the enclaves. All of these improved relations imply that there were no other disputed issues, but this was not the case. Without the shift in Spain's policy toward the Polisario in the Western Sahara and further concessions in terms of fishing rights, Morocco was in no position to drop its claims to the enclaves or offer any form of concessions. Despite the pledge not to push the claim, Moroccan leaders have still continued to use the dispute to gain concessions in other issues.

Finally, in July 2005, Morocco agreed to a four-year fisheries agreement with the EU, only allowing 120 fishing boats (compared to 600 from 1995 to 1999) and favoring Spanish and Portuguese fishing vessels, in exchange for $173 million. The delay in the agreement allowed for the replenishment of fish in Morocco's territorial waters and the development of Morocco's own fishing fleet (Afrol News 2005). Clearly Morocco gained significant concessions from the EU as a result of its delay tactics and Spain's pressure on the EU to provide Morocco with concessions in order to get its fishing fleet employed again. It is not clear how much Morocco's threats regarding the enclaves and other disputed issues had to do with the pressure felt by Spain, but in the end, if it played a role, the issue linkage and coercive diplomacy worked.

In fall 2005, the Spanish government had to deal with a crisis of sub-Saharan African migrants attempting to cross from Morocco into the enclaves to gain European residency. Illegal immigration is considered to be the most pressing political problem for the socialist government, based on Spain's vicinity to the African continent, even ahead of rising unemployment and terrorism (Narayanswamy 2005). In late September and early October 2005, thousands of migrants swarmed the border security fences into Ceuta, and eleven migrants were killed attempting to climb the fences.[4] Spain demanded that Morocco take more responsibility in preventing the tens of thousands of migrants who had made it to Morocco from getting to the enclaves' borders. Taking advantage of the immigration crisis and Morocco's continued claim on the enclaves, the Moroccan government responded by saying that it lacked the proper security forces, and what was needed was a modern Marshall Plan in which Spain would provide Morocco with economic aid.

Using issue linkage and coercive diplomacy, King Mohammed demanded that Spain provide economic funding for Moroccan development before Moroccan security forces would be able to help Spain with the immigration crisis (Africa News 2005). By making such a demand, Morocco was able to use the territorial dispute by threatening to allow the migrants to get to the borders of the enclaves in order to gain concessions on another issue, economic aid. Spanish prime minister Zapatero responded to the demand by promising to consider increased economic aid to Morocco. Two days after the Moroccan king made his demand, Zapatero responded by saying, "We must contribute to reducing the prosperity gap between Spain and Morocco," attacking the skepticism of the opposition party, the Popular Party. Zapatero also stated that he would ask the EU for economic aid for Morocco at the next European Council meeting (*La Razon* 2005). Morocco's strategy had worked. To protect the more important issue of sovereignty and security of the enclaves and prevent illegal immigration, Spain was willing to give a minor concession to Morocco. Morocco was able to use the enclaves issue as bargaining leverage, which provided the king with the opportunity to request increased economic aid from Spain and the EU.

Eventually, Spain had a change of position regarding the Western Sahara since it offered support for an April 2007 Moroccan proposal to provide limited autonomy to the Saharawi people in parts of the Western Sahara. Since then, Spain has maintained a position of "positive neutrality" regarding the Western Sahara, but there is no guarantee that a new Spanish government will not revert back to supporting a referendum for the Saharawi people. Again, it is not clear whether Moroccan linkage of the enclaves to Spanish support for the Western Sahara played a role, but Morocco gained Spanish support on the issue, meaning that the Western Sahara issue ceased to exist as another disputed issue between Spain and Morocco, at least for the time.

Since mid-2007, there has only been one issuance of a diplomatic threat regarding the enclaves, but no use of coercive diplomacy. In November 2007, Morocco reiterated its claim specifically in response to an announcement that the Spanish king and queen would visit the enclaves for the first time to signal their attachment to the citizens. Upon hearing the news, Moroccan prime minister Abbas el Fassi expressed his shock at their intention to visit "the two robbed cities, Ceuta and Melilla," and made another explicit claim that the territory was Moroccan and "their return to the motherland will be completed through direct negotiations with neighboring Spain as was the case with regard to Tarfaya, Sidi Ifni and the Moroccan Sahara" (RTM TV Rabat 2007). The next day, the Moroccan Foreign Ministry announced the decision by King Mohammed to recall Morocco's ambassador to Spain, heightening tensions to the worst point they had been since Zapatero came into office in 2004. The recall was followed by a letter of protest written by the Moroccan speakers of the House of Representatives and Chamber of Counselors to the Spanish ambassador in Rabat. In the letter, they made implicit threats by calling on

> the Spanish constitutional institutions to stop causing harm to Morocco and to reconsider their stands which will, no doubt, have negative consequences on bilateral relations and also on the common interests of the two countries . . . the Moroccan people, who are attached to their total territorial integrity, aspire to a serious and immediate dialogue in order to close this chapter of the decolonization of Ceuta and Melilla and the occupied islands [Leila], an approach which they regard as a responsible prelude to the continuation and consolidation of relations between the two countries and to building these relations on healthy and solid grounds, free from domestic political calculations and the base of which should be cooperation and good neighborliness. (Maghreb Arabe Presse 2007b)

Despite the protests, the royal visit to the enclaves occurred on November 5 and 6. In response, King Mohammed openly threatened Spain with consequences and strongly condemned the visit, claiming that "we hold the Spanish authorities responsible for jeopardizing the future and the progress of bilateral relations" (Maghreb Arabe Presse 2007a). The king admitted that the recall of the Moroccan ambassador from Spain was to signal Morocco's serious dissatisfaction with the Spanish royal visit to the enclaves. In this conflict, there was no specific issue linkage besides the general threats of bilateral relations being affected. Morocco's actions were most likely as strong as they were because they did not want to signal acquiescence to Spain about the royal visit. Diplomatic relations were reinstalled in January 2008 when the Spanish foreign minister visited King Mohammed in Morocco. No other diplomatic or militarized threats have since occurred.

CONCLUSIONS

Overall, the theory of territorial disputes as bargaining leverage provides a strong explanation for Moroccan strategies in the enclaves dispute. Without any significant value, tangible or intangible, in the enclaves for Morocco, it appears that the value of the disputed territory is not what is driving Moroccan strategies. Similarly, domestic accountability and mobilization opportunities have not really been pursued by Moroccan leaders using the enclaves dispute. Rather, the emphasis has been on domestic mobilization using the Western Sahara territory, a much more salient piece of territory for Morocco and one that unites all aspects of Moroccan society. The pattern demonstrated here is that Moroccan officials have pursued diplomatic threats and avoided making any territorial concessions because they were able to gain bargaining leverage using issue linkage and coercive diplomacy with regard to the enclaves. As long as other serious disputed issues have existed between Morocco and Spain, mainly the Spanish position on the Western Sahara, fishing rights in Moroccan waters, and illegal immigration, Moroccan leaders have had no incentive to work toward resolution of the enclaves dispute and less incentive to give up their opportunities to issue diplomatic threats to Spain by reasserting Morocco's territorial claim for the enclaves. By maintaining the claim, using occasional coercive diplomacy, and not considering any form of territorial concessions, Morocco has been able to use the dispute as bargaining leverage against Spain with regard to other disputed issues, as long as they continued to be problems for Morocco.

As the challenger state in this territorial dispute, Morocco has been successful in taking advantage of this dispute with Spain by linking it with other bilateral issues disputed with Spain. By far the most important dispute linkage has been Morocco's attempts to influence Spanish support for their position in the Western Sahara against the Polisario Front. Moroccan officials have consistently linked the two disputes, reminding Spain that Morocco could threaten the enclaves if Spain did not withdraw support for the Polisario Front and its objective of independence. Despite Spain's resolve in supporting the Western Sahara's independence and not the Moroccan position, Moroccan officials continued to link the two disputes in order to provide Morocco with bargaining leverage that it otherwise would not have.

Morocco has been most successful in achieving bargaining gains from Spain in the form of economic and other concessions in the fishing rights dispute. Starting in the mid-1980s, each time the contract for Spanish/EU fishing rights in the waters off the coast of Morocco came close to expiring, Moroccan officials deliberately let the contract expire, claiming that the conditions set by the previous contract were no longer sufficient. Moroccan officials would then conveniently reassert the claim for the enclaves around the same time, using the enclaves dispute as a bargaining chip in the fishing rights dispute. By linking the enclaves dispute with the fishing rights dispute, Morocco was successful in acquiring extra concessions from Spain and the EU as part of their renegotiated fishing rights contracts. Most recently, Moroccan officials linked the enclaves dispute with a dispute over illegal immigrants in Spain. Though few concessions have been won, there have been some gains made by Morocco, and Morocco has so far avoided being the recipient of threatened Spanish economic sanctions. Thus, the dispute linkage has been worthwhile. As with the fishing rights issue, Moroccan officials have used the enclaves as a bargaining chip to signal resolve to Spain on an issue in which they otherwise do not have much bargaining strength.

As the weaker state with less bargaining power, Morocco has chosen an effective strategy, coercive diplomacy and issue linkage, which has paid off over the years when other disputed issues have arisen. Due to the significant concessions Morocco has achieved by using the territorial dispute as bargaining leverage, as long as other disputed issues with Spain continue to exist, there should be little incentive for Morocco to attempt to peacefully resolve the territorial dispute by dropping its claim for the enclaves. The likelihood of the enclaves dispute enduring for some time is high, at least as long as Morocco can use the dispute as bargaining leverage in other disputed issues, mainly the Western Sahara issue and renewed fishing rights negotiations. Both of these issues are ongoing and have the potential to flare up again, when Spain takes an action regarding support for the Western Sahara or when fishing rights contracts expire and negotiations start again. For Spain, this means that Morocco's territorial claim will likely continue to act as a thorn in its bilateral relations with Morocco. Unless Spain wants to risk Morocco following through with threats about the enclaves, Spain will have to continue to comply with Moroccan demands on other disputed issues.

This territorial dispute between Morocco and Spain should be of particular concern to policy makers since the enclaves often act as a bridge from Africa to Europe for illegal immigrants, drugs, and other smuggling. In recent years, there have been several crises resulting from mass numbers of sub-Saharan African migrants attempting to cross from Morocco into the enclaves to gain

European residency. Illegal immigration is considered to be the most press-ing political problem for the socialist government, based on Spain's vicinity to the African continent, even ahead of rising unemployment and terrorism (Narayanswamy 2005, A08). Because of Spain's membership in the EU, this im-migration crisis affects not only Spain but also all other EU member states, who by law cannot extradite the migrants to their home countries. Therefore the disputed enclaves act as the doorstep for Europe's immigration crisis. Perhaps a more significant security concern is the fact that the enclaves, Melilla in par-ticular, are sources of Islamic extremism and a key location for jihadist recruit-ment for terrorism in Spain. In August 2006, two men in Melilla were arrested on suspicion of carrying out the 2003 Casablanca bombings, and the following month, eleven Islamic extremists were arrested in Ceuta for having links with al-Qaida. The diplomatic tensions caused by Moroccan claims for the enclaves continue to negatively affect bilateral cooperation between Morocco and Spain on immigration, terrorism, and other salient issues. Until major disputed is-sues, mainly the Western Sahara dispute, fishing rights negotiations, and ille-gal immigration, are settled once and for all, the likelihood of resolution of this dispute is low.

CHAPTER EIGHT

The Sino-Soviet/Russian Border and Territorial Dispute

I n March 1969, two nuclear powers, the People's Republic of China (PRC) and the Union of Soviet Socialist Republics (USSR), came close to full-scale war after major armed clashes occurred along their disputed border. Almost forty years later, after several decades of hostility and unwillingness to resolve the dispute, these two major powers settled their longstanding territorial dispute in July 2008. This territorial dispute is worthy of study not only because it was so enduring and finally resolved, a stronger test for the theory, but also because it caused significant tension between two of the world's greatest powers. The resolution of this dispute has a direct impact on the status of the international system since Chinese-Russian relations have grown stronger over the past decade as both states agreed to work toward resolution. More importantly, the resolution of the dispute takes off the table the potential of armed conflict between these two nuclear powers. For several decades, the dispute played a key role in the tensions between the PRC (China henceforth) and the USSR (Soviet Union henceforth), and the disputed border was labeled "one of the most explosive international boundaries in the world" (An 1973, 13).

Even though major armed conflict occurred only in the 1960s, minor clashes continued through the 1970s, and the border was consistently manned with dozens of heavily armed divisions and deployed nuclear weapons on each side of the border throughout the 1980s.[1] A Chinese scholar argued in the early 1980s, "In view of both the enduring nature of the conflict and the importance of the political roles the PRC and the USSR play in the world arena, the Sino-Soviet boundary dispute has caused world concern and deserves scholarly attention" (Tsui 1983) (see also An 1973; Chew 1970; Doolin 1965; Ellison 1982; Ginsburgs and Pinkele 1978; Hinton 1976; Jackson 1962; Robinson 1970, 1971; Watson 1966). Though policy makers no longer need to worry about the potential for armed conflict related to the territorial dispute, there are significant lessons to be learned from this dispute, making it very worthy of study.

The main questions examined in this chapter are why China, as the challenger state, was unwilling to attempt settlement of its border dispute with the Soviet Union/Russia for so many decades, why it initiated diplomatic and militarized threats on occasion, but not at other times, and why it offered territorial concessions on occasion, but not at other times, including major concessions that eventually led to the final settlement of the dispute. I examine monthly data on all actions taken regarding the border dispute—settlement attempts and diplomatic or militarized threats and uses of force from 1960, when the dispute was initiated, to 2008, when the dispute was resolved, and any other disputed issues that existed or were resolved between China and the Soviet Union/Russia during this time period. As with the other chapters, I also examine the potential role of the value of territory and domestic accountability and mobilization as alternative explanations.

The overall findings in this chapter demonstrate that China was unwilling to attempt settlement or offer concessions when other disputed issues existed, mainly those dubbed the "three obstacles," but once these were resolved, China was finally willing to work toward settlement of the border dispute. Over the years, China deliberately and explicitly linked the settlement of the border dispute to these three other disputed issues, as well as broader geostrategic concerns about relative power, using diplomatic and militarized threats and uses of force in the territorial dispute and demanding that the Soviet Union resolve these other outstanding disputed issues that were of concern regarding China's national security. China's strategy of issue linkage worked well; not only did the Soviet Union effectively address China's concerns eventually, but China immediately agreed to negotiations and territorial concessions once the other disputed issues were resolved, resulting in final settlement in 2008.

THE SINO-SOVIET/RUSSIAN BORDER

Though often referred to as a border dispute, China also claimed a significant amount of territory controlled by the Soviet Union for much of the dispute. Therefore, it is more accurate to label this dispute as a border and territorial dispute. The dispute over the border, covering 4,500 miles, the longest land border in the world, focused on two sections, east and west, divided by the presence of Mongolia. The eastern part of the border totals approximately 2,670 miles,

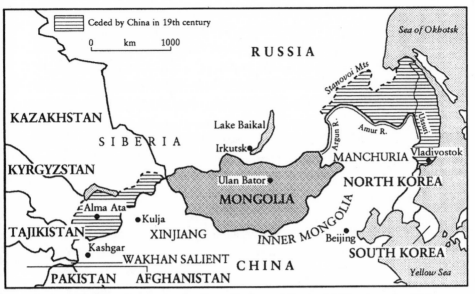

Figure 4. The Sino-Russian border. From *Border and Territorial Disputes,* 4th edition, Peter Calvert, ed., London: John Harper Publishing, 2004.

while the western border, in Central Asia, totals about 1,865 miles. Most of the eastern border comprises rivers and islands that were disputed between the two states, including the Amur/Heilong River, the Ussuri/Wusuli River, and the Argun/Erhkuna River.[2] The western border mainly comprises mountain ranges including the Altai and Pamir Mountains, one of the highest mountain ranges in the world.

The border dispute was mainly about a disagreement over the location of the boundary in the rivers, whether it was the deepest channels (Thalweg principle), one shore line or the other, or the middle of the river. The river boundary disputes also influenced the sovereignty of around seven hundred islands located in the disputed rivers, including the Damansky/ Zhenbao Island where the major border conflict took place in 1969 and Bolshoy Ussuriysky/Heixiazi Island, an island of about 135 square miles, which was the last island dispute to be resolved. In addition to the disputed boundary, in the 1960s and part of the 1970s China claimed hundreds of thousands of square miles of Soviet controlled territory, stating it was unfairly annexed by the Russian Empire in past centuries due to unfair treaties.

The dispute dates to the seventeenth century when tsarist Russia expanded territorially toward the Pacific Ocean as well as southward toward Central Asia and China. According to a Chinese scholar, it is well known that some of the territory that became part of Russian, then Soviet, territory was once Chinese (Tsui 1983). An American scholar agrees, noting, "From a historical point of view, the Chinese have several just grievances, at least in terms of prior claims and occupation" (Fitzgerald 1967, 683). Through the centuries Russia and China signed several treaties to determine the border between their two territories, the first of which was the 1689 Treaty of Nerchinsk/Nipchu, followed by the Bur Treaty in 1727 and the Treaty of Kiakhta in 1728, which focused on the western portion of the border.

Tsarist Russia pursued a second stage of southward expansion in the mid-nineteenth century, acquiring territory formerly recognized by the Treaty of Nerchinsk/Nipchu as Chinese, mainly along the Amur/Heilong River.[3] A third treaty, the Treaty of Aigun, was signed by China's military governor of Heilongjiang Province in 1858 in the midst of the second Opium War, while the British and French were threatening major Chinese cities. In the treaty, China ceded to Russia a significant amount of territory, including sixty-four Chinese villages and about 232,000 square miles along the border. As a reward for providing good offices to negotiate a peaceful settlement of the Opium Wars, in 1860 the Russian tsar also demanded territory east of the Ussuri/Wusuli River, to which the Chinese agreed in the Treaty of Beijing. The Treaty of Peking followed in 1860, in which China accepted Russian annexation of the region around the Ussuri/Wusuli River, an area of around 155,000 square miles. In Central Asia, China also ceded 135,000 square miles to Russia around Xinjiang Province in the Sino-Russian Protocol of Cheguchak/Tarbagatai in 1864, followed by the ceding of more territory in subsequent treaties signed in the 1880s (Tsui 1983).

The dispute came to the forefront in 1911, when Dr. Sun Yat-sen, leader of the newly declared Republic of China, demanded that the previously signed treaties from the nineteenth century be abrogated since they were unequal and thus null and void. In the same year, Russia demanded that the eastern portion of the border be delineated again, and as a result the Treaty of Tsitsihar was signed by a provincial governor in December 1911, in which Russians annexed an additional 600 square miles from the Chinese side of the border. The treaty was not ratified, however, so it was considered null and void by the Chinese national government (Tsui 1983). According to the Chinese government, as a result of China's weakness during the Opium Wars, Chinese officials were forced to sign the Treaty of Aigun in 1858 and the Treaty of Peking in 1860, ceding significant amounts of territory to Russia. More problematic is that the treaties left some degree of ambiguity, placing close to 130,000 square miles between the Ussuri/Wusuli River and the Pacific Ocean under joint Sino-Russian sovereignty "pending a future decision on the matter" (Hobday 1987, 261).

The first real tensions regarding the border dispute occurred near Outer Mongolia from 1911 to 1913, when the militaries of the two countries clashed and came close to war due to Russian attempts to annex further Chinese territory. Chinese leaders claimed that Russia took advantage of political chaos in China at the time, and Russian attempts to re-delimit the border actually led to boundary markers being moved and the subsequent annexation of territory on the Chinese side of the border. After two decades of Manchu rule by China, the Mongols declared independence and requested Russian support and protection, which led to protests by the new Chinese republican government (An 1973). In 1915, Russia agreed to recognize Chinese sovereignty over that particular disputed territory in the Russian-Chinese Mongolian Treaty (Tsui 1983). The new Soviet Union agreed in July 1919 to declare most treaties with China signed by former "bourgeoisie" Russian governments (led by tsars) null and void, but the Treaties of Aigun and Beijing were not cited, claiming that the people living in the affected territories could decide in which state they wished to live (Calvert 2004). Talks were held in 1924 and 1926 to demarcate the border but resulted in no agreement, with the border ambiguity left as the status quo for several decades. In subsequent decades, China was engulfed in civil conflict and war against Japan, so the border dispute with the Soviet Union was a nonissue.

From the birth of the People's Republic of China in 1949 to the 1960s, Sino-Soviet relations were relatively friendly and positive, as indicated by the 1950 Treaty of Friendship, Alliance, and Mutual Assistance, which included no reference to any dispute over the border and instead made reference to respect for each other's territorial integrity. Though the new PRC government declared that all treaties signed with foreign governments prior to 1949 would be abrogated or would need revision or confirmation, Chinese officials made no actual attempt to claim territory annexed by the Russians/Soviets. For the sake of building positive relations with the Soviet Union, China "refrained from making public expression of disagreements on territorial questions," but there was always some degree of resentment about the treatment of the border and how it was shaped by Russian tsars (An 1973, 58). A brief reference was made in the friendship treaty requesting mutual respect for sovereignty and territorial integrity, but no actual dispute was noted. It is believed that Chinese leaders brought up the territorial issue when Nikita Khrushchev visited China in 1954, and again in 1957 Chinese prime minister Zhou Enlai officially noted the border question on a visit to Moscow, where he requested that the Soviet Union "make proper arrangements for the territorial issues covering Japan, China, and the Middle East," along with European states bordering the Soviet Union (Ginsburgs and Pinkele 1978, 9). An analysis of this statement concluded that China's intention was not "detaching large chunks of peripheral Soviet territory and parceling them out among the interested contiguous states," but instead was an attempt to signal grievances about the Sino-Soviet border based on past treaties (Ginsburgs and Pinkele 1978, 11). In response, the Soviets simply took the statement to mean that the Soviet Union should maintain the territorial status quo with its neighboring states.

In April 1960, Zhou Enlai again cited the Sino-Soviet border in a speech in Nepal, in which he noted that the border and territorial disputes were considered "insignificant divergences on the maps" that would be "easy to solve peacefully" (Calvert 2004, 160). This was not an actual claim to disputed territory, but only part of a series of Chinese attempts with all of its neighbors to delineate and demarcate its borders. Only in August and September 1960 did the first official territorial claim occur when the Chinese government proposed to the Soviet government that negotiations be held "on the settlement of the pending issues regarding the Sino-Soviet boundary delineation" (Foreign Broadcast Information Service [FBIS] Daily Report 1969). According to a Chinese specialist of the dispute, the initiation of the dispute "was obviously prompted by the fact that some border troubles had already occurred" in areas in the western border region (Tsui 1983, 33).

The Soviet response in October 1960 was that no dispute actually existed, a typical response from target states when first confronted by challenger states in territorial disputes. This Soviet attitude, to claim that no border dispute existed (especially between communist brethren), continued until late 1963 when Soviet officials accepted Chinese proposals to begin border negotiations as a result of several border clashes that had occurred (Tsui 1983). As late as 1974, Soviet premier Leonid Brezhnev denied any legitimate Chinese claim: "Peking, in fact, puts forth, as a preliminary condition, no more no less than the demand of withdrawal of the Soviet frontier guards from a number of areas of our territory, to which the Chinese leaders now decided to lay claims, which they began to call 'disputed areas.' And Peking declares outright that it will only agree to negotiations on frontier questions after its demands about these 'disputed areas' are satisfied. Comrades, it is absolutely clear that this position is totally untenable and we reject it . . . for us there are no 'disputed areas'" (Brezhnev 1975, 90).

DISPUTE STRATEGIES

Since 1960, China and the Soviet Union actively disputed the placement of their border and surrounding territory until they resolved the dispute with finality in 2008. During this time, as the claimant or challenger state, China made sixteen diplomatic threats and pursued dozens of militarized threats or uses of force, primarily from October 1964 to March 1969 (Tsui 1983); twenty-two of the main militarized threats or actions are listed in table 10.[4] From 1960 to 2008, China made twelve attempts to settle the border and territorial dispute, listed in table 11, by offering and agreeing to territorial concessions; only one offer or concession occurred in the 1960s, and the remaining ones took place after 1987. China initiated and agreed to many rounds of border negotiations in the 1970s, but it was unwilling to agree to or offer any territorial concessions.

It was only in the early 1960s that border incidents began occurring. Though the dispute had been on the back burner for both states for many decades, in the early 1960s the border dispute became a major cause of the subsequent Sino-Soviet rift and a key determinant of future bilateral relations between the two great powers (Tsui 1983). The first major incident occurred when a provincial Chinese government ordered hundreds of cattle herders to cross deep into Soviet territory and settle there in the fall and winter of 1960, despite demands by Soviet border guards to return to China. In April 1962, both China and the Soviet Union reinforced their military garrisons in their respective border regions, upping the ante. There were allegedly thousands of incursions by Chinese citizens across the border each year in the early 1960s, all by the order or encouragement of Chinese officials (Ginsburgs and Pinkele 1978). This strategy is similar to the Chinese government's encouragement of citizen groups or fishermen sailing to the disputed Senkaku/Dioayu Islands in the East China Sea to provoke Japan in the 1970s through 1990s.

In March 1963 the Chinese government–run *People's Daily* specifically cited the unequal treaties with the Soviet Union, the first time the dispute was discussed publicly, and asked, "In raising questions of this kind do you intend to raise all the questions of unequal treaties and invite a general settlement?"—interpreted by the Soviets as an indication that China was reserving the right to reinitiate the territorial claim in the near future (Hobday 1987, 262). The Soviet

Table 10. Chinese diplomatic actions and militarized threats/uses of force, 1960–2008

DATE	TYPE	CHINESE ACTION	REASON FOR ACTION
Fall/Winter 1960	Diplomatic	Hundreds of Chinese settlers ordered to cross into and settle in Soviet territory	Start of rift in bilateral relations
April 1962	Militarized	Reinforced garrisons along the border	Growing rift in bilateral relations
March 1963	Diplomatic	Restated threat for claim along disputed border	Growing rift in bilateral relations
February 1964	Diplomatic	Territorial claim expanded	Growing rift in bilateral relations
July 1964	Diplomatic	Mao threatened territorial claim; border talks suspended	Chinese concerns about Soviet attack on China's nuclear installations
November 1964	Militarized	Border clashes	Armies provoked each other
1965	Militarized	Deployment of troops on border increased	Disagreement about escalation of conflict in Vietnam
October 1966	Militarized	Chinese troops opened fire at Soviet ships in Amur River	Positional issue—concerns about Soviet power relative to China
February 1967	Militarized	600,000 Chinese troops put on alert at border	Geostrategic concerns about Soviet power relative to China
Late 1967	Militarized	Fighting on Damansky/Zhenbao Island	Geostrategic concerns about Soviet power relative to China
1968	Militarized	Fighting on Damansky/Zhenbao Island	Soviet intervention in Czechoslovakia/ Brezhnev Doctrine
March 2, 1969	Militarized	Chinese troops opened fire on Soviet border guards	Geostrategic concerns about Soviet power relative to China
March 15, 1969	Militarized	Fighting on Damansky/Zhenbao Island	Geostrategic concerns about Soviet power relative to China
April 1969	Militarized	Fighting along Central Asian border	Geostrategic concerns about Soviet power relative to China
August 1969	Militarized	Fighting along Central Asian border	Geostrategic concerns about Soviet power relative to China
December 1969	Militarized	Deployments of troops increased to 28 divisions	Increasing concern about border defense
December 1970	Militarized	4 more divisions added to border deployment	Increasing concern about border defense
1973	Diplomatic	China withdrew cooperation on navigational issues	Chinese resolve for claim
March 1974	Militarized	Chinese forces captured Soviet helicopter; held crew	Soviet incursion into Chinese territory

Table 10. (*continued*)

DATE	TYPE	CHINESE ACTION	REASON FOR ACTION
May 1974	Diplomatic	China withdrew cooperation on navigational issues	Chinese resolve for claim
August 1977	Militarized	Border clashes at Xinjiang province border	Armies provoked each other
September 1977	Militarized	China threatened to impose a counterblockade in rivers	Chinese resolve for claim
February 1978	Diplomatic	Demand for withdrawal of Soviets from disputed border region	Chinese rejection of Soviet proposed joint statement on principles
May 1978	Militarized	Fighting on Chinese side of border	Initiation of force by Soviet patrol landing on Chinese bank of Ussuri River
February 1979	Militarized	Chinese border troops put on alert	Soviet support of Vietnam in Sino-Vietnamese war
March 1979	Militarized	Chinese border troops put on alert	Soviet support of Vietnam in Sino-Vietnamese war
April 1979	Diplomatic	Cancellation of friendship treaty; demanded reduction of Soviet border troops	Soviet troops stationed in Outer Mongolia
July 1979	Militarized	Border clash	Armies provoked each other
January 1980	Diplomatic	Cancellation of negotiations	Soviet invasion of Afghanistan in December 1979
April 1980	Diplomatic	Refusal to engage in border negotiations	Three obstacles—Soviet occupation of Afghanistan; Soviet troops in Mongolia; Soviet support of Vietnam's occupation of Cambodia
October 1980	Militarized	Border clashes	Large Soviet deployment to border
June 1981	Diplomatic	Refusal to accept Soviet attempts to reopen border negotiations	Soviet-Afghan border treaty signed in June 1981
1982	Diplomatic	Refusal to accept Soviet attempts to reopen border negotiations	Three obstacles cited
March 1983	Diplomatic	China refused to sign nonaggression pact and measures to restore confidence on the border	Three obstacles cited
October 1983	Diplomatic	Refusal to move further in normalization talks without removal of ss-20 missiles and reduction of troops along border	Three obstacles cited

Table 10. (*continued*)

DATE	TYPE	CHINESE ACTION	REASON FOR ACTION
March 1984	Diplomatic	Refusal to move further in normalization talks without removal of ss-20 missiles and reduction of troops along border	Three obstacles cited
October/ November 1984	Diplomatic	Refusal to move further in normalization talks without removal of ss-20 missiles and reduction of troops along border	Three obstacles cited
July 1985	Militarized	Chinese patrol opened fire in Soviet territory	Armies provoked each other

interpretation was accurate; in 1960 China had begun an official policy of mass Chinese settlement in the disputed border region, and in response the Soviets claimed that the Chinese military and civilians were violating the Soviet border in attempts to develop Soviet territory.

Though not publicly disclosed at the time, the Soviets offered to negotiate territorial concessions in May 1963. China responded with a vague proposal in August 1963 in which the Chinese stated that negotiations rather than force should be used to resolve the dispute. In November 1963, China consented to participate in the Soviet-proposed border talks but strongly requested that the forthcoming talks be kept out of the media, noting that they should be considered as consultations, not negotiations (Ginsburgs and Pinkele 1978). The consultations occurred in February 1964, where Chinese representatives reasserted their claim and demanded that the Soviet Union officially recognize that the nineteenth-century treaties were unequal. The Soviets rejected the demand and denied that any border dispute even existed, leading to an impasse in the talks (Tsui 1983). The Soviets then publicly blamed the Chinese for the breakdown in talks, claiming that "the 1964 consultations showed that the Chinese side had no intention of reaching an agreement" (Ginsburgs and Pinkele 1978, 101). According to materials released more recently, Chinese and Soviet representatives actually made some significant progress in the dispute and agreed to a delimitation of the eastern border (Fravel 2005). This agreement, though it was not pursued again until 1991, was the only territorial concession made by China (and the Soviet Union) until 1987.

Table 11. Chinese settlement attempts/territorial concessions, 1960–2008

DATE	CAUSE OF CONCESSIONS	OUTCOME OF NEGOTIATIONS
May 1964	To get Soviets to agree to recognition of unequal treaties	Impasse, due to lack of Soviet recognition of unequal treaties
February 1987	Vladivostok speech—Gorbachev's offer of concessions to China on other disputed issues	20 percent reduction of Soviet troops from Mongolia in the spring and summer; continuation of talks
August 1987	Second round of talks	Agreement to redraw river boundaries
November 1988	Proposed Soviet withdrawal from Afghanistan by February 1989; Soviet acquiescence to Chinese control of the Spratly Islands	Continuation of talks
May 1989	Soviet pressure on Vietnam to resolve the Cambodia dispute	Demilitarization of border
June 1990	Violence in Xinjiang	Increased cross-border trade
May 1991	Compromise achieved	Establishment of official river borders; Russian concession of 700 islands and 1,500 hectares of land to China; Chinese agreement to drop territorial claim in Russia's Far East
September 1994	Significant reduction in size of Soviet forces	
November 1997	Compromise achieved	Continuation of talks
April 1999	Compromise achieved	1,163 islands in the Amur River were agreed to be Russian; 1,281 islands agreed to be Chinese
July 2001	Compromise achieved	Treaty of Good-Neighbourliness, Friendship, and Cooperation signed
2004	Compromise achieved	Russian offer of two islands to China
July 2008	Compromise achieved	Last two disputed islands delimited and demarcated

In a July 1964 speech, Chairman Mao Zedong of China expanded the territorial claim, adding 580,000 square miles, based on the unequal treaties of the nineteenth century. In addition to the territorial claim, Mao also questioned Soviet territorial integrity by challenging the Soviet right to the Kurile Islands/Northern Territories, disputed with Japan, as well as parts of Romania, Poland, and East Germany (Griffith 1967). Khrushchev's response pointed out that China had no political right to a territorial claim, nor did they have any right to question Soviet territorial integrity, but the Soviets were willing to discuss the border dispute dealing with ethnic rights of local peoples. The failure of the border talks in early 1964 appears to have acted as a major turning point in the large-scale deployment of troops on both sides of the border (Tsui 1983). The first militarized use of force by China since the reinitiation of the claim occurred in November 1964. From the summer of 1965 to 1969, border tensions increased significantly, including dozens of Soviet flyovers of Chinese territory, mass deployments of troops on both sides of the border, and incursions of troops on both sides, ultimately leading to armed clashes in the spring and summer of 1969. For example, in October 1966, Chinese troops opened fire on Soviet ships in the Amur River on a number of occasions. Chinese troops numbering six hundred thousand were put on alert at the border in February 1967, and many minor clashes occurred throughout 1967 and 1968. The number of Soviet troops also increased into the Far East region of Siberia starting in the latter half of 1967.

The largest-scale fighting in the dispute occurred on March 2 and 15, 1969, provoked by Chinese border patrols that were ordered to patrol the disputed Damansky/Zhenbao Island in the Ussuri/Wusuli River, where they were expected to provoke Soviet troops, which they did. As early as January 1968, the Military Council of the CCP Central Committee had sent instructions to Chinese military districts along the border to build up troops in key regions along the eastern sector of the border and ensure critical preparations for an offensive attack against the Soviets, waiting for the right circumstances. Plans for the actual attack were drawn up in January 1969, with the timing meant to undermine a planned meeting of communist parties led by the Soviet Union. Zhenbao Island was chosen since this island had been one of the territories the Chinese considered turning over in the 1964 talks, so it had less value for the Chinese. At the same time, it was estimated that an attack on this particular island would incite a response by the Soviets. Meticulous planning occurred up to the end of February 1969, and the strike occurred on March 2 (Danhui 2005).

In response to the fighting, both governments justified their territorial claims and actions and issued venomous attacks on the other side, such as the Chinese claim that Khrushchev and other Soviet leaders were "a herd of swine" and that the Soviet Union was "a traitor to the sacred cause of communism" (Jones and Kevill 1985, 95). Mass demonstrations of hundreds of thousands of people occurred in both Beijing and Moscow, protesting the actions of the adversarial state. Fighting also occurred in April and then again in August 1969 along the western border just five days after border negotiations regarding river navigation. It is believed that this time the Soviets initiated the armed conflict to keep China off balance (An 1973).

In the years prior to the armed conflict, China had refused to even meet at the bargaining table to discuss the border dispute. After the March, April, and August 1969 conflicts, the Soviet Union "suddenly became the 'eager' party for resolving the boundary disputes between the PRC and the USSR" (Tsui 1983, 64). The Soviets again proposed talks in April and then again in June 1969, while the Chinese remained uncommitted. Further fighting occurred in August 1969, allegedly pursued mainly by the Soviets to compel China to resolve the border dispute and work toward normalization. This was followed by a rapid Soviet troop buildup along the border and threats of imminent military invasion deep into China to destroy nuclear weapons installations (Sutter 1986). The conflict ended and talks resumed upon the September death of Vietnamese leader Ho Chi Minh, who had issued a statement during the fighting, appealing for "the restoration of unity among the fraternal parties" (Calvert 2004, 160). A brief meeting occurred in Beijing when Soviet Premier Aleksei Kosygin made a detour to China on his way home from Ho Chi Minh's funeral to meet with Zhou Enlai. At the meeting, China agreed to resume border negotiations. However, though China in principle agreed to negotiations, the following month the Chinese reiterated their firm stance on the border question, a move that was intended to signal that China had no intentions to compromise or consider territorial concessions (Sutter 1986; Tsui 1983).

Several rounds of border talks took place, first from the end of October to the end of December 1969, then from January to April 1970, and again from January to the summer of 1971. At each round, the two adversaries had difficulty even figuring out the agenda due to their differing views on the existence of a border dispute, and they began each round with uncompromising positions (An 1973). During the last round of talks, the Soviet Union made a territorial concession offer to China to partially accept the Chinese position regarding the boundary in the Amur/Heilong and Ussuri/Wusuli rivers, which was "apparently the best 'offer,' so far, the Soviet side rendered" (Tsui 1983, 71). The Soviets also offered to hand over several islands in the Ussuri/Wusuli River, particularly the recently fought over Damansky/Zhenbao Island (Quested 1984). Yet Chinese officials rejected the concessions, made it clear that their position had not changed since 1964, and demanded the unconditional return of all islands in the disputed rivers. The Soviets responded by attempting to justify their prior annexation and ownership of allegedly disputed territories claimed by China (Tsui 1983). At the same time as the ongoing negotiations, China was increasingly concerned about border defense, increasing its deployment of military divisions on the Chinese side in December 1969 and December 1970.

A fourth round of talks occurred in the spring of 1972, with both sides firmly holding to their positions. In these talks, the Soviets offered further concessions in the hope that such concessions would improve Sino-Soviet relations and prevent détente and improving relations between China and the US from continuing. The timing of the Soviet visit to Beijing for border talks was deliberate since President Richard Nixon had visited China in February and was scheduled to return in May (Quested 1984). In the fifth round of border talks, held from March to June 1973, the Soviet government attempted to persuade the Chinese government to sign a nonaggression pact, which Chinese officials rejected, mainly due to the Soviet refusal to withdraw troops from the border and the increase in military divisions deployed to the border during this time (Gaiduk 2008). Concessions offered by the Soviets and rejected by the Chinese in this round were also intended to influence Sino-American détente. No progress was made in the following two rounds of border talks, held in the summer of 1974 and spring of 1975, mainly because a Soviet helicopter had crossed into Chinese territory in March 1974, ratcheting up tensions between the two states. In 1973 and 1974, China made two diplomatic threats and used force once regarding the disputed border. On the first two occasions, China withdrew and refused to cooperate regarding navigational issues along the disputed rivers (Maxwell 1978). Throughout the 1970s, both China and the Soviet Union continued to deploy increasing numbers of troops to the border, and it is reported that hundreds of incidents occurred each year, though most of these were not made public (Tsui 1983).

Subsequent rounds of talks, a diplomatic threat, and a use of force occurred in 1976, 1977, and 1978. The only progress made regarding the border dispute was the decision at an October 1977 session of a joint commission for navigation on the border rivers to agree on the navigation of Chinese ships on the eastern shipping lane when water in the other shipping lane (on the Chinese side of the river) was too low (Hobday 1987). This outcome was a result of a decision the month before by the Soviets to lift a river blockade that had been imposed since 1969, which itself had been the Soviet reaction to a Chinese threat to impose a counterblockade. As Maxwell (1978, 144) notes, "The message clearly intimated that Soviet vessels could not expect to continue to use that passage unhindered unless the Soviets lifted their blockade down-river." Even though the Chinese had shifted their overall position toward the Soviet Union after the death of Chairman Mao in September 1976, the Chinese position on the border and territorial dispute did not shift, and by the end of the ninth round of talks held in April 1978, neither side had modified its position, leaving the dispute at an impasse (Segal 1985).

No other border talks occurred until 1987. Instead, China shifted its focus to overall bilateral relations with the Soviet Union, and talks occurred every year or so throughout the 1980s. In February 1978, China demanded that the Soviets withdraw from the border region, rejecting a Soviet proposed joint statement on principles. Fighting occurred on the border in May 1978 as a result of a Soviet patrol landing on the Chinese bank of Ussuri/Wusuli River. Tensions ratcheted again in the spring of 1979, with several militarized threats occurring, including Chinese forces stationed along the border put on alert in February and March 1979. In April 1979, Chinese officials made an offer to the Soviets to hold talks in which they would discuss "the solution of outstanding issues and the improvement of relations between the two countries" (Tretiak 1979, 764–65). At the same time, China notified the Soviet Union of its intention not to extend their friendship treaty and demanded a reduction of Soviet troops along the border. Another round of talks was held focusing on bilateral relations, but they ended at the beginning of December without any progress having been made (Segal 1985). In the meantime, a border clash occurred in July 1979, resulting in the death of a Chinese soldier, but both sides claimed that the other initiated the incident (Segal 1985).

The Soviet Union's invasion of Afghanistan at the end of December 1979 prevented any further talks, and it would take many concessions on the part of the Soviet Union to get China to agree to reinstate border talks in the latter 1980s. In January 1980, after the Soviet Union had invaded Afghanistan, Chinese officials canceled scheduled meetings dealing with bilateral relations and the border dispute in particular, stating that they would have to be put off since it was considered an inappropriate time for such negotiations (Calvert 2004). Chinese officials also refused to meet with the Soviets in negotiations in April 1980. The border dispute worsened when a Chinese border patrol opened fire in Soviet territory in July 1980, and then border clashes occurred in October 1980, and again in 1981 when the Soviets mobilized the largest number of troops ever along the disputed border. In June 1981, Chinese officials announced that they would not agree to border negotiations, followed by several Soviet attempts to restart negotiations in 1981 and 1982, which China refused to consider. When the Soviets offered a nonaggression pact with China in 1983, China refused, along with proposed measures to restore confidence on the border. Later that year, in October, China refused to move forward in normalization talks without the removal of ss-20 missiles and a reduction of troops along the border. Chinese officials also withdrew from normalization talks for the same reasons in March and October/ November 1984. The last militarized use of force occurred in July 1985 when a Chinese patrol opened fire on Soviet troops, but it is not clear what provoked the soldiers to open fire.

After several years of no border talks, the two adversaries finally met to discuss sovereignty issues in August 1987. Both sides agreed to consider redrawing the disputed river boundary, the first time China agreed to consider any territorial concessions. Though significant progress was made on determining the river boundary, further progress was stalled due to the existence of hundreds of disputed islands, allowing the dispute to persist. China agreed to continue border talks, which were held in November 1988, where both sides agreed to further territorial concessions. Sino-Soviet relations were normalized in May 1989 with a historic meeting of Mikhail Gorbachev and Deng Xiaoping. In May 1991, Russia and China signed the Sino-Soviet Border Agreement at the end of negotiations to establish the deepest channel of the Argun/Erhkuna, Ussuri/ Wusuli, and Amur/Heilong rivers as the official border in the east. Russia also agreed to concede 700 islands and 1,500 hectares of land to China along its border, and China provided a major territorial concession by agreeing to drop any territorial claim in Russia's Far Eastern region. This major breakthrough essentially resolved most of the eastern border with Russia. The treaty was ratified by the Supreme Soviet of the Russian Federation in February 1992 and approved by the Chinese National Assembly in March 1992 (Bakshi 2001). The outcome of the border negotiations led to the resolution of 98 percent of the border disputes (Calvert 2004), resulting in the persistence of only a small part of the border disputes. Upon the breakup of the Soviet Union, China then had to resolve border disputes with several new states, including Kazakhstan, Kyrgyzstan, and Tajikistan, as well as Russia.

Through the early 1990s, both states worked to delimit and demarcate the exact location of the border, placing markers along the settled boundary. Yet no attempt was made by China until September 1994 to deal with the disputed islands. In that month, the two states agreed to demarcate the western border, which had been greatly reduced due to the fact that most of the disputed border now belonged to former Soviet republics that would deal directly with China. In December 1994, China ratified the agreement resolving the western border dispute, and Russia ratified the agreement in May 1995 (Bakshi 2001). The next round of talks occurred in November 1997 and finally in April 1999, where 1,163 islands in the Amur/Heilong River were agreed to be under Russian control and another 1,281 islands under Chinese control (Bakshi 2001). The two former adversaries announced in December 1999 that the border dispute was primarily resolved, with all but three islands assigned, leaving only a tiny portion of the dispute unresolved.

In July 2001, the two former adversaries signed the Treaty of Good-Neighbourliness, Friendship, and Cooperation based on strong bilateral relations and shared security interests in the region and international system, which included final provisions for settlement of the territorial dispute. The status of the three remaining disputed islands was resolved in 2004 when Vladimir Putin offered two of the three islands to China, despite protests from local governors, as part of the Complementary Agreement between the People's Republic of China and the Russian Federation on the Eastern Section of the China-Russia Boundary, signed by both Russia and China. In the agreement, Russia agreed to turn over Yinlong Island and half of Bolshoy Ussuriysky/Heixiazi Island to China. By signing the agreement, China dropped its claim to the other half of Bolshoy Ussuriysky/Heixiazi Island. The legislatures of both states approved the Complementary Agreement in 2005. The foreign ministers of both states signed an agreement in Beijing on July 21, 2008, for the final demarcation of the border. On October 14, 2008, Russia officially ceded half of Bolshoy Ussuriysky/Heixiazi Island, turning it over to Chinese troops, which served as the symbolic and formal end of the decade-long settlement process. Currently, the two states are working to set up a free trade zone on the island for easier transfer of products between the two states.

VALUE OF TERRITORY

Overall, the value of the islands in the disputed rivers and the disputed territory occupied by the Soviet Union in eastern Siberia is relatively minor. On the salience scale ranging from 1 to 12, with 12 being the most salient, the Sino-Soviet border has a score of only 3 (Hensel and Mitchell 2005). With regard to intangible value, the disputed region is part of the Chinese homeland and not colonial territory, and it has a permanent population, but it was and still is sparsely populated. In terms of tangible value, the disputed border region is part of the mainland, but is a border region at the same time. There is not significant economic value in the disputed areas along the border, mainly because they are desolate with limited populations, and there are no actual natural resources in the formerly disputed areas. The only limited economic value that the river islands provided for China was in terms of shipping access to the Pacific Ocean from the northern parts of Manchuria. One of the last islands to be divided in the resolution of the dispute, Bolshoy Ussuriysky/Heixiazi, does have some value for Russia in that it is the main source of drinking water for the second largest city in that region, it is close to the main channel of the Amur/Wusuli River, and, probably least important, it is the location of family gardens where potatoes are harvested for citizens of a nearby city (Bakshi 2004). Lowenthal (1971, 513) describes the disputed border:

> The disputed islands themselves are worthless. The prospect of a multiplication of similar incidents along the endless frontier offered to the Soviets no possible gain, but the nightmare of having to tie down large forces for recurring, indecisive battles against an enemy specializing in hit-and-run warfare and disposing of inexhaustible manpower. The Chinese, on the other hand, whose propagandist exploitation of the incidents was far better prepared—with detailed maps—could make excellent use of them for maintaining the "besieged fortress" spirit in general and popular hostility to the "new Tsars" in particular beyond the end of the cultural revolution.

It is believed that economic value makes attempts at settlement more likely and armed conflict less likely, yet this factor was consistent while settlement attempts and militarized threats varied significantly, regardless of the limited economic value.

If anything, the only tangible value attributable to the disputed border region was strategic. As China increasingly viewed the Soviet Union as more of a national security threat through the 1960s, the heavily militarized border grew in strategic value, making attempts of settlement less likely and militarized threats and uses of force more likely. Not only were troop divisions deployed along the border, but the military balance between China and the Soviet Union was shifting and growing, both in conventional and nuclear terms. During the 1960s and 1970s while China was embroiled in its Cultural Revolution and its economy stagnated, Soviet nuclear capabilities increased significantly. On average, the Soviets deployed 150 new intercontinental ballistic missiles (ICBMs) each year, some targeted directly at China. The Soviet Union also deployed medium-range nuclear missiles along the disputed border, therefore giving strategic value to the disputed territory. China, though inferior in terms of nuclear capabilities, also deployed about twenty medium-range nuclear missiles in regions near the border (Tsui 1983).

Limitations of the Value of Territory Explanation

China's initiation of numerous diplomatic and militarized threats and uses of force and the variation in attempts at settlement can only partially be attributed to the value of the disputed territory. The disputed border is likely to have had strategic value only because it was militarized, therefore making this factor endogenous. This is likely the case since any alleged strategic value dropped when the border was demilitarized in the late 1980s during the negotiations. Yet the presence of nuclear missiles along the border would have been likely regardless of whether the border was disputed, so there is some credence to the argument that the border itself was salient due to the presence and severe threat of nuclear missiles. The imbalance of military capabilities can explain the lack of willingness of China to use force to resolve the dispute in the 1970s (Tsui 1983), but not necessarily at other times.

The strategic value cannot explain the lack of settlement attempts, except for the possibility that tensions were so high due partially to the nuclear deployments along the border that China was unwilling to consider territorial concessions at that time. In fact, nuclear deployments were also reduced along with military troops by both sides in the 1980s because the two states were working toward normalization and then eventually dispute resolution, so again it is difficult to know whether the strategic value of the border region caused or was the result of the attempts to resolve the dispute in the latter 1980s. Even if strategic value was a major factor for Chinese dispute strategies, the problem is that dispute strategies varied during the time when strategic value remained the same.

It could be argued that the ethnic value of the disputed territory, based on an overlap of Chinese minority ethnic groups living across the border, played a role in influencing the likelihood of settlement attempts. However, this factor is not likely since the Soviet Union had invited these minority groups to migrate into Soviet territory due to Chinese repression. Along the eastern part of the border, the population was sparse and there were very few Chinese residents in the disputed territory. In the western region, there were also no established Chinese inhabitants (Fitzgerald 1967).[5] More importantly, no Chinese claims for the territory occupied by tsarist Russia in earlier centuries ever cited the reunification of Chinese people, which is the strongest evidence that ethnic links really played no role in Chinese strategies in the dispute.

It is possible that the disputed territory had symbolic, nationalist value for China, making it salient and thus less likely for China to attempt settlement, but this is difficult to prove. None of the claims made for the disputed territory made any mention about the salience of the territory as part of the homeland, as Chinese rhetoric about other territorial disputes has, focusing instead on the unequal treaties that tsarist Russia made Chinese officials sign in the nineteenth century. Overall, value of territory has a difficult time explaining the variation in Chinese settlement attempts and diplomatic and militarized threats or uses of force because, besides strategic value, there was no variation in value from the 1960s to the 1990s. There were, however, major shifts in strategy regarding attempts at settlement and threats and uses of force made by China regarding the territorial dispute. Additionally, the strategic value was mainly endogenous to the dispute, so once the dispute was resolved, the strategic value went away.

DOMESTIC ACCOUNTABILITY AND MOBILIZATION

There is limited evidence of Chinese officials using the border dispute with the Soviet Union as a means to mobilize domestic support. An argument could be made that the border dispute was part of China's drive to reassert its control over historically lost territories. For example, in the early twentieth century Sun Yat-sen cited the Heilong and Wusuli river basins as territory that once belonged to China, and in the 1940s Mao cited his bitterness toward the Soviet

Union for "encroachment on Chinese territorial sovereignty" (An 1973, 61–62). There are several occasions when domestic mobilization did occur based on the border dispute, most strongly in March 1969 when the border conflict occurred. When the dispute first began in 1960, the Chinese government discussed the dispute in school textbooks, spreading Chinese territorial nationalist sentiment and anti-Soviet sentiment, much as it later would do with the Senkaku/Diaoyu Islands and anti-Japanese sentiment. This mobilization was typical of Chinese strategy, but it does not necessarily suggest that the dispute was reinitiated in order to mobilize domestic support for the government for the sake of mobilization, but rather to rally Chinese citizens against the Soviet Union.

Another instance of domestic mobilization was in the summer of 1966, at the beginning of the Cultural Revolution in China, when an estimated two million Chinese people participated in mass demonstrations along the Soviet border to show support for China's territorial claims. Chinese officials also organized thousands of students to protest outside the Soviet embassy in August 1966, but these protests were in direct response to Soviet requests for the Chinese to retract attacks on the embassy by the Red Guards (Jones and Kevill 1985). This means that the mobilization did not occur as a plan to increase domestic support for the government, but rather as a signal of resolve to the Soviets. The domestic populace also showed strong support for China's territorial claims against the Soviet Union in February 1967 when members of the Red Guards attacked the Soviet embassy in Beijing over a two-week period in support of Chinese troops halting an alleged Soviet attempt to attack China through Manchuria. The deployment of hundreds of thousands of troops to the border coincided with this event in Beijing, but once the embassy incident had ended, the troops were withdrawn from the border.

There is strong evidence that part of the reason why Mao and company initiated the March 1969 armed border conflict with the Soviets was as a means of domestic diversion and mobilization at the height of the Cultural Revolution. Perhaps the strongest evidence that Mao in particular chose this tactic is his statement that "we should let them come in, which will help us in our mobilization" (K. Yang 2000, 30). As was the case with the Soviet use of the conflict to mobilize domestic support, Mao was able to divert the Chinese public from internal chaos that had resulted from the Cultural Revolution by doing some "foreign dog-baiting" (An 1973 99). Chinese leaders were also able to use the conflict to stir up Chinese patriotism, which had been badly affected by the

Cultural Revolution in past years, and to mobilize massive anti-Soviet demonstrations, which provided support for the regime in Beijing. This was particularly important in terms of strengthening loyalty and stability among the PLA, whose reputation had also been negatively affected by the Cultural Revolution. Mobilizing domestically provided the national cohesion sought after by the regime in time for the Ninth Party Congress of the CCP as well.

Mao had decided to strike the Soviet Union prior to the opening of the party congress in order to demonstrate the fight against revisionism and to help stabilize the domestic situation in China (Danhui 2005). One high-ranking leader, PLA head Lin Biao, directly benefited from the border conflict by gaining prominence at the Congress and becoming Mao's second in command and heir to power (Quested 1984). According to a Chinese scholar, "stirring up the nationalistic fervor that spilled blood provoked is always good for a group battling to stay in power. Accordingly, Peking tried to use the Ussuri incident at the Ninth Party Congress to show that China was truly surrounded by foes. Furthermore, Peking hoped to emphasize that national unity behind the leadership of Mao Tse-tung was now a necessity as never before" (An 1973, 98–99). Shortly after the border conflict, when China was preparing for potential war with the Soviet Union, the preparations also appear to have served Mao's domestic needs to restore some degree of order and national unity, which had been disrupted by the Cultural Revolution (An 1973). Though war preparation likely did help Mao domestically in the midst of the Cultural Revolution, it is almost certain that such war preparations were made not only for the purpose of mobilizing domestic support but also to actually prepare for the potential of war. There is little doubt, though, that the 1969 border conflict was used partly for domestic mobilization purposes: "the organization of border conflicts and their use for strengthening the state's domestic solidarity and alleviating internal contradictions was capable of providing short-term results" (Danhui 2005, 92). Eventually, such mobilization would die down, but for a short time, the border conflict did benefit the government.

On the other hand, Fravel (2008) points out that the armed conflict was only one incident that occurred during a long period of domestic unrest and instability, when it would have been useful for Mao to frequently mobilize the populace through provocations with the Soviet Union, but this was not the case. It is also not clear why the Chinese leaders chose to use diversion with the Soviets rather than another adversary if they were using armed conflict to mobilize domestically. It is likely that Chinese officials partially refused settlement and also initiated militarized threats and uses of force to satisfy the domestic populace in these cases, but there is no other evidence of a link between the border dispute and domestic accountability or mobilization in China. Besides the very likely use of the 1969 border conflict and occasional other threats of force against the Soviet Union as means of domestic mobilization during the Cultural Revolution in China, domestic mobilization and accountability are unable to satisfactorily account for the variation in dispute strategies of Chinese leaders and, more importantly, the lack of territorial concessions between 1964 and 1987.

Limitations of the Domestic Accountability and Mobilization Explanations

Unlike value of territory, domestic accountability and mobilization partially explain the lack of settlement attempts in the 1960s to 1980s, but they cannot explain the attempts to settle in the 1990s. According to the domestic accountability theory, Chinese officials should be less likely to attempt settlement or engage in threats or uses of force when they are most vulnerable to domestic punishment—when a coup has recently occurred, when there is political unrest, when there are high levels of authoritarianism, or when there are steps toward democratization. In terms of recent coups in China, the only situations like a coup occurred in 1971 when Lin Biao attempted to take power from Mao and in 1976 after the death of Chairman Mao when the Gang of Four attempted to take power. At these times and in subsequent years, China was engaged in border negotiations, but made no offers of territorial concessions until 1987. This is consistent with the domestic accountability explanation, but it is not clear that the attempted coups played a significant role in influencing decisions of Chinese officials regarding the border and territorial dispute. At the same time, China did engage in militarized threats, which could have been costly if the domestic populace did not back the government.

The domestic accountability theory also suggests that when political unrest is occurring, leaders are more susceptible and less likely to engage in costly behavior in territorial disputes. Yet China made its only offer of a territorial concession prior to the late 1980s—in 1964 at a time of "acute regime insecurity for China's leaders" (Fravel 2008, 58). This situation means that Chinese leaders did exactly the opposite of what the domestic accountability explanation would predict. On the other hand, during the years of the Cultural Revolution, 1966 to 1976, when political unrest was at its height in China, Chinese officials made no offers of territorial concessions, thought they did engage in the highest number of rounds of talks during this time. Though this is consistent with the predictions of the domestic accountability theory, it does not demonstrate that domestic unrest prevented the offer of territorial concessions since, as is the case with the Senkaku/Diaoyu Islands dispute, it is impossible to falsify. At the same time, Chinese officials engaged in armed conflict with the Soviet Union on several occasions, including the large-scale 1969 border conflict, which is contrary to the domestic accountability theory.

During most of the time period observed, China was a highly authoritarian state with Polity IV scores ranging from −8 at the worst and −7 at the best, with 10 being most democratic and −10 being most authoritarian. Despite shifts in domestic policy as early as 1978–79 when Deng Xiaoping came into power in China, there was no similar shift in foreign policy toward the Soviet Union (Sutter 1986). The only shift in Polity score occurred at the end of the Cultural Revolution in 1976, when China moved from a −8 to a −7, but this could hardly be considered democratization. In the second part of the 1980s, China did begin to operate democratically on some issues, but only in a very limited sense, with Deng Xiaoping allowing limited intellectual freedoms, political reform, semi-autonomous judiciary, greater autonomy for trade unions, and direct elections at the county level. This, however, cannot really be considered democratization either due to the continued features of authoritarian rule by the CCP. The domestic accountability theory predicts that Chinese officials would be less likely to engage in territorial dispute strategies that might be costly from a domestic audience perspective. Yet it is precisely during the height of democratization when Chinese officials first began to agree to and offer territorial concessions in China's dispute with the Soviet Union. Democratization and a shifting domestic political context in the post-Mao era may have actually encouraged Chinese officials to consider concessions. In any case, Chinese democratization cannot explain the decision to shift strategies and begin agreeing to and offering territorial concessions in the latter part of the 1980s. After 1987, the Soviet Union began to democratize somewhat, shifting from a Polity IV score of −7 to a score of 6. This shift in democratization likely accounts for the Soviet Union's willingness to attempt settlement of the border dispute through territorial concessions, but it cannot account for China's willingness to do so, and not in the way the domestic accountability theory predicts. As with China, it is likely that the Soviet Union's democratization was part of Gorbachev's overall revamping of Soviet policies, both domestic and international, in the latter 1980s, and therefore the shift in democratization partially accounts for the decision for Soviet concessions and subsequently China's willingness to agree to such concessions in border negotiations. Overall, the domestic accountability theory cannot explain China's dispute strategies. Rather, the only match for domestic factors is Fravel (2008), who argues that Chinese leaders are more likely to attempt settlement of territorial disputes when there is domestic unrest or vulnerability. Therefore, these explanations provide only limited effectiveness to explain China's strategies in the border dispute with the Soviet Union.

BARGAINING LEVERAGE

According to the theory of coercive diplomacy and issue linkage, China should have been unwilling to attempt settlement of the dispute through territorial concessions, and more likely to initiate diplomatic and militarized threats when other disputed issues existed with the Soviet Union. Throughout the duration of the dispute, many other disputed issues occurred, and most were explicitly linked, but sometimes only implicitly linked to the border and territorial dispute. Overall, the evidence shows that China used explicit and implicit issue linkage and coercive diplomacy to attain bargaining leverage to compel the Soviet Union to shift its positions on several other disputed issues throughout the dispute. The general Chinese strategy was to link the border dispute with other disputed issues as a form of coercive diplomacy. In this way, "the boundary dispute was intensified, blown up and taken to a feverish pitch at particular points of time to serve China's larger political objectives. . . . Bigger claims are advanced with the purpose of acquiring bargaining chips for reaching more realistic settlements that would take care of China's substantive interests" (Bakshi 2001, 1834). Of the thirty-eight diplomatic and militarized threats or uses of force, 66 percent involved issue linkage and coercive diplomacy, linking the dispute with other disputed issues, while the remaining threats or uses of force were pursued due to direct threats or Soviet actions regarding the disputed border. The most commonly linked issues, listed in table 12, were a growing rift in bilateral relations, Soviet support of Vietnam, Soviet involvement in Afghanistan, Soviet troops stationed in Mongolia, and Soviet power relative to Chinese power.

There were occasional times early in the dispute when China pursued diplomatic or militarized threats, but explicit issue linkage did not occur, even when

Table 12.   Soviet/Russian issues linked by China to territorial dispute

DISPUTED ISSUE	NUMBER OF LINKAGES
Geostrategic concerns about Soviet power relative to China	8
Soviet support of Vietnam in Sino-Vietnamese war/Cambodia	8
Soviet occupation of Afghanistan	8
Soviet troops in Mongolia	7
Growing rift in bilateral relations	4
Chinese concerns about Soviet attack on China's nuclear installations	1
Chinese rejection of Soviet-proposed joint statement on principles	1

other disputed issues existed. In the first decade of the dispute, Chinese decision makers led by Mao pursued such threats or uses of force as coercive diplomacy, only learning that they could use the dispute as bargaining leverage as
they went along. China also sometimes used issue linkage without the type of
coercive diplomacy as predicted by the theory, but instead as part of border negotiations. In other words, on several occasions Chinese officials made explicit
links to other disputed issues as part of border talks, not just through refusals
to negotiate or militarized threats or uses of force.

Even though the territorial dispute was not yet a severe problem, the late
1950s was "never anything but a tattered quilt, hiding deep historical splits
based on natural rivalry between two massive empires" (Segal 1985, 3). Initial evidence suggests that only when other disputed issues began to arise and
cracks began to spread in the Sino-Soviet relationship did the dispute come to
the forefront, and Chinese officials began making claims and demands about
the border and territorial dispute. As Fitzgerald (1967, 683) explains, "What
began as an ideological dispute may have become inflamed by territorial ambitions or resentments." From 1956 to 1959, Chinese citizens had illegally crossed
into Soviet territory on a frequent basis, yet border guards had dealt with
these crossings in a businesslike manner, never letting the situations escalate.
In 1960, however, when Chinese officials instigated a mass Chinese crossing
into Soviet territory, the incident did escalate, so that "what had been viewed a
nuisance henceforth became a provocation," "premeditated malice," and a "deliberate violation" by China (Ginsburgs and Pinkele 1978, 16). Unlike previous
border incidents, the 1960 incident was "qualitatively different from this earlier
spate of border 'irregularities' in that the Soviets perceived it as having been
deliberately staged at the instigation of the PRC government . . . and that the

PRC officialdom had used the occasion to formulate a territorial claim against the Soviet Union. . . . An adversary situation had thus been created, which, the Soviets said, signaled the beginning of a new phase in Sino-Soviet border relations and ushered in a period marked by a PRC policy of conscious and systematic violation of the frontier between the two countries" (Ginsburgs and Pinkele 1978, 14).

Reinitiating the territorial claim and "raising old scores against Tsarist Russia serves to underline current propaganda, painting the Soviet Union as a sham communist state, riddled with bourgeois reaction and revisionism; and not only at home. . . . It would seem that the main Chinese motive in calling the Soviet border into question is to carry on a polemical war against Russian revisionism rather than actively to press for lost territory" (Fitzgerald 1967, 692). There is little doubt that the Chinese deliberately reinitiated the border dispute to serve as a means of signaling growing frustration with the Soviet Union and not just to reclaim lost territory. As a Chinese scholar explains, the dispute actually began as an ideological dispute in 1960, which "degenerated into a nationalistic clash based on territorial issues" (An 1973, 13). He continues: "In the wake of the deteriorating Sino-Soviet relations in the early 1960s, however, the respective Communist powers became more nationalistic, and frontier frictions began to develop as the momentous Sino-Soviet split started to widen in other spheres" (An 1973, 73). Such commentary suggests that the reinitiation of the territorial claim in 1960 had more to do with other disputed issues, and therefore the territorial dispute was brought up only in the context of difficult bilateral relations. This is consistent with the argument that territorial disputes are used as bargaining tools with other disputed issues. The use of the border dispute would serve China well over the next few decades with regard to other disputed issues.

By the end of the 1950s, major splits were beginning to occur as disputed issues arose. The first major dispute was a series of disagreements about military strategy and cooperation. Growing tensions led the Soviets to deploy troops to the border region, which then led China to do the same. A disputed issue that came about in the late 1950s was China's growing dissatisfaction with some degree of Soviet détente with the US. As a result of this Soviet move, China became concerned that the Soviet Union was not sufficiently supporting the communist movement (Segal 1985). In the late 1950s, China also openly rejected the Soviet economic model, furthering the Sino-Soviet split that would last to the

1980s. Though not stated explicitly at the time, later statements revealed that Chinese officials reinitiated the border and territorial dispute and instigated the 1960 border incident in response to growing problems with the Soviet Union, specifically in this case the recall of 1,390 Soviet technical experts from China in July and August 1960. The Soviet government had unilaterally decided to withdraw the experts as part of the growing rift between the two states regarding disagreements about the role of the Soviet Union in the club of international communist states. The withdrawal deeply affected the Chinese economy, when it was already struggling, leading to a harsh Chinese reaction (Jones and Kevill 1985, 21). Many other incidents followed as a systematic means of signaling Chinese intentions regarding growing tense relations with the Soviet Union. In other words, as the theory suggests, China did not randomly choose to reinitiate the border dispute and territorial claim and instigate the first of many militarized provocations. Rather, Chinese officials figured out that they could use the border dispute as bargaining leverage in response to the increasingly negative political context that resulted due to other disputed issues.

Though the Chinese insisted on border negotiations in 1960, it appeared that officials had no intention of actually attempting to resolve the dispute, instead discussing generalities and avoiding specifics. This suggests that the dispute was reinitiated, not to resolve it as rhetoric claimed, but to use the dispute for other purposes, mainly as future leverage regarding other disputed issues. According to analysts studying the conflict:

> The inference is that while the Buz-Aigyr business [border incident] was a separate item and severable from the territorial phenomenon, the Chinese were determined to link the two elements and through this medium harness the potency of local border tensions to the job of extracting a global frontier accommodation (without, in the process, necessarily sacrificing the corollary goal of securing favorable on-the-spot border 'corrections'). To play the game successfully, the border issue could not be allowed to acquire an independent existence, for then it might have proved susceptible to ad hoc treatment and failed as an ancillary weapon in the territorial context, and an easy way of avoiding that contingency was by not volunteering any vital statistics concerning the purported claim and keeping the relevant contextual format as vague as possible. (Ginsburgs and Pinkele 1978, 18)

This pattern continued through the 1960s, as the Sino-Soviet split went into full swing, with China making demands on the border and territorial dispute, while simultaneously condemning the Soviets as colluding with the US and complaining about other issues, particularly Soviet intentions in other communist states and interactions with China's other adversaries.

Sino-Soviet Split, Early 1960s

During this time period, China was increasingly suspicious of Soviet intentions at a geostrategic level, such as a Soviet agreement in the summer of 1962 to sell MiG fighter planes to another of China's adversaries, India, with whom it was also involved in a border and territorial dispute. Though the planes were not delivered until after the Sino-Indian War in October 1962, "the agreement caused great offence in China, in view of her strained relations with India" (Jones and Kevill 1985, 27). Though it is difficult to prove issue linkage explicitly, there are several other disputed issues that arose during this time that likely explain the lack of settlement attempts and the Chinese initiation of diplomatic and militarized threats. Based on the evidence available, there is little doubt among observers that China directly linked the border and territorial dispute to other disputed issues: "the direct confrontation of Soviet and Chinese troops only developed after the open Sino-Soviet political/ideological split of the early 1960s" (Segal 1985, 4). Therefore, bargaining leverage theory likely explains the lack of settlement attempts through territorial concessions and the militarized threats and uses of force during the 1960s.

China's concerns about Soviet interference in other communist states was a major factor in the split, leading to several other disputed issues that China linked to the territorial dispute. In addition to Chinese concerns about Soviet interference in Albania and Yugoslavia in 1961, Chinese officials were strongly provoked by the Soviet deployment of nuclear missiles in Cuba in 1962, because they were opposed to "the sacrifice of another country's sovereignty [Cuba] as a means of reaching a compromise with imperialism" (Jones and Kevill 1985, 29). Chinese officials harshly criticized Soviet decisions in the Cuban missile crisis in October 1962, mainly what was viewed as a capitulation to US demands and compromise of dismantling Soviet bases on the island (Jones and Kevill 1985). Soviet Premier Nikita Khrushchev responded in December 1962 by criticizing China for its lack of action in Hong Kong and Macau compared to India's retaking of Goa from Portugal. In this war of words, the border dispute became a pawn in which the Soviets attempted to publicly reveal what had been mainly a private discussion of the border and territorial claims and demands for negotiations. In this way, "Khrushchev finally succumbed to the temptation to try to pin his Chinese opponents on the cross of Hong Kong and Macau and thus risk injecting the territorial theme into the Sino-Soviet shouting match" (Ginsburgs and Pinkele 1978, 42). When the Chinese considered a February 1963 Soviet proposal to restart talks over bilateral issues including the border dispute, the Chinese government stated that for such talks to occur, "necessary preconditions" would include the resolution of several other disputed issues, namely "the ending of attacks on the Chinese and Albanian parties, coupled with condemnation of the Yugoslavs as 'traitors to the Communist cause'" (Jones and Kevill 1985, 31). The first public mention of the border dispute by the Chinese occurred in March 1963 in direct response to Khrushchev's December 1962 speech (Jones and Kevill 1985, 29), a clear instance of issue linkage and an attempt by the Chinese to gain bargaining leverage against the Soviet Union.

A few months later, in June 1963, China presented a letter to the Soviet Union with twenty-five points to discuss at future bilateral talks, including references to the Cuban missile crisis, Albania, and Yugoslavia, as well as the border dispute. The Soviets responded to the letter with their own viewpoints, furthering the split. Adding to the already tense relations, in July 1963 another related disputed issue arose with the Soviet Union's signing of the Partial Nuclear Test Ban Treaty (PTBT) with the US, which China criticized as colluding with imperialism (Worden, Savada, and Dolan 1987). Hostile letters published in the press continued to be sent back and forth in a tit-for-tat fashion into early 1964. On the Soviet side, in addition to addressing other disputed issues, the letters complained about the thousands of Chinese excursions across the border each year from 1960 to 1963. There is no doubt these other disputed issues widened the rift between China and the Soviet Union, but the question is whether these actions provoked the Chinese claim of additional territory and the breakdown of border negotiations in May 1964, as well as the July 1964 threat by Chairman Mao to reacquire Soviet territory.

In February 1964, the two adversaries exchanged increasingly acrimonious letters, with China calling for a split in the international communist movement and the Soviet Union accusing China of interfering. At the end of the month, China made an explicit link between other disputed issues and the border dispute when the Central Committee of the CCP expressed its intention to deal with the border issue in the context of disagreements about Albania, Yugoslavia, and the end of Soviet technical and economic aid to China, among others

(Jones and Kevill 1985). While this war of words was escalating, border nego-tiations were held from February to May 1964, where representatives actually did make progress in agreeing to demarcation of the border. Border talks were suspended in May because the Soviets refused to give in to a Chinese demand to recognize the inequality of the nineteenth-century treaties.

The Chinese had three options regarding how to deal with the dispute: to set aside the problem of the unfair treaties and sign an agreement with conces-sions, to uphold their position but continue talks, or to aggravate the situation by making further demands. Clearly, Mao chose the last option (Danhui 2005). By May 1964, despite the agreement to demarcate the border, the Chinese were dissatisfied with the Soviet unwillingness to recognize the unequal treaties, and talks were halted. Since China did offer territorial concessions at these talks, it would appear that China would actually seek resolution of the dispute. Yet the addition of the demand for the Soviet Union to recognize unequal treaties after the demarcation agreement suggests that the Chinese did not necessarily in-tend to resolve the dispute after all, knowing, as they must have, that the Soviets would not agree to such a demand. Despite the progress made in the talks, the demand about recognizing the unequal treaties and Mao's July 1964 claim for Soviet territory led to a toughening of the Soviet position. Hostile letters con-tinued to be exchanged throughout the spring and summer of 1964, culminat-ing with Mao's claim to an additional 580,000 square miles of Soviet territory in July 1964. Therefore, the one and only territorial concession offered by the Chinese prior to the late 1980s was followed by issue linkage and coercive di-plomacy. The offer of a territorial concession is not consistent with the theory, but its retraction and the following diplomatic threat are. Apparently, domestic divisions within the Chinese government led to varying diplomatic tracks, with Mao ultimately trumping Zhou Enlai.

In just two short months, China had shifted from offering territorial con-cessions to claiming vast amounts of Soviet territory, changing the border dis-pute into a territorial dispute as well. Though it appears on the surface that Mao contradicted Zhou Enlai's statements made in the border negotiations regard-ing China's willingness to resolve the dispute, it turns out that Mao deliber-ately made the claim as a form of pressure on the Soviet Union. The objective appeared to be "to temporarily postpone reaching an agreement with the So-viet Union on the border problem in order to retain a certain amount of pres-sure on the Soviet Union and maintain a certain level of tension in Sino-Soviet relations, thus keeping the U.S.S.R. among the likely adversaries threatening China's national security" (Danhui 2005, 86).

In his July 1964 comments, Mao pursued a bargaining strategy when he "aggravated the situation on his own initiative, threw his counterpart off balance, made him nervous, then after taking the initiative into his own hands, began slowly releasing the pressure, gradually bringing the situation to the desired denouement" (Goncharov and Danhui 2004, 98). In other words, Mao's territorial threat was a tactical bargaining move that was intended to put pressure on the Soviet Union regarding their aggravated bilateral relations and not an actual territorial claim. Later in the fall of 1964, Mao himself even admitted on at least three occasions that he was using empty words, and the goal was to "take the offensive in the border talks" and make them nervous, not the return of 580,000 square miles of Soviet territory (Goncharov and Danhui 2004, 102).

Though Mao did not explicitly admit the purpose of the pressure on the Soviets, it is believed that under the circumstances of the time, the pressure was related to other disputed issues. For example, one analyst argues that the territorial threat made by Mao "clearly was not [about] a Soviet attempt at territorial conquest, but [about] a preventive strike at China's fledgling nuclear installations" (Lowenthal 1971, 511). The diplomatic threat issued by Mao in July 1964 appears to have had more to do with other security concerns, mainly potential Soviet threats to China's nuclear program and the Soviet treaty with the US, two greater geostrategic concerns, than an actual intent to resolve the border dispute. Chinese expansion of the territorial claim as part of the tit-for-tat hostile exchanges between the two states demonstrates the direct attempt to bring a territorial dispute to the forefront of tense relations due to other disputed issues. Such issue linkage and coercive diplomacy is consistent with the bargaining leverage theory.

Further evidence is the fact that Soviet officials interpreted Chinese stubbornness regarding the recognition of the unequal treaties in the border talks and Mao's expanded territorial claim as bargaining ploys. When border negotiations failed in May 1964, the Soviets suspected China of refusing to make any progress in negotiations on the border dispute for political purposes. As expressed in a statement given in September 1964: "The Soviet Government has invited the Chinese Government a number of times to hold consultations on the question of ascertaining separate sections of the border line, to exclude any possibility of misunderstanding. The Chinese side, however, evades such consultations while continuing to violate the border. This cannot but make us wary. . . . However, the artificial creation of any territorial problems in our times, especially between socialist countries, would be tantamount to embarking on a very dangerous path" (Hobday 1987, 263). Another similar point is that it was not until March 1969 when Chinese officials actually used legal arguments based on treaties of 1919 and 1920, which would have strengthened China's position in border negotiations. The lack of a real effort to defend its legal claim to the disputed border and territory is supplemental evidence that China did not likely engage in border negotiations to actually shift the territorial status quo, let alone offer territorial concessions. Rather, it appears that China engaged in such negotiations to address other disputed issues with the Soviet Union.

It could be argued that China was unwilling to actually resolve its border and territorial disputes with any of its neighbors for fear of losing territory, and this is why Chinese officials withdrew from the 1964 talks with the Soviet Union. However, prior to those talks, China had already signed a border treaty with Mongolia in December 1962 and similar treaties with Burma in 1960, Nepal in 1961, and Pakistan and Afghanistan in 1963, providing territorial concessions in those negotiations (Fravel 2008). At the same time, China also engaged in a border conflict with India in 1962, "a step that can only be described as a grand demonstrative gesture" (Ginsburgs and Pinkele 1978, 55), and then resolved the Sino-Indian border and territorial dispute in 1963. China demonstrated its strategy to use issue linkage to attain bargaining leverage by resolving its disputes with Burma and Nepal specifically to signal its ability "to work out a reciprocally satisfactory arrangement with a pair of smaller neighbors as compared to India's apparent intransigence, and exert pressure on the Indian government to also come to terms" with China's demands (Ginsburgs and Pinkele 1978, 56). The Chinese intention for the resolution of these two disputes in particular was that Zhou Enlai hoped to persuade India to agree to a similar peaceful settlement in their border dispute (Fravel 2004). Likewise, China was willing to resolve its dispute with Pakistan to persuade it to withdraw from its allegiance to the Southeast Asian Treaty Organization (SEATO) and its dispute with Mongolia in an attempt to convince Mongolia to move away from its pro-Soviet position. No other disputed issues appear to have existed at this time in these other territorial disputes, making resolution through territorial concessions possible.

Buildup to the 1969 Border Conflict

Throughout the remainder of the decade, other issues furthered the split to the point where China viewed the Soviet Union as its main threat. In early 1965, the two states strongly disagreed about the escalation of conflict in Vietnam (Jones and Kevill 1985). A year later, the Soviets signed a defense treaty with Mongolia, expanding the number of troops deployed there (Fravel 2008). It was also at this time that China began to shift its national security threat away from the US to the Soviet Union. China publicly expressed concern that the Soviet Union was colluding with the US, which was contrary to Chinese national interests. As one observer at the time remarked, "the pattern of world affairs became definitely 'triangular' with the open break between the two communist powers" (Lowenthal 1971, 507). In 1966, the Chinese Communist Party broke off ties with the Soviet Communist Party, worsening bilateral relations.

Another Chinese concern was the 1968 Soviet invasion of Czechoslovakia, which it believed was an ominous sign of social imperialism (Country Studies 1987), and which Zhou Enlai called "the most barefaced and typical specimen of fascist power politics played by the Soviet revisionist clique against its so-called allies" (Jones and Kevill 1985, 84), along with the declaration in November 1968 of the Brezhnev Doctrine, which allowed for Soviet interference in socialist states where interference was needed to maintain socialism. The implication was that if the Soviet Union wished, it could coerce China, as a socialist state, into regime change, and the troops stationed along the border could be the force to incite such change (Fravel 2008). Despite Chinese aversion to the Czechoslovakian liberals who provoked the Soviet intervention, the Chinese viewed the intervention and the Brezhnev Doctrine "as an alarming portent" (Quested 1984, 138) and "absolutely not coincidental" to violations of Chinese airspace (Fravel 2008, 208). Based on the growing suspicion that these actions signaled Soviet intentions to invade China across their disputed border, the Chinese immediately linked the Soviet actions with the border dispute, with particular concern regarding Soviet troop buildup along the border (Sutter 1986). The general idea was that the Chinese wanted to deploy massive numbers of troops to the border to deter a potential Soviet invasion, but the deployment was done in the name of the border dispute. By using the border dispute as an excuse, China was able to justify the deployment and secure its borders to avoid any potential Soviet incursion that the Chinese feared because of the Soviet intervention in Czechoslovakia and the subsequent announcement of the

Brezhnev Doctrine. Otherwise, a Chinese deployment of military divisions to the border without justification could have led to a security dilemma and likely provoked armed conflict. Thus, the border dispute was placed into a larger geostrategic arena and indirectly used as a pawn as part of China's growing rivalry with the Soviet Union and its position in the international system, even though China did not make the linkage explicit.

Border confrontations started to occur shortly after the Soviet intervention in Czechoslovakia, with several confrontations being violent (Fravel 2008). The evidence strongly suggests that China was framing the territorial dispute and specifically the armed conflict as part of larger geostrategic concerns with the Soviet Union throughout the 1960s, just as it had when it reinitiated the claim in 1960:

> This dispute, though narrow in its territorial scope, has profound implications for relations between the two neighbors. The Chinese would see any coerced surrender of their treaty rights as a return to the old relationship of superiority and inferiority, which could be applied in other realms of Sino-Soviet dealings and certainly in other sectors of their borders. Assertion of right of access to the rivers thus appears to Peking as crucial to China's whole relationship to the Soviet Union and therefore its standing in the world. That perception, not, as some analysts concluded, an exaggerated concern for a tiny and useless patch of territory, led China in March 1969 to give battle on Chenpao [Zhenbao] Island. (Maxwell 1978, 141)

By the late 1960s, there is little doubt that the border dispute was playing a central role in the rivalry with the Soviet Union, and it was difficult to separate out the territorial dispute from other disputed issues that caused the rivalry (Fravel 2008).

It is likely that China initiated the use of force in March 1969 partly as a form of domestic mobilization, discussed earlier, and partly as a form of coercive diplomacy linked to China's broader adversarial relationship with the Soviet Union in terms of relative power, and not only as a means to acquire "a tiny and useless patch of territory." Mao's plan was to seek neither war nor peace, but instead to put pressure on the Soviet Union to maintain some degree of tension, prompted by "the need to streamline China's foreign political strategy, maintain pressure on the Soviet Union, and play the border card; and on the other, it was beneficial for resolving domestic problems. This essentially meant transforming the talks on border issues into a tactical technique of struggle against the enemy, which was not conducive to the development of relations between China and a foreign state" (Danhui 2005, 91–92). In terms of coercive diplomacy, one of the reasons for the use of force was to expose Soviet "savagery" to other communist bloc states and African and Asian states "by equating Soviet savagery on the Chinese border in March 1969 with the Soviet invasion of Czechoslovakia in August 1968 . . . evidently timed to influence the outcome of the international Communist conference in Moscow that was to be held in June 1969" (An 1973, 101). Another alleged motive was to create a second front in Asia in order to humiliate the Soviets regarding the recent Berlin crisis.

Both states had downplayed the large number of previous border clashes, yet when the March 1969 clashes occurred, both sides issued strong protests and were "quick to turn the March 1969 border clashes to propaganda purposes" (An 1973, 17). This suggests that some other factors besides the actual border clashes existed to make both states so strongly protest the conflict and escalate it. The general themes of the Chinese anti-Soviet propaganda after the border conflict not only discussed how the Soviets "repeatedly nibbled at China's 'sacred soil'" but also made direct references to Soviet interest in Mongolia and the Soviet invasion of Czechoslovakia in 1968 as "an attempt to set up a colonial empire of the czarist type," and Soviet intentions regarding nuclear weapons (An 1973, 17).[6] Fighting in August 1969 occurred along the western border just five days after border negotiations regarding river navigation. It is believed that this time the Soviets initiated the armed conflict to keep China off balance (An 1973). The Soviets believed that the initiation of the border conflict was just "a link in the chain of hostile actions taken by the Peking leaders, who have not given up their absurd territorial claims against the Soviet Union" (An 1973, 106), which would potentially have been met by nuclear war (Quested 1984, 139). Mao responded that if the Soviets were to use nuclear missiles, so would China (An 1973).

During the 1969 border conflict, when the Soviet government made several attempts to reinitiate border negotiations, the Chinese government rejected most offers, primarily because "they were not in a good position to initiate boundary negotiations. In view of the immense Soviet military pressure they were facing, a Chinese call for resumption of border talks immediately after the Chenpao incidents could well have been interpreted as a Chinese 'surrender,' at least technically so. The Chinese, nevertheless, constantly insisted on the clarification of the boundary" (Tsui 1983, 65), keeping up pressure on the border. It appears that they agreed to negotiations, but not concessions, in order to prevent an escalation of the border conflict into war with the Soviet Union. Though the Chinese had initiated the armed conflict, they were cautious to prevent it from escalating since they knew such large-scale conflict would be detrimental. Instead, Chinese leaders demanded full withdrawal of Soviet troops from the disputed territory, but since the disputed territory was controlled completely by the Soviets, such withdrawal would have involved a unilateral concession that the Soviets were unwilling to give (Bakshi 2001).

Even though the Chinese government was genuinely concerned with a preemptive strike by the Soviet Union, due to "a fanatic Maoist rigidity of self-righteousness," the Beijing government was "unable or unwilling to back away on the border dispute and in the ideological conflict. In other words, the Peking regime was walking a very tight rope. It could not afford to push Moscow around too much, but it was equally unable to capitulate. China risked Soviet military action in either case—in response to excessive Chinese provocation or in response to evidence of Peking's weakness. To extricate itself from such a painful dilemma, there seemed to be only one solution: to maintain an essentially defensive posture toward the Soviet Union while agreeing to resume border talks simply to buy time to get through a highly dangerous phase in the conflict" (An 1973, 108). This posture suggests that Chinese decision makers led by Mao were willing to keep up the dispute for bargaining purposes but still had to engage in negotiations to prevent escalation. At the same time, there is no indication that China was willing to offer or accept any territorial concessions, and none were exchanged. Rather, by engaging in talks, but demanding that the Soviets fully acknowledge the unequal treaties of the nineteenth century, "the Chinese appear to have hit on a means for keeping the frontier question open, and thus maintaining popular hostility, without dangerously provoking the Russians by actual fighting" (Lowenthal 1971, 514).

Further evidence demonstrates not just a deliberate delay in resolution of the border dispute, but also the use of issue linkage. It turns out that China engaged in the October 1969 border negotiations partly to prevent a Soviet-American détente. Just days after the negotiations, Mao began signaling interest in talks with the US, pursued since "it apparently wanted to play off Moscow against Washington to achieve maximum negotiating leverage at the border talks" (An 1973, 111). Thus, China pursued the border negotiations as an attempt to prevent nuclear war and to play Moscow against Washington. It should be no surprise under these circumstances that China not only had no intention of offering territorial concessions, but it also expected that the Soviet Union would not make any concessions either, due to the Soviet military and nuclear superiority over China. Rather, Chinese leaders preferred to draw out the border dispute and negotiations as long as possible to avoid an armed conflict with the relatively superior Soviet military (An 1973). In this case, Chinese officials pursued negotiations as part of issue linkage, a slightly different prediction than the theory of bargaining leverage.

Postconflict Negotiations and Bilateral Relations, 1970s

In the 1970s, bilateral relations continued to be tense. Though war was unlikely, resolution of the dispute was just as unlikely (Gaiduk 2008). In fact, one scholar studying the dispute labeled the decade of the 1970s as "a new stage characterized by an unprecedented level of military confrontation, fruitless negotiations and academic warfare" (Tsui 1983, 10–11).[7] Another scholar of Sino-Soviet relations noted that the late 1970s was a time when "signs were extraordinarily confusing" (Segal 1985, 2). The prospect of resolving the dispute was at its lowest point since neither side was willing to make even minor compromises or offer territorial concessions as a means of moving toward resolution. At the time, the reality was that "deterioration of relations between the two powers has now reached the point where both adversaries would regard any kind of concession as a shameful defeat" (An 1973, 121). Throughout the decade, despite attempts to work toward normalization of bilateral relations and engagements in border negotiations, relations worsened due to new disputed issues that arose during this time period.

It was during the 1970s that one of the disputed issues eventually labeled by the Chinese as the "three obstacles" arose, Soviet support and aid to the Democratic Republic of Vietnam (North Vietnam). As early as 1973, the Soviets had begun to provide significant financial and military aid to North Vietnam in the form of military advisors, money and equipment, and training for army officers, and they had also been actively involved in diplomatic efforts to bring a resolution to the war with the US and South Vietnam. The purpose of the Soviet military aid to North Vietnam was "not to help it eliminate the pro-American regime in South Vietnam, which was doomed anyway. The Soviet leaders were primarily concerned about the policy followed by Beijing which, after 1972, adopted a two-faced position with respect to the events to the south of its borders" (Gaiduk 2008, 120). With the involvement of the Soviet Union in Indochina, China began to consider the Soviet policy toward Vietnam as threatening to its regional role, and as a result, the Soviet-Vietnamese relationship became another disputed issue between the Soviet Union and China. Beijing was particularly concerned about ensuring that Cambodia and Laos be independent from Vietnam, and Chinese leaders were determined to prevent Soviet influence regarding this concern. By the end of the war in Vietnam in 1975, Soviet influence in Vietnam greatly outweighed Chinese influence, Laos had decided to align with the Soviets, and both Vietnam and Laos had agreed to Soviet military presence in their states, which was "primarily aimed at China" (Gaiduk 2008, 121). Chinese leaders would not link the border and territorial dispute with the Vietnam issue until later, but eventually the issue linkage would become explicit and direct.

A second disputed issue that would become part of the three obstacles, Soviet troops deployed in Outer Mongolia, also began to influence Sino-Soviet relations in the early 1970s. Though Soviet troops had been deployed to Mongolia as early as 1963 (Danhui 2005), from 1970 to 1971 the number of Soviet divisions increased from thirty to forty-four in Mongolia, supported by around a thousand combat aircraft and a coordinated defense air system (Ostermann 1995). Since the early 1960s, Mongolia had maintained close relations with the Soviet Union, straining Sino-Soviet relations further. The deployment of Soviet troops to Mongolia immediately became linked to the Sino-Soviet border dispute (Jones and Kevill 1985). The deployment became a disputed issue for China because it was concerned that the increase in Soviet military deployments and realignment of military districts in Central Asia, particularly in Mongolia, would be an encroachment on China.

Other Chinese concerns during this time included the Soviet regimes imposed in Angola in 1975, Ethiopia in 1978, and South Yemen in 1978 (Hilali 2001), as well as the Soviet-Vietnamese friendship treaty signed in November 1978, which was arranged specifically to counter Chinese influence in Indochina. A further Chinese concern was Soviet influence over Vietnam's decision to invade Kampuchea (Cambodia) at that time in February 1979 (Gaiduk 2008). China was also concerned in the mid-1970s about developing states having to choose between siding with China or the Soviet Union. Most states were choosing the Soviet Union, which tilted the balance of power toward the Soviet side due to alliances and alignments. By 1976, as one observer noted, "Sino-Soviet relations were obviously hostile—some might argue that the two countries were then at a peak of hostility" (Segal 1985, 6). Relations continued to be tense when Chairman Mao died in China, to the point that the CCP rejected a condolence note sent by the Soviet Communist Party in 1976, as well as Leonid Brezhnev's first message to Hua Guofeng as the new chairman of the CCP. Despite a brief thaw when Deng Xiaoping came into power, followed by China filling its vacant ambassador posting in Moscow in August 1976, by the end of 1977 when Sino-Vietnamese relations along the border began heating up, Sino-Soviet relations again worsened.[8] In response to these worsening relations, Soviet officials made an offer to China of a joint statement of principles, which was not only rejected but explicitly linked to Soviet troop withdrawals from the border as a precondition of normalization of bilateral relations (Segal 1985). The Soviet invasion of Afghanistan at the end of December 1979 "promptly created a third precondition for China's agreement to normalize Sino-Soviet relations" and thus deal with the border dispute (Segal 1985, 8–9).

According to the theory of territorial disputes as bargaining leverage, China should not have attempted settlement of the border dispute through the offer of territorial concessions during this time since there were many other disputed issues. Chinese officials did participate in several rounds of border negotiations, as discussed earlier, but their position never shifted, and they made no offers of concessions or even considered concessions made by the Soviet Union. The lack of concession offers during these talks is consistent with the predictions of the theory and not surprising considering the existence of several other disputed issues. Though border talks were held, neither side was willing to budge its position regarding resolution of the border and territorial dispute.

At the same time, China should also have been expected to pursue coercive diplomacy to use the border and territorial dispute as bargaining leverage to compel the Soviets to shift their policies on these other disputed issues. During this decade, China and the Soviet Union both increased their deployments of troops stationed on each side of the border, and there were also frequent border clashes, some resulting in deaths of troops. In the early 1960s, Chinese divisions numbered about twenty-four, but by 1975, the divisions numbered about seventy-eight (Tsui 1983).[9] In the early 1970s it was estimated that both sides had a combined two million troops deployed along the disputed border, many on combat alert and preparing for "a war of aggression" (An 1973, 19). In addition, in the years following the 1969 border conflict, the Chinese increased army and militia training, stockpiled supplies and food along the border, and constructed tunnels and air-raid shelters in preparation for a potential war with the Soviet Union (An 1973). In terms of uses of force, though there were allegedly hundreds of minor border clashes throughout the 1970s, consistent with the use of coercive diplomacy, it appears that neither state was willing to use force in an attempt to resolve the border dispute, also consistent with the theory. As the theory of bargaining leverage predicts, uses of force must be relatively low cost and not be likely to escalate to war in order for them to be used effectively as bargaining leverage. If uses of force were large scale or led to war, the costs would likely be too high despite any gains of bargaining leverage, which would be inefficient for challenger states. In the case of China and the Soviet Union, after the 1969 border conflict both sides acknowledged that "such large scale frontier strife, if continued, could eventually bring the two countries to a general war which neither side could possibly afford" (Tsui 1983, 50). Minor border incidents did continue though, initiated by both sides.

Since most of the uses of force by both sides were not made public, it is difficult to know if China used any force during the 1970s as coercive diplomacy for the purposes of bargaining leverage. In many cases, particularly the incidents of March 1974, May 1978, and June 1979, the Chinese used force in response to Soviet incursions into Chinese territory, such as in March 1974 when a Soviet helicopter flew seventy miles into Chinese territory, landing several times, and Chinese forces captured the helicopter and its crew and held them until December 1975 (Tsui 1983). During the Sino-Vietnamese war in February 1979, Chinese troops were put on alert on the Sino-Soviet border, a militarized threat aimed at the Soviet Union, but no actual combat occurred. It is not clear that China was making any attempt at issue linkage, but the shift in balance of power likely influenced an issue linkage by the Chinese. According to Segal (1985, 20), military balance played a significant role in determining how China acted during the Sino-Vietnamese war, not only along the border, but also inside Vietnam: "Unlike in 1969, China had no illusions about her ability to 'punish' the Soviet Union for her support for Vietnam, and the PLA obviously respected superior Soviet military force. Indeed, the violence and scope of China's attack on Vietnam [in 1979] was limited from the start for fear of Soviet reaction. Thus, in practice, China was never likely to be able to teach Vietnam a very substantial lesson, and the Soviet Union could be pleased with the indirect deterrent role of her armed forces."

China also attempted issue linkage through negotiations, not coercive diplomacy, on several occasions, as it had in latter 1969. According to one analyst, in the early 1970s "Beijing had managed to use the Sino-Soviet border talks to help reduce the Soviet threat against China" (Sutter 1986, 29). Another instance of issue linkage used in negotiations was in 1979 when Chinese officials attempted to discuss Soviet support for Vietnam, Soviet aid to Vietnam, and Soviet troop withdrawals from the border during normalization talks. By the 1980s, it was reported that the Soviets were providing more than $1 million per day to Vietnam to keep the economy going and support its occupation of Cambodia (Segal 1985). The only potential use of coercive diplomacy at this time was the increased deployment of Chinese military divisions along the border, but it is not clear that the Chinese explicitly linked increased deployments at the border with Soviet support of Vietnam or other disputed issues. In the talks, Soviet officials focused instead on bilateral relations and were not willing to discuss a shift in their positions regarding the border dispute or their support of Vietnam.

This indicates that though China was using issue linkage, it was not necessarily using militarized coercive diplomacy as bargaining leverage, but hoping instead to persuade Soviet officials through diplomatic forms of coercive diplomacy by linking border negotiations to other disputed issues. By 1978, Chinese officials had begun to explicitly link Soviet withdrawal of troops from Mongolia to the border dispute by making the withdrawal a key condition for talks to occur (Jones and Kevill 1985). Therefore, the theory can explain China's unwillingness to attempt settlement through territorial concessions, and its use of diplomatic threats, but not necessarily militarized threats or uses of force pursued by China in the 1970s. This pattern of using the border dispute as bargaining leverage continued into the next decade, until a major shift occurred in 1987.

The Three Obstacles

In April 1979, China notified the Soviet Union that it did not plan to renew the 1950 treaty of friendship and alliance when it expired the following year, and it simultaneously requested border talks. Relations were increasingly deteriorating as a result of growing troop deployment along the disputed border and in Mongolia, as well as the Soviet support of Vietnam's invasion of Cambodia in December 1978 and the overthrow of the Daoud regime in Afghanistan by Soviet-supported communist forces. As a result, "China found itself threatened and it became defensive towards the Soviet Union" (Hilali 2001, 329). As part of the notification not to renew the treaty of friendship, China linked the end of the friendship treaty to a call for reducing Soviet troops on their disputed border and a demand to withdraw troops from Mongolia and Afghanistan. It was a clear instance of Chinese decision makers explicitly linking the border dispute to other disputed issues and attempting to use the dispute as bargaining leverage. As with earlier attempts, border talks that took place from September to December 1979 were not meant to actually move forward on reconciliation, but to provide an opportunity for China to link the border dispute with other disputed issues. At the talks, Beijing "demanded that the Soviets remove 'obstacles' to improved relations before China would agree to a statement on principles governing Sino-Soviet relations" (Sutter 1986, 95). The Chinese representatives demanded that the Soviets withdraw troops from Mongolia, halt all support of Vietnam's occupation of Cambodia, and reduce Soviet troops deployed along the Sino-Soviet border to the level of the 1960s. The Soviet response was that policy changes on other issues could not be made at the expense of other states, as the Chinese demanded, in order to make progress in the border dispute (Sutter 1986).

Through much of the 1980s, China used the strategy of coercive diplomacy and issue linkage with the Soviet Union when China refused to work toward settlement of their border dispute unless the specifically cited "three obstacles" were addressed through concessions made by the Soviet Union. These three obstacles—other disputed issues that China directly linked to the resolution of the border dispute—were the presence of Soviet troops in Mongolia, Soviet support of Vietnam and Vietnam's occupation of Cambodia, and Soviet intervention in Afghanistan. Though the other issues mentioned earlier were also noted, these three particular issues held the most salience for China, and Chinese officials explicitly cited them as such. All of these issues were frequently cited by China through much of the 1980s, publicly and privately at meetings between the two adversaries. In addition to demanding that the Soviet Union put pressure on Vietnam to withdraw from Cambodia, China also insisted that the resolution of the border dispute be linked to the withdrawal of Soviet troops from Mongolia and the Soviet withdrawal from Afghanistan. A broader concern was the presence of ss-20 missiles along the border and in the far eastern part of the Soviet Union. Such an "impressive Soviet military buildup," which continued for several years into the 1980s, "underlined Soviet objectives that went beyond past concern with inhibiting China from challenging the border with the ussr" (Sutter 1986, 89). All of these issues were major national security concerns for China, which feared them as signs of Soviet encirclement of the country.

In order for China to be able to influence Soviet support in Southeast Asia, Mongolia, and Afghanistan, issues with which China had little leverage itself, China used the leverage it had by refusing to make progress on resolving the border dispute with the Soviet Union and continuing to maintain troops at the border, all of which meant that normalization of relations would not occur anytime in the near future unless the Soviet Union reconsidered and changed its policies on a number of other disputed issues. In fact, "Mongolia, like Afghanistan and Vietnam, was concerned that the Soviet Union might 'sell her out' for the sake of a broader Sino-Soviet deal" (Segal 1985, 24), which implies that decision makers in these states were fully aware of China's use of issue linkage with regard to disputed issues related to Soviet policies and actions in these three states and the normalization of Sino-Soviet relations, and hence the border dispute.

China's concern with the Soviet intervention in Afghanistan was two tiered: concern with Soviet wishes to expand its role as regional hegemon and concern with Soviet encroachment on territory bordering the Sino-Afghan border and a direct threat to Chinese security, perceived as encirclement of China. The Chinese reaction to the Soviet invasion of Afghanistan was strong; China believed the invasion was intolerable: a "great threat to peace and security in Asia and the whole world" and a "wanton violation of all norms of international relations" (*Beijing Review* 1980). China worked vehemently to diplomatically isolate the Soviet Union and attempted to weaken Soviet power, particularly through strengthened relations with the US (Hilali 2001). According to an official at the Chinese Ministry of Foreign Affairs as announced to the Soviet ambassador the week after the invasion, "Afghanistan is China's neighbor . . . and therefore the Soviet armed invasion of that country poses a threat to China's security. This cannot but arouse the grave concern of the Chinese people" (*Beijing Review* 1980, 3). In addition to feeling encircled (along with Mongolia and Vietnam), China was mostly concerned that the Soviets would be able to use their enhanced power to destabilize China (Hilali 2001) and expand its power and influence. When the Soviet Union attempted to restart border negotiations in April 1980, China rejected the attempt, again explicitly citing "Sino-Soviet differences over Vietnam, Afghanistan, Mongolia, and the Sino-Soviet border" (Sutter 1986, 122).

The other of China's main concerns regarding Soviet involvement in Afghanistan was directly linked to a June 1981 treaty signed between the Soviet Union and Afghanistan recognizing as Soviet a strip of territory near China. The treaty, which was signed the same day that the Soviet military occupied the Wakhan salient, a strip of strategically salient territory at the conjunction of the Chinese-Afghan-Soviet borders, led to Chinese and Western suspicions of Soviet plans to annex the disputed territory. China's official response to the Soviet-Afghan treaty was hostile and negative, stating that the treaty was null and invalid since the Soviet Union did not have a right to sign a border treaty regarding territory located between China and Afghanistan, territory that had been disputed and resolved between the two states in 1963. The Chinese also complained that the territory bordered disputed Soviet territory claimed by China (Jones and Kevill 1985). If the Soviets were to annex the Wakhan salient, this would be a direct strategic threat to China on its western border, an outcome that China did not want to see. Thus, not only did China disapprove of the Soviet intervention in Afghanistan based on power relations and spheres of influence, but China was also concerned with Soviet intentions in Afghanistan that directly impacted the Chinese-Afghan border. By linking these two disputes together, China explicitly linked resumption of border talks to Soviet intervention in Afghanistan. Chinese officials explicitly linked the border dispute with the problem of Soviet involvement in Afghanistan, claiming that if negotiations were to occur, the Soviets had to promise to consider the withdrawal of Soviet troops from the Chinese border and Afghanistan (Jones and Kevill 1985). Since the Soviets made no attempts to appease China, as a result no border talks occurred until the latter 1980s when Soviet policies shifted regarding Afghanistan, Mongolia, and Vietnam's occupation of Cambodia.[10]

As noted earlier, the Soviet Union made several attempts to restart border negotiations in 1981 and 1982, but Chinese officials refused, each time citing the three unresolved obstacles. For example, when the Soviet government proposed the resumption of border talks in September 1981, Chinese officials replied there had been inadequate preparations, referring to the fact that the Soviets were still present in Mongolia and nothing had changed regarding their involvement in Afghanistan. When another attempt was made by the Soviet Union in February 1982, the Chinese response was that no border talks would occur until the Soviet Union "renounced its policy of hegemonism and expansionism" and withdrew its troops from Afghanistan (Hobday 1987, 268). When the Chinese did actually agree to meet for normalization talks, held in October 1982, Chinese officials demanded the withdrawal of six hundred thousand Soviet troops from the Chinese border and also cited concerns about Soviet support of Vietnam in Cambodia and Soviet intervention in Afghanistan (Jones and Kavill 1985). Chinese statements also warned that it was unlikely that any breakthrough would occur since the Soviets had stated that they were unwilling to meet conditions set by China regarding the three obstacles in particular

(Sutter 1986). The Soviet response was that they wished to confine the talks to only bilateral issues, but clearly China was unwilling to take advantage of the Sino-Soviet dispute to affect other disputed issues.

Even though Chinese officials were willing to work toward normalized relations with the Soviet Union in 1981 and 1982 due to China's relations with the US, which provided some leverage for China, they calculated that they could use that leverage to pressure the Soviets on the three obstacles and nuclear missile deployment. During the early 1980s, not only did Chinese officials not offer or accept any territorial concessions, but they also did not even engage in border negotiations. Instead, Chinese spokesmen repeatedly noted the resolution of the three obstacles as necessary conditions for talks, specifically citing each of the three Chinese concerns regarding Soviet involvement in Mongolia, Afghanistan, and Vietnam/Cambodia, along with Soviet troops on the Chinese border (Jones and Kavill 1985; Quested 1984). Since the Soviet Union's response to such demands was refusal to link such issues to the border talks, no talks occurred, let alone discussion of potential resolution. If China had agreed to territorial concessions to resolve the dispute, it would not have had sufficient leverage to pressure the Soviets on these other disputed issues. Hence the persistence of the dispute was a useful bargaining tool for China due to the existence of several other disputed issues.

With regard to Vietnam, China "repeatedly insisted that before it would agree to regularized diplomatic exchanges and to a Sino-Soviet summit, Moscow would have to cease supporting Vietnam's Cambodia policy. Deng Xiaoping personally insisted that Moscow would have to resolve the issue of Vietnam's occupation of Cambodia before China would agree to a summit" on their border dispute (Ross 1991, 1174). For some time, the Soviets had considered Vietnam their most important Asian ally due to its size, its strategic location, its influence over Cambodia and Laos, and its position as a potential buffer against Chinese expansion into Southeast Asia (Young 1988). The Soviet-backed Vietnamese control of Cambodia was so despised by China that it invaded Vietnam in February 1979 to "teach Vietnam a lesson" and to roll back Vietnamese forces from Cambodia, an attempt at coercive diplomacy that ultimately failed (Ross 1991, 1172). By 1983, Soviet officials began to offer the first of several concessions to China. First, in August 1983, Soviet President Andropov offered China a concession in the form of reduced deployment of ss-20 medium-range ballistic missiles, "primarily in an attempt to appease China while super-power relations were going from bad to worse" (Segal 1985, 13). A few months earlier, in May 1983, Chinese officials had officially cited the presence of Soviet ss-20 missiles in the Far East as a direct threat to China, which was another disputed issue in addition to the three obstacles. An analysis of this move claimed that it was unlikely that China had a sudden concern for Soviet nuclear capabilities, but instead, it seemed to be "an attempt to 'put down the marker' in Sino-Soviet talks to prevent the Soviet Union ignoring the nuclear dimension in any agreement on troop reductions" (Segal 1985, 22). Based on this analysis, it seems that China used issue linkage between the ss-20s and the border dispute, but not coercive diplomacy.

Despite China's willingness to meet to discuss bilateral relations in October 1983, no real progress was made on improving relations because according to Chinese Foreign Minister Wu Xuequian, the Soviets had refused to discuss "third states' interests," referring to Afghanistan and Vietnam primarily (Segal 1985, 13). Only after Yuri Andropov became ill in the latter part of 1983 did Sino-Soviet relations worsen again. Chinese officials subsequently shifted tactics when they realized that not only had Soviet deployment of troops and nuclear missiles continued to increase, but the incoming Soviet premier, Konstanin Chernenko, was even more rigid and uncompromising. China had also become concerned that softening toward the Soviet Union might not be consistent with China's efforts to maintain positive relations with the us. Several incidents in particular had also provoked China during this time period: the deployment of Soviet medium bombers in Cam Ranh Bay, Vietnam, in late 1983; the February 1984 deployment of two Soviet aircraft carriers to the western part of the Pacific Ocean, one of which passed closely by Chinese waters; and Soviet use of an aircraft carrier task force as part of a joint training exercise with Vietnam conducted near Chinese waters in March 1984 (Sutter 1986). As a result of these incidents and the reversed Chinese attitude toward the Soviet Union, anti-Soviet rhetoric began again, focused on both the Soviet threat on the border, nuclear missiles, and the three obstacles. Through most of 1984, China continued to insist that the three obstacles first be resolved before any bilateral relations with the Soviets could be normalized. Deng Xiaoping did note on one occasion in February 1984 that China would be willing to move forward on normalization talks while the three obstacles remained on the side. Yet when talks occurred the following month in March, the three obstacles were again cited, and no progress on normalization was made (Segal 1985).

Border Détente, Mid-1980s

In 1985, after Mikhail Gorbachev came into power in the Soviet Union, China continued to insist that withdrawal of Soviet troops from the Sino-Soviet border was a precondition of normalized relations and that the three obstacles be addressed. Though Gorbachev would eventually shift positions, initially he insisted that there could be no preconditions for normalizing relations, and that if there were to be reductions in troops along the border, they must be mutual and balanced. From the mid-1970s to the mid-1980s, troop deployments had remained fairly consistent, with an average of seventy-four Chinese divisions and forty-nine Soviet divisions along the border (Segal 1985). There was also no initial willingness to consider unilateral Soviet concessions to China to address the three obstacles.

Yet, Gorbachev eventually shifted positions and began to consider and then offer concessions related to the three obstacles. Realizing that Sino-Soviet relations had to be improved, Gorbachev recognized the need to begin rapprochement with China, which would involve making a number of significant concessions to satisfy Chinese demands. The economic cost of maintaining the Soviet empire and the intensified competition with the US in the 1980s had led to an economic and military crisis that forced Gorbachev to seriously reconsider Soviet relations with China. Gorbachev hoped that improved relations with China would halt the decline in the Soviet position in the international community (Fravel 2008). With the decline of the Soviet economy and military in the years just prior to the eventual collapse of the Soviet Union, Gorbachev realized that military confrontation with China was not feasible and that improved relations were necessary. In this changing geopolitical atmosphere, the Chinese government was willing not only to agree to resolve the dispute through concessions but also to drop the demand for Russian acknowledgment about the unfair status of the nineteenth-century treaties (Bakshi 2001). Gorbachev's initiatives would eventually open the door to the resolution of the territorial dispute.

It is believed that Gorbachev's initiatives are directly the result of China's counterstrategy in the 1980s (Fravel 2008; Hilali 2001), and therefore they played a key role in the eventual settlement of the dispute. What this suggests is that Chinese pressure on the Soviet Union through issue linkage and coercive diplomacy played a role in persuading Gorbachev to reconsider the three obstacles with regard to China because Chinese deployment on the border was too risky for the Soviets at the time. In July 1986, Gorbachev announced in a speech given at Vladivostok, aimed primarily at China, that the Soviet Union was prepared, "at any time and at any level, to discuss with China additional measures for creating a good-neighbourly atmosphere," citing a number of salient issues disputed with China, including troop reductions along the Chinese border, a promise not to increase Soviet ss-20 missiles in Asia, another promise that ss-20 missiles in Eastern Europe not be transferred to Asia, a pledge to consider a Soviet withdrawal from Mongolia, and another pledge that six Soviet regiments would be withdrawn from Afghanistan by the end of the year (Thakur and Thayer 1987). In August 1985, Mongolia's anti-Chinese leader had been replaced, which eased Sino-Mongolian relations, the main reason why Soviet troops had been deployed to Mongolia (Segal 1985). Gorbachev believed that offering disarmament concessions would "prove attractive" to China and help with political rapprochement (Young 1988, 323). The one issue not mentioned was Soviet support for Vietnamese occupation of Cambodia. China welcomed the pledges but stated that they still fell short of removing the three obstacles, the other disputed issues that needed to be resolved before China would consider attempting settlement of the border dispute and normalizing relations. In September and October 1986, the Chinese and Soviet foreign ministers met to discuss normalizing relations and resolution of their other disputed issues in order to move toward settlement of the border dispute. At the second meeting, the two foreign ministers agreed that border dispute talks would resume in February 1987, an agreement that "was generally believed to have resulted from Gorbachev's initiative in his Vladivostok speech" (Calvert 2004, 162).

The border talks that occurred in August 1987 led to significant progress in continuing to resolve the three obstacles, including a 20 percent reduction of Soviet troops in Mongolia in the spring and summer. Gorbachev also ordered the reduction of Soviet troops in the far eastern Soviet Union near the disputed border, which allowed for a joint commission to begin work on discussing the boundary in the Amur/Heilong and Ussuri/Wusuli rivers (Bakshi 2004). The reduction in troops was believed by political observers to be linked to the overall improvement of Sino-Soviet relations: "The purpose of this withdrawal is to show that Gorbachev is sincere about improving relations with Beijing" (FBIS 1987, C1). By 1988, Sino-Soviet relations had improved significantly, and border talks were held in November to discuss the eastern part of the border. Relations had improved mainly due to the proposed Soviet withdrawal from Afghanistan by February 1989, the acquiescence of the Soviets to Chinese control of the disputed Spratly Islands in the South China Sea, and increased efforts by the Soviet

Union to put pressure on Vietnam to resolve the Cambodia dispute. During this time, the Soviet Union began phasing out aid programs to Vietnam, encouraging Vietnamese flexibility on Cambodia in an effort to improve bilateral relations with China, and reducing Soviet deployment of ships in Cam Ranh Bay. All of these concessions were sought by the Soviet Union when it realized that Chinese relations were more salient than good relations with Vietnam, and to signal to China that it was serious about improving Sino-Soviet relations (Buszynski 1992; Hilali 2001; Ross 1991).

In February 1989, at a Sino-Soviet meeting, the Soviets agreed to a full withdrawal of Vietnamese troops, and in March 1989, the Soviet Union announced it was withdrawing 75 percent of its troops in Mongolia. As a result of these moves by the Soviet Union, all three of the obstacles were finally resolved, and Soviet deployment of troops and missiles along the border and in the Far East had been reduced. Therefore, there was no further incentive for China to withhold making and agreeing to territorial concessions to resolve the border dispute. Once significant progress on these issues had been made, China officially denounced its policy of antihegemonism against the Soviet Union and announced it was ready to agree to border dispute negotiations and actual concessions. At a summit held in May 1989, at which Gorbachev visited Beijing, the two states agreed to increase trade and pledged to transform the formerly militarized border into a border of peace and good neighborliness. By the early 1990s, after the breakup of the Soviet Union, Russia had made significant progress in the reduction of its military, a particular concern of China. The two states signed the Agreement on Guiding Principles for the Mutual Reduction of Military Forces Along the Sino-Soviet Boundary and the Strengthening Confidences in the Military in April 1990, further evidence of the intentions of both sides to move forward in resolving the border dispute. This reduction is believed to have had an impact on the Chinese decision to continue pursuing border talks. According to one observer, the border negotiations held during this time had "become linked to wider issues," mainly large-scale force reductions (Buszynski 1992, 504).

There were many shifts throughout the 1980s as Chinese and Soviet officials considered and eventually accepted détente. The theory of bargaining leverage clearly explains much of China's actions since it frequently and explicitly applied issue linkage and coercive diplomacy. China's strategy of coercive diplomacy in the 1980s was not through the use of militarized threats or uses of force as in the 1960s and 1970s, but instead through the use of diplomatic threats, mainly refusal to negotiate the border and drop its territorial claim for Soviet territory. This pattern suggests that the shift in military balance and the changing balance in the international system throughout the 1980s may have played a role, as it did during the Chinese decision to limit its use of violence in the Sino-Vietnamese war, for fear of provoking a Soviet reaction, as discussed earlier. The reduced tensions at the border were clearly linked to other disputed issues and political conflict between China and the Soviet Union, as an observer of Sino-Soviet relations suggested: "It seemed clear that, far from being a cause of Sino-Soviet disputes, the military tension along the frontier was largely a reflection of broader political differences. When political tension eased, so did the military situation" (Segal 1985, 20).

Territorial Concessions and Settlement of the Dispute

With the removal of the main disputed issues, China and Russia were able to work toward the resolution of the dispute through a number of negotiations and concessions throughout the 1990s and 2000s. By the early 2000s, bilateral relations were at an all-time high due to efforts by Jiang Zemin of China and Boris Yeltsin and then Vladimir Putin of Russia, resulting in the Treaty of Good-Neighborliness, Friendship, and Cooperation signed in July 2001, improved economic relations, and cooperation on several international issues. Most importantly, by the mid-2000s, there were no serious disagreements about other issues that had haunted Sino-Soviet/Russian relations for decades (B. Lo 2004). The territorial concession made by Russia in 2004 when it turned over two of three of the remaining disputed islands was allegedly done to ease China's potential anger regarding Putin's decision to build a pipeline with Japan rather than China and also to help persuade China to support Russia's entry into the World Trade Organization (WTO) (Buszynski 2006). Russia's offer of the two islands linked to two other issues is an example of positive issue linkage as the target state, unlike China's negative use of issue linkage as the challenger state. Since the resolution of the dispute in 2008, not only have the relations between the two former adversaries improved, but the settlement has also allowed for further growth in bilateral relations, including record amounts of trade (a 65 percent increase from 2000 to 2007) and investment, the ability to construct a cross-border pipeline for natural gas from Siberia to energy-hungry China, military sales, joint military research and development, and common positions on issues such as Taiwan and US missile defense (Iyer 2008; Pirchner 2008).

Interestingly, the 2001 treaty expires in twenty years, and some Russian analysts are nervous about an expiration date for the settlement of the territorial dispute and China's future intentions. Such concerns have been expressed regarding China's ability to shift its position: "China is currently a friendly country, but in the future, as has already been the case before, its political and military reference points could change sharply and a truly realistic threat to our security could emerge" (Tsygichko 2001). There is even growing concern among Russian policy makers that Chinese migration and settlement in Far Eastern Russia and depopulation of Russians could lead to future Chinese claims of parts of Siberia (Buszynski 2006). Therefore, even though the territorial dispute has been officially resolved, some Russians fear that there is a potential for China to reopen its territorial claims along the border and again use the dispute as bargaining leverage in its relationship with Russia. As one analyst notes, "For the moment, Russia and China are useful to each other" (Pirchner 2008, 319–20), but this is not necessarily guaranteed for the long term. Both states are hesitant to claim the "unbreakable friendship" of the 1950s during the Stalin-Mao era, but instead present a more realist image of their relations (B. Lo 2004).

The timing of the path to settlement of the border dispute was not highly intentional. With improved bilateral relations and the resolution of other disputed issues, Chinese decision makers were willing to work toward settlement and agree to drop China's claims to numerous islands along the border. Though it is impossible to know with certainty, it is likely that decision makers in Beijing concluded that the resolution of the three obstacles and subsequent geostrategic shifts in the status quo were significant enough to resume border negotiations, and with improved relations the potential for other disputed issues would be significantly reduced. Since the resolution of the dispute, "somewhat remarkably, given the historical record, there are currently no serious disagreements" between Russia and China (B. Lo 2004, 296), and relations have continued to improve.

It is also likely that Chinese decision makers felt confident enough to settle the border dispute because China is currently the stronger of the two states militarily, economically, and in overall influence in the world (Bakshi 2001; Buszynski 2006; Pirchner 2008). Not only did the Soviet Union effectively resolve the other disputed issues with China, but the relative balance of power between the two states also shifted with the breakup of the Soviet Union. As one scholar has pointed out, the "geopolitical weight of Moscow in the region and the world at large went down while that of China greatly increased. In the changed circumstances, Beijing could afford to be more relaxed and confident and, what was more, responsible and *status quo* oriented" (Bakshi 2001, 1848). With stronger overall leverage relative to Russia, China no longer needs to use the border dispute as bargaining leverage as it did when its leverage was weaker relative to the Soviet Union, making resolution not only feasible but attractive for China, a state that was ready to move on from its tense relations with Russia and work toward a new improved relationship.

CONCLUSIONS

The territorial dispute between China and the Soviet Union/Russia demonstrates how challenger states can use the strategy of issue linkage and coercive diplomacy to gain bargaining leverage with other disputed issues. The case also validates the claim that when other disputed issues are resolved, threats and uses of force should be less likely, while settlement attempts through territorial concessions should be more likely to occur, leading to ultimate resolution of territorial disputes. The theories of value of territory and domestic mobilization do provide some explanation for China's lack of territorial concessions prior to 1987 on occasion, along with its threats and uses of force, but the theories are falsified the majority of the time. Because these factors are primarily static or rarely changed over time, they cannot explain much of the variation in Chinese dispute strategies. The only real value of the disputed territory was strategic, and that was primarily the case only because the two adversaries deployed troops to the border to defend their respective territorial claims, making the strategic value endogenous to the dispute. While Chinese leaders were able to piggyback on threats or uses of force initiated for other reasons to mobilize domestic support, the limited times when domestic vulnerability of leaders existed in China cannot provide a suitable explanation for decades of no territorial concessions and hundreds of threats and uses of forces. Sometimes the strategy of offering concessions was made when it appeared that Chinese leaders were the most vulnerable domestically in the 1980s.

The resolution of other salient disputed issues—the withdrawal of Soviet troops from Mongolia and Afghanistan and the Soviet pressure on Vietnam to withdraw from Cambodia, in particular—allowed China and the Soviet Union to move forward in the late 1980s on the resolution of their decades-old territorial dispute. As long as other disputed issues existed, China was unwilling to resolve the border dispute, which prevented normalized bilateral relations. The critical point is that China was able to use the border dispute as bargaining leverage to compel the Soviet Union to change its foreign policies in other disputed issues that negatively affected China. It is believed that China's pressure on the Soviet Union through diplomatic threats was enough to persuade Gorbachev to realize in the mid-1980s that normalized relations with China, and therefore settlement of the territorial dispute, were necessary. Without the previous militarized and diplomatic threats and uses of force regarding the territorial dispute, China would have had little leverage to pressure the Soviet Union on the other disputed issues. These findings are consistent with the theory of bargaining leverage. However, the historic record also demonstrates that China used border negotiations to compel the Soviet Union on other disputed issues, not just coercive diplomacy through diplomatic or militarized threats or uses of force as expected. This finding indicates that states can be creative in how they pursue coercive diplomacy, and it may not only be through threats or uses of force. This pattern also suggests that challenger states may engage in territorial dispute negotiations not necessarily to attempt resolution of the dispute, but specifically to make their adversaries deal with other disputed issues. Though the bargaining leverage theory presented in this study did not predict such behavior, it is nevertheless consistent with the overall objective of the study, which is to demonstrate that states can take advantage of territorial disputes and, therefore, can have little incentive to resolve them.

Once the border dispute was resolved, the Soviet Union/Russia was able to make significant gains by improving its bilateral relations with China. Such improved relations would not have been possible without settlement of the territorial dispute and, indirectly, settlement of other disputed issues. China has also benefited from the resolution of the territorial dispute, particularly from arms sales with Russia, but the resolution of the other disputed issues was more salient to China at the time compared to resolution of the border dispute. Only with the resolution of the "three obstacles" and other disputed issues was China willing to drop its linkage of the border dispute to those issues and begin work toward settlement of the border dispute. This particular case provides observers in international relations with the ability to understand how challenger states like China can deliberately maintain a territorial dispute while other disputed issues are on the table, and how once these issues are resolved, the likelihood of resolution of a territorial dispute increases.

CHAPTER NINE

The Resolution of Enduring Territorial Disputes

Territorial disputes cause instability in the international system, threatening tensions, crises, and even wars. Millions of people living in states involved in territorial disputes are affected either directly or indirectly by border clashes, ethnic conflict, terrorism, martial law, militarized occupation, forced transfers, refugee status, fear of invasion, and, in some cases, nuclear war. These threats are part of regular life for South Koreans, Taiwanese, Indians, Pakistanis, Georgians, Israelis, Cypriots, and others. The endurance of these disputes, or the lack of peaceful settlement, has multiple costs that put a strain not only on the states involved but also on the international community as a whole.

The endurance of territorial disputes can be very costly in both financial and nonfinancial terms for states involved. China, India, Pakistan, and North Korea have all invested heavily in conventional and nuclear weapons in part to deal with their territorial disputes with other states. Hundreds of thousands of US troops are stationed in Japan and South Korea to assist with potential attacks rooted in territorial disputes (Taiwan, South Korea, Senkaku/Diaoyu Islands). Disputed borders have to be guarded, enclosed, and tightened, all of which is a cost for states involved in border disputes. Troop mobilization, deployment of ships or submarines to disputed waters, and flyovers by fighter jets, radar planes, and helicopters over disputed territory and waters are other common expenditures.

States often incur long-term military costs of having to maintain or prepare for troop mobilization, armament preparations, or ship or submarine deployments in waters near the disputed territory, distressing economies so that resources are diverted from other domestic needs such as social welfare, education, infrastructures, as well as economic development, investment, or other important issues. The settlement of territorial disputes reduces significant costs of maintaining the disputes, reducing the need for higher military expenditures and resources, and contributes to overall positive bilateral relations between states. Not only do territorial disputes force states to spend finances on military capabilities and actions, but often these disputes also prevent potential economic gains such as exploitation of natural gas and oil, fishing rights, minerals, water, and other natural resources in the disputed territories. Because of territorial disputes over the Spratly Islands, Senkaku/Diaoyu Islands, Suriname, and the Falkland/Malvinas Islands, all territories that are expected to have significant amounts of oil resources, each state involved in a particular dispute cannot attempt to profit from the resources until the dispute is settled. Most oil companies are extremely hesitant to invest billions of dollars into disputed territories, which could provoke armed conflict.

Enduring territorial disputes are the most troublesome type of interstate dispute in international relations today. Their endurance and lack of settlement have consequences that resonate around the world, directly affecting the foreign policies of dozens of states and indirectly involving many states in the international system. Territorial dispute tensions jeopardize regional security and limit the ability of regional and international organizations to act effectively in dealing with salient issues. When disputes do escalate to war, many other states, both regional and nonregional, are dragged into the dispute as allies or states having to make recommendations via UN Security Council resolutions or mediation attempts. Contiguous states feel the brunt of such conflicts through overflows of refugees and, in some cases, guerrilla groups based in neighboring states. In these cases, territorial wars force states to shift their focus from other salient issues to resolving a crisis.

Even when territorial disputes do not cause crises or wars, the tensions that result from the persistence of an enduring territorial dispute often damage normal bilateral relations beyond the other disputed issues that may also exist. Without normalized bilateral relations, joint cooperation on issues such as economic development, trade, shared water resources, energy and the environment, migration, and efforts to halt the smuggling of drugs, weapons, and other illegal resources is threatened. Trade relations are often halted or limited, leading to increased costs for imports in some cases, or lost markets for exports (Simmons 1999). When territorial disputes are resolved, trade tends to increase (Simmons 2005). Other benefits of settled territorial disputes are that they increase the potential for democratization to occur (Gibler 2007), and demilitarization is more likely, since large standing armies are difficult to justify without the existence of external territorial threats (Gibler 2010; Gibler and Tir 2010). Most importantly, long periods of peace are directly associated with the existence of fewer territorial disputes (Vasquez and Henehan 2010), providing significant incentive for the global community to work toward helping states resolve territorial disputes.

The management of enduring territorial disputes should therefore be a major priority of international security for all states in the international community, and understanding the endurance of these disputes is paramount. Though ideal, the resolution of all territorial disputes is unlikely. Rather, the focus of policy makers and scholars alike should be to figure out the best means of conflict management and the prevention of conflict. As this study has demonstrated, it may not be the territorial disputes that are driving dispute strategies, but instead other disputed issues that are linked to territorial disputes, particularly in the case of challenger states. Recent findings in the rivalry literature point to a similar pattern—that territorial disputes may not be the main variable influencing dispute strategies, but rather, territorial disputes may be embedded in rivalries, which then influence dispute strategies (Colaresi, Rasler, and Thompson 2007). In a similar sense, it is not necessarily territorial disputes, but rather other disputed issues, that are the most salient to challenger states, influencing their dispute strategies. The implication is that the peaceful resolution of territorial disputes—and other disputed issues linked to such disputes—is critical to preventing further armed conflicts and maintaining peace.

This study has attempted to explain the reasons why there are so many enduring territorial disputes remaining in the twenty-first century by examining dispute strategies. The predominant explanations in previous research on territorial disputes have been based primarily on the value of the disputed territory and domestic accountability or mobilization. Explanations about value of territory can help explain variation in dispute strategies in terms of probabilities, but since there is little variation over time, such explanations cannot sufficiently explain variation in disputed strategies at different times. Likewise, the contradictory findings in previous literature regarding value of territory, both tangible and intangible, making armed conflict and attempted settlement both more and less likely, indicate that this area of research needs further examination.

The domestic accountability and mobilization explanations likewise help to explain variance in dispute strategies in many disputes, but not in others where the territorial dispute is not salient enough or leaders have not pursued domestic mobilization using the disputed territory. Though there are extreme cases where domestic accountability and mobilization have played a significant role in influencing territorial dispute strategies, like the Argentine claim for the Falklands/Malvinas Islands, the Guatemalan claim for Belize, and the Chinese claim for Taiwan, many territorial disputes just do not have enough salience or the domestic populace is not focused enough on such disputed territory to potentially punish or support leaders based on territorial dispute strategies. Likewise, there are many months and years in which domestic vulnerability exists in many states, but dispute strategies do not match what the theories predict.

The research in this book was undertaken to provide a theory that helps explain the variation of dispute strategies and the subsequent endurance of territorial disputes not explained by previous theories. Many territorial disputes do not arise because of the territory itself, or only because of the territory, but rather because the disputes can be used for other gains. Recent research on territorial disputes and domestic politics has examined how leaders can achieve domestic gains, not through mobilization, but by their ability to centralize power as well as build up armies when external territorial threats exist (Gibler 2010; Gibler and Tir 2010). Yet, this explanation can adequately explain the dispute strategies just of target states, not challenger states that are issuing the territorial threat. By providing an explanation for challenger state strategies, this theory complements the theory of domestic gains through external threats, as well as previous findings about domestic mobilization and accountability and value of territory. Together, these findings provide a much more complete picture of territorial dispute strategies.

Even when challenger states claim that the disputed territory is highly significant and can never be negotiated, many states are playing a game using the dual strategy of coercive diplomacy and issue linkage. By examining four territorial disputes in depth, I have shown how these states were able to actually benefit from the endurance of their territorial disputes and, therefore, how they have had little or no incentive to peacefully resolve such disputes when other disputed issues existed. By persisting in territorial disputes and occasionally confronting target states diplomatically or militarily, challenger states can pursue a dual strategy of coercive diplomacy and issue linkage in order to use the territorial dispute as bargaining leverage in other disputed issues. The findings of this research suggest that it may not be the territorial dispute that is driving certain dispute strategies but rather the bargaining gains that can be achieved by linking the territorial dispute to other disputed issues.

One may ask why challenger states use territorial disputes as bargaining leverage linking them to other disputed issues instead of dealing with the other disputed issues independently. In other words, why do states bother to link territorial dispute threats with other disputed issues? As I have shown in this study, states can use territorial dispute threats as leverage when they lack the upper hand in the other salient disputed issues. When a challenger state has weak leverage in one area, it can link the upper hand it has by claiming a target state's territory and hope that a threat in the territorial dispute will be sufficient to compel a target state to make a change in some other policy or action unrelated to the territorial dispute itself. The assumption is that the disputed territory has more salience for the target state, not necessarily because of any tangible or intangible value, but merely because the threat of a territorial claim is a threat to the sovereignty and security of the state, and maintenance of sovereignty and security of one's territory is a critical priority for any state. Therefore, the ideal conditions for the strategy are when the other disputed issues are more salient for the challenger state, but less salient for the target state.

In most cases, the dual strategy of coercive diplomacy and issue linkage works for the challenger state. The target state complies with the demands of the challenger state on issues less salient to the target state relative to a threat to its territorial integrity and sovereignty because the costs of doing so are lower than the costs of a threat to the target state's sovereign territory. Challenger states know that the target state will likely comply with their demands, making the strategy an attractive and easy one. All over the world, dozens of diplomatic and militarized threats are being issued by states claiming territory of another sovereign state. Sometimes these threats turn into actual armed conflict, such as the 1982 Falklands War or the 2006 Lebanon War. In most cases, however, the threats are de-escalated and never pursued by the challenger states. This does not mean the threats and persistence in the dispute do not involve any costs, but they are seemingly low enough for challenger states, and the gains from using the territorial disputes as bargaining leverage are sufficiently high enough to make the endurance of territorial disputes worthwhile.

The four cases examined in this study illustrate the validity of the theory of bargaining leverage as an explanation for varied dispute strategies in territorial disputes. As with all other research on conflict management and international relations, this theory cannot explain every instance of diplomatic or militarized threats or uses of force, but rather demonstrate that certain conditions make such strategies more likely. No theory is perfect, and I do not claim that this theory is perfect either. In these cases, the existence of other disputed issues made diplomatic or militarized threats or uses of force much more likely. Not only are there correlations in terms of timing, but a careful reading of qualitative evidence indicates that there is a clear causal mechanism in play in these four cases. Though I cannot show that a certain strategy is x times more or less likely through statistical models, this in-depth research provides ample evidence that coercive diplomacy and issue linkage is at play in these disputes, and likely in many others.

In each case, a different type of territory is disputed: uninhabited islands and territorial waters, border disputes, and inhabited territories. In all four cases, the challenger states clearly benefited from the endurance of the disputes, with little incentive to attempt peaceful resolution, as long as other disputed issues existed. Bargaining leverage accounted for the majority of dispute strategies the majority of the time, some more than others, depending on the case. When other disputed issues existed, the challenger states were more willing to pursue issue linkage and coercive diplomacy and avoid attempted settlement. On the other hand, in months and years when other disputed issues lapsed and bilateral relations improved, challenger states were less likely to pursue diplomatic or militarized threats or uses of force. In the one case where all other disputed issues were resolved, the challenger state offered territorial concessions toward settlement. China's issue linkages of the Senkaku/Diaoyu Islands were almost always implicit, but clearly understood by Japan. Issue linkages made by Morocco against Spain and Hezbollah/Lebanon against Israel were almost always explicit and clearly linked. China's use of issue linkage against the Soviet Union/Russia was relatively consistent and mostly explicit. In all four cases, the target states—Japan, Spain, Israel, and the Soviet Union/Russia—complied with demands regarding other disputed issues the majority of the time.

SENKAKU/DIAOYU ISLANDS

For China, the Senkaku/Diaoyu Islands provide an opportunity for the Chinese government to gain concessions from Japan in other disputed issues. By threatening Japan diplomatically and militarily for almost forty years, China has successfully compelled Japan to shift or halt some policy or action perceived by China as damaging or threatening. China knows that Japan values the disputed territory, so China expects that Japan will comply with most Chinese demands if they are reasonable and are cheaper and easier than risking that China will follow through on its territorial threats. In particular, China has used the territorial dispute as bargaining leverage to compel Japan to shift its actions in regard to nationalist issues, the use of the Japanese military abroad, and economic aid to China. In each of these cases, China was able to make some implicit or explicit threat about the islands dispute and link the threat indirectly to other disputed issues.

The continued endurance of the Senkaku/Diaoyu Islands dispute has a number of important policy ramifications that are significant not only for China and Japan but also for Taiwan and the US in particular. For the US, Japan, and Taiwan, China's claim for the disputed islands is directly related to a much larger military strategy to spread its naval capabilities eastward. This has been particularly important for China since the US and Japan announced that China's threat to Taiwan was a mutual security concern in February 2005, a move that China strongly rejected. The disputed islands sit right in the middle of the likely sea route between US forces that would be deployed to Taiwan from Okinawa, a factor of which China is keenly aware. Any actions taken on the disputed islands therefore indirectly affect US military capabilities and Taiwan's status. Since Taiwan also claims the disputed islands and China's claim to the islands is mostly based on its claim to Taiwan (since the islands are closest to Taiwan), these two disputes are closely linked. Taiwan's claims to the islands could also further complicate Taiwanese relations with China and Japan.

Another policy problem is that until the dispute is fully resolved, the full potential of oil and gas resources cannot be realized for energy hungry China and Japan. The current ongoing development of natural gas resources in the East China Sea is only a small part of the anticipated oil and gas resources, which cannot be exploited until the dispute is fully settled. China will inevitably continue to claim that its EEZ extends to the continental shelf, while Japan will continue to claim that the median line between the two states determines each state's EEZ zones. The islands dispute is critical in determining rights to EEZ zones and therefore oil and gas resources, as well as fishing and other maritime resources.

By far the most important policy consequence is the potential for the dispute to continue to trigger tense and difficult relations between China and Japan. Though the proposed joint gas project in the East China Sea has recently promoted friendlier relations, this does not mean that bilateral relations could not sour again due to landings of Chinese activists on the islands or other opportunities China may have to use the islands to gain leverage in another disputed issue. Until the dispute is settled in finality, there will always be some degree of risk of harming critical economic and diplomatic relations in a region where these two states are the major movers and shakers. Japan must work with China to ensure that other disputed issues are resolved before settlement can occur.

CEUTA/SEBTA AND MELILLA/MELILIA

In the dispute over the enclaves of Ceuta/Sebta and Melilla/Melilia between Morocco and Spain, Morocco has also repeatedly gained concessions from Spain in other disputed issues by using threats about the enclaves as bargaining leverage. Despite rhetorical claims by Morocco about its wish to change the status quo and reunite the enclaves with the rest of Morocco after centuries of Spanish rule, the actions taken by Moroccan decision makers have not supported such assertions. Moroccan officials have made repeated calls for a working group or bilateral negotiations to discuss sovereignty, but none of these calls have been serious enough to be perceived as attempts at settlement. Rather, they represent actions taken in the dispute to signal resolve to Spain with regard to the dispute itself and other disputed issues.

The findings have provided substantial support for the idea that Moroccan leaders have chosen to persevere rather than actively attempt settlement primarily because Morocco has been able to achieve numerous concessions and bargaining gains on other disputed issues with Spain, mainly with fishing rights and illegal immigration of Moroccans into Spain. Even though Spain recognizes the bargaining leverage that the enclaves provide for Morocco, Spanish officials have had little choice but to give in to demands on other disputed issues in most instances and sometimes pursue a strategy of appeasement in order to prevent Morocco from threatening the security of the enclaves. Unless Spain can find a way to prevent Morocco from achieving bargaining gains through dispute linkage, it is unlikely that Morocco will halt its attempts to use the enclaves dispute to achieve other gains they otherwise would not have been able to realize.

For policy makers, this dispute may seem less worrisome than the other disputes examined in this study. Though the likelihood of armed conflict is very low, the endurance of this dispute is nevertheless concerning. Because of the location of the enclaves and their role as bridges for illegal immigration of Africans into the EU, as well as a recruitment and coordination location for radical Islamic terrorists, the enclaves dispute should be on the radar of policy makers. For the US, this dispute has interfered with bilateral relations with the states involved, both of which are US allies, and it will likely play a role in future UN decisions about the status of the Western Sahara. This dispute should be carefully observed, and any attempt to resolve it must be cognizant of the benefits that Morocco gets from keeping the dispute ongoing. Without such knowledge, any attempt at resolution will likely fail miserably.

SHEBAA FARMS

Of the four territorial disputes reviewed in this book, the dispute over Shebaa Farms is by far the most volatile and disconcerting for policy makers, partly because of its geostrategic location and partly because it involves a violent non-state actor that has engaged in terrorism and insurgency supported by rogue states Iran and Syria. Not only has this dispute involved dozens of militarized uses of force, but it also escalated into a full-scale war, involving the deaths of more than a thousand civilians. Though the Lebanese government made the official territorial claim for the small territory along the border, Shebaa Farms, it has not pursued militarized threats itself. Instead, Lebanon has relied on and allowed Hezbollah to confront Israel since the dispute's initiation in the summer of 2000. In just six short years, Hezbollah and IDF troops clashed on two dozen occasions, involving the deaths of some 140 Israeli soldiers and several hundred Hezbollah fighters, as well as more than a thousand Lebanese civilians and a few dozen Israeli civilians. Since the end of the 2006 war, Hezbollah has kept to its agreement not to confront Israel militarily, but this does not mean the dispute is over. Rather, Hezbollah has rearmed and recruited new members of its military wing, which is still located in southern Lebanon, though not right along the border.

The incentives for Hezbollah, and indirectly Lebanon, to keep the dispute over Shebaa Farms going are not as direct as in the cases of China and Morocco in their respective disputes. In this case, based on a complicated power-sharing arrangement, Lebanon has allowed Hezbollah, and to some degree Syria, to achieve their shared objectives regarding Israel. First of all, the endurance of the Shebaa Farms dispute has allowed Hezbollah to justify its continued armed resistance against Israel. Without Shebaa Farms, there would have been no real justification for Hezbollah's presence along the border in south Lebanon or its armament. Other issues that were explicitly linked to militarized threats on Shebaa Farms included releases of Lebanese prisoners, support for the Palestinian cause, Hezbollah's objective to challenge Israel's security overall, and the Israeli-occupied Syrian Golan Heights. The Lebanese government has acknowledged having similar goals as Hezbollah, with regard to the release of Lebanese prisoners and pressure on the state of Israel regarding a Palestinian state. Therefore, though the Lebanese government itself did not pursue threats or uses of force, the allowance and sometimes support of Hezbollah's actions to seek similar goals suggest that both actors were working together to some degree. Despite major differences on other issues, particularly Syrian influence on Lebanese politics, both the majority and opposition governments in Lebanon, which include Hezbollah as a political party, have agreed on the status of Shebaa Farms.

Hezbollah's use of the Shebaa Farms dispute as bargaining leverage against Israel has set an unfortunate precedent—that Israel is willing to negotiate with violent nonstate actors and comply with their demands. The problem with Israel repeatedly conceding to Hezbollah's demands is that Hezbollah has little incentive to give up any bargaining leverage it has over Israel, including Shebaa Farms. Policy makers involved in mediation attempts with Lebanon, as well as Syria, and Israel must understand the use of Shebaa Farms as bargaining leverage and Israel's willingness to comply with demands. Israel's 2006 attempt to destroy Hezbollah would have allowed Israel to stop complying with its demands, but since Israel failed to thwart the group's continued existence, this means Hezbollah still maintains the stronger hand, as long as Lebanon continues to maintain its territorial claim for Shebaa Farms. The most important lesson from this dispute is that nonstate actors can act as proxies for challenger states, and therefore policy makers must consider actions by nonstate actors like Hezbollah in conjunction with state decisions and actions. Examining the Lebanese government's actions and Hezbollah's actions separately would provide an inaccurate and incomplete picture of the dispute. Acknowledging that a nonstate actor can play a major role in a territorial dispute between sovereign states is significant for future studies of territorial disputes, particularly those involving insurgency and terrorism.

Until other more significant issues are resolved, it is unlikely that the Lebanese government would be willing to negotiate its claim for Shebaa Farms and engage in peace talks with Israel. The animosity is just too convenient for Lebanon and Hezbollah, as well as Syria. Shebaa Farms may be a seemingly small, irrelevant piece of land that has no real value, but in reality, it is the epicenter of the larger Arab-Israeli dispute, involving the Golan Heights and Syria's animosity toward Israel, and the Palestinian issue, including terrorism conducted by Hamas and Islamic Jihad, groups that Hezbollah supports.

SINO-SOVIET/RUSSIAN BORDER DISPUTE

Unlike the other three disputes examined in this study, the Sino-Soviet/Russian border dispute was resolved with finality in 2008. This dispute, which lasted for forty-eight years, played a major role in the bilateral relations of two major powers during the Cold War. China and the Soviet Union engaged not only in threats of force but also in significant uses of force, including major border clashes in 1969 on disputed islands in the Ussuri River. China made one offer of a territorial concession in the 1960s but did not offer any other concession until the latter 1980s, when negotiations began that would eventually lead to the resolution of the dispute. As the state involved in the largest number of territorial disputes in the latter part of the twentieth century, China resolved many of them in the 1960s, but not this dispute. Rather, China used multiple attempts of issue linkage and coercive diplomacy with the border dispute, delaying settlement.

As the challenger state, China was able to express its dissatisfaction with other disputed issues in Sino-Soviet relations all throughout the dispute when other disputed issues arose, affecting bilateral relations. In the 1960s, China was primarily concerned with the growing rift in bilateral relations between the two communist powers followed by geostrategic concerns about Soviet power relative to China. Later, in the 1970s and 1980s, China linked the border dispute to other disputed issues that were referred to by China as the "three obstacles"— Soviet troops in Mongolia, the Soviet invasion and occupation of Afghanistan, and Soviet support for Vietnam and its invasion of Cambodia. It was only after these three major issues of contention were near resolution that China was willing to engage in negotiations involving offers of territorial concessions in the latter 1980s.

There are several lessons to be learned from studying this resolved dispute. First, this dispute shows that resolution between adversaries disputing territory over several decades is possible. Most importantly, it shows that effectively resolving other disputed issues opened the possibility for China as the challenger state to consider territorial concessions and eventual settlement of the dispute. This case also demonstrates how major rivals can use territorial disputes to gain bargaining leverage on other more salient disputed issues that tend to exist in rivalries, such as the disagreements over relative power and ideological influence in this case. It also suggests that though territorial disputes play a role in rivalries, they may not be the only dispute or even the most salient dispute, as current research on territorial disputes and rivalries suggests. It may be that multiple issues make rivalries more difficult to manage (Dreyer 2010; Dreyer and Wiegand 2010). Finally, the resolution of the dispute suggests that decision makers in target states need to seriously consider how they deal with other disputed issues, if they are salient enough to them, or whether the disputed territory is more salient.

REAL-WORLD IMPLICATIONS

Without a large-N analysis, it is difficult to generalize the theory of territorial disputes as bargaining leverage across all cases. In fact, it is certain that this theory can explain many enduring territorial disputes, but not all. However, I do not believe this is a major limitation since future research can take the theory suggested here and test it on other disputes. Eventually, a large-N study can be conducted once significant data are collected on other disputed issues existing in each territorial dispute in every month or year throughout their duration. Several previous studies have shown that certain values of territory and domestic accountability and mobilization in particular make states involved in territorial disputes less likely to attempt settlement. This study does not claim these theories are invalid, but instead that there is an additional pattern of causality in territorial dispute strategies, leading to a problem of enduring disputes.

The theory of territorial disputes as bargaining leverage can help to explain more about the variation in territorial dispute strategies regarding conflict management. There are likely many other enduring territorial disputes in which the challenger state is unwilling to attempt settlement, instead using the dispute as bargaining leverage. One such dispute is that between Eritrea and Ethiopia, in which Ethiopia has indirectly admitted that its pressure on the border dispute is pursued as bargaining leverage to ensure that Eritrea allows Ethiopia, now a landlocked state, to use Eritrean ports. In East Asia, the Spratly Islands have been used by several involved players—China, Vietnam, Malaysia, and the Philippines—as bargaining leverage in greater Asian power politics. Though there is little doubt that Syria would certainly like to reacquire the Israeli-occupied Golan Heights, the disputed territory has served a greater purpose in justifying Syrian antipathy toward Israel and complaints that Israel is the aggressor state in the region, not Syria. It is not necessarily the case that these states do not actually want to (re)acquire disputed territory, but rather their strategies suggest that pursuing diplomatic and militarized threats or uses of force and avoiding settlement attempts through territorial concessions is a more effective strategy overall while other disputed issues exist between disputing states.

States' use of territorial disputes as bargaining leverage should be considered as a key factor in attempts by policy makers and mediators to resolve these disputes. The benefits of using threats or minor uses of force in territorial disputes as bargaining leverage for other disputed issues are just too attractive to challenger states that have opportunities to achieve such leverage. As long as other disputed issues are considered more salient than the territorial claim itself, there is little incentive to drop the claim. Based on the research in this study, it seems that enduring territorial disputes will be a long-term problem for international relations scholars and policy makers alike unless other issues disputed between adversaries are resolved. When disputed issues accumulate, as often happens in rivalries, resolution of such disputes becomes more difficult, and we are more likely to observe higher levels of tension, rivalry, and armed conflict (Dreyer 2010).

Unfortunately, this is a relatively pessimistic view of territorial disputes, which demonstrates why attempted settlement of territorial disputes is not always the best option for challenger states, while diplomatic and militarized threats and limited uses of force can be a better option for challenger states. This study shows that territorial disputes can actually be efficient for some states, as long as the costs to maintain the disputes do not outweigh the benefits of using them as bargaining leverage. States will cooperate with each other when rational decision makers recognize that the benefits of cooperation outweigh the costs (Fearon 1995, 1998). In the case of territorial disputes, as long as other salient disputed issues exist, which challenger states can link to territorial disputes to gain bargaining leverage, the benefits will outweigh the costs. Disputes will become inefficient if no other salient disputed issues exist, making the strategy of issue linkage and coercive diplomacy useless. If disputes are likely to escalate to armed conflict, the costs affiliated with conflict will also outweigh any benefits, making the disputes inefficient. As long as states only pursue threats or limited uses of force and avoid armed conflict, disputes can remain efficient. In most of the enduring disputes today, the benefits apparently continue to outweigh the costs since other disputed issues continue to prevail, and very few involve militarized actions. When they are militarized, they are relatively minor and not very costly.

An implication of this research is that states cannot only continue to take

advantage of current territorial disputes, but other states can also initiate territorial claims when they see fit to use such claims as bargaining leverage against
their adversaries in other disputed issues. For example, China used force to
seize the Crescent Group of islands in the Paracel Islands, islands not claimed
previously, specifically in response to South Vietnamese and Philippine actions in the Spratly Islands in January 1974. The objective in this case was to
strengthen China's position in all of its offshore island disputes (Fravel 2008),
not necessarily to acquire the Crescent Group of islands. The Shebaa Farms case
is another example of a territorial claim activated for the purpose of achieving
bargaining leverage, as discussed earlier. The findings of this book suggest that
theorists and policy makers need to be more cognizant of the benefits of enduring territorial disputes when attempting to negotiate, mediate, arbitrate, or
adjudicate resolutions in territorial disputes. Understanding that states can use
territorial disputes as bargaining leverage will help policy makers better manage international conflicts to prevent triggering military force.

On a more optimistic note, attempts to peacefully resolve territorial disputes
are feasible, as shown by the dozens of successfully settled territorial disputes.
The majority of territory disputes in the second half of the twentieth century
have been successfully and peacefully resolved, which suggests that settlement
is not only possible but feasible under the right conditions. The good news is
that previous studies show that once territorial disputes are resolved, and states
accept the outcome of negotiations or other peaceful resolution methods, territorial disputes are not likely to arise again, and peace will dominate the formerly adversarial relationship (Simmons 1999). Likewise, even when other salient issues arise in the future, once territorial disputes are settled, long periods
of peace will likely occur (Vasquez 1993). More importantly, if boundaries are
peacefully changed to accommodate settlement (Tir 2003, 2006), or if neighboring states legally accept their boundaries (Kocs 1995), the likelihood of militarized conflict is reduced significantly. Such findings suggest that once territorial disputes are resolved, they are less likely to again become problems or lead
to future armed conflict. Therefore, the international community should work
hard to help provide conditions for states that are suitable to settlement involving territorial concessions.

To make progress in resolving territorial disputes and to apply lessons learned
from this study, resolution attempts should involve discussions on the actual
territorial disputes and must also involve other disputed issues that challenger
states have linked to the disputes. I have attempted to show in the cases ex-

amined that the resolution of other disputed issues is critical to achieve the willingness of challenger states to halt all diplomatic or militarized threats or uses of force and to consider attempting settlement of their territorial disputes through territorial concessions. Thus, perhaps the most effective way for mediators to help states to resolve their territorial disputes is to encourage resolving other disputed issues first, so that challenger states do not need to use territorial dispute threats to achieve concessions in these other issues. As with rivalries, where multiple disputed issues tend to exist, states involved in territorial disputes can work to remove one issue at a time, like peeling the layers of an onion, eventually resolving all disputed issues, including the territorial disputes.

Though many of the other disputed issues are more salient than the disputed territory, policy makers can help states build confidence to first resolve those issues. This suggests that states should take small steps that act as confidence-building measures (CBMs), leading to cooperation first on smaller issues, then working toward larger, more salient issues. Cooperation on other less salient issues is beneficial in several ways—it increases interaction, reduces uncertainty and distrust, and expands the shadow of the future in which further cooperation is required. First, more frequent cooperation provides a higher number of iterations, so that the disputing states have to meet regularly to discuss disputed issues (Axelrod 1984; Keohane 1984; Oye 1985). A higher number of meetings means that decision makers in the disputing states increase their interactions, they learn more about the bargaining tactics of their opponent, and the level of distrust and uncertainty is reduced (Leng 1983; Lipson 1993; Wiegand and Powell forthcoming). By decreasing distrust and uncertainty about negotiating tactics on one issue, the challenger state is able to build trust and reduce uncertainty for the target state. By cooperating more frequently on long-term issues such as water resources or drug trafficking across the border, the shadow of the future is also expanded so that future cooperation is necessary. Even when cooperation does not occur, attempts to cooperate provide further interactions, reducing uncertainty and distrust.

Each of these factors is believed to breed a better negotiating environment, increase the level of mutual trust between the disputing states, and increase the level of bilateral relations, which an enduring dispute would continuously threaten. As the frequency of cooperation on other bilateral issues occurs, such cooperation acts as CBMs that weaken the level of distrust inherent in territorial disputes. Over time, more frequent cooperation is expected to increase interactions between decision makers of the disputing states, providing more opportunity to discuss and resolve other disputed issues and, eventually, the territorial disputes.

Though scholars have not fully recognized the link between other bilateral issues and territorial disputes, policy makers understand that in order to improve the chances of meeting at the negotiating table to discuss the most difficult disputed issue, it is helpful to first be able to take smaller steps that act as confidence-building measures. CBMS, commonly discussed in the literature on disarmament and regional security policies, are designed to provide reassurances about intentions, reduce uncertainty between the disputing states, and increase predictability of future actions (Asada 1988; Kang and Kaseda 2000; Rathmell 2000). They also improve transparency of capabilities and intentions of the disputing states, reducing the likelihood of unintentional armed clashes that result from miscalculation or suspicion. Most importantly, CBMS are expected to encourage disputing states to move forward on negotiations regarding more ambitious initiatives rather than the issues with which the CBMS are dealing. Cooperation on other bilateral issues such as trade, linked infrastructure, and cultural exchanges act as CBMS in the hopes that the disputing states will recognize that such cooperation can pave the way toward mutual interests on more salient disputed issues.

By engaging in cooperation on other bilateral issues that act as CBMS, such as providing concessions or signaling trust by joining a shared alliance, signing a treaty on another issue, or increasing trade or investment, target states in particular can attempt to build confidence with challenger states so that they are more willing to work toward resolution of other more salient disputed issues, such as fishing rights or support for third-party adversaries. For example, if Spain can provide additional alternative concessions to Morocco in lieu of pressure by Morocco on the EU for concessions for Spanish fishing rights in Moroccan waters, then Morocco should have no reason to link its territorial dispute with Spain each time the contract expires. If the fishing rights issue were nonexistent, there would be less incentive for Morocco to use coercive diplomacy and issue linkage in the enclaves dispute.

By resolving the other disputed issues, challenger states should have incentive to engage in territorial dispute settlement attempts or even be willing to drop their territorial claims, unless the value of the territory makes it so salient that settlement is a nonoption. By working to resolve other disputed issues, target states offer a carrot to challenger states in order to bring the latter to the territorial disputes negotiation table, and once they get there, the target state can hope that the bilateral cooperation on other issues impresses the challenger enough to potentially "soften" its position on the territorial claim (Wiegand and Powell forthcoming). For example, in the years prior to the settlement of their territorial dispute, Bahrain and Qatar actively cooperated with each other regarding collective security as a part of the Gulf Cooperation Council Charter, specifically with regard to possible aggression by Iraq or Iran, by participating in joint training exercises and sharing military equipment. Such actions acted as CBMs to reduce the bilateral tension and other salient issues related to their long-standing rivalry, helping to move the states to a place where they were willing to resolve their territorial dispute. Honduras and Nicaragua also used CBMs as part of a mediation attempt by the Organization of American States in an attempt to settle their dispute over five thousand square miles along their border before it was brought to the ICJ (Conaway 2001). In the mid-1980s, the Soviets and Chinese began to engage in CBMs, such as advance notice of troop movement, military exercises in the border regions, border trade, exchange of production technology, technical training, and exchange of scientific experts (Sutter 1986), which influenced the first major breakthrough in border negotiations a few years later.

The use of CBMs is frequently noted in press statements about territorial dispute settlement attempts, which indicates that policy makers directly involved in settlement attempts are aware of the benefits of CBMs and are attempting to apply them to deal with other disputed issues and, subsequently, particular territorial disputes. If states involved in territorial disputes can use CBMs to improve other bilateral relations outside of the territorial dispute, they can hopefully persuade challenger states to consider settlement attempts or provide concessions in upcoming territorial dispute settlement attempts. This can be the case particularly if the challenger states see that target states are serious about changing their positions or offering concessions on other disputed issues that the challenger states have linked the territorial dispute as bargaining leverage.

By working to delink territorial disputes with other disputed issues, there is some hope for the settlement of territorial disputes. In the meantime, policy makers must recognize the significant role that bargaining leverage plays in territorial disputes, particularly in challenger threats against the target states, in addition to value of territory and domestic factors. This research has shown how bargaining leverage helps to explain dispute strategies and, therefore, the endurance of territorial disputes. Together with the findings of previous studies about value of territory and domestic vulnerability, the findings in this study provide scholars with a richer understanding of the strategies pursued by states involved in territorial disputes and provide policy makers with the ability to use this consolidated research to better manage and resolve such disputes.

NOTES

CHAPTER ONE. The Endurance of Territorial Disputes

1. To be amenable to both realists and liberal institutionalists, I use the terms "states" and "decision makers" interchangeably. Clearly, government officials are the ones who actually make decisions about strategies, and most of the time I refer to officials, decision makers, or leaders, but for the sake of simplicity I sometimes refer to such decision makers as states, such as China or Morocco. This does not, however, imply an assumption of the unitary actor model.

2. Though the term "endurance" implies duration of disputes, this study does not attempt to explain duration in terms of years, but rather it focuses on lack of settlement and any diplomatic or militarized threats or uses of force occurring during the years of the dispute. The term "enduring" is used similarly to its use in "enduring rivalries," which are disputes that involve militarized conflict and have lasted for a minimum of at least ten years (Goertz and Diehl 1992; 1995; Tir and Diehl 2002). I use the ten-year minimum to label territorial disputes as enduring, but unlike enduring rivalries, enduring territorial disputes need not involve militarized conflict. The objective of this study is to explain the lack of settlement in territorial disputes, which can lead to enduring territorial disputes. Therefore, I include all ongoing disputes, including those that have lasted only a year or so, because these disputes can become enduring territorial disputes if settlement does not occur in the near future. Only three ongoing disputes today are not enduring.

3. In atlases produced in India, the territory of Kashmir and Jammu is clearly marked as Indian. A colleague purchased a world atlas in India, and during the customs check, Indian officials stamped "Kashmir and Jammu are Indian territory" on every page of the atlas, regardless of whether it was a map of the United States, Latin America, or South Asia.

4. For detailed information about the Kashmir and Jammu territorial dispute and resulting wars between India and Pakistan, see Behera 2006; Choudhury 1968; Ganguly 2002; Thomas 1992.

5. Argentine leaders claimed then and now that the intent for the armed provocation was to compel the UK to agree to sovereignty negotiations, in which they were reluctant

to engage at the time. The failure of negotiations was one of the last straws for Argentina, "depriving the junta of the much needed recognition of their wishes as an egalitarian partner" (Femenia 1996, 93). Facing "this lack of clout, and to engage Britain in serious negotiations," the junta decided to invade, which "would capture the attention of both the United Kingdom and the U.S. and would lead to resumption of negotiations" (93), which Argentina claimed to be its ultimate goal.

6. Target states can also cease control of disputed territory and cede territory to the challenger state without engaging in negotiations or a third-party resolution method.

CHAPTER TWO. Previous Research on Territorial Dispute Strategies

1. Agriculture and business are not considered as economic value since such means of income can be relocated to another suitable territory within a state. Using this measure would also be inefficient since every tract of territory on earth could potentially become economically valuable.

2. Although most of the literature on public opinion and foreign policy is on American presidents and Congress, there is also literature examining similar trends in democracies including Germany, Canada, and the United Kingdom, and some in Latin America. See Aldrich, Sullivan, and Borgida (1989); Brace and Hinckley (1992); Fagan (1960); Laulicht (1965); Page and Shapiro (1983).

3. According to former Argentine Foreign Minister Costa Mendez, the junta had hoped that "the peaceful and bloodless occupation of the Islands would make the Argentine will to negotiate the solution of the underlying conflict evident" to the British (Femenia 1996, 93). Mendez explained that the initial stages of planning led to an objective of a touch-and-go operation in which the military would land in the Malvinas and then leave, so that it was perceived not as a military conquest but rather as the means to gain publicity for their sovereignty dispute. The plan had been to restart bilateral negotiations that had been abandoned in 1968. The operation was to be a "show of military teeth followed by a turn to the negotiation table," which would be feasible based on Argentina's capabilities at that time (Busser 1987, 16).

CHAPTER THREE. Territorial Disputes as Bargaining Leverage

1. See "Research Using ICOW: Project Data," http://www.paulhensel.org/icowcites .html, for a list of publications that use the ICOW data.

2. See also Evans, Jacobsen, and Putnam (1993).

3. There is general agreement among scholars that the Chinese attack across the border in February 1979 was not intended as a full-scale invasion, despite media reports to the contrary. Mulvenon (1995, 74) notes that if the Chinese had planned the attack to be a

full-scale invasion, "the Chinese could have thrown a much larger force at the Vietnamese, completely overwhelming their border defense," and that the attack was more like a signal and not like conquering.

4. See Gaiduk (2008) for further support of this argument. The Vietnamese invasion of Cambodia provoked China because China regarded Southeast Asia as its own sphere of influence, and Vietnam had attempted to assert hegemony there, and because Cambodia was one of China's few ideological allies.

5. This argument that disputed territory is salient is specifically compared to other disputed issues *across issues* and does not refer to whether disputed territory itself has value such as economic resources or strategic value *within issues*.

6. This is a general assumption about salience of territory and is not necessarily true across *all* dyads. As with any assumption in IR theory, the purpose of this assumption that territory has more salience for target states is necessary for the logic of the theory. Of course, it is always possible that the target state or specific leaders perceive other issues such as nuclear threat or removal of a leader as more salient. Yet these issues are generally the result of threats by challenger states that involve the disputed territory, so it is difficult to separate them from issue linkage and coercive diplomacy pursued by challenger states. In the end, survival of the state is the most important issue for any state, and prevention of loss of sovereign territory is a key component of the survival of the state. In some cases, like Guatemala's claim for Belize, the entire territory of the target is threatened, and there is no doubt that territorial sovereignty is critical to the state's survival.

7. The key point is that dispute strategies pursued by the challenger state are *more* or *less* likely based on the assumptions of relative issue salience across issues for both the challenger and target states, not that *all* dispute strategies can be explained sufficiently. There are certainly cases where target states do not comply with demands of challenger states, but these are the exception.

8. It may seem difficult to infer implicit issue linkage, but in the case studies, I only claim that issue linkage actually occurred when there is later admission of such linkage, or the coercive diplomacy and issue linkage actually led to a shift in the target's behavior or policy choices, indicating that the target understood that the challenger pursued issue linkage.

CHAPTER FOUR. Characteristics of Territorial Disputes

1. King, Keohane, and Verba (1994, 44–45) make the case that descriptions in case studies are: "fundamental to social science.... In fields such as comparative politics or international relations, descriptive work is particularly important because there is a great deal we still need to know, because our explanatory abilities are weak, and because

good description depends in part on good explanation. . . . A purported explanation of some aspect of world politics that assumes the absence of strategic interaction and anticipated reactions will be much less useful than a careful description that focuses on events that we have reason to believe are important and interconnected. Good description is better than bad explanation."

2. It should be noted that China has been involved in twenty-three territorial disputes since World War II, making it the state with the highest number of territorial disputes (Fravel 2008). Therefore, the inclusion of two disputes in which China is involved is more reflective of the high number of disputes rather than a selection bias.

3. See chapter 1 for a detailed definition of "enduring territorial disputes."

4. Jordan was a challenger against Israel from 1950 to 1994 and Israel was a challenger against Jordan from 1949 to 1967. The reciprocal claims of these two states account for the reason why there are eight dyads cited but nine disputes.

5. This number excludes the four bilateral treaties in which the target withdrew from the territory completely, discussed earlier. In those cases, treaties were the result of a unilateral decision by the target to cease its ownership of the territory, rather than the result of bilateral negotiations and territorial concessions.

6. All but three of the ongoing disputes described in this section are enduring, lasting ten years or more. I included the three nonenduring disputes in the data because they have good potential to become enduring. Although Taiwan is not a sovereign state, it is included in this study because it has several independent territorial claims on other territories that are separate from its dispute with China.

7. These disputes could be considered as examples of "negative peace" (Gibler and Tir 2010; Klein, Goertz, and Diehl 2008), in which the states have not actively settled the dispute, but they are not actively pursuing the territorial claim either.

CHAPTER FIVE. The Senkaku/Diaoyu Islands Dispute

1. By September 1972, Japan had broken diplomatic relations with the ROC, or Taiwan, and established relations with China. Though Taiwan is still an active claimant of the disputed islands to this day, the dispute is officially between China and Japan because Japan does not recognize Taiwan as a sovereign entity. Therefore, this study excludes interactions between Japan and Taiwan regarding the dispute because they are unique to the dispute with the PRC. If Taiwan played an influential role in the dispute between Japan and China, reference is made in the study.

2. The term "joint" is used by observers of the agreement, but not by the disputants themselves since this would imply recognition of each other's territorial claims. Despite some views that the June 2008 agreement was a diplomatic breakthrough, it is important to note that the agreement is only on general principles to work toward a treaty, which

will require many more difficult negotiations. The current agreement only allows Japan to invest in and claim proportional profits from the Chinese gas fields already set up. See Drifte (2008a) for support of this argument.

3. Since the start of the dispute, Chinese-Japanese negotiations have focused only on joint development of oil resources in waters *outside* of the disputed zone, hence preventing development of oil resources inside the disputed zone.

4. In November 1967, Taiwan, South Korea, and the Philippines formed the Committee for Coordination of Joint Prospecting for Mineral Resources in Asian Offshore Areas. The committee was sponsored by the UN Economic Commission for Asia and the Far East (ESCAFE) and was assisted by the US Naval Oceanographic Office.

5. By July 1970, Taiwan granted drilling rights to a Japanese subsidiary of a US oil company over a seabed area that included the disputed islands. However, the drilling never occurred.

6. The COW Militarized Interstate Dispute data lists only four MIDS, yet table 4 lists fourteen. The discrepancy is because table 4 splits up MIDS within a year into several MIDS depending on the month of initiation, because several MIDS occurred after 2001, the last year of the COWS MIDS data collection, and one MID in the table is targeted at Japanese nonstate actors and is thus not coded by the COWS MID data.

7. China also criticized the treatment of Taiwanese activists who had attempted to land on the islands on October 21.

CHAPTER SIX. The Shebaa Farms Border Dispute

1. The inclusion of this northeast finger of territory was included as a concession to the British due to an Arab attack on Tel Hai, killing eight Jewish settlers, which had taken place just three months before in March 1920.

2. None of the MIDS listed in table 1 are in the COW Militarized Interstate Dispute data since all were initiated by a nonstate actor Hezbollah from 2000 to 2006.

3. For detailed information on the war, see Achcar (2007) and Harel and Issacharoff (2008).

4. The scores for the years 2000 to 2005 are nonexistent in the Polity IV data.

5. It is more likely that the Syrian and Iranian governments had some role in Hezbollah decision making.

6. The exact number of Lebanese prisoners held in Israeli prisons was not certain. In addition to the nineteen named prisoners, it was believed an additional thirty prisoners were also in Israel, but their release was not sought by Hezbollah.

7. Samir Kuntar was involved in a 1979 killing of four Israelis in the Israeli town of Nahariya, including two children.

8. The kidnapping occurred along the border about fifteen miles from the sea.

CHAPTER SEVEN. The Ceuta/Sebta and Melilla/Melilia Enclaves Dispute

1. One of the two MIDS, from 1975, is listed in the COW MID data. The MID from 2002 is not yet coded in the MID data.

2. The Polisario Front (Popular Front for the Liberation of the Saguia el Hamra and Rio de Oro) is an independence movement that has been fighting for recognition of Sahrawi Democratic Republic in the Saharan territory occupied by both Morocco and Mauritania until 1979, and then by just Morocco, which annexed the territory left by Mauritania, to the present.

3. The purpose of the deployment of tanks was to use them as a deterrent on the border with Algeria, the state sponsor of the Polisario Front.

4. It was not clear whether the migrants were shot by Spanish or Moroccan guards.

CHAPTER EIGHT. The Sino-Soviet/Russian Border and Territorial Dispute

1. According to Segal (1985), even when Sino-Soviet détente gained ground in the mid-1980s, Soviet troops along the border had to treat China with some caution as "a potential enemy with a large population, irredentist claims on Soviet territory and, at least in the 1970s, a tendency to join forces with the United States."

2. The first name listed is Russian, the second name listed is Chinese. This format is consistent throughout the chapter.

3. During the 1840s and 1850s, while Russia expanded into formerly Chinese territory, China's power was severely diminished due to the Taiping Rebellion and the Opium Wars fought against Britain and France.

4. The COW Militarized Interstate Dispute data lists sixteen MIDS from 1960 to 2001, yet the data listed in table 10 lists twenty-two MIDS. Some MIDS in the COW data are not specifically about the Sino-Soviet border, but about other issues such as the disputed Mongolian border. Some MIDS in Table 10 are not in the COW MID data because my data split up MIDS further than the COW MID data. The only real discrepancy is the deployment of four divisions to the Soviet border in 1970, which is missing in the COW MID data.

5. Estimates for Chinese residents in the far eastern part of Russia along the border place the number at about 100,000. No villages or settlements have predominant Chinese populations (B. Lo 2004). Along the western border, the Soviet government granted emigrant status to a number of Chinese citizens who departed from Xinjiang Province across the border into the Soviet Union. There were also approximately 140,000–160,000 Soviet residents who had emigrated into China, primarily in Xinjiang Province, but they were forced by the Chinese government to return across the border by the mid-1960s (Danhui 2005).

6. In response, the Soviet propaganda compared Mao to Hitler and portrayed him as a killer of Russian soldiers.

7. After the 1969 border conflict, both the Soviet and Chinese governments sponsored a large number of reports and studies about the border dispute in an attempt to justify their claims (Tsui 1983).

8. China's posting of an ambassador to Moscow occurred three days after a visit by the US secretary of state Cyrus Vance, which "did not go well" (Segal 1985, 7). It appears that Chinese officials posted the ambassador to Moscow as part of the balance of power game played by the Soviets, Chinese, and Americans during the Cold War.

9. Soviet divisions increased from twelve to fourteen in the early 1960s to forty-eight in the late 1970s (Segal 1985; Tsui 1983).

10. In an interesting twist of irony, on the same day that the Soviet-Afghan treaty was publicized, June 17, 1981, an article appeared in the *People's Daily* announcing willingness to negotiate the disputed border with the Soviet Union if certain conditions were met. The purpose of the announcement was to serve as a warning to the US that China might work to improve relations with the Soviet Union. The same day, US Secretary of State Alexander Haig departed Beijing after failed talks discussing US arms sales to Taiwan. It appears that China was using the border dispute as leverage against the US in this case, but before officials knew of the Soviet-Afghan treaty. Once the Soviet-Afghan treaty was publicized, the Chinese withdrew their offer, which was not a major deal. They had no real intention of negotiating with the Soviets anyway since the offer to negotiate had been only a bargaining ploy with the US.

REFERENCES

ABC.es. 2001. Morocco seizes Spanish fishing vessel. November 30. http://www.abc.es/.

Achcar, Gilbert. 2007. *The 33-day war: Israel's war on Hezbollah in Lebanon and its consequences.* With Michel Warschawski. Boulder, Colo.: Paradigm.

Africa News. 2005. Morocco; from the Berlin Wall to Ceuta and Melilla. October 5.

Afrol News. 2005. Morocco-EU fisheries deal finally renewed. July 28.

Agence France Presse. 1996a. Chinese war games warning to Japan, protest boat leaves Hong Kong. September 22.

———. 1996b. Japan tells China Hashimoto won't visit controversial shrine: Report. September 27.

———. 1996c. Japan urged to draw lessons from cunning Chinese. September 26.

———. 2000. Spain's Aznar accused of appeasement over North African enclaves. January 9.

———. 2001a. Illegal immigration sparks new friction between Morocco, Spain. August 23.

———. 2001b. Spain rejects Moroccan protest amid worsening Madrid-Rabat ties. November 27.

Aldrich, John H., John L. Sullivan, and Eugene Borgida. 1989. Foreign affairs and issue voting: Do presidential candidates "waltz before a blind audience"? *American Political Science Review* 83 (1): 123–41.

Algerian Radio. 1994. Polisario says Morocco is putting pressure on Spain to accept UN Sahara report. March 3.

al-Haruji, Khalid. 2003. Hezbollah official discusses political stance, regional ties, others. *al-Majallah*, August 17.

Allcock, John, ed. 1992. *Border and territorial disputes.* 3rd ed. Essex, UK: Longman.

Allee, Todd L., and Paul K. Huth. 2006. The pursuit of legal settlements to territorial disputes. *Conflict Management and Peace Science* 23 (4): 285–307.

al-Manar Television. 2008. Sheikh Qassem: We welcome Shebaa liberation. June 21.

Amer, Ramses. 1994. Sino-Vietnamese normalization in the light of the crisis of the late 1970s. *Pacific Affairs* 67 (3): 357–83.

An, Tai Sung. 1973. *The Sino-Soviet territorial dispute.* Philadelphia: Westminster Press.

Anderson, James. 1988. Nationalist ideology and territory. In *Nationalism, self-determination, and political geography,* ed. R. J. Johnston, P. Knight, and E. Kofman. New York: Croom Helm.

Anderson, John Ward. 2003. Hezbollah shells kill Israeli boy, injure 4; cross-border strikes are stepped up. *Washington Post*, August 11, A12.

Anderson, Malcolm. 1996. *Frontiers: Territory and state formation in the modern world*. Oxford: Polity Press.

ArabicNews.com. 1999. Spain refuses Moroccan request over Sebta, Mellila. August 16.

Asada, Masahiko. 1988. Confidence-building measures in East Asia: A Japanese perspective. *Asian Survey* 28 (5): 489–508.

Associated Press. 1978. Rabat, Morocco. November 7.

———. 1991. Hezbollah-Israeli prisoner-body exchange. December 4.

———. 1996. China accuses Japan of promoting right-wing revival. August 29.

Axelrod, Robert. 1984. *Evolution of cooperation*. New York: Basic Books, 1984.

Bakshi, Jyotsna. 2001. Russia-China boundary agreement: Relevance for India. *Strategic Analysis* 24 (10): 1833–59.

———. 2004. *Russia-China Relations: Relevance for India*. Dehli, India: Shipra.

Baogang, He. 2004. China's national identity: A source of conflict between democracy and state nationalism. In *Nationalism, democracy and national integration in China*, ed. Leong H. Liew and Shaoguang Wang, 170–95. New York: Routledge Curzon.

Behera, Navnita Chadha. 2006. *Demystifying Kashmir*. Washington, D.C.: Brookings Institution.

Beijing Review. 1980. Vice Minister of Foreign Affairs Zhang Haifeng. January 7, 3.

Beirut Research and Information Centre. 2004. Poll results. February. http://www.beirutcenter.info.

———. 2006. Poll finds support for Hizbullah's retaliation. July 29. http://www.beirutcenter.info.

Bennett, Scott D. 1998. Integrating and testing models of rival duration. *American Journal of Political Science* 42 (4): 1200–32.

Ben-Yehuda, Hemda. 2004. Territoriality and war in international crises: Theory and findings, 1918–2001. *International Studies Review* 6 (4): 85–105.

Bercovitch, Jacob. 1999. The structure of international conflict management: An analysis of the effects of intractability and mediation. *International Journal of Peace Studies* 4 (1): 1–20.

Bercovitch, Jacob, and Jeffrey Z. Rubin. 1992. *Mediation in international relations: Multiple approaches to conflict management*. New York: St. Martin's Press.

Blanchard, Jean-Marc F. 2000. The U.S. role in the Sino-Japanese dispute over the Diaoyu (Senkaku) Islands, 1945–1971. *China Quarterly* no. 161: 95–123.

Blanford, Nicholas. 2001a. In Lebanon, resentment rises over 17 detainees in Israel. *Christian Science Monitor*, August 28, 8.

———. 2001b. Why regional conflict molders in south Lebanon. *Christian Science Monitor*, May 25, 8.

———. 2002a. Lebanon border nears crisis point. *Christian Science Monitor*, April 3, 6.

———. 2002b. Lebanon border tensions raise second front fear. *Times* (London), April 4.

———. 2005. IDF, Hizbullah clash in Shebaa Farms. *Jane's Defense Weekly*, July 6, 6.

———. 2008. Shebaa Farms: Key to stability? *Christian Science Monitor*, July 8, 6.

Blechman, B., and S. Kaplan. 1978. *Force without war: U.S. armed forces as a political instrument*. Washington, D.C.: Brookings Institution.

Blum, Gabriela. 2007. *Islands of agreement: Managing enduring armed rivalries*. Cambridge, Mass.: Harvard University Press.

Bonilla, Adrian. 1999. The Ecuador-Peru dispute: The limits and prospects for negotiation and conflict. In *Security cooperation in the Western Hemisphere: Resolving the Ecuador-Peru conflict*, ed. Gabriel Marcella and Richard Downes, 67–89. Miami: North-South Center Press.

Brace, Paul, and Barbara Hinckley. 1992. *Modern presidents*. New York: Basic Books.

Brezhnev, Leonid. 1975. The Sino-Soviet dispute: Speech by Secretary General Brezhnev, November 6, 1974. *Survival* 17 (2): 89–90.

British Broadcasting Corporation (BBC) *News*. 1979a. Deng-Suzuki meeting: China's interest in Senkaku Islands. June 7.

———. 1979b. Sahara: Moroccan attack on Suarez' statement in Algiers. May 10.

———. 1979c. Spanish-Moroccan relations. May 5.

———. 1983a. In brief: Spanish-Moroccan relations. April 9.

———. 1983b. Polisario official calls for Spanish intercession with Morocco. November 24.

———. 1983c. Spanish exercises off Morocco. February 18.

———. 1983d. "Storms looming" in Spanish-Moroccan relations. April 8.

———. 1990. Morocco general strike ends in violence; 33 reportedly dead in Fez. December 17.

———. 1998a. Minister says Morocco wants enclaves issue settled "in most civilized way." February 20.

———. 1998b. Morocco: Prime Minister Youssoufi addresses Parliament. April 19.

———. 1999. China intensifies activities near islands disputed with Japan. May 24.

———. 2000a. Argentina: Foreign ministry reaffirms sovereign rights to Falkland Islands. January 4.

———. 2000b. Morocco reportedly not consulted by Spain on drawing Canary Islands border. December 16.

———. 2001. Moroccan king's visit. November 11.

———. 2002. Spain island landing "like war declaration." July 17.

———. 2004. Chinese officer cautions Japan over U.S. military realignment. October 26.

———. 2005. China forms "special" East China naval fleet—Japanese agency. September 17, 38.

———. 2009. Regions and territories: Ceuta and Melilla. http://news.bbc.co.uk/2/hi/europe/country_profiles/4209538.stm.

Brody, Richard. 1984. International crises: A rallying point for the president? *Public Opinion* 6 (6): 41–43.

Bronner, Ethan, and Robert F. Worth. 2008. Israel offers Lebanon talks on peace, and land. *New York Times*, June 19, 6.

Bueno de Mesquita, Bruce, James D. Morrow, Randolph M. Siverson, and Alastair Smith. 1999. Policy failure and political survival: The contribution of political institutions. *Journal of Conflict Resolution* 43 (2): 147–61.

Bueno de Mesquita, Bruce, and Randolph Siverson. 1995. War and the survival of political leaders. *American Political Science Review* 89 (4): 841–55.

Bueno de Mesquita, Bruce, Randolph Siverson, and Gary Woller. 1992. War and the fate of regimes. *American Political Science Review* 86 (2): 638–46.

Burns, Christopher. 1995. Morocco's King Hassan II plays high-stakes game for Western Sahara. Associated Press. December 18.

Burton, Bruce. 1978/79. Contending explantations of the 1979 Sino-Vietnamese War. *International Journal* 34 (4): 699–722.

Busser, Carlos. 1987. *Malvinas: La guerra inconclusa.* Buenos Aires: Ediciones Fernández Reguera.

Buszynski, Leszek. 1992. Russia and the Asia-Pacific region. *Pacific Affairs* 64 (4): 486–509.

———. 2006. Oil and territory in Putin's relations with China and Japan. *Pacific Review* 19 (3): 287–303.

Butcher, Tim. 2005. Border dispute farms reap a bitter harvest; UN rebuff Hizbollah frontier claim. *Daily Telegraph* (London), March 14, 12.

Calvert, Peter, ed. 2004. *Border and territorial disputes of the world.* 4th ed. London: John Harper.

Carly, Christian, and Akiko Kashiwagi. 2006. A risky game of chicken; Japan and China's growing assertiveness in the East China Sea could start a military skirmish—or worse. *Newsweek*, September 18.

Cassese, Antonio. 2005. *International law.* 2nd ed. Oxford: Oxford University Press.

Central Intelligence Agency. 1995–2008. *CIA World Factbook.* https://www.cia.gov/library/publications/the-world-factbook/index.html.

Chehabi, H. E. 1985. Self-determination, territorial integrity, and the Falkland Islands. *Political Science Quarterly* 100 (2): 215–25.

Chen, King C. 1987. *China's war with Vietnam, 1979: Issues, decisions, and implications.* Stanford, Calif.: Hoover Institution Press.

Chew, Allen F. 1970. *An atlas of Russian history: Eleven centuries of changing borders.* New Haven, Conn.: Yale University Press.

China Central Television. 1990. China's "stern representations" to Japan over islands and SDF. October 27.

Chiozza, Giacomo, and Ajin Choi. 2003. Guess who did what: Political leaders and the management of territorial disputes, 1950–1990. *Journal of Conflict Resolution* 47 (3): 251–78.

Chiozza, Giacomo, and Henk E. Goemans. 2004. Avoiding diversionary targets. *Journal of Peace Research* 41 (4): 423–43.

Chiu, Hungdah. 1996/97. An analysis of the Sino-Japanese dispute over the T'iaoyutai Islets (Senkaku Gunto). In *Chinese yearbook of international law and affairs*, ed. Hungdah Chiu, 15: 9–31. Taipei: Chinese Society of International Law.

———. 1999. *An Analysis of the Sino-Japanese dispute over the Tiaoyutai Islets*. Occasional Papers, Series in Contemporary Asian Studies, no 1. Baltimore: School of Law, University of Maryland, 2–27.

Choudhury, G. W. 1968. *Pakistan's relations with India, 1947–66*. New York: Praeger.

Chung, Chien-peng. 1998. The Diaoyutai/Senkaku Islands dispute: Domestic politics and the limits of diplomacy. *American Asian Review* 16 (3): 135–64.

———. 2004. *Domestic politics, international bargaining and China's territorial disputes*. New York: Routledge Curzon.

Cia, Yang. 2005. High tension without war: Interpreting Taiwan Strait relations from 1990 to 2005. Master's thesis, Georgia State University.

CNN.com. 2004. Israel, Hezbollah swap prisoners. January 29. www.cnn.com.

———. 2008. U.S. takes N. Korea off terror list. October 15. www.cnn.com.

Colaresi, Michael P., Karen Rasler, and William R. Thompson. 2007. *Strategic rivalries in world politics: Position, space and conflict escalation*. Cambridge: Cambridge University Press.

Colaresi, Michael P., and William R. Thompson. 2005. Alliances, arms buildups and recurrent conflict: Testing a steps-to-war model. *Journal of Politics* 67 (2): 345–64.

Collier, David, and James Mahoney. 1996. Insights and pitfalls: Selection bias in qualitative research. *World Politics* 49 (1): 56–91.

Conaway, Janelle. 2001. A mission of confidence. *Americas* 53 (5).

Curtin, J. 2005. Stakes rise in Japan, China gas dispute. *Asia Times*, October 19. www.atimes.com.

Daily Star (Beirut). 2007. Siniora: Extended army control will trigger prosperity. July 30.

———. 2008. UNIFIL denies latest talks with Lebanese and Israeli armies dealt with. June 18.

Daily Yomiuri (Tokyo). 1996. Japan, China to discuss Senkaku Islands row. September 20.

———. 2004. Beijing should stop trying to exploit Yasukuni issue. April 4, 4.

Dakroub, Hussein. 1998. Prisoners arrive home after Israel and Lebanon swap bodies. Associated Press. June 26.

Damis, J. 1998. Morocco's 1995 fisheries agreement with the European Union. *Mediterranean Politics* 3 (2): 61–73.

Danhui, Li. 2005. On some aspects of Sino-Soviet relations in the 1960s. *Far Eastern Affairs* 33 (2): 74–92.

Day, Alan J. 1987. *Border and territorial disputes*, 2nd ed. Essex, UK: Longman.

Deans, Phil. 2000. Contending nationalisms and the Diaoyutai/Senkaku dispute. *Security Dialogue* 31 (1): 119–31.

del Pino, Domingo. 1983. *La ultima Guerra con Marruecos: Ceuta y Melilla.* Barcelona: Editorial Argos Vergara.

———. 2002. Análisis del real instituto—Morocco-Spain: A relationship difficult to repair. *Real Instituto Elcano de Estudios Internationales y Estratégicos.* November 11.

Deutsch, Morton. 1973. *The resolution of conflict.* New Haven, Conn.: Yale University Press.

Deutsche Presse-Agentur. 1996a. China reiterates claim to islands, plays up naval exercise. September 25.

———. 1996b. Don't let islands dispute damage ties, Li tells Japan. September 30.

———. 1997a. Spain downplays Melilla celebration after pressure from Morocco. September 15.

———. 1997b. Spain celebrates 500 years in Melilla to Moroccan protests. September 17.

———. 1999. Aznar rules out talks with Morocco on Ceuta and Melilla. August 16.

———. 2000a. Israel begins withdrawal from Shebaa area of Lebanon. May 26.

———. 2000b. Lebanon calls for Israeli pullout from the farms of Shebaa. May 12.

———. 2000c. U.N. representative calls for release of prisoners. October 7.

———. 2001. Spain threatens reprisals against Morocco after failure of fisheries agreement. April 26.

de Vasconçelos, Alvaro. 2002. Análisis del real instituto—Perejil/Leila: Lessons for Europe. Why have all failed? *Real Instituto Elcano de Estudios Internationales y Estratégicos.* July 19.

Diehl, Paul. 1991. Geography and war: A review and assessment of the empirical literature. *International Interactions* 17 (1): 1–27.

———. 1992. What are they fighting for? The importance of issues in international conflict research. *Journal of Peace Research* 29 (3): 333–44.

Diehl, Paul F., and Gary Goertz. 1988. Territorial changes and militarized conflict. *Journal of Conflict Resolution* 32 (1): 103–22.

Dixon, William J. 1986. Reciprocity in United States–Soviet relations: Multiple symmetry or issue linkage? *American Journal of Political Science* 30 (2): 421–45.

Doolin, D. J. 1965. *Territorial claims in the Sino-Soviet conflict.* Hoover Institution Studies, no. 7. Stanford, Calif.: Hoover Institution, Stanford University.

Downing, David. 1980. *An atlas of territorial and border disputes*. London: New English Library.

Downs, Erica Strecker, and Phillip C. Saunders. 1998. Legitimacy and the limits of nationalism: China and the Diaoyu Islands. *International Security* 23 (3): 114–46.

Downs, George W., and David M. Rocke. 1994. Conflict, agency, and gambling for resurrection: The principal-agent problem goes to war. *American Journal of Political Science* 38 (2): 362–80.

Dreyer, David R. 2010. Issue accumulation and the dynamics of strategic rivalry. *International Studies Quarterly* 54 (3): 779–95.

Dreyer, David R., and Krista E. Wiegand. 2010. Multidimensional rivalry: Issue accumulation, linkages, and coercive Diplomacy. Paper presented at the Annual Meeting of the International Studies Association, New Orleans.

Drifte, Reinhard. 2002. Engagement Japanese style. In *Chinese-Japanese relations in the twenty-first century*, ed. M. Soedererg, 52–68. New York: Routledge.

———. 2008a. From "sea of confrontation" to "sea of peace, cooperation and friendship"? Japan facing China in the East China Sea. *Japan Aktuell*, no. 3.

———. 2008b. *Japanese–Chinese territorial disputes in the East China Sea—between military confrontation and economic cooperation*. London School of Economics Asia Research Center Working Paper 24. London: Asia Research Centre, London School of Economics and Political Science.

Dutton, Peter. 2007. Carving up the East China Sea. *Naval War College Review* 60 (2): 45–68.

Economist. 1978. Western Sahara. October 21, 82.

———. 1979. Morocco and Spain: About turn. May 12, 76.

———. 1984. The Andulusian Gulf. September 1, 34.

———. 1990. Senkaku Islands; a sporting effort. October 27, 37.

———. 2005. Oil and gas in troubled waters; Japan and China. October 8.

———. 2010. Getting their goat: Trouble over some caprine islands. September 16.

Edwards, Steven. 2002. War may spill into Lebanon: Hezbollah renews attacks on Israel's northern border. *National Post* (Canada), April 4, A14.

el-Hakim, Ali. 1979. *The Middle Eastern states and the law of the sea*. Manchester: Manchester University Press.

Ellison, Herbert J., ed. 1982. *The Sino-Soviet conflict*. Seattle: University of Washington Press.

Ellman, Paul. 1985. Spanish intend to cling to their African foothold: The future of Ceuta in Morocco. *Guardian* (London), December 6.

———. 1987a. Madrid pulls out. *Guardian* (London), August 1.

———. 1987b. Moroccan waters turn choppy for Spain. *Guardian* (London), July 11.

Ellsberg, Daniel. 1959. Theory and practice of blackmail. *RAND Corporation Paper P-3883.* http://www.rand.org/pubs/papers/P3883/.

El Mundo. 2001. Moroccan foreign affairs minister calls Ceuta and Melilla "occupied cities." November 1, 20.

El Pais. 2001a. Government and PSOE blame Morocco for not controlling illegal immigration. September 5, 12.

———. 2001b. Mohammed VI rejects Spanish blame for immigrant problem. September 4, 3.

———. 2001c. Morocco asks for Spain's support on Saharan autonomy. November 14, 27.

———. 2001d. Morocco unilaterally postpones summit it arranged with Spain. October 31, 28.

———. 2002. Madrid and Rabat formalize the return of the small and barren island of Perejil to the status quo. July 22.

Ephron, Dan. 2004. Israel, Hezbollah exchange prisoners. *Boston Globe,* January 30, A18.

Evans, Peter B., Harold K. Jacobsen, and Robert D. Putnam. 1993. *Double-edged diplomacy: International bargaining and domestic politics.* Berkeley: University of California Press.

Facts on File World News. 1980. Spain recognizes Polisario. December 31, 995 (C3).

Fagan, Richard. 1960. Some assessments and uses of public opinion in diplomacy. *Public Opinion Quarterly* 24 (3): 448–57.

Faiola, Anthony. 2004. Isles become focus for old antagonism; Japan's neighbors, resentful since war, view a rise in nationalism with worry. *Washington Post,* March 27, A13.

Fearon, James D. 1994. Domestic political audiences and the escalation of international disputes. *American Political Science Review* 88 (2): 577–92.

———. 1995. Rationalist explanations for war. *International Organization* 49 (3): 379–414.

———. 1998. Bargaining, enforcement, and international cooperation. *International Organization* 52 (2): 269–305.

———. 2004. Why do some civil wars last so much longer than others? *Journal of Peace Research* 41 (3): 275–301.

Femenia, Nora. 1996. *National identity in times of crises: The scripts of the Falklands-Malvinas War.* Commack, N.Y.: Nova Science.

Fesyun, Andrei. 2008. China, Japan agree on East China Sea gas deposits. Russian News and Information Agency. June 23.

Financial Times. 1998. Morocco protest broken up. October 27, 1.

———. 2001. Spain views renewed fishing talks with Morocco as suicide. April 24, 54.

Fisk, Robert. 2000. Hopes of peace in Mr. Pinter's maps; a redrawing of borders has become a major part of the Israeli-Lebanese conflict. *Independent* (London), May 7, 21.

———. 2001. Hizbollah vows to make Shebaa the last battleground. *Independent* (London), May 15, 13.

———. 2004. Why Israel will do business in the hostage bazaar. *Independent* (London), January 30, 15.

Fitzgerald, C. P. 1967. Tension on the Sino-Soviet border. *Foreign Affairs* 45 (4): 683–94.

Foreign Broadcast Information Service (*FBIS*) Daily Report. 1969. Statement of the government of the People's Republic of China, May 24, 1969. May 26.

———. 1987. On Soviet troops withdrawal from Mongolia. *Hong Kong Ta Kung Pao*, January 17. Reported in FBIS-China-87-012, January 20, C1.

Forsberg, Thomas. 1996. Explaining territorial disputes: From power politics to normative reasons. *Journal of Peace Research* 33 (4): 433–49.

Fravel, M. Taylor. 2005. Regime insecurity and international cooperation: Explaining China's compromises in territorial disputes. *International Security* 30 (2): 46–83.

———. 2007. Power shifts and escalation: Explaining China's use of force in territorial disputes. *International Security* 32 (3): 44–83.

———. 2008. *Strong borders, secure nation: Cooperation and conflict in China's territorial disputes*. Princeton, N.J.: Princeton University Press.

Frazier, Derrick V. 2006. Third party characteristics, territory, and the mediation of militarized interstate disputes. *Conflict Management and Peace Science* 23 (4): 267–84.

Freedman, Lawrence, ed. 1998. *Strategic coercion: Concepts and cases*. Oxford: Oxford University Press.

Fuhrmann, Matthew, and Jaroslav Tir. 2009. Territorial dimensions of enduring internal rivalries. *Conflict Management and Peace Science* 26 (4): 307–29.

Gaiduk, Ilya. 2008. The failed détente in the Asia-Pacific region. *International Affairs* 54 (1): 113–28.

Ganguly, Sumit. 2002. *Conflict unending: India-Pakistan tensions since 1947*. Oxford: Oxford University Press.

Gelpi, Christopher, and Joseph Grieco. 2001. Democracy, leadership tenure, and the targeting of militarized challenges. *Journal of Conflict Resolution* 45 (6): 794–817.

George, Alexander L. 1991. *Forceful persuasion: Coercive diplomacy as an alternative to war*. Washington, D.C.: U.S. Institute of Peace Press.

———. 1994. Coercive diplomacy: Definition and characteristics. In *The limits of coercive diplomacy*, ed. A. L. George and W. E. Simons. Boulder, Colo.: Westview Press.

George, Alexander L., and Andrew Bennett. 2005. *Case studies and theory development in the social sciences*. Cambridge, Mass.: MIT Press.

George, Alexander L., David K. Hall, and William E. Simons. 1971. *The limits of coercive diplomacy: Laos, Cuba, Vietnam*. Boston: Little, Brown.

George, Alexander L., and William Simons. 1994. *The limits of coercive diplomacy*. Boulder, Colo.: Westview Press.

George, Alexander L., and Richard Smoke. 1974. *Deterrence in American foreign policy: Theory and practice*. New York: Columbia University Press.

Gibler, Douglas M. 2007. Bordering on peace: Democracy, territorial issues, and conflict. *International Studies Quarterly* 51 (3): 509–32.

———. 2010. Outside-in: The effects of external threat on state centralization. *Journal of Conflict Resolution* 54 (4): 519–42.

Gibler, Douglas M., and Jaroslav Tir. 2010. Settled borders and regime type: Democratic transitions as consequences of peaceful territorial transfers. *American Journal of Political Science* 54 (4): 951–68.

Giles, Ciran. 2001. Spain "surprised" as Morocco recalls ambassador. Associated Press, October 30.

Gillespie, Richard. 1999. *Spain and the Mediterranean: Developing a European policy towards the south.* Basingstoke,UK: Macmillan.

Ginsburgs, George, and Carl F. Pinkele. 1978. *The Sino-Soviet territorial dispute, 1949–1964.* New York: Praeger.

Gochman, C. S., and R. J. Leng. 1983. Realpolitik and the road to war: An analysis of attributes and behavior. *International Studies Quarterly* 27 (1): 97–120.

Gochman, C. S., and Zeev Maoz. 1984. Militarized interstate disputes, 1816–1976: Procedures, patterns, and insights. *Journal of Conflict Resolution* 28 (4): 585–616.

Goddard, Stacie. 2010. *Indivisible territory and the politics of legitimacy: Jerusalem and Northern Ireland.* Cambridge: Cambridge University Press.

Goemans, Hein. 2000. *War and punishment: The causes of war termination and the First World War.* Princeton, N.J.: Princeton University Press.

Goertz, Gary, and Paul F. Diehl. 1992. *Territorial changes and international conflict.* New York: Routledge.

———. 1995. The initiation and termination of enduring rivalries: The impact of political shocks. *American Journal of Political Science* 39 (1): 30–52.

Gold, Peter. 2000. *Europe or Africa? A contemporary study of the Spanish North African enclaves of Ceuta and Melilla.* Liverpool: Liverpool University Press.

———. 2005. *Gibraltar: British or Spanish?* New York: Routledge.

Goncharov, Sergei, and Li Danhui. 2004. On territorial claims and inequitable treaties in Russian Chinese relations: Myth and reality. *Far Eastern Affairs* 32 (3): 94–106.

Gottman, Jean. 1973. *The significance of territory.* Charlottesville: University Press of Virginia.

Gozani, Ohad. 2000. Militants killed in Israeli ambush; commado unit traps Arabs after soldier dies in bombing near Lebanese border. *Daily Telegraph* (London), November 27, 14.

Gries, Peter Hays. 2004. *China's new nationalism: Pride, politics, and diplomacy.* Berkeley: University of California Press.

Griffith, William E. 1967. *Sino-Soviet relations, 1964–1965.* Cambridge, Mass.: MIT Press.

Guy, Ron. 2004. Western Sahara: The wall of shame. *Green Left Weekly*, Global Policy Forum.

Hagstrom, Linus. 2005. Quiet power: Japan's China policy in regard to the Pinnacle Islands. *Pacific Review* 18 (2): 159–88.

Halpern, Orly, and Nicholas Blanford. 2006. A second front opens for Israel. *Christian Science Monitor*, July 13, 1.

Hamboyan, Sarkis D. 1968. The historical background of the Moroccan territorial claims. PhD diss., American University of Beirut.

Hamilos, P. 2002. Behind the parsley farce. *Guardian* (London), July 23.

Harel, Amos, and Avi Issacharoff. 2008. *34 Days: Israel, Hezbollah, and the war in Lebanon*. New York: Palgrave Macmillan.

Hassner, Ron E. 2003. To halve and to hold: Conflicts over sacred space and the problem of indivisibility. *Security Studies* 12 (4): 1–33.

———. 2009. *War on sacred ground*. Ithaca, N.Y.: Cornell University Press.

Henderson, Daniel. 2006. Israel strikes after kidnaps; new front opens up as Hezbollah abducts troops. *Herald* (Glasgow), July 13, 15.

Henehan, Marie T., and John A. Vasquez. 2011. The changing probability of interstate war, 1816–1992. In *Territory, war, and peace*, ed. J. A. Vasquez and M. T. Henehan, 179–94. New York: Routledge.

Hensel, Paul. 1996. Charting a course to conflict: Territorial issues and interstate conflict, 1816–1992. *Conflict Management and Peace Science* 15 (1): 43–73.

Hensel, Paul. 1999. Charting a course to conflict: Territorial issues and interstate conflict, 1816–1992. In *The road map to war*, ed. Paul Diehl, 115–46. Nashville, Tenn.: Vanderbilt University Press.

———. 2001. Contentious issues and world politics: The management of territorial claims in the Americas, 1816–1992. *International Studies Quarterly* 45 (1): 81–109.

Hensel, Paul R., Michael Allison, and Ahmed Khanani. 2009. Territorial integrity treaties and armed conflict over territory. *Conflict Management and Peace Science* 26 (2): 120–43.

Hensel, Paul R., and Sara McLaughlin Mitchell. 2005. Issue indivisibility and territorial claims. *GeoJournal* 64 (4): 275–85.

Hensel, Paul R., Sara McLaughlin Mitchell, Thomas E. Sowers II, and Clayton L. Thyne. 2008. Bones of contention: Comparing territorial, maritime, and river issues. *Journal of Conflict Resolution* 52 (1): 117–43.

Hernando de Larramendi, Miguel. 1992. Perception espagnole du Maghreb et politique étrangère de l'Espagne Démocratique, *Le Maghreb, l'Europe et la France*. Paris: Centre Nationale de la Recherche Scientifique (CNRS).

Hernando de Larramendi, M., and J. A. Nunez Villaverde. 1996. *La politica exterior y de cooperacion de Espana en el Maghreb*. Madrid: Los Libros de la Catarata.

Herz, John. 1957. Rise and demise of the territorial state. *World Politics* 9 (4): 473–93.

Hezbollah Central Press Office. 1985. Nass al-risala al-maftuha allati wajahaha Hezbollah ila-l-mustad'afin fi Lubnan wa-l-alam [Open letter to the downtrodden in Lebanon and the world]. *al-Safir*, February 16.

Hilali, A. Z. 2001. China's response to the Soviet invasion of Afghanistan. *Central Asian Survey* 20 (3): 323–51.

Hinton, Harold C. 1976. *The Sino-Soviet confrontation: Implications for the future.* New York: Crane, Russak.

Hirst, David. 2000. Israelis expected to use diplomacy to get hostages. *St. Petersburg (Fla.) Times,* October 10, 6A.

———. 2001. Middle East conflict: Analysis: Lebanon: War's playground once more: Beirut fears Israel-Hezbollah conflict could bring collapse if scale of reprisals escalates. *Guardian* (London), April 17, 12.

Hobday, Charles. 1987. China-Soviet Union. In *Border and territorial disputes,* ed. Alan J. Day. Detroit: Gale Research.

Hockstader, Lee. 2000. Israel begins Lebanon pullout; 22 year occupation of southern zone may end quickly. *Washington Post,* May 22, A1.

Hoekman, Bernard. 1989. Determining the need for issue linkages in multilateral trade negotiations. *International Organization* 43 (4): 693–714.

Hof, Frederic C. 1985. *Galilee divided: The Israel-Lebanon frontier, 1916–1984.* Boulder, Colo.: Westview Press, 1985.

Hoffman, Fred S. 1982. Plans for Marine landing in Morocco upset Spain. Associated Press. November 8.

Holsti, Kal J. 1991. *Peace and war: Armed conflicts and the international order, 1648–1989.* Cambridge: Cambridge University Press.

Hood, Steven J. 1992. *Dragons entangled: Indochina and the China-Vietnam War.* Armonk, N.Y.: M. E. Sharpe.

Horowitz, Donald L. 1985. *Ethnic groups in conflict.* Berkeley: University of California Press.

Human Rights Watch. 2007. *Why they died: Civilian casualties during the 2006 Lebanon War.* Human Rights Watch, September 5, http://www.hrw.org/.

Huth, Paul. 1996. *Standing your ground: Territorial disputes and international conflict.* Ann Arbor: University of Michigan Press.

———. 1997. Reputations and deterrence: A theoretical and empirical assessment. *Security Studies* 7 (1): 72–99.

Huth, Paul K., and Todd L. Allee. 2002. *The democratic peace and territorial conflict in the twentieth century.* Cambridge: Cambridge University Press.

Huth, Paul K., and Bruce Russett. 1984. What makes deterrence work: Cases from 1900 to 1980. *World Politics* 36 (4): 496–526.

Ibrahim, Sheikh Attalah. 2000. Interview with author. Central Information Office of Hezbollah, Haret Hreik, Beirut, Lebanon, June 30.

Ijiri, Hidenori. 1996. Sino-Japanese controversy since the 1972 diplomatic normalization. In *China and Japan: History, trends, and prospects*, ed. C. Howe, 60–82. Oxford: Clarendon Press.

Ilke, Fred C. 1964. *How nations negotiate*. New York: Harper and Row.

Immigration and Refugee Board of Canada. 2000. Morocco/Western Sahara: Whether the Polisario Front is active in El Ayoun and other cities in Western Sahara. *United Nations High Commission on Refugees*, September 20.

Info-Prod Research. 1997. New credits lines to Morocco approved by Spain. December 11.

International Boundary Research Unit News Archive. 2010. http://www.dur.ac.uk/ibru/.

International Court of Justice. 2010. List of Cases. http://www.icj-cij.org/.

International Crisis Group. 2007. Western Sahara: The cost of conflict. *Middle East/North Africa Report no. 65*. June 11.

Islam, Shada. 1995. Morocco-Europe: Fishing pact follows trade and aid outline deal. Inter Press Service, November 13.

Iyer, Pallavi. 2008. China, Russia end border dispute. *Hindu*, July 22. http://www.hindu.com/2008/07/22/stories/2008072260091300.htm.

Jackson, W. A. D. 1962. *The Russo-Chinese borderlands: Zone of peaceful contact or potential conflict?* Princeton, N.J.: D. Van Nostrand.

Jakobsen, Peter Viggo. 1998. *Western use of coercive diplomacy after the cold war: A challenge for theory and practice*. New York: St. Martin's Press.

James, Patrick, Johann Park, and Seung-Whan Choi. 2006. Democracy and conflict management: Territorial claims in the Western Hemisphere revisited. *International Studies Quarterly* 50 (4): 803–17.

Jansen, Michael. 2006. Hizbullah pressure on Israel to exchange prisoners. *Irish Times* (Dublin), July 13, 11.

Japan Defense Agency. 1989. *Defense of Japan, 1988*. Tokyo: Japan Times.

Japan Times Online. 2010a. Hatoyama Asia community plan places China, Japan at the core. April 14. http://search.japantimes.co.jp/cgi-bin/nn20100414a6.html.

———. 2010b. Seabed exploration to rile China. http://search.japantimes.co.jp/cgi-bin/nb20100428a4.html.

Jiji Press. 1996. Japan, China agree to handle isle row calmly. September 25.

Johnson, Carter. 2008. Partitioning to peace: Sovereignty, demography, and ethnic civil wars. *International Security* 32 (4): 140–70.

Johnson, Tim. 2005. Japan-China tensions rising, threatening region's stability. *Philadelphia Inquirer*, February 20, A03.

Jones, Daniel, Stuart Bremer, and J. David Singer. 1996. Militarized interstate disputes,

1816–1992: Rationale, coding rules, and empirical patterns. *Conflict Management and Peace Science* 15 (2): 163–213.

Jones, Peter, and Sian Kevill. 1985. *China and the Soviet Union, 1949–1984*. Essex, UK: Longman.

Kacowicz, Arie M. 1994. *Peaceful territorial change*. Columbia: University of South Carolina Press.

Kamm, Henry. 1984. Several deaths suspected in Morocco rioting. *New York Times*, January 22, 4.

Kang, C. S. Eliot, and Yoshinori Kaseda. 2000. Confidence and security building between South Korea and Japan. *Journal of Political and Military Sociology* 28 (1): 93–109.

Katada, Saori N. 2001. Why did Japan suspend foreign aid to China? Japan's foreign aid decision-making and sources of aid sanctions. *Social Science Japan Journal* 4 (1): 39–58.

Kaufman, Asher. 2002. Who owns the Shebba Farms? Chronicle of a territorial dispute. *Middle East Journal* 56 (4): 576–96.

———. 2004. Understanding the Shebaa Farms dispute: Roots of the anomaly and prospects of resolution. *Palestine-Israel Journal of Politics, Economics, and Culture* 11 (1): 37–43.

Kaufmann, Chaim. 1996. Possible and impossible solutions to ethnic civil wars. *International Security* 20 (4): 136–75.

———. 1998. When all else fails: Ethnic population transfers and partitions in the twentieth century. *International Security* 23 (2): 120–56.

Keohane, Robert O. 1984. *After hegemony: Cooperation and discord in the world political economy*. Princeton, N.J.: Princeton University Press.

Keohane, Robert O., and Joseph Nye. 1977. *Power and interdependence*. Boston: Little, Brown.

Kifner, John. 2000. Whose holy land? The Lebanon-Israel frontier; 3 Israelis are now pawns in a growing deal. *New York Times*, October 10, A16.

Kimura, Masato, and David Welch. 1998. Specifying "interests": Japan's claim to the northern territories and its implications for international relations theory. *International Studies Quarterly* 42 (2): 213–44.

Kin, Kwan Weng. 2004. Japan sketches scenarios for a Chinese attack; report reflects concerns over dealing with a rising China. *Straits Times* (Singapore), November 9.

King, Gary, Robert Keohane, and Sidney Verba. 1994. *Designing social inquiry: Scientific inference in qualitative research*. Princeton N.J.: Princeton University Press.

Kingdom of Morocco Radio. 1998. Joint statement issued with Spain on need to strengthen relations. April 27.

Klein, James P., Gary Goertz, and Paul Diehl. 2008. The peace scale: Conceptualizing and operationalizing non-rivalry and peace. *Conflict Management and Peace Science* 25 (1): 67–80.

Knight, David B. 1983. The dilemma of nations in a rigid state structured world. In *Pluralism and political geography: People, territory, and state*, ed. N. Kliot and S. Waterman, 114–37. London: Croon Helm.

———. 1984. Geographical perspectives on self-determination. In *Political geography: Recent advances and future directions*, ed. P. Taylor and J. House, 168–90. London: Croon Helm.

Kocs, Stephen. 1995. Territorial disputes and interstate war, 1945–1987. *Journal of Politics* 57 (1): 159–75.

Kopnov, Alexander. 1996. China may send troops to Diaoyudao Islands. Russian Information Agency (ITAR/TASS), September 12.

Kratochwil, Friedrich. 1985. *Peace and disputed sovereignty: Reflections on conflict over territory*. Lanham, Md.: University Press of America.

Kristof, Nicholas D. 1990. China, reassessing its roes, views Japan warily. *New York Times*, October 23, A12.

Kumar, Radha. 1997. The troubled history of partition. *Foreign Affairs* 76 (1): 22–34.

Kyodo News Service. 1990a. Chinese authorities probing anti-Japan rallies. December 19.

———. 1990b. Spokesman favors leaving Senkaku issue to posterity. October 23.

———. 1992. Chinese law says Senkaku Islands are its territory. February 26.

———. 1996a. China blasts Ikeda's remarks on Senkaku Islands. August 29.

———. 1996b. China calls on Japan to be "sensible" over Senkaku. September 24.

———. 1996c. China makes protest to Japan over disputed isles. September 10.

———. 1996d. Sino-Japanese relations are good, but could be better. November 16.

———. 2004a. Japan, China cancel sea treaty talks after island row. March 31.

———. 2004b. Japanese agency cites Chinese media on "provocative" defense plans. November 10.

Lacy, Dean, and Emerson M. S. Niou. 2004. A theory of economic sanctions and issue linkage: The roles of preferences, information, and threats. *Journal of Politics* 66 (1): 25–42.

La Razon. 2005. Spain's Zapatero to visit Melilla and Ceuta. October 7.

Laulicht, Jerome. 1965. Public opinion and foreign policy decisions. *Journal of Peace Research* 2 (2): 147–60.

Lauren, Paul Gordon. 1994. Coercive diplomacy and ultimata: Theory and practice in history. In *The limits of coercive diplomacy*, ed. A. George and W. Simons, 23–50. Boulder, Colo.: Westview Press.

Lee, Jae-Hyung. 2002. China's expanding maritime ambitions in the Western Pacific and the Indian Ocean. *Contemporary Southeast Asia* 24 (3): 549–68.

Lee, Seokwoo. 2002. Territorial disputes among Japan, China and Taiwan concerning the Senkaku Islands. *Boundary and Territory Briefing* 3 (7): 1–8.

Leeborn, David W. 2002. Linkages. *American Journal of International Law* 96 (1): 5–27.

Leng, Russell J. 1983. Will they ever learn? Coercive bargaining in recurrent crises. *Journal of Conflict Resolution* 27 (3): 379–419.

Levy, Jack S., and Lily I. Vikili. 1992. Diversionary action by authoritarian regimes: Argentina in the Falklands/Malvinas case. In *The internationalization of communal strife*, ed. Manus I. Midlarsky, 121–23. London: Routledge.

Lipson, Charles. 1993. Achieving cooperation under anarchy: Strategies and institutions. In *Neorealism and neoliberalism: The contemporary debate*, ed. D. Baldwin, 60–84. New York: Columbia University Press.

Lloyd, Richard. 2005. War crimes apology is welcomed by China. *Times* (London), April 23, 48.

Lo, Bobo. 2004. The long sunset of strategic partnership: Russia's evolving China policy. *International Affairs* 80 (2): 295–309.

Lo, Chi-Kin. 1989. *China's policy towards territorial disputes: The case of the South China Sea Islands.* London: Routledge.

Lockhart, Charles. 1979. *Bargaining in international conflicts.* New York: Columbia University Press.

López García, B., A. Planet, and A. Ramírez, eds. 1996. *Atlas de la inmigración Magrebí a España.* Madrid: Ediciones de UAM.

Lowenthal, Richard. 1971. Russia and China: Controlled conflict. *Foreign Affairs* 49 (3): 507–18.

Luard, E. 1970. *The international regulation of frontier disputes.* New York: Praeger.

Macleod, Hugh. 2006. Israelis exchange fire with Hezbollah in disputed area. *Independent* (London), February 4, 26.

Maghreb Arabe Presse. 1999a. Morocco: Papers call for end of Spanish "colonial" rule of northern enclaves. December 21.

———. 1999b. Morocco: Unemployed graduates organize protest march in Rabat. October 27.

———. 2002a. Morocco: Major trade union to stage protest marches. June 28.

———. 2002b. Morocco: People protest Spanish "invasion" of islet. July 18.

———. 2007a. Moroccan king condemns Spanish monarch visit. November 6.

———. 2007b. Moroccan parliament speakers hand protest letter to Spanish ambassador. November 5.

Mandel, Robert. 1980. Roots of the modern interstate border dispute. *Journal of Conflict Resolution* 24 (3): 427–54.

———. 1986. The effectiveness of gunboat diplomacy. *International Studies Quarterly* 30 (1): 59–76.

Mansbach, Richard, and John A. Vasquez. 1981. *In search of theory: A new paradigm for global politics.* New York: Columbia University Press.

Maroc 2020. 2002. The 2002 parliamentary elections: Attitudes and expectations of the Moroccan public. International Republican Institute. http://www.iri.org.

Martinez-Soler, Ana. 1983. Spain gets caught between "the rock" and Morocco. *Christian Science Monitor*, March 16, 4.

Mathews, Jay. 1978. China's row with Japan may peril ties to U.S. *Washington Post*, April 22, A20.

Maxwell, Neville. 1978. Why the Russians lifted the blockade at Bear Island. *Foreign Affairs* 57 (1): 138–45.

Mazza, Michael. 2010. China and the lost pearls. *American*, April 23. http://www.american.com/archive/2010/april/china-and-the-lost-pearls.

McCabe, Aileen. 2010. China's tight security, Web blackout keep anti-Japanese protests in check. *Vancouver (British Columbia) Sun*, September 18.

McCurry, Justin, and Jonathan Watts. 2004. China's angry young focus their hatred on old enemy: Anti-Japanese fury is rising among Internet users—a trend the state is keen to encourage. *Guardian* (London), December 30, 14.

McGinnis, Michael D. 1986. Issue linkage and the evolution of international cooperation. *Journal of Conflict Resolution* 30 (1): 141–70.

McLean, Renwick. 2006. Zapatero stirs anger of Morocco; Spanish leader tours an African enclave. *International Herald Tribune*, February 1, 3.

MCOT *English News.* 2008. Japan, China agree on investment, joint gas project in E. China Sea. June 18. www.mcot.net/EnglishNews.

Melendez, Federico. 1984. *The Falklands: A study in international confrontation.* Carlsbad, Calif.: Arcadia.

Middle East Economic Digest. 1995. Morocco: EU association agreement in sight. October 13, 19.

Midlarsky, Manus. 1975. *On war: Political violence in the international system.* New York: Free Press.

Miks, Jason. 2007. Chinese premier's visit to Japan marks major thaw. *Christian Science Monitor*, April 11, 5.

———. 2008. With Hu visit, leaders look to continue thaw in Japan-China relations. *World Politics Review*, May 2.

Mitchell, Sara McLaughlin. 2002. A Kantian system? Democracy and third party conflict resolution. *American Journal of Political Science* 46 (4): 749–59.

Mitchell, Sara McLauglin, and Cameron G. Thies. Forthcoming. Issue rivalries. *Conflict Management and Peace Science.*

Mitnick, Joshua, and Nicholas Blanford. 2006. Behind the dispute over Shebaa Farms. *Christian Science Monitor*, August 22, 10.

Moneyclips. 1999. Toward a fishing agreement with Spain. May.

Morgan, Clifford. 1990. Issue linkages in international crisis bargaining. *American Journal of Political Science* 34 (2): 311–33.

Morgan, Forrest E. 2003. *Compellence and the strategic culture of imperial Japan: Implications for coercive diplomacy in the twenty-first century.* Westport, Conn.: Praeger.

Morris, Nomi. 2008. On edge at border: Lebanese forces, UN maintain calm by preventing refugees from protests against Israel. *Gazette* (Montreal), October 10, B1.

Morrison, Charles. 1997. A clear case for preventive diplomacy in East Asian waters. *International Herald Tribune* (New York), May 13, 8.

Moscow Home Service. 1979. Deng-Suzuki meeting: China's interest in Senkaku Islands. June 7.

Mueller, John. 1973. *War, presidents, and public opinion.* New York: Wiley.

Mulvenon, James. 1995. The limits of coercive diplomacy: The 1979 Sino-Vietnamese border war. *Journal of Northeast Asian Studies* 14 (3): 68–89.

Murphy, Alexander. 1990. Historical justifications for territorial claims. *Annals of the Association of American Geographers* 80 (4): 531–48.

———. 1991. Territorial ideology and international conflict: The legacy of prior political formations. In *The Political geography of conflict and peace*, ed. N. Kliot and S. Waterman, 126–41. London: Belhaven Press.

Narayanswamy, Anupama. 2005. European Union confronts immigration; border control, development lead remedies. *Washington Times*, November 6, A08.

Nasrallah, Hassan. 2006. Press conference with Hassan Nasrallah. al-Manar Television, July 12.

Nathan, Andrew J., and Robert S. Ross. 1997. *The Great Wall and the empty fortress: China's search for security.* New York: W. W. Norton.

Newman, David. 1999. Real spaces, symbolic spaces: Interrelated notions of territory in the Arab-Israeli conflict. In *A road map to war: Territorial dimensions of international conflict*, ed. P. Diehl, 3–34. Nashville, Tenn.: Vanderbilt University Press.

New York Times. 1981. Violence reported in Morocco. June 23, A8.

New Zealand Herald (Auckland). 2008. Prisoner swap frees notorious killer. July 1.

Norton, A. R. 2000. Hezbollah and the Israeli withdrawal from southern Lebanon. *Journal of Palestine Studies* 30 (1): 22–35.

Ostermann, Christian F. 1995. East German documents on the border conflict, 1969. *Cold War International History Bulletin 7.*

Ostrom, Charles W., and Dennis Simon. 1985. Promise and performance: A dynamic model of presidential popularity. *American Political Science Review* 79 (2): 334–58.

Oye, Kenneth A. 1979. The domain of choice: International constraints and Carter administration foreign policy. In *Eagle entangled: U.S. foreign policy in a complex world*, ed. K. Oye, D. Rothschild, and R. Lieber, 3–33. New York: Longman, 1979.

———. 1985. Explaining cooperation under anarchy: Hypotheses and strategies. *World Politics* 38 (1): 1–24.

Page, Benjamin I., and Robert Y. Shapiro. 1983. Effects of public opinion on policy. *American Political Science Review* 77 (1): 175–90.

Pan, Zhongqi. 2007. Sino-Japanese dispute over the Diaoyu/Senkaku Islands: The pending controversy from the Chinese perspective. *Journal of Chinese Politics* 12 (1): 71–89.

Pan Orient News. 2010. Okada brushes off Beijing's demand. September 12. http://www.panorientnews.com.

Pape, Robert. 1990. Coercive air power in the Vietnam War. *International Security* 15 (2): 103–146.

———. 1997. Why economic sanctions do not work. *International Security* 22 (2): 90–136.

———. 1998. Why economic sanctions still do not work. *International Security* 23 (1): 66–77.

Percebal, Juan Luis. 1994. The Spanish enclaves that time forgot: A decision to approve self-rule for two cities in Morocco has fueled a centuries old dispute. *Guardian* (London), September 22, 15.

Percival, Debra. 1995. Morocco-Europe: EU faces new fish war on a front closer to home. Inter Press Service, April 24.

Ping, Lo. 1990. Bowing to Japanese yen has angered the masses. *Cheng Ming,* November 1, 6–7.

Pirchner, Herman. 2008. The uncertain future: Sino-Russian relations in the twenty-first century. *Demokratizatsiya* 16 (4): 309–22.

Potter, Williams. 1980. Issue area and foreign policy analysis. *International Organization* 34 (3): 405–27.

Powell, Emilia J., and Krista E. Wiegand. 2010. Legal systems and peaceful attempts to resolve territorial disputes. *Conflict Management and Peace Science* 27 (2): 129–51.

Powell, Robert. 1999. *In the shadow of power.* Princeton, N.J.: Princeton University Press.

Prados, Alfred B. 2001. The Shib'a farms dispute and its implications. *CRS Report for Congress.* Washington, D.C.: Library of Congress, August 7.

Press (Christchurch, New Zealand). 2006. Border clashes worsen. May 30, 2.

Pruitt, Dean G. 1981. *Negotiation behavior.* New York: Academic Press, 1981.

Quested, R. K. I. 1984. *Sino-Russian relations: A short history.* Boston: George Allen & Unwin.

Rabil, Robert G. 2003. *Embattled neighbors: Syria, Israel, and Lebanon.* Boulder, Colo.: Lynne Rienner.

Radcliffe, Sarah. 1998. Frontiers and popular nationhood: Geographies of identity in the 1995 Ecuador-Peru border dispute. *Political Geography* 17 (3): 273–93.

Radin, Charles A. 2002. On Lebanese border, tinder of regional war is lit. *Boston Globe,* April 10.

Radio Exterior de España Servicio Mundial. 1994. Spanish Foreign Ministry assessing King Hassan's remarks on Ceuta and Melilla. March 7.

Radio France Internationale. 1996. Morocco agrees to receive African illegal immigrants held in Spanish enclaves. December 20.

Radio Lebanon. 1996. Hezbollah-Israeli prisoner-body exchange. July 22.

———. 1999. Five released Hezbollah members welcomed at Beirut Airport. December 30.

Radio Nur. 2002. Deputy secretary general Naim Qassem. May 15.

Randle, Robert. 1987. *Issues in the history of international relations.* New York: Praeger.

Rasler, Karen A., and William R. Thompson. 2006. Contested territory, strategic rivalries, and conflict escalation. *International Studies Quarterly* 50 (1): 145–67.

Rathmell, Andrew. 2000. Building confidence in the Middle East: Exploiting the information age. *Journal of Palestine Studies* 29 (2): 5–19.

Reeves, Phil. 2000. Syria clashes with UN over Golan Heights dispute. *Independent* (London), June 1, 15.

Rézette, Robert. 1976. *Les enclaves espagnoles au Maroc.* Paris: Nouvelle Editions Latines.

Rice, Xan. 2005. After 70,000 deaths, Eritrea and Ethiopia prepare for war again. *Times* (London), December 8.

Rich, Norman. 2003. *Great power diplomacy since 1914.* New York: McGraw Hill.

Richardson, Lewis. 1960. *Statistics of deadly quarrels.* Pittsburgh: Boxwood Press.

Robinson, T. W. 1970. *The Sino-Soviet border dispute: Background, development, and the March 1969 clashes.* Santa Monica, Calif.: RAND.

———. 1971. *The border negotiations and the future of Sino-Soviet-American relations.* Santa Monica, Calif.: RAND.

Rosenau, James. 1966. Pre-theories and theories of foreign policy. In *Approaches to comparative and international politics*, ed. R. B. Farrell, 27–92. Evanston, Ill.: Northwestern University Press.

———. 1967. Foreign policy as an issue area. In *Domestic sources of foreign policy*, ed. James Rosenau, 11–50. New York: Free Press.

Ross, Robert S. 1988. *The Indochina tangle: China's Vietnam policy, 1975–1979.* New York: Columbia University Press.

———. 1991. China and the Cambodian peace process: The value of coercive diplomacy. *Asian Survey* 31 (12): 1170–85.

RTM TV Rabat. 1998. Morocco and Spain set up joint commission on illegal immigration. January 24.

———. 2007. Moroccan government opposes Spanish king's scheduled visit to enclaves. November 1.

Ruggie, John G. 1993. Territoriality and beyond: Problematizing modernity in international relations. *International Organization* 47 (1): 139–74.

Russett, Bruce. 1990. *Controlling the sword*. Cambridge, Mass.: Harvard University Press.

Sanz, P., and J. C. Egurbide. 2002. Rabat wants to negotiate all subjects of conflict with Spain. *El Pais* (Madrid), July 22.

Sasajima, Masahiko. 1996. Storm over Senkakus: How to deal with hot nonissue. *Daily Yomiuri* (Tokyo), October 2, 7.

Sasajima, Masahiko, and Chiharu Mori. 1996. Japan silent amid China protest over Senkaku. *Daily Yomiuri* (Tokyo), September 21, 3

Schelling, Thomas. 1960. *The strategy of conflict*. Cambridge, Mass.: Harvard University Press.

———. 1966. *Arms and influence*. New Haven, Conn.: Yale University Press.

Schneider, Howard. 2000. Israeli, Lebanese forces move to border; diplomats scurry to defuse crisis triggered by Hezbollah seizure of 3 soldiers. *Washington Post*, October 9, A18.

———. 2001. On Lebanese border, a lasting flash point: Israel, Hezbollah still contest Shebaa area. *Washington Post*, January 30, A13.

Schweid, Barry. 1991. Hostage releases follow years of frustrating diplomacy. Associated Press, December 4.

Sebenius, James K. 1983. Negotiation arithmetic: Adding and subtracting issues and parties. *International Organization* 37 (2) 281–316.

Segal, Gerald. 1985. *Sino-Soviet relations after Mao*. London: International Institute for Strategic Studies.

Senese, Paul D. 1996. Geographic proximity and issue salience: The effects on the escalation of militarized conflict. *Conflict Management and Peace Science* 15 (2): 133–61.

———. 1999. Geographical proximity and issue salience: Their effects on the escalation of militarized interstate conflict. In *The road map to war*, ed. Paul Diehl, 147–78. Nashville, Tenn.: Vanderbilt University Press.

———. 2005. Territory, contiguity, and international conflict: Assessing a new joint explanation. *American Journal of Political Science* 49 (4): 769–79.

Senese, Paul D., and John A. Vasquez. 2003. A unified explanation of territorial conflict: Testing the impact of sampling bias, 1919–1992. *International Studies Quarterly* 47 (2): 275–98.

Senese, Paul D., and John A. Vasquez. 2008. *The steps to war: An empirical study*. Princeton, N.J.: Princeton University Press.

Shambaugh, David. 1996. China and Japan: Towards the twenty-first century: Rivals for pre-eminence or complex interdependence? In *China and Japan: History, trends, and prospects*, ed. C. Howe, 83–97. Oxford: Clarendon Press.

Shaw, Han-yi. 1999. *The Diaoyutai/Senkaku Islands dispute: Its history and an analysis of the ownership claims of the PRC, ROC, and Japan*. Occasional Papers, Series in Contemporary Asian Studies, no 3. Baltimore: School of Law, University of Maryland.

Shaw, Malcolm. 2003. *International law*, 5th ed. Cambridge: Cambridge University Press.

Simmons, Beth A. 1999. See you in "court"? The appeal to quasi-judicial legal processes in the settlement of territorial disputes. In *A roadmap to war: Territorial dimensions of international conflict*, ed. P. F. Diehl, 205–37, Nashville, Tenn.: Vanderbilt University Press.

Simmons, Beth A. 2002. Capacity commitment and compliance: International institutions and territorial disputes. *Journal of Conflict Resolution* 46 (6): 829–55.

———. 2005. Rules over real estate: Trade, territorial conflict, and international borders as institutions. *Journal of Conflict Resolution* 49 (5): 823–48.

Smith, Alastair. 1998. International crises and domestic politics. *American Political Science Review* 92 (3): 623–38.

Snyder, Glenn H. 1961. *Deterrence and defense: Toward a theory of national security.* Princeton, N.J.: Princeton University Press.

Snyder, Glenn H., and Paul Diesing. 1977. *Conflict among nations: Bargaining, decision making, and system structure in international crises.* Princeton, N.J.: Princeton University Press.

Soh, Felix. 1996. China sent 2 submarines to disputed Diaoyu isles. *Straits Times* (Singapore), August 24, 17.

Solsten, Eric, and Sandra W. Meditz, eds. 1988. *Spain: A country study.* Washington, D.C.: Government Printing Office for the Library of Congress.

Sontag, Deborah. 2000. Whose holy land? The overview: Arab-Israeli conflict spreads to border with Lebanon. *New York Times*, October 8, 1.

Souva, Mark, and Jessica Montgomery. 2010. A theory and test of effective threats. Paper presented at the Southern Political Science Association Annual Conference, Atlanta, January.

Starr, Harvey. 1978. "Opportunity" and "willingness" as ordering concepts in the study of war. *International Interactions* 4 (4): 363–87.

Starr, Harvey, and Benjamin Most. 1976. The substance and study of borders in international relations research. *International Studies Quarterly* 20 (4): 581–620.

———. 1980. Diffusion, reinforcement, geopolitics and the spread of war. *American Political Science Review* 74 (4): 932–46.

———. 1983. Contagion and border effects on contemporary African conflicts. *Comparative Political Studies* 16 (1): 92–117.

Straits Times (Singapore). 1990. Islands of contention. October 27.

———. 2008. China, Taiwan slam Japan MPs' survey of disputed isles. July 2.

Stuckey, Maurice S. 1975. *The Senkakus: Black gold or black powder?* Maxwell Air Force Base, Ala.: Air War College, Air University.

Suganuma, Unryu. 2000. *Sovereign rights and territorial space in Sino-Japanese relations.* Honolulu: University of Hawaii Press.

Sunday Telegraph (Sydney). 2001. New deaths could ignite border war. February 18, 52.

Surface Forces. 2010. Chinese fleet closes in on Okinawa. April 15. http://www.strategy page.com/htmw/htsurf/articles/20100415.aspx.

Sutter, Robert G. 1986. *Chinese foreign policy: Developments after Mao.* New York: Praeger.

Tarvainen, Sinikka. 1997. Spain holds on to Melilla after 500 Years. Deutsche Presse-Agentur, September 11.

Taylor, Catherine. 2002. War roars back into Lebanese politics. *Australian* (Sydney), April 9, 8.

Thakur, Ramesh, and Carlyle A. Thayer. 1987. *The Soviet Union as an Asian Pacific power: Implications of Gorbachev's 1986 Vladivostok initiative.* Boulder, Colo.: Westview Press.

Thomas, Raju G. C., ed. 1992. *Perspectives on Kashmir: The roots of conflict in South Asia.* Boulder, Colo.: Westview Press, 1992.

Thompson, William R. 1995. Principal Rivalries. *Journal of Conflict Resolution* 39 (2): 195–223.

———. 2001. Identifying Rivals and Rivalries in World Politics. *International Studies Quarterly* 45 (4): 557–86.

Tir, Jaroslav. 2002. Letting secessionists have their way: Can partitions help end and prevent ethnic conflicts? *International Interactions* 28 (3): 261–92.

———. 2003. Averting armed international conflicts through state-to-state territorial transfers. *Journal of Politics* 65 (4): 1235–57.

———. 2005a. Dividing countries to promote peace: Prospects for long-term success of partitions. *Journal of Peace Research* 42 (5): 545–62.

———. 2005b. Keeping the peace after secession: Territorial conflicts between rump and secessionist states. *Journal of Conflict Resolution* 49 (5): 713–41.

———. 2006. *Redrawing the map to promote peace: Territorial dispute management via territorial changes.* Lanham, Md.: Lexington Books.

———. 2010. Territorial diversion: Diversionary theory of war and territorial conflict. *Journal of Politics* 72 (2): 413–25.

Tir, Jaroslav, and Paul F. Diehl. 2002. Geographic dimensions of enduring rivalries. *Political Geography* 21 (2): 263–86.

Tir, Jaroslav, and John Vasquez. 2010. Recent theory and research on geography, territory, and conflict: A compendium essay. Paper presented at the Annual Meeting of the International Studies Association, February 2010, New Orleans.

Toft, Monica Duffy. 2002. Indivisible territory, geographic concentration, and ethnic war. *Security Studies* 12 (2): 82–119.

———. 2003. *The geography of ethnic violence: Identity, interests, and the indivisibility of territory.* Princeton, N.J.: Princeton University Press.

Tollison, Robert D., and Thomas D. Willet. 1979. An economic theory of mutually advantageous issue linkages in international negotiations. *International Organization* 33 (4): 425–49.

Tremlett, Giles. 1995. Spain agrees to $16 million fishing aid. United Press International, April 28.

———. 1996. Spain might renegotiate Moroccan debt. United Press International, February 5.

———. 1999. Morocco seeks return of Spanish enclaves. *Scotsman* (Edinburgh), August 13, 13.

Tretiak, Daniel. 1978. The Sino-Japanese treaty of 1978: The Senkaku incident prelude. *Asian Survey* 13 (12): 1235–49.

Tretiak, Daniel. 1979. *1977–78 Sino-Cambodian relations and their impact on the third Indochina war.* Seoul: Institute of Social Sciences, Seoul National University.

Tsui, Tsien-hua. 1983. *The Sino-Soviet border dispute in the 1970s.* Oakville, Ont.: Mosaic Press.

Tsvetov. 1979. Fishing boats "dangerously close" to Senkakus: China's sabre-rattling. April 7.

Tsygichko, Vitaly. 2001. Academic: Russia should accept Bush partnership offer, counter China threat. *Nezavisimaya Gazeta*, June 9.

Ueki, Yasuhiro. 1988. Politics of issue linkage and delinkage: An analysis of Japanese-Soviet negotiations. PhD diss., Columbia University.

United Nations Security Council. 2001. Report of the Secretary General on the United Nations Interim Force in Lebanon (for the period from July 18, 2000 to January 18, 2001), S/2001/66.

United Nations Security Council Resolution 1701. 2006. http://www.un.org/News/Press/docs/2006/sc8808.doc.htm.

United States Energy Information Administration. 2010. World oil transit chokepoints. http://www.eia.doe.gov/cabs/World_Oil_Transit_Chokepoints/Full.html.

Vagts, A. 1956. *Defense and diplomacy: The soldiers and the conduct of foreign relations.* New York: King's Crown Press.

Valencia, Mark J. 2000. *Domestic politics fuels northeast Asian maritime disputes.* Asia Pacific Issues, no. 3. Honolulu: East-West Center.

———. 2005. Pouring oil on the East China Sea. *International Herald Tribune* (New York), February 24.

Vasquez, John. 1993. *The war puzzle.* Cambridge: Cambridge University Press.

———. 1996. Distinguishing rivals that go to war from those that do not: A quantitative case study of the two paths to war. *International Studies Quarterly* 40 (4): 531–58.

Vasquez, John, and Marie T. Henehan. 2001. Territorial disputes and the probability of war, 1816–1992. *Journal of Peace Research* 38 (2): 123–38.

———. 2010. Peace, globalization, and territoriality. In *Territory, war, and peace*, ed. John A. Vasquez and Marie T. Henehan, 195–205. New York: Routledge.

Vasquez, John A., and Brandon Valeriano. 2008. Territory as a source of conflict and a road to peace. In *Sage handbook on conflict resolution*, ed. Jacob Bercovitch and I. William Zartman. Newbury Park, Calif.: Sage.

Wagner, Harrison. 2000. Bargaining and war. *American Science Political Review* 44 (3): 469–84.

Wallace, William. 1976. Issue linkage among Atlantic governments. *International Affairs* 52 (2): 163–79.

Wallensteen, Peter. 1984. Incompatibility, confrontation, and war: Four models and three historical systems, 1816–1976. *Journal of Peace Research* 18 (1): 57–90.

Walter, Barbara. 2003. Explaining the intractability of territorial conflict. *International Studies Review* 5 (4): 137–53.

Watson, F. 1966. *The frontiers of China*. New York: Praeger.

Weekend Australian. 2004. Israel, Hezbollah in border firefight. May 8, 12.

Weymouth, Lally. 2001. This land is our land. *Washington Post*, April 29, B1.

White, David. 1983. Tension in Spain over Moroccan land claim. *Financial Times* (London). February 12, 2.

———. 1987a. Spain in talks on enclaves. *Financial Times* (London), July 3.

———. 1987b. Spain rejects Moroccan overture on enclaves. *Financial Times* (London), January 23.

White, George. 1995. *Nationalism and territory: Constructing group identity in southeastern Europe*. New York: Rowman & Littlefield.

White, Gregory W. 1996. The Mexico of Europe? Morocco's partnership with the European Union. In *North Africa: Development and reform in a changing global economy*, ed. D. Vandewalle, 111–28. New York: St. Martin's Press.

Whiting, Allen. 1989. *China eyes Japan*. Berkeley: University of California Press.

Wiegand, Krista E. 2005. Nationalist discourse and domestic incentives to prevent settlement of the territorial dispute between Guatemala and Belize. *Nationalism and Ethnic Politics* 11 (3): 349–83.

———. 2011. Militarized territorial disputes: States' attempts to transfer reputation for resolve. *Journal of Peace Research* 48 (1): 101–13.

Wiegand, Krista E., and Emilia Justyna Powell. 2011. Past experience, quest for the best forum, and peaceful attempts to resolve territorial disputes. *Journal of Conflict Resolution* 55 (1): 33–59.

———. Forthcoming. Unexpected companions: Bilateral cooperation between states involved in territorial disputes. *Conflict Management and Peace Science*, 28 (3).

Wilson, Scott. 2005. Hezbollah, Israeli forces clash on Lebanese border. *Washington Post*, November 22, A25.

Winograd Commission on the War in Lebanon report. 2008. Washington, D.C.: Council on Foreign Relations.

Witte, Griff. 2008. Israel proposes talks with Lebanon; offer on eve of cease-fire gets cool reception, but diplomatic flurry is called "extraordinary." *Washington Post*, June 19.

Woodwell, Douglas. 2004. Unwelcome neighbors: Shared ethnicity and international conflict during the Cold War. *International Studies Quarterly* 48 (1): 197–223.

Worden, Robert L., Andrea Matles Savada, and Ronald E. Dolan, eds. 1987. *A country study: China*. Washington, D.C.: Government Printing Office for the Library of Congress.

Xide, Jin. 2002. The background and trend of the partnership. In *Chinese-Japanese relations in the twenty-first century*, ed. M. Soedererg, 103–13. New York: Routledge.

Xinhua News Agency. 1983. Morocco, Spain reach fishing agreement. August 20.

———. 1995. Spain threatens to reconsider ties with Morocco. August 28.

———. 1996. Spanish prime minister visits Morocco. May 27.

———. 2000. Lahoud drafts Lebanon's position at coming Arab summit. October 18.

———. 2001. Talks on captive swap between Hezbollah and Israel underway. January 2.

———. 2004a. China again summons Japan's charge d'affaires in islands dispute. March 25.

———. 2004b. China demands Japan 'unconditionally' release island activists. March 25.

Yang, Daquing. 2002. Mirror for the future or the history card? In *Chinese-Japanese relations in the twenty-first century*, ed. M. Soedererg, 10–31. New York: Routledge.

Yang, Kuisong. 2000. The Sino-Soviet border clash of 1969: From Zhenbao Island to Sino-American Rapprochement. *Cold War History* 1 (1): 21–52.

Yee, Herbert. 1980. The Sino-Vietnamese border war: China's motives, calculations, and strategies. *China Report*, 15–32.

Young, Stephen M. 1988. Gorbachev's Asian policy: Balancing the new and the old. *Asian Survey* 28 (3): 317–39.

Zeng, Ka. 2004. *Trade threats, trade wars: Bargaining, retaliation, and American coercive diplomacy*. Ann Arbor: University of Michigan Press.

Zimmerman, William. 1973. Issue area and foreign policy process. *American Political Science Review* 67 (4): 1204–12.

Zisser, Eyal. 2006. Hizballah and Israel: Strategic threat on the northern border. *Israel Affairs* 12 (1): 86–106.

Zunes, Stephen. 2002. Indigestible lands? Comparing the fates of Western Sahara and East Timor. In *Right-sizing the state: The politics of moving borders*, ed. B. O'Leary, I. S. Lustick, and T. Callaghy, 289–317. Oxford: Oxford University Press.

INDEX